安徽省高等学校省级质量工程
一流教材建设项目成果
21世纪高等院校英语专业系列规划教材

Selected Readings in American Literature

美国文学选读

（第3版）

主　编　郝涂根　梁亚平
副主编　汪　宇
编　者　瞿宁霞　胡光宇
　　　　胡明涛　皮振雷
　　　　邓　莉　姜艳艳
　　　　曹良成

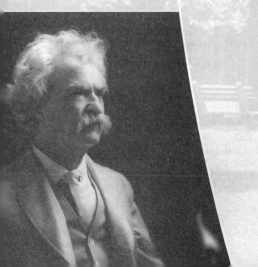

北京师范大学出版集团
BEIJING NORMAL UNIVERSITY PUBLISHING GROUP
安徽大学出版社

图书在版编目（CIP）数据

美国文学选读 / 郝涂根, 梁亚平主编 .—3 版 .—合肥：安徽大学出版社，2024.1
ISBN 978-7-5664-2691-8

Ⅰ.①美… Ⅱ.①郝… ②梁… Ⅲ.①英语—阅读教学—高等学校—教材 ②文学—作品—介绍—美国 Ⅳ.① H319.4：I

中国版本图书馆 CIP 数据核字（2023）第 212724 号

美国文学选读（第 3 版）
Meiguo Wenxue Xuandu

主编　郝涂根　梁亚平

出版发行：	北京师范大学出版集团	
	安 徽 大 学 出 版 社	
	（安徽省合肥市肥西路3号　邮编230039）	
	www.bnupg.com	
	www.ahupress.com.cn	
印　　刷：	安徽利民印务有限公司	
经　　销：	全国新华书店	
开　　本：	710 mm × 1010 mm 1/16	
印　　张：	23	
字　　数：	634 千字	
版　　次：	2024 年 1 月第 3 版	
印　　次：	2024 年 1 月第 1 次印刷	
定　　价：	57.90 元	
ISBN 978-7-5664-2691-8		

策划编辑：李　雪			美术设计：李　军	
责任编辑：李　雪			装帧编辑：李　军	
责任校对：高婷婷			责任印制：赵明炎	

版权所有　侵权必究

反盗版、侵权举报电话：0551-65106311
外埠邮购电话：0551-65107716
本书如有印装质量问题，请与印制管理部联系调换。
印制管理部电话：0551-65106311

修订前言

为使教材满足新时代英语类专业人才培养的新需求,编者对第三版《美国文学选读》做了如下修订:

1. 为贯彻"课程思政"这一核心理念,选择更有利于落实立德树人根本任务的美国文学名家的作品。例如,将霍桑所著的《牧师的黑面纱》替换为《拉普契尼博士的女儿》,引导学生正确理解现代科技的作用;将惠特曼的诗《我听见美国在歌唱》替换为《我坐而眺望》,客观地展现19世纪美国的社会现实;将海明威的作品《白象似的群山》替换为《一个干净明亮的房间》,揭示战争对人性的摧残。

2. 考虑到教学课时有限,将教材压缩为24节(第1、2版均为26节)。

3.《美国文学选读》可与吴定柏编著的国家级规划教材《美国文学大纲》配套使用。《美国文学大纲》共17章。考虑到美国文学不同时期的特点和教学的实际需要,本书从《美国文学大纲》每一章所介绍的作家中选取一至两位最有代表性的作家。因此,删去了 Ralph Waldo Emerson、Emily Dickinson、Ezra Pound 和 John Updike 4 位作家,新增了 J·D·Salinger 和 Toni Morrison 2 位作家。

4. 根据《普通高等学校本科外国语言文学类专业教学指南(上)》的要求,在 **Knowledge of Literature** 部分介绍了小说、诗歌、戏剧三类文学体裁的基本要素,以及西方马克思主义、生态主义、女性主义、接受美学、后殖民批评等现代西方文学分析与批评理论,并附有运用相关批评理论解读作品的文章，引导学生关注学术前沿，提高文学批评能力。

5. 基于打造金课的需要，适当增加了思考题和赏析部分的难度，旨在培养学生的思辨和创新能力。

6. 为帮助学生理解作品，适当增加了中文注释的比重，并标注所选篇目译文的出处。

7. 在 **Topics for Further Study** 部分增加了一些有利于融入思政元素的讨论题，旨在帮助学生塑造正确的人生观、价值观和世界观。

参加此次修订工作的有安庆师范大学郝涂根、汪宇、瞿宁霞、胡光宇老师和亳州学院梁亚平、胡明涛、皮振雷老师。

尽管编者付出了努力，但书中的错误仍难以避免。恳请使用本教材的老师和学生提出意见和建议，以便编者不断将其改进和完善。

郝涂根

2023 年 10 月 24 日

前　言

1783年，美国独立战争结束不久，知名辞典编撰家诺亚·韦伯斯特（Noah Webster）呼吁："美国必须像在政治上获得独立一样，在文学上也要谋求自主。"他的话也是众多美国人的心声。此时的美国文学仍带有鲜明的模仿痕迹，富兰克林、弗瑞诺等知名作家或多或少地沿袭了欧洲文学的样式或风格。然而，随着时间的推移，韦伯斯特的愿望变为了现实。在短短的两个世纪中，美国文学以令人叹为观止的速度摆脱了欧洲文学的束缚和影响，不断探索并开创了一条具有本土特色的道路，显现出独特的气质和成熟的风格，跃升为世界文学中重要的一支。迄今为止，已经有10名美国作家荣获诺贝尔文学奖。美国文学正以其多元化、多样性和多维度的特质呈现出勃勃生机，并在世界文坛上发挥着重要作用。

我国自改革开放以来，对美国文学的研究日益重视，各本科和高职院校纷纷开设了美国文学课程，有关教材也相继问世，为高校美国文学教学和研究提供了宝贵的参考依据。然而在多年的教学实践中，我们发现，由于编写年代较早或面向读者群不同等原因，很多美国文学教材只选录18、19世纪的经典作家作品，对20世纪特别是二战后的作品涉及甚少。此外，部分教材趣味性不强，难度太大，注释偏少，不能有效地激发学生的兴趣，同时也给教师的讲解带来了一定的困难。

本书在参考国内同类书籍的基础上，针对英语专业复合型人才培养的特定需要和教学的实际情况，精选了从殖民地时期到20世纪末的24位重要作家的代表作品，在体裁上兼顾小说、诗歌、戏剧与散文。全书按照历史发展顺序展开，涵盖了从本杰明·富兰克林到托马斯·品钦等美国文学各重要时期代表作家的作品，内容包括作者简介、作品选读、作品注释、赏析思考题和文学知识等。

本书的编写凝聚着集体的心血，由安庆师范大学郝涂根教授和阜阳师范大学梁亚平教授担任主编，安徽大学李梅编审担任副主编。参与编写的有安庆师范大学汪宇、邓莉老师和阜阳师范大学姜艳艳、曹良成老师。

此外，书中借鉴了国内外学者的若干著述，这些著述都在不同程度上帮助和启发了本书的编写和完善，在此一并表示衷心的感谢。

鉴于编者水平有限，书中谬误和不足在所难免，恳请同行专家和广大读者不吝赐教。

郝涂根

2013 年 5 月 18 日

修订于 2019 年 7 月

Table of Contents

Chapter 1　American Literature Before the Nineteenth Century 1

 Benjamin Franklin (1706~1790) 2

  Autobiography 3

Chapter 2　American Literature in the Romantic Period 12

 Washington Irving (1783~1859) 12

  Rip Van Winkle 14

 Henry David Thoreau (1817~1862) 28

  Walden 30

 Edgar Allen Poe (1809~1849) 45

  The Raven 47

  Annabelle Lee 52

 Nathaniel Hawthorne (1804~1864) 57

  Dr. Rappaccini's Daughter 60

 Walt Whitman (1819~1892) 86

  I Sit and Look Out 90

  One's-Self I Sing 91

Chapter 3 American Literature of the Realist and Naturalistic Periods 95

Mark Twain (1835~1910) 96
    The Adventures of Huckleberry Finn 98
Henry James (1843~1916) 109
    Daisy Miller 110
Theodore Dreiser (1871~1945) 124
    Sister Carrie 126

Chapter 4 American Literature in the Modern Period 139

T. S. Eliot (1888~1965) 140
    The Love Song of J. Alfred Prufrock 141
Robert Frost (1874~1963) 150
    The Road Not Taken 152
    Mending Wall 154
F. Scott Fitzgerald (1896~1940) 158
    The Great Gatsby 159
Ernest Hemingway (1899~1961) 175
    A Clean Well-lighted House 178
William Faulkner (1897~1962) 185
    A Rose for Emily 188
Eugene O'Neill (1888~1953) 200
    Long Day's Journey into Night 202

Chapter 5 American Literature After World War II 231

Tennessee Williams (1911~1983) 232
    A Streetcar Named Desire 234
J. D. Salinger (1919~2010) 249

The Catcher in the Rye	251
Thomas Pynchon (1937~)	260
Entropy	261
Allen Ginsberg (1926~1997)	280
A Supermarket in California	281
Toni Morrison (1931~2019)	285
Home	287
Isaac Bashevis Singer (1904~1991)	291
Gimpel the Fool	293
Saul Bellow (1915~2005)	309
A Father-To-Be	311
Maxine Hong Kingston (1940~)	323
Woman Warrior: Memoirs of a Girlhood among Ghosts	325
Alice Walker (1944~)	341
Everyday Use	342
Bibliography	354

Chapter 1
American Literature Before the Nineteenth Century

　　严格意义上来讲，今天我们所说的美国文学并不是美洲大陆所孕育的最初文学形式。早在17世纪初欧洲殖民者登陆之前，北美印第安人就创造了令人叹为观止的口头文学。这种世代相传的本土文学极富想象力，内容丰富多彩，涵盖各部落的神话传说、典仪祝词和劳动歌曲等，充分展现了印第安人独特的部落文化和生活风貌。但随着欧洲移民对印第安人的残酷迫害，这一文学传统遭到了毁灭性的打击，逐渐销声匿迹，湮没在历史长河中。取而代之的白人英语文学，开始在美洲大陆生根发芽，并最终成为美国文学的源头。较之同时代的英国文学，这一时期的美国文学水平低下，形式单一，主要包括游记、日记、书信、宗教著作和少量诗歌。这些带有浓厚宗教色彩的作品以简单朴实的语言展现了美洲大陆的自然风光，记载了早期移民在新大陆上辛勤开拓、建立家园的曲折经历，也倾诉了这些移民，尤其是清教徒对上帝无限的虔诚和崇敬之情。

　　18世纪下半叶，在独立战争和启蒙运动的影响下，美国文学开始摆脱宗教的羁绊和控制，回归世俗生活，为本国的政治独立和文化启蒙服务。这一时期的很多作家如潘恩（Thomas Paine）、杰弗逊（Thomas Jefferson）等以纸笔为刀枪，创作了大量观点鲜明、慷慨激昂的政论文、演说词和爱国诗篇。富兰克林（Benjamin Franklin）更是用自己传奇的一生和脍炙人口的《自传》（*Autobiography*）极好地诠释了启蒙运动和美国梦的精髓，激励世世代代的美国人追寻心中的梦想。值得一提的是，这一时期的美国文学已有文学独立的苗头。例如，弗瑞诺（Philip Freneau）在诗歌中热情讴歌美国本土自然风光和印第安人的生活。但总的来说，这一时期的美国文学尚未取得独立，带有明显的模仿痕迹，诸如富兰克林、弗瑞诺（Philip Freneau）等知名作家的作品或多或少地沿袭了欧洲文学的形式与风格。

Benjamin Franklin (1706~1790)

About the Author

Franklin was born in Boston, Massachusetts. He received very little education, but through a lot of reading and other ways of self-education he became a brilliant and versatile man. In 1718, at the age of 12 he became an apprentice of his brother in printing. Starting as a poor boy in a family of 17 children, he became famous on both sides of the Atlantic as a statesman, scientist, and writer. Despite his fame, he always remained a man of industry and simple tastes.

Franklin's writings range from informal sermons on thrift to urbane essays. He wrote gracefully as well as clearly with a wit that often gave an edge to his words. Though the style he formed came from imitating two noted English essayists, Addison and Steele, he made it into his own. His most famous work is his *Autobiography*. Before his autobiography, his *Poor Richard's Almanac* (1733~1758) became popular, containing many proverbs like "Early to bed, and early to rise, makes a man healthy, wealthy and wise".

In 1771, while living in England and serving as ambassador for most of the colonies, Franklin began his autobiography as a letter to his son, William. He got as far as the year 1730 (including his arrival in Philadelphia) when the writing was interrupted by "the affairs of the Revolution". In 1784, while living in Passy, France, then a suburb of Paris, he extended his *Autobiography* through 1731. The bulk of the remainder of the work was added in 1788 and the final few pages were written in 1790, the year of his death. None of them was published while Franklin lived. Shortly after his death, a French translation of his life to 1731 (the first two sections that Franklin wrote) was published. Though this was soon translated into English and published in London, the official text did not appear until 1818, as part of the works of Benjamin Franklin, edited by his grandson William Temple Franklin. The first "complete" *Autobiography*—with the pages written in 1790—did not appear until 1868, edited by John Bigelow, who had bought Franklin's original manuscript from a Franklin family the previous year.

Autobiography covers Franklin's life only until 1757 when he was 51 years old, well before his major accomplishments as a diplomat. The work as a whole was written by a man well beyond the normal age of retirement, yet it is not the less lively for that fact. Franklin's mastery of a prose style characterized by clarity, concision, flexibility and order was central to his fame as a great man of letters.

Autobiography

About the Work

Franklin's *Autobiography* contains many things. First of all, it is an inspiring account of a poor boy's rise to a high position. Franklin tells his story modestly, omitting some of his misdeeds. He is resigned to the fact that his misdeeds will often receive a punishment of one sort or another. Viewing himself with objectivity, Franklin offers his life story as a lesson to others. It is a positive lesson that teaches the reader to live a useful life. In fact, *Autobiography* is a how-to-do-it book, a book on the art of self-improvement.

From *Autobiography*

CONTINUATION OF THE ACCOUNT OF MY LIFE.
BEGUN AT PASSY, NEAR PARIS 1784.

…

It was about this time I conceiv'd the bold and arduous Project of arriving at moral Perfection. I wish'd to live without committing any Fault at anytime; I would conquer all that either Natural Inclination, Custom, or Company might lead me into. As I knew, or thought I knew, what was right and wrong, I did not see why I might not *always* do the one and avoid the other. But I soon found I had undertaken a Task of more Difficulty than I had imagined: While my Care was employ'd in guarding against one Fault, I was often surpris'd by another. Habit took the Advantage of Inattention. Inclination was sometimes too strong for Reason. I concluded at length, that the mere speculative Conviction that it was out Interest to be completely virtuous, was not sufficient to prevent our Slipping; and that the contrary Habits must be broken and good Ones acquired and established, before we can have any Dependence on a steady uniform Rectitude of Conduct. For this purpose I therefore contriv'd the following Method.

In the various Enumerations of the moral Virtues[①] I had met with in my Reading, I found the Catalogue more or less numerous, as different Writers included more or fewer Ideas under the same Name. Temperance, for Example, was by some confin'd

---

① the moral Virtues: According to the Christian tradition, there are seven virtues and seven vices. The seven virtues are: Faith, Hope, Charity, Prudence, Justice, Fortitude and Temperance. The seven vices are: Pride, Wrath, Envy, Lust, Gluttony, Avarice and Sloth.

to Eating and Drinking, while by others it was extended to mean the moderating every other Pleasure, Appetite, Inclination or Passion, bodily or mental, even to our Avarice and Ambition. I propos'd to myself, for the sake of Clearness, to use rather more Names with fewer Ideas annex'd to each, than a few Names with more Ideas; and I included after Thirteen Names of Virtues all that at that time occurr'd to me as necessary or desirable, and annex'd to each a short Precept, which fully express'd the Extent I gave to its Meaning[①].

These Names of Virtues with their Precepts were

1. TEMPERANCE

Eat not to Dullness. Drink not to Elevation.[②]

2. SILENCE

Speak not but what may benefit others or yourself.[③] Avoid trifling Conversation.

3. ORDER

Let all your Things have their Places. Let each Part of your Business have its Time.

4. RESOLUTION

Resolve to perform what you ought. Perform without fail what you resolve.

5. FRUGALITY

Make no Expense but to do good to others or yourself: i.e., Waste nothing.

6. INDUSTRY

Lose no Time. Be always employ'd in something useful. Cut off all unnecessary Actions.

7. SINCERITY

Use no hurtful Deceit. Think innocently and justly; and, if you speak, speak accordingly.

---

① which fully express'd the Extent I gave to its Meaning: which gave each of my virtues a full and accurate definition.
② Eat… to elevation: Don't eat so much as to get stupefied. Don't drink so much as to become wild.
③ Speak… yourself: Only say what may be good for others or yourself. The word "but" here means "except".

8. JUSTICE

Wrong none, by doing Injuries or omitting the Benefits that are your Duty.

9. MODERATION

Avoid Extremes. Forbear resenting Injuries so much as you think they deserve.

10. CLEANLINESS

Tolerate no Uncleanness in Body, Clothes or Habitation.

11. TRANQUILITY

Be not disturbed at Trifles, or at Accidents common or unavoidable.

12. CHASTITY

Rarely use Venery but for Health or Offspring; Never to Dullness, Weakness, or the Injury of your own or another's Peace or Reputation.

13. HUMILITY

Imitate Jesus and Socrates.

My intention being to acquire the *Habitude* of all these Virtues, I judg'd it would be well not to distract my Attention by attempting the whole at once, but to fix it on one of them at a time, and when I should be Master of that, then to proceed to another, and so on till I should have gone thro' the thirteen. And as the previous Acquisition of some might facilitate the Acquisition of certain others, I arrang'd them with that View as they stand above. *Temperance* first, as it tends to produce that Coolness and Clearness of Head, which is so necessary where constant Vigilance was to be kept up, and Guard maintained, against the unremitting Attraction of ancient Habits, and the Force of perpetual Temptations. This being acquir'd and establish'd, *Silence* would be more easy, and my Desire being to gain Knowledge at the same time that I improv'd in Virtue, and considering that in Conversation it was obtain'd rather by the Use of the Ears than of the Tongue, and therefore wishing to break a Habit I was getting into of Prattling, Punning and Joking, which only made me acceptable to trifling Company, I gave *Silence* the second Place. This, and the next, *Order*, I expected would allow me more Time for attending to my Project and my studies; RESOLUTION, once become habitual, would keep me firm in my Endeavors to obtain all the subsequent Virtues; *Frugality* and *Industry*, by freeing me from my remaining Debt, and producing Affluence and Independence, would make more easy the Practice of Sincerity and

Justice, etc., etc. Conceiving then that agreeable to the Advice of Pythagoras① in his Golden Verses, daily Examination would be necessary, I contriv'd the following Method for conducting that Examination.

    I made a little Book in which I allotted a Page for each of the Virtues. I rul'd each Page with red Ink so as to have seven Columns, one for each Day of the Week, marking each Column with a Letter for the Day. I cross's these Columns with thirteen red Lines, marking the beginning of each Line with the first Letter of one of the Virtues, on which Line and in its proper Column I might mark by a little black Spot every Fault I found upon Examination, to have been committed respecting that Virtue upon that Day.

    I determined to give a Week's strict Attention to each of the Virtues successively. Thus in the first Week my great Guard was to avoid every the least Offence against Temperance, leaving the other Virtues to their ordinary Chance, only marking every Evening the Faults of the Day. Thus if in the first Week I could keep my first Line marked T clear of Spots, I suppos'd the Habit of that Virtue so much strengthen'd and its opposite weaken'd, that I might venture extending my Attention to include the next, and for the following Week keep both Lines clear of Spots. Proceeding thus to the last, I could go thro' a Course complete in Thirteen Weeks, and four Courses in a Year. And like him who having a Garden to weed, does not attempt to eradicate all the bad Herbs at once, which would exceed his Reach and his Strength, but works on one of the Beds at a time, and having accomplish'd the first proceeds to a second; so I should have, (I hoped) the encouraging Pleasure of seeing on my Pages the Progress I made in Virtue, by clearing successively my Lines of their Spots, till in the End by a Number of Courses, I should be happy in viewing a clean Book after a thirteen Weeks' daily Examination.

...

Form of the Pages

TEMPERANCE.							
Eat not to Dullness. *Drink not to Elevation.*							
	S	M	T	W	T	F	S
T							

---

① Pythagoras (c.580~500 BC): a Greek philosopher and mathematician who founded the Pythagorean school which believed that the soul imprisoned in the body could be purified by study. He followed a strict discipline of purity and self-examination.

Chapter 1 American Literature Before the Nineteenth Century

(continued)

S	* *	*		*		*		
O	*	*	*		*	*	*	
R			*			*		
F		*			*			
I				*				
S								
J								
M								
Cl								
T								
Ch								
H								

The Precept of Order requiring that every Part of my Business should have its allotted time, one Page in my little Book contain'd the following Scheme of Employment for the Twenty-four Hours of a natural Day.

The Morning. *Question.* What Good shall I do this Day?	5 6 7	Rise, wash, and address *Powerful Goodness*; contrive Day's Business and take the Resolution of the Day; Prosecute the present Study, and breakfast.
	8 9 10 11	Work.
Noon.	12 1	Read, or overlook my Accounts, and dine.
	2 3 4 5	Work.
Evening. *Question.* What Good have I done today?	6 7 8 9	Put Things in their Places, Supper, Music, or Diversion, or Conversation, Examination of the Day.

Night.	10	
	11	
	12	
	1	Sleep.
	2	
	3	
	4	

  I entrer'd upon the Execution of this Plan for Self-Examination, and continu'd it with occasional Intermissions for some time. I was surpris'd to find myself so much fuller of Faults than I had imagined, but I had the Satisfaction of seeing them diminish. To avoid the Trouble of renewing now and then my little Book, which by scraping out the Marks on the Paper of old Faults to make room for new Ones in a new Course, became full of holes: I transferr'd my Tables and Precepts to the Ivory Leaves of a Memorandum Book, on which the Lines were drawn with red Ink that made a durable Stain, and on those Lines I mark'd my Faults with a black Lead Pencil, which Marks I could easily wipe out with a wet Sponge. After a while I went thro' one Course only in a Year, and afterwards only one in several Years; till at length I omitted them entirely, being employ'd in Voyages and Business abroad with a Multiplicity of Affairs, that interfered. But I always carried my little Book with me.

  My Scheme of ORDER, gave me the most Trouble, and I found, that tho' it might be practicable where a Man's Business was such as to leave him the Disposition of his Time, that of a Journeyman Printer for instance, it was not possible to be exactly observ'd by a Master, who must mix with the World, and often receive People of Business at their own Hours. *Order* too, with regard to Places for Things, Papers, etc., I found extremely difficult to acquire. I had not been early accustomed toit, and having an exceeding good Memory, I was not so sensible of the Inconvenience attending Want of Method. This Article therefore cost me so much painful Attention and my Faults in it vex'd me so much, and I made so little Progress in Amendment, and had such frequent Relapses, that I was almost ready to give up the Attempt, and content myself with a faulty Character in that respect. Like the Man who in buying an Ax of a Smith my Neighbor, desired to have the whole of its Surface as bright as the Edge; the Smith consented to grind it bright for him if he would turn the Wheel. He turn'd while the Smith press'd the broad Face of the Ax hard and heavily on the Stone, which made the Turning of it very fatiguing. The man came every now and then from the Wheel to see how the Work went on; and at length would take his Ax as it was without farther

Grinding. No, says the Smith, Turn on, turn on; we shall have it bright by and by; as yet 'tis only speckled. Yes, says the man; but—*I think I like a speckled Ax best.*—And I believe this may have been the Case with many who having for want of some such Means as I employ'd found the Difficulty of obtaining good, and breaking bad Habits, in other Points of Vice and Virtue, have given up the Struggle, and concluded that *a speckled Ax was best.* For something that pretended to be Reason was every now and then suggesting to me, that such extreme Nicety as I exacted of myself might be a kind of Foppery in Morals, which if it were known would make me ridiculous; that a perfect Character might be attended with the Inconvenience of being envied and hated; and that a benevolent Man should allow a few Faults in himself, to keep his Friends in Countenance.

In Truth I found myself incorrigible with respect to *Order*; and now I am grown old, and my Memory bad, I feel very sensibly the want of it. But on the whole, tho' I never arrived at the Perfection I had been so ambitious of obtaining, but fell far short of it, yet I was by the Endeavour a better and a happier Man than I otherwise should have been, if I had not attempted it; As those who aim at perfect Writing by imitating the engraved Copies, tho' they never reach the wish'd for Excellence of those Copies, their Hand is mended by the Endeavour, and is tolerable while it continues fair and legible.

...

译文链接：https://www.thn21.com/Article/chang/18809.html

Questions for Understanding

1. What reason does Franklin give for putting Temperance first on his list of virtues?
2. How does Franklin define Resolution, Frugality and Tranquility? Try to use your own words in your answer.
3. What are the three types of Cleanliness that Franklin considers important?
4. What can you infer about Franklin's character from the thirteen virtues and the "timetable"?
5. Why did the Scheme of Order give him trouble?

Aspects of Appreciation

1. *Autobiography* is a Puritan document. It is Puritan because it is a record of self-examination and self-improvement. Reading *Autobiography*, one sees an old man, serene and cool, casting a backward glance, looking intensely into his past life

and, pen in hand, carefully noting down his experience as if in this way, he could communicate with God.

2. *Autobiography* is also an eloquent elucidation of the fact that Franklin was the spokesman for the new order of the eighteen-century enlightenment, representing in America all its ideas that man is basically good and free and that man is endowed by God with certain inalienable rights to life, liberty and the pursuit of happiness.

3. Franklin believed that America was a land of opportunities and that "one man of tolerable abilities will work great changes and accomplish great affairs among mankind". Thus through telling a success story of self-reliance, the book celebrates the fulfillment of the American dream.

Suggested Further Reading

Poor Richard's Almanac (1729); *The Way to Wealth* (1758).

Topics for Further Study

1. What motivated Franklin to write his autobiography? How did he go about it?
2. What was Franklin's childhood like? How did his upbringing influence his later life?
3. How did Franklin develop his strong work ethic? What did he learn from his early experiences as an apprentice?
4. What role did Franklin play in the founding of the United States? How did his contributions to the American Revolution shape his legacy?
5. What were Franklin's most important inventions and discoveries? How do they impact our life?
6. What were Franklin's personal beliefs and values? How did they influence his actions and decisions?
7. How did Franklin's views on religion and spirituality evolve over the course of his life? How did he reconcile his beliefs with the scientific discoveries of his time?
8. What were the challenges and setbacks that Franklin faced throughout his life? How did he manage to achieve success?

Knowledge of Literature

Autobiography（自传）

An autobiography is a person's account of his or her life. Generally written in the first person, with the author speaking as "I", autobiographies present life events as the writer views them. In addition to providing inside details about the writer's life, autobiographies offer insight into the beliefs and perceptions of the author. Autobiographies also offer glimpses of what it was like to live in the author's time, and often provide a view of historical events that people can not find in history books. Benjamin Franklin's *Autobiography* set the standard for what was then a new genre of American literature.

Chapter 2
American Literature in the Romantic Period

　　19世纪上半期，随着美国在政治、经济上的独立和崛起，美国文学也迎来了第一个繁荣时期——浪漫主义时期。以欧文（Washington Irving）、库珀（James Fennimore Cooper）、布赖恩特（William Cullen Bryant）为代表的早期浪漫主义作家不再满足于对欧洲文学亦步亦趋的模仿，开始将目光转向本土瑰丽多姿的自然风光和人文风貌，积极挖掘和拓展具有鲜明民族特色的文学题材和形式。他们的创新和努力不仅为美国文学赢得了欧洲文学界的认可，也激励着一大批作家继续为争取本国的文学独立而奋斗。

　　19世纪30年代在新英格兰地区兴起的超验主义（Transcendentalism）更是将美国浪漫主义文学推向了高潮。这一时期，以爱默生（Ralph Waldo Emerson）、梭罗（Henry David Thoreau）、惠特曼（Walt Whitman）为代表的作家谱写了众多气势恢弘、脍炙人口的篇章，讴歌壮美秀丽的自然景色和生机勃勃的新世界，赞美充满活力和热情的新一代亚当与夏娃，并满怀希望地憧憬新世界的美好未来。然而，在这种乐观向上的主旋律之外，也响起了一股阴郁低沉的变奏。坡（Edgar Allan Poe）、霍桑（Nathaniel Hawthorne）、麦尔维尔（Herman Melville）等作家以冷峻理性的笔触审视人性和现实社会，探讨其中所隐藏的危险和阴暗面。

　　至19世纪中期，美国文学业已摆脱历史和传统的束缚，以独立的姿态彰显自身独特的魅力，跻身于世界文学之林。

Washington Irving (1783~1859)

About the Author

　　Washington Irving is called "the first American man of letters". He is best known for the short stories "The Legend of Sleepy Hollow" and "Rip Van Winkle".

　　As the favorite and last of 11 children of an austere Presbyterian father and a genial Anglican mother, young and frail Irving grew up in an atmosphere of indulgence. He escaped a college education, which his father required of his elder sons, but read intermittently at the law, notably in the office of Josiah Ogden Hoffman, with whose pretty daughter Matilda he early fell in love. He wrote a series of whimsically satirical essays, published in Peter Irving's newspaper *Morning Chronicle* in 1802~1803. He made several trips up the Hudson, and took an extended tour of Europe in 1804~1806.

On his return, he passed the bar examination late in 1806 and soon set up as a lawyer. But during 1807~1808, his chief occupation was to collaborate with his brother William and James K. Paulding in the writing of a series of periodical essays entitled "Salmagundi". Concerned primarily with passing phases of contemporary society, the essays retain significance as an index to the social milieu.

Irving's *A History of New York by Diedrich Knickerbocker*(1809) was a comic history of the Dutch regime in New York, prefaced by a mock-pedantic account of the world from creation onward. Its writing was interrupted in April 1809 by the sudden death of Matilda Hoffman, as grief incapacitated him. In 1811 he moved to Washington, D.C., as a lobbyist for the Irving brothers' hardware-importing firm, but his life seemed aimless for some years. He prepared an American edition of Thomas Campbell's poems, edited *Analectic Magazine*, and acquired a staff colonelcy during the War of 1812. In 1815, he went to Liverpool to look after the interests of his brothers' firm. In London he met Sir Walter Scott, who encouraged him to renew his effort of writing. The result was *The Sketch Book of Geoffrey Crayon, Gent* (1819~1820), a collection of stories and essays that mix satire and whimsicality with fact and fiction. Most of the book's 30-odd pieces concern Irving's impressions of England, but six chapters deal with American subjects. Of these, the tales "The Legend of Sleepy Hollow" and "Rip Van Winkle" have been called the first American short stories. They are both Americanized versions of German folktales. The main character of "Rip Van Winkle" is a henpecked husband who sleeps for 20 years and awakes as an old man to find his wife dead, his daughter happily married, and America now an independent country. The tremendous success of *The Sketch Book* in both England and the United States assured Irving that he could live by his pen. In 1822, he produced *Bracebridge Hall*, a sequel to *The Sketch Book*. He traveled in Germany, Austria, France, Spain, the British Isles, and later in his own country.

Early in 1826, he accepted the invitation of Alexander H. Everett to attach himself to the American legation in Spain, where he wrote his *Columbus* (1828), followed by *The Companions of Columbus* (1831). Meanwhile, Irving had become absorbed in the legends of the Moorish past and wrote *A Chronicle of the Conquest of Granada* (1829) and *The Alhambra* (1832), a Spanish counterpart of *The Sketch Book*.

After a 17-year absence, Irving returned to New York in 1832, where he was warmly received. He made a journey west and produced in rapid succession *A Tour of the Prairies* (1835), *Astoria* (1836), and *The Adventures of Captain Bonneville* (1837). Except for four years (1842~1846) as minister to Spain, Irving spent the rest of his life at his home, "Sunnyside", in Tarrytown, on the Hudson River, where he devoted himself to literary pursuits.

Rip Van Winkle

About the Story

Rip is an old farmer, but he does not like farm work. He often stays in the village tavern to talk with others. He is afraid of his talkative and shrewish wife. One day he takes his gun to go to the mountain followed by his dog. On the way he meets a man with a keg. The man invites Rip to go with him. In the deep mountain they arrive at a place where two old men are playing chess. Rip watches them and drinks the wine. Soon he falls asleep. When he wakes up, his dog is gone and his gun rusted. He finds his way home. But to his surprise, none of the people can he recognize. It is nearly twenty years since he fell asleep. Great changes have taken place. The British flag has been replaced by the American star-ribbon flag. His wife died long ago. His daughter has been married. She takes Rip home. Rip still stays at the village tavern and tells his tales to other people.

Rip Van Winkle

Whoever has made a voyage up the Hudson must remember the Kaatskill mountains. They are a dismembered branch of the great Appalachian family, and are seen away to the west of the river, swelling up to a noble height, and lording it over the surrounding country. Every change of season, every change of weather, indeed, every hour of the day, produces some change in the magical hues and shapes of these mountains, and they are regarded by all the good wives, far and near, as perfect barometers. When the weather is fair and settled, they are clothed in blue and purple, and print their bold outlines on the clear evening sky; but sometimes, when the rest of the landscape is cloudless, they will gather a hood of gray vapors about their summits, which, in the last rays of the setting sun, will glow and light up like a crown of glory.

At the foot of these fairy mountains, the voyager may have descried the light smoke curling up from a village, whose shingle-roofs gleam among the trees, just where the blue tints of the upland melt away into the fresh green of the nearer landscape. It is a little village, of great antiquity, having been founded by some of the Dutch colonists, in the early times of the province, just about the beginning of the government of the good Peter Stuyvesant① (may he rest in peace!) and there were some of the houses of the original settlers standing within a few years built of small yellow bricks brought from Holland, having latticed windows and gable fronts, surmounted with weathercocks.

In that same village and in one of these very houses (which, to tell the precise truth, was sadly time-worn and weather-beaten), there lived many years since, while the country was yet a province of Great Britain, a simple good-natured fellow, of the name of Rip Van Winkle. He was a descendant of the Van Winkles who figured so gallantly in the chivalrous days of Peter Stuyvesant, and accompanied him to the siege of Fort Christina②. He inherited, however, but little of the martial character of his ancestors. I have observed that he was a simple good-natured man; he was, moreover, a kind neighbor, and an obedient hen-pecked husband. Indeed, to the latter circumstance might be owing that meekness of spirit which gained him such universal popularity, for those men are most apt to be obsequious and conciliating abroad, who are under the discipline of shrews at home. Their tempers, doubtless, are rendered pliant and malleable in the fiery furnace of domestic tribulation, and a curtain lecture③ is worth all the sermons in the world for teaching the virtues of patience and long-suffering. A termagant wife may, therefore, in some respects, be considered a tolerable blessing; and if so, Rip Van Winkle was thrice blessed.

Certain it is that he was a great favorite among all the good wives of the village, who, as usual with the amiable sex, took his part in all family squabbles; and never failed, whenever they talked those matters over in their evening gossiping, to lay all the blame on Dame Van Winkle. The children of the village, too, would shout with joy whenever he approached. He assisted at their sports, made their playthings, taught them to fly kites and shoot marbles④, and told them long stories of ghosts, witches, and Indians. Whenever he went dodging about the village, he was surrounded by a troop of them hanging on his skirts, clambering on his back, and playing a thousand tricks on him with impunity; and not a dog would bark at him throughout the neighborhood.

The great error in Rip's composition was an insuperable aversion to all kinds

---

① Peter Stuyvesant: the last Dutch governor of New Netherland, which was divided into the English colonies of New York and New Jersey in 1664. He held the position from 1647 to 1664.
② Fort Christina: a Swedish fort on the Delaware River, captured by Stuyvesant in 1665 when he took possession of the colony of New Sweden.
③ curtain lecture: a scolding or rebuke given in private, esp by a wife to her husband(床头训诫).
④ shoot marbles: a game played by children with small balls of glass, clay or stone.

of profitable labor. It could not be from the want of assiduity or perseverance; for he would sit on a wet rock, with a rod as long and heavy as a Tartar's① lance, and fish all day without a murmur, even though he should not be encouraged by a single nibble. He would carry a fowling-piece on his shoulder for hours together, trudging through woods and swamps, and uphill and down dale, to shoot a few squirrels or wild pigeons. He would never refuse to assist a neighbor even in the roughest toil, and was a foremost man at all country frolics for husking Indian corn, or building stone fences; the women of the village, too, used to employ him to run their errands, and to do such little odd jobs as their less obliging husbands would not do for them. In a word, Rip was ready to attend to anybody's business but his own; but as to doing family duty, and keeping his farm in order, he found it impossible.

In fact, he declared it was of no use to work on his farm; it was the most pestilent little piece of ground in the whole country; everything about it went wrong, and would go wrong, in spite of him. His fences were continually falling to pieces; his cow would either go astray, or get among the cabbages; weeds were sure to grow quicker in his fields than anywhere else; the rain always made a point of setting in just as he had some outdoor work to do; so that though his patrimonial estate had dwindled away under his management, acre by acre, until there was little more left than a mere patch of Indian corn and potatoes, yet it was the worst conditioned farm in the neighborhood.

His children, too, were as ragged and wild as if they belonged to nobody. His son Rip, an urchin begotten in his own likeness, promised to inherit the habits, with the old clothes, of his father. He was generally seen trooping like a colt at his mother's heels, equipped in a pair of his father's cast-off galligaskins② which he had much ado to hold up with one hand, as a fine lady does her train in bad weather.

Rip Van Winkle, however, was one of those happy mortals③, of foolish, well-oiled dispositions, who take the world easy, eat white bread or brown, whichever can be got with least thought or trouble, and would rather starve on a penny than work for a pound. If left to himself, he would have whistled life away in perfect contentment; but his wife kept continually dinning in his ears about his idleness, his carelessness, and the ruin he was bringing on his family. Morning, noon, and night, her tongue was incessantly going, and everything he said or did was sure to produce a torrent of household eloquence. Rip had but one way of replying to all lectures of the kind, and that, by frequent use, had grown into a habit. He shrugged his shoulders, shook his

---

① Tartar: 鞑靼人。
② galligaskins: loose hose or breeches worn in the 16th and 17th centuries(宽松马裤)。
③ mortals: human beings.

head, cast up his eyes, but said nothing. This, however, always provoked a fresh volley from his wife; so that he was fain to draw off his forces, and take to the outside of the house—the only side which, in truth, belongs to a hen-pecked husband.

Rip's sole domestic adherent was his dog Wolf, who was as much hen-pecked as his master; for Dame Van Winkle regarded them as companions in idleness, and even looked upon Wolf with an evil eye, as the cause of his master's going so often astray. True it is, in all points of spirit, befitting an honorable dog, he was as courageous an animal as ever scoured the woods—but what courage can withstand the ever-during and all-besetting terrors of a woman's tongue? The moment Wolf entered the house, his crest fell, his tail drooped to the ground, or curled between his legs, he sneaked about with a gallows air, casting many a side-long glance at Dame Van Winkle, and at the least flourish of a broomstick or ladle, he would fly to the door with yelping precipitation.

Times grew worse and worse with Rip Van Winkle as years of matrimony rolled on; a tart temper never mellows with age, and a sharp tongue is the only edged tool that grows keener with constant use. For a long while he used to console himself, when driven from home, by frequenting a kind of perpetual club of the sages, philosophers and other idle personages of the village; which held its sessions on a bench before a small inn, designated by a rubicund portrait of His Majesty George the Third①. Here they used to sit in the shade through a long lazy summer's day, talking listlessly over village gossip, or telling endless sleepy stories about nothing. But it would have been worth any statesman's money to have heard the profound discussions that sometimes took place, when by chance an old newspaper fell into their hands form some passing traveler. How solemnly they would listen to the contents, as drawled out by Derrick Van Bummel, the schoolmaster, a dapper learned little man, who was not to be daunted by the most gigantic word in the dictionary; and how sagely they would deliberate upon public events some months after they had taken place.

The opinions of this junto② were completely controlled by Nicholas Vedder, a patriarch of the village, and landlord of the inn, at the door of which he took his seat from morning till night, just moving sufficiently to avoid the sun and keep in the shade of a large tree; so that the neighbors could tell the hour by his movements as accurately as by a sundial. It is true he was rarely heard to speak, but smoked his pipe incessantly. His adherents, however (for every great man has his adherents), perfectly

---

① His Majesty George the Third: the king of England from 1760 to 1820 who lost the fight to keep control over the American colonies.
② junto: a club founded by Benjamin Franklin in 1727 for people to debate moral, political and philosophical issues and to exchange knowledge about business matters. Here the word is used by the writer in a jocular way.

understood him, and knew how to gather his opinions. When anything that was read or related displeased him, he was observed to smoke his pipe vehemently, and to send forth short, frequent, and angry puffs, but when pleased he would inhale the smoke slowly and tranquilly, and emit it in light and placid clouds; and sometimes, taking the pipe from his mouth, and letting the fragrant vapor curl about his nose, would gravely nod his head in token of perfect approbation.

From even this stronghold the unlucky Rip was at length routed by his termagant wife, who would suddenly break in upon the tranquility of the assemblage and call the members all to naught; nor was that august personage, Nicholas Vedder himself, sacred from the daring tongue of this terrible virago, who charged him outright with encouraging her husband in habits of idleness.

Poor Rip was at last reduced almost to despair; and his only alternative, to escape from the labor of the farm and clamor of his wife, was to take gun in hand and stroll away into the woods. Here he would sometimes seat himself at the foot of a tree, and share the contents of his wallet with Wolf, with whom he sympathized as a fellow-sufferer in persecution. "Poor Wolf," he would say, "thy mistress leads thee a dog's life of it; but never mind, my lad, whilst I live thou shalt never want a friend to stand by thee!" Wolf would wag his tail, look wistfully in his master's face, and if dogs can feel pity, I verily believe he reciprocated the sentiment with all his heart.

In a long ramble of the kind on a fine autumnal day, Rip had unconsciously scrambled to one of the highest parts of the Kaatskill mountains. He was after his favorite sport of squirrel-shooting, and the still solitudes had echoed and re-echoed with the reports of his gun. Panting and fatigued, he threw himself, late in the afternoon, on a green knoll, covered with mountain herbage, that crowned the brow of a precipice. From an opening between the trees he could overlook all the lower country for many a mile of rich woodland. He saw at a distance the lordly Hudson, far, far below him, moving on its silent but majestic course, with the reflection of a purple cloud, or the sail of a lagging bark, here and there sleeping on its glassy bosom, and at last losing itself in the blue highlands.

On the other side he looked down into a deep mountain glen, wild, lonely, and shagged, the bottom filled with fragments from the impending cliffs, and scarcely lighted by the reflected rays of the setting sun. For some time Rip lay musing on this scene; evening was gradually advancing; the mountains began to throw their long blue shadows over the valleys; he saw that it would be dark long before he could reach the village, and he heaved a heavy sigh when he thought of encountering the terrors of Dame Van Winkle.

As he was about to descend, he heard a voice from a distance, hallooing, "Rip Van

Winkle! Rip Van Winkle!" He looked round, but could see nothing but a crow winging its solitary flight across the mountain. He thought his fancy must have deceived him, and turned again to descend, when he heard the same cry ring through the still evening air: "Rip Van Winkle! Rip Van Winkle!" —At the same time Wolf bristled up his back, and, giving a loud growl, skulked to his master's side, looking fearfully down into the glen. Rip now felt a vague apprehension stealing over him; he looked anxiously in the same direction, and perceived a strange figure slowly toiling up the rocks, and bending under the weight of something he carried on his back. He was surprised to see any human being in this lonely and unfrequented place; but supposing it to be some one of the neighborhood in need of his assistance, he hastened down to yield it.

On nearer approach he was still more surprised at the singularity of the stranger's appearance. He was a short, square-built old fellow, with thick bushy hair and a grizzled beard. His dress was of the antique Dutch fashion—a cloth jerkin, strapped round the waist—several pair of breeches, the outer one of ample volume, decorated with rows of buttons down the sides, and bunches at the knees. He bore on his shoulder a stout kegthat seemed full of liquor, and made signs for Rip to approach and assist him with the load. Though rather shy and distrustful of this new acquaintance, Rip complied with his usual alacrity; and mutually relieving each other, they clambered up a narrow gully, apparently the dry bed of a mountain torrent. As they ascended, Rip every now and then heard long rolling peals, like distant thunder, that seemed to issue out of a deep ravine, or rather cleft, between lofty rocks, towards which their rugged path conducted. He paused for an instant, but supposing it to be the muttering of one of those transient thunder-showers which often take place in mountain heights, he proceeded. Passing through the ravine, they came to a hollow, like a small amphitheater, surrounded by perpendicular precipices, over the brinks of which impending trees shot their branches, so that you only caught glimpses of the azure sky and the bright evening cloud. During the whole time Rip and his companion had labored on in silence, for though the former marveled greatly what could be the object of carrying a keg of liquor up this wild mountain; yet there was something strange and incomprehensible about the unknown, that inspired awe and checked familiarity.

On entering the amphitheater, new objects of wonder presented themselves. On a level spot in the center was a company of odd-looking personages playing at ninepins[①]. They were dressed in a quaint outlandish fashion; some wore short doublets, others jerkins, with long knives in their belts, and most of them had

---

① ninepins: a game played with nine pins, or pieces of wood, set on end, at which a wooden ball is thrown to knock them down.

enormous breeches, of similar style with that of the guide's. Their visages, too, were peculiar; one had a large head, broad face, and small piggish eyes; the face of another seemed to consist entirely of nose, and was surmounted by a white sugar-loaf hat, set off with a little red cock's tail. They all had beards, of various shapes and colors. There was one who seemed to be the commander. He was a stout old gentleman, with a weather-beaten countenance; he wore a laced doublet, broad belt and hanger[①], high-crowned hat and feather, red stockings, and high-heeled shoes, with roses in them. The whole group reminded Rip of the figures in an old Flemish painting[②], in the parlor of Dominie[③] Van Shaick, the village parson, and which had been brought over from Holland at the time of the settlement.

What seemed particularly odd to Rip was, that though these folks were evidently amusing themselves, yet they maintained the gravest faces, the most mysterious silence, and were, withal[④], the most melancholy party of pleasure he had ever witnessed. Nothing interrupted the stillness of the scene but the noise of the balls, which, whenever they were rolled, echoed along the mountains like rumbling peals of thunder.

As Rip and his companion approached them, they suddenly desisted from their play, and stared at him with such fixed, statue-like gaze, and such strange, uncouth, lack-luster countenances, that his heart turned within him, and his knees smote together. His companion now emptied the contents of the keg into large flagons, and made signs to him to wait upon the company. He obeyed with fear and trembling; they quaffed the liquor in profound silence, and then returned to their game.

By degrees Rip's awe and apprehension subsided. He even ventured, when no eye was fixed upon him, to taste the beverage, which he found had much of the flavor of excellent Hollands. He was naturally a thirsty soul, and was soon tempted to repeat the draught. One taste provoked another; and he reiterated his visits to the flagon so often, that at length his senses were overpowered, his eyes swam in his head, his head gradually declined, and he fell into a deep sleep.

On waking, he found himself on the green knoll whence he had first seen the old man of the glen. He rubbed his eyes—it was a bright sunny morning. The birds were hopping and twittering among the bushes, and the eagle was wheeling aloft, and breasting the pure mountain breeze. "Surely," thought Rip, "I have not slept here all night." He recalled the occurrences before he fell asleep. The strange man with a keg

---

① hanger: a short sword, hung from the belt.
② Flemish painting: painting produced in the area of Flanders, northern Belgium.
③ Dominie: Priest.
④ withal: (archaic) moreover.

of liquor the mountain ravine-the wild retreat among the rocks—the woebegone party at nine-pins—the flagon— "Oh! That flagon! That wicked flagon!" Thought Rip; "what excuse shall I make to Dame Van Winkle?"

He looked round for his gun, but in place of the clean well-oiled fowling-piece, he found an old firelock lying by him, the barrel incrusted with rust, the lock falling off and the stock worm-eaten. He now suspected that the grave roysters of the mountain had put a trick upon him, and, having dosed him with liquor, had robbed him of his gun. Wolf, too, had disappeared, but he might have strayed away after a squirrel or partridge. He whistled after him, and shouted his name, but all in vain; the echoes repeated his whistle and shout, but no dog was to be seen.

He determined to revisit the scene of the last evening's gambol, and, if he met with any of the party, to demand his dog and gun. As he rose to walk he found himself stiff in the joints, and wanting in his usual activity. "These mountain beds do not agree with me," thought Rip; "and if this frolic should lay me up with a fit of the rheumatism, I shall have a blessed time with Dame Van Winkle." With some difficulty he got down into the glen: he found the gully up which he and his companion had ascended the preceding evening; but to his astonishment, a mountain stream was now foaming down it—leaping from rock to rock, and filling the glen with babbling murmurs. He, however, made shift to scramble up its sides, working his toilsome way through thickets of birch, sassafras, and witch-hazel, and sometimes tripped up or entangled by the wild grape-vines that twisted their coils or tendrils from tree to tree, and spread a kind of network in his path.

At length he reached to where the ravine had opened through the cliffs to the amphitheater; but no traces of such opening remained. The rocks presented a high impenetrable wall, over which the torrent came tumbling in a sheet of feathery foam, and fell into a broad, deep basin, black from the shadows of the surrounding forest. Here, then, poor Rip was brought to a stand. He again called and whistled after his dog; he was only answered by the cawing of a flock of idle crows, sporting high in air about a dry tree that overhung a sunny precipice; and who, secure in their elevation, seemed to look down and scoff at the poor man's perplexities. What was to be done?—the morning was passing away, and Rip felt famished for want of his breakfast. He grieved to give up his dog and his gun; he dreaded to meet his wife; but it would not do to starve among the mountains. He shook his head, shouldered the rusty firelock, and, with a heart full of trouble and anxiety, turned his steps homeward.

As he approached the village he met a number of people, but none whom he knew, which somewhat surprised him, for he had thought himself acquainted with everyone in the country round. Their dress, too, was of a different fashion from that to which he was accustomed. They all stared at him with equal marks of surprise, and, whenever they cast their eyes upon him, invariably stroked their chins. The constant recurrence of this gesture induced Rip, involuntarily, to do the same—when, to his astonishment, he found his beard had grown a foot long!

He had now entered the skirts of the village. A troop of strange children ran at his heels, hooting after him, and pointing at his gray beard. The dogs, too, not one of which he recognized for an old acquaintance, barked at him as he passed. The very village was altered; it was larger and more populous. There were rows of houses which he had never seen before, and those which had been his familiar haunts had disappeared. Strange names were over the doors—strange faces at the windows—everything was strange. His mind now misgave him; he began to doubt whether both he and the world around him were not bewitched. Surely this was his native village, which he had left but the day before. There stood the Kaatskill mountains—there ran the silver Hudson at a distance—there was every hill and dale precisely as it had always been. Rip was sorely perplexed. "That flagon last night," thought he, "has addled my poor head sadly!"

It was with some difficulty that he found the way to his own house, which he approached with silent awe, expecting every moment to hear the shrill voice of Dame Van Winkle. He found the house gone to decay—the roof fallen in, the windows shattered, and the doors off the hinges. A half-starved dog that looked like Wolf, was skulking about it. Rip called him by name, but the cur snarled, showed his teeth, and passed on. This was an unkind cut indeed—"My very dog", sighed poor Rip, "has forgotten me!"

He entered the house, which, to tell the truth, Dame Van Winkle had always kept in neat order. It was empty, forlorn, and apparently abandoned. The desolateness overcame all his connubial fears—he called loudly for his wife and children—the lonely chambers rang for a moment with his voice, and then all again was silence.

He now hurried forth, and hastened to his old resort, the village inn—but it too was gone. A large, rickety, wooden building stood in its place, with great gaping windows, some of them broken and mended with old hats and petticoats, and over the door was painted, "The Union Hotel, by Jonathan Doolittle." Instead of the great tree that used to shelter the quiet little Dutch inn of yore, there was now reared a tall naked pole, with something on the top that looked like a red nightcap[①], and from it was fluttering a flag, on which was a singular assemblage of stars and stripes—all this was strange and incomprehensible. He recognized on the sign, however, the ruby face

---

① a red nightcap: the liberty cap. Because the caps were once worn by Roman liberated slaves, they were a symbol of liberty.

of King George, under which he had smoked so many a peaceful pipe; but even this was singularly metamorphosed. The red coat was changed for one of blue and buff①, a sword was held in the hand instead of a scepter, the head was decorated with a cocked hat, and underneath was painted in large characters, General Washington.

There was, as usual, a crowd of folks about the door, but none that Rip recollected. The very character of the people seemed changed. There was a busy, bustling, disputatious tone about it, instead of the accustomed phlegm and drowsy tranquility. He looked in vain for the sage Nicholas Vedder, with his broad face, double chin, and fair long pipe, uttering clouds of tobacco-smoke instead of idle speeches; or Van Bummel, the schoolmaster, doling forth the contents of an ancient newspaper. In place of these, a lean, bilious-looking fellow, with pockets full of handbills was haranguing vehemently about rights of citizens—elections—members of Congress—liberty— Bunker's Hill②—heroes of seventy-six—and other words, which were a perfect Babylonish jargon③ to the bewildered Van Winkle.

The appearance of Rip, with his long grizzled beard, his rusty fowling-piece, his uncouth dress, and an army of women and children at his heels, soon attracted the attention of the tavern politicians. They crowded round him, eyeing him from head to foot with great curiosity. The orator bustled up to him, and, drawing him partly aside, inquired "On which side he voted?" Rip stared in vacant stupidity. Another short but busy little fellow pulled him by the arm, and, rising on tiptoe, inquired in his ear, "Whether he was Federal or Democrat④?" Rip was equally at a loss to comprehend the question; when a knowing, self-important old gentleman, in a sharp-cocked hat, made his way through the crowd, putting them to the right and left with his elbows as he passed, and planting himself before Van Winkle, with one arm akimbo, the other resting on his cane, his keen eyes and sharp hat penetrating, as it were, into his very soul, demanded in an austere tone, "What brought him to the election with a gun on his shoulder, and a mob at his heels, and whether he meant to breed a riot in the village?" —"Alas! Gentlemen," cried Rip, somewhat dismayed, "I am a poor quiet man, a native of the place, and a loyal subject of the king, God bless him!"

Here a general shout burst from the bystanders—"A tory⑤! A tory! A spy! A refugee! Hustle him! Away with him!" It was with great difficulty that the self-important man in the cocked hat restored order; and, having assumed, a tenfold

---

① blue and buff: the uniform of then American soldiers.
② Bunker's Hill: 邦克山。邦克山战役为美国独立战争第一场战斗。
③ Babylonish jargon: unintelligible language; nonsense.
④ Federal or Democrat: the two political parties during George Washington's administration (1789~1797).
⑤ A tory: an American backing the English side during the American Revolution.

austerity of brow, demanded again of the unknown culprit, what he came there for, and whom he was seeking? The poor man humbly assured him that he meant no harm, but merely came there in search of some of his neighbors, who used to keep about the tavern.

"Well—who are they?—name them."

Rip bethought himself a moment, and inquired, "Where's Nickolas Vedder?"

There was a silence for a little while, when an old man replied in a thin piping voice, "Nicholas Vedder why, he is dead and gone these eighteen years! There was a wooden tombstone in the churchyard that used to tell all about him, but that's rotten and gone too."

"Where's Brom Dutcher?"

"Oh, he went off to the army in the beginning of the war; some say he was killed at the storming of Stony Point[①]—others say he was drowned in a squall at the foot of Antony's Nose. I don't know—he never came back again."

"Where's Van Bummel, the schoolmaster?"

"He went off to the wars too, was a great militia general, and is now in Congress."

Rip's heart died away at hearing of these sad changes in his home and friends, and finding himself thus alone in the world. Every answer puzzled him too, by treating of such enormous lapses of time, and of matters which he could not understand; war—Congress—Stony Point—he had no courage to ask after any more friends, but cried out in despair, " Does nobody here know Rip Van Winkle?"

"Oh, Rip Van Winkle!" exclaimed two or three, "Oh, to be sure that's Rip Van Winkle yonder, leaning against the tree."

Rip looked, and beheld a precise counterpart of himself, as he went up the mountain: apparently as lazy, and certainly as ragged. The poor fellow was now completely confounded. He doubted his own identity, and whether he was himself or another man. In the midst of his bewilderment, the man in the cocked hat demanded who he was, and what was his name?

"God knows," exclaimed he, at his wits' end; "I'm not myself—I'm somebody else—that's me yonder—no—that's somebody else got into my shoes—I was myself last night, but I fell asleep on the mountain, and they've changed my gun, and everything's changed, and I'm changed, and I can't tell what's my name, or who I am!"

The bystanders began now to look at each other, nod, wink significantly, and tap their fingers against their foreheads. There was a whisper, also, about securing

---

① Stony Point: a village to the southeast of New York; the site of a battle during which a British fortification was attacked.

the gun, and keeping the old fellow from doing mischief, at the very suggestion of which the self-important man in the cocked hat retired with some precipitation. At this critical moment a fresh comely woman pressed through the throng to get a peep at the gray-bearded man. She had a chubby child in her arms, which, frightened at his looks, began to cry. "Hush, Rip," cried she, "hush, your little fool; the old man won't hurt you." The name of the child, the air of the mother, the tone of her voice, all awakened a train of recollections in his mind.

"What is your name, my good woman?" asked he.

"Judith Gardenier."

"And your father's name?"

"Ah, poor man, Rip Van Winkle was his name, but it's twenty years since he went away from home with his gun, and never has been heard of since—his dog came home without him; but whether he shot himself, or was carried away by the Indians, nobody can tell. I was then but a little girl."

Rip had but one question more to ask; but he put it with a faltering voice, —

"Where's your mother?"

"Oh, she too had died but a short time since; she broke a blood-vessel in a fit of passion at a New-England pedlar."

There was a drop of comfort, at least, in this intelligence. The honest man could contain himself no longer. He caught his daughter and her child in his arms. "I am your father!" cried he—"Young Rip Van Winkle once—old Rip Van Winkle now!—Does nobody know poor Rip Van Winkle?"

All stood amazed, until an old woman, tottering out from among the crowd, put her hand to her brow, and peering under it in his face for a moment, exclaimed, "Sure enough! it is Rip Van Winkle—it is himself! Welcome home again, old neighbor—Why, where have you been these twenty long years?"

Rip's story was soon told, for the whole twenty years had been to him but as one night. The neighbors stared when they heard it; some were seen to wink at each other, and put their tongues in their cheeks: and the self-important man in the cocked hat, who, when the alarm was over, had returned to the field, screwed down the corners of his mouth, and shook his head—upon which there was a general shaking of the head throughout the assemblage.

It was determined, however, to take the opinion of old Peter Vanderdonk, who was seen slowly advancing up the road. He was a descendant of the historian of that name, who wrote one of the earliest accounts of the province. Peter was the most ancient inhabitant of the village, and well versed in all the wonderful events and tradition of the neighborhood. He recollected Rip at once, and corroborated his story in the most satisfactory manner. He assured the company that it was a fact, handed down from his ancestor the historian, that the Kaatskill mountains had always been haunted by strange beings. That it was affirmed that the great Hendrick Hudson, the first discoverer of the river and country, kept a kind of vigil there every twenty years, with his crew of the Halfmoon, being permitted in this way to revisit the scenes of his enterprise, and keep a guardian eye upon the river, and the great city called by his name. That his father had once seen them in their old Dutch dresses playing at nine-pins in a hollow of the mountain; and that he himself had heard, one summer afternoon, the sound of their balls, like distant peals of thunder.

To make a long story short, the company broke up, and returned to the more important concerns of the election. Rip's daughter took him home to live with her; she had a snug, well-furnished house, and a stout cheery farmer for her husband, whom Rip recollected for one of the urchins that used to climb upon his back. As to Rip's son and heir, who was the ditto of himself, seen leaning against the tree, he was employed to work on the farm; but evinced an hereditary disposition to attend to anything else but his business.

Rip now resumed his old walks and habits; he soon found many of his former cronies, though all rather the worse for the wear and tear of time; and preferred making friends among the rising generation, with whom he soon grew into great favor.

Having nothing to do at home, and being arrived at that happy age when a man can be idle with impunity, he took his place once more on the bench at the inn door, and was reverenced as one of the patriarchs of the village, and a chronicle of the old times "before the war". It was some time before he could get into the regular track of gossip, or could be made to comprehend the strange events that had taken place during his torpor. How that there had been a revolutionary war—that the country had thrown off the yoke of Old England—and that, instead of being a subject of His Majesty George the Third, he was now a free citizen of the United States. Rip, in fact, was no politician; the changes of states and empires made but little impression on him; but there was one species of despotism under which he had long groaned, and that was—petticoat government. Happily that was at an end; he had got his neck out of the yoke of matrimony, and could go in and out whenever he pleased without dreading the tyranny of Dame Van Winkle. Whenever her name was mentioned, however, he shook his head, shrugged his shoulders, and cast up his eyes; which might pass either for an expression of resignation to his fate, or joy at his deliverance.

He used to tell his story to every stranger that arrived at Mr. Doolittle's hotel. He was observed at first to vary on some points every time he told it, which was, doubtless, owing to his having so recently awaked. It at last settled down precisely to the tale I have related, and not a man, woman, or child in the neighborhood but knew if by heart. Some always pretended to doubt the reality of it, and insisted that Rip had been out of his head, and that this was one point on which he always remained flighty. The old Dutch inhabitants, however, almost universally gave it full credit. Even to this day they never hear a thunder-storm of a summer afternoon about the Kaatskill, but they say Hendrick Hudson and his crew are at their game of nine-pins; and it is a common wish of all hen-pecked husbands in the neighborhood, when life hangs heavy on their hands, that they might have a quieting draught out of Rip Van Winkle's flagon.

译文链接: https://www.vrrw.net/wx/43919.html

Questions for Understanding

1. What kind of person is Rip Van Winkle?
2. What does he do in the mountain?
3. How many years does he sleep?
4. What changes have taken place when he returns to his village?
5. What are the themes of the story?
6. What is Irving's attitude toward the past? What does he prefer, the days before the War of Independence or those after the war?

Aspects of Appreciation

1. This is a tale about an American dream which is different from others. This dream focuses on Rip's confused state of mind when he wakes from his sleep. What this American dream says is that many Americans (the early colonists) were so confused about the changes brought about by the American Revolution that they, like Rip, felt they were twenty years behind. The confusion was a psychological difficulty Americans at the time felt in understanding their own recent national history.

2. The creation of Rip Van Winkle as a prototypical American male entails some problems from a feminist point of view. The humor of the tale is achieved at the expense of Rip's wife, Dame Van Winkle. Rip's newly acquired independence is not from the tyranny of England or the patriarch in the village, but from the yoke of his wife who is now dead. Because of the influence the tale has on later male writers, gender-conscious critics identify it as the origin of an androcentric narrative type.

Suggested Further Reading

"The Legend of Sleepy Hollow" (1820); *Life of George Washington* (1842~1846).

Topics for Further Study

1. Irving is remembered for his literary innovations. Can you explain what inspired him, and why he could make so many significant innovations?

2. The authenticity of the story of "Rip Van Winkle" is open to debate, although Irving affirmed, in the mouth of D.K., the narrator, that the story was a real one. What do you think of the meaning of the story if you take it for granted?

Knowledge of Literature

An Element of Fiction: Character（人物）

A character is usually a person in a narrative. Sometimes, as in fantasy fiction, a character may be an animal, a robot, or a creature from outer space, but the author endows it with some human qualities. Characters can be divided into flat (simple) and round (complex) characters. Flat characters have only one or two personality traits and are easily recognizable as stereotypes. Round characters have multiple personality traits and therefore resemble real people. Characters who remain the same throughout a work are static. Those who change are dynamic characters. Usually, round characters change and flat characters remain the same, but not always. Overall, characters help to create a rich and engaging story that readers can relate to and empathize with.

推荐阅读的论文：
[1] 周莉丽. 以女性主义视角对温克尔太太形象的重新解读 [J]. 新乡学院学报，2016, 33(08).
[2] 刘婕，杨保林. 华盛顿·欧文笔下的女性形象解析 [J]. 兰州交通大学学报，2013, 32(02).

Henry David Thoreau (1817~1862)

About the Author

Thoreau was born in Concord, a village near Boston where many of the literary figures of the 19th century, including Emerson, lived. After graduating from Harvard and teaching school for a few years, Thoreau went to live with Emerson both to study with him and to work as a handyman. Later in his life, he traveled a little, but in general Thoreau stayed near his home. He had a strong attachment to his family, and he preferred to travel through books. The trips he did take were often camping trips, for he enjoyed the outdoors and was a skillful woodsman.

Both Thoreau's Transcendental philosophy and his scientific knowledge contributed to his love of nature. In *A Week on the Concord and Merrimack Rivers*, he wrote about a canoeing trip he made with his brother. Later he built himself a cabin in the woods by Walden Pond, and lived there for two years, reporting on his experiences in *Walden*. He wanted to live alone and depend on his own mental and physical resources. He raised his own food and spent very little money, devoting most of his time to study and reflection.

Thoreau's style is often conversational in tone, similar to that found in Emerson's journals, so on the surface his books seem to be nothing more than casual accounts of his trips. In fact, however, they are carefully arranged, their design helping to convey Thoreau's meaning.

Walden is deceptively casual. Thoreau condensed his two and a half years in the woods into one year, stressing the unifying theme of seasonal changes as he progressed from the summer growth of his bean crop to its harvest, and to the death of the plants and replanting in the spring. Thoreau used the little world around Walden Pond to illustrate his philosophy and observations about life.

Through his writing Thoreau wanted to illustrate that the pursuit of material things had no value. He desired a life of contemplation, of being in harmony with nature, and of acting on his own principles. His study of Eastern religions contributed to his desire for a simple life, while his reaction against such Yankee pragmatists as Benjamin Franklin is also apparent. Both Franklin and Thoreau advocated thrift and hard work, but while Franklin expected the frugal to get richer and richer, Thoreau thought physical labor and a minimum of material goods made men more sensitive and kept them closer to nature.

In 1847 Thoreau was imprisoned briefly for refusing to pay a tax while the government supported a war he considered unjust. His refusal to pay was consistent with his belief in using civil disobedience to protest government actions, a philosophy he explains in his essay, "Civil Disobedience". He was also strongly opposed to slavery. Thoreau was very much an individualist, distrusting group action and preferring to depend on individual reform for the improvement of society.

Walden

About the Work

Walden is a book unique in its analysis of life and criticism of customs. In this book, there are many pages of beautiful and detailed depictions. There are some pages of incisive and enlightening reasoning. Although it was written more than a hundred years ago, it has not lost its significance.

On the surface, *Walden* speaks only of the practical side of living alone in the woods, of the plants, animals and insects one finds there, and of the changing seasons. But in fact it is a completely Transcendentalist work. Thoreau rejects the things ordinary people desire in life, such as money and possessions. Instead, he emphasizes the search for true wisdom. True enjoyment comes only when one throws off all unnecessary things. *Walden* is a hopeful book, encouraging people to lead sincere, joyous, and meaningful lives.

Where I Lived, and What I Lived For

At a certain season[①] of our life we are accustomed to consider every spot as the possible site of a house. I have thus surveyed the country on every side within a dozen miles of where I live. In imagination I have bought all the farms in succession, for all were to be bought and I knew their price. I walked over each farmer's premises, tasted his wild apples, discoursed on husbandry with him, took his farm at his price, at any price, mortgaging it to him in my mind; even put a higher price on it—took every thing but a deed of it—took his word for his deed, for I dearly love to talk—cultivated it, and him too to some extent, I trust, and withdrew when I had enjoyed it long enough, leaving him to carry it on. This experience entitled me to be regarded as a sort of real-estate broker by my friends. Wherever I sat, there I might live, and the landscape radiated from me accordingly. What is a house but a sedes[②], a seat?—better if a country seat. I discovered many a site for a house not likely to be soon improved, which some might have thought too far from the village, but to my eyes the village was too far from it. Well, there I might live, I said; and there I did live, for an hour, a summer and a winter life; saw how I could let the years run off, buffet the winter through[③], and see the spring come in. The future inhabitants of this region, wherever

---

① season: Here it means "period" or "stage"(时期).
② sedes: (Latin) chair(座位).
③ buffet the winter through: go through the winter(挨过了冬天).

they may place their houses, may be sure that they have been anticipated. An afternoon sufficed to lay out the land into orchard, wood-lot and pasture, and to decide what fine oaks or pines should be left to stand before the door, and whence each blasted tree could be seen to the best advantage①; and then I let it lie, fallow perchance, for a man is rich in proportion to the number of things which he can afford to let alone.

My imagination carried me so far that I even had the refusal of several farms—the refusal was all I wanted—but I never got my fingers burned by actual possession. The nearest that I came to actual possession was when I bought the Hollowell Place②, and had begun to sort my seeds, and collected materials with which to make a wheelbarrow to carry it on or off with; but before the owner gave me a deed of it, his wife—every man has such a wife—changed her mind and wished to keep it, and he offered me ten dollars to release him. Now, to speak the truth, I had but ten cents in the world, and it surpassed my arithmetic to tell, if I was that man who had ten cents, or who had a farm, or ten dollars, or all together.③ However, I let him keep the ten dollars and the farm too, for I had carried it far enough; or rather, to be generous, I sold him the farm for just what I gave for it, and, as he was not a rich man, made him a present of ten dollars, and still had my ten cents, and seeds, and materials for a wheelbarrow left. I found thus that I had been a rich man without any damage to my poverty. But I retained the landscape, and I have since annually carried off what it yielded without a wheelbarrow. With respect to landscapes,—

"I am monarch of all I survey,

My right there is none to dispute." ④

I have frequently seen a poet withdraw, having enjoyed the most valuable part of a farm, while the crusty farmer supposed that he had got a few wild apples only. Why, the owner does not know it for many years when a poet has put his farm in rhyme⑤, the most admirable kind of invisible fence, has fairly impounded it, milked it, skimmed it, and got all the cream, and left the farmer only the skimmed milk.

The real attractions of the Hollowell farm, to me, were its complete retirement, being about two miles from the village, half a mile from the nearest neighbor, and separated from the highway by a broad field; its bounding on the river, which the owner said protected it by its fogs from frosts in the spring, though that was nothing to

---

① and whence each blasted tree...best advantage: 从何处可以十分清楚地看见每一棵枯萎的树。
② Hollowell Place: name of a place.
③ it surpassed...all together: 这使我算不上来，弄不清我自己是否真有十分钱，或有个农庄，或有十元钱，或拥有这一切。(指这一变故使他不知所措。)
④ "I am...to dispute.": "我是眺望一切美景的君王，我的权力不容争辩。" The two lines are quoted from the poem "Verses Supposed to Be Written by Alexander Selkirk" by English poet William Cowper (1731~1800).
⑤ has put his farm in rhyme: 诗人已将他的农场写进了诗。

me; the gray color and ruinous state of the house and barn, and the dilapidated fence, which put such an interval between me and the last occupant; the hollow and lichen-covered apple trees, gnawed by rabbits, showing what kind of neighbors I should have; but above all, the recollection I had of it from my earliest voyages up the river, when the house was concealed behind a dense grove of red maples, through which I heard the house-dog bark. I was in haste to buy it, before the proprietor finished getting out some rocks, cutting down the hollow apple trees, and grubbing up some young birches which had sprung up in the pasture, or, in short, had made any more of his improvements. To enjoy these advantages I was ready to carry it on; like Atlas[①], to take the world on my shoulders—I never heard what compensation he received for that—and do all those things which had no other motive or excuse but that I might pay for it and be unmolested in my possession of it; for I knew all the while that it would yield the most abundant crop of the kind I wanted if I could only afford to let it alone. But it turned out as I have said.

All that I could say, then, with respect to farming on a large scale, (I have always cultivated a garden,) was, that I had had my seeds ready. Many think that seeds improve with age. I have no doubt that time discriminates between the good and the bad; and when at last I shall plant, I shall be less likely to be disappointed. But I would say to my fellows, once for all, as long as possible live free and uncommitted. It makes but little difference whether you are committed to a farm or the county jail.[②]

Old Cato[③], whose "De Re Rustic"[④] is my "Cultivator", says, and the only translation I have seen makes sheer nonsense of the passage, "When you think of getting a farm, turn it thus in your mind, not to buy greedily; nor spare your pains to look at it, and do not think it enough to go round it once. The oftener you go there the more it will please you, if it is good." I think I shall not buy greedily, but go round and round it as long as I live, and be buried in it first, that it may please me the more at last.

The present was my next experiment of this kind, which I purpose to describe more at length; for convenience, putting the experience of two years into one. As I have said, I do not propose to write an ode to dejection, but to brag as lustily as chanticleer in the morning, standing on his roost, if only to wake my neighbors up.[⑤]

When first I took up my abode in the woods, that is, began to spend my nights

---

① Atlas: 阿特拉斯，希腊神话中以肩顶天的巨神。常喻指肩负重担的人。
② as long as possible...country jail: 你们要自由自在地生活，无拘无束地生活，能多久，就多久，热衷于农场与关在县府大牢，二者没有多大区别。
③ Cato: Marcus Porcius Cato (234 BC~149 BC), ancient Roman politician, general and writer.
④ De Re Rustic:《乡村篇》。It was written by Cato.
⑤ if only to wake my neighbors up: 哪怕只是为了唤醒我的邻居。

as well as days there, which, by accident, was on Independence Day, of the fourth of July, 1845, my house was not finished for winter, but was merely a defence against the rain, without plastering or chimney, the walls being of rough weather-stained boards, with wide chinks, which made it cool at night. The upright white hewn studs and freshly planed door and window casings gave it a clean and airy look, especially in the morning, when its timbers were saturated with dew, so that I fancied that by noon some sweet gum would exude from them. To my imagination it retained throughout the day more or less of this auroral character[①], reminding me of a certain house on a mountain which I had visited the year before. This was an airy and unplastered cabin, fit to entertain a traveling god, and where a goddess might trail her garments. The winds which passed over my dwelling were such as sweep over the ridges of mountains, bearing the broken strains, or celestial parts only, of terrestrial music. The morning wind forever blows, the poem of creation is uninterrupted; but few are the ears that hear it. Olympus is but the outside of the earth every where.[②]

The only house I had been the owner of before, if I except a boat, was a tent, which I used occasionally when making excursions in the summer, and this is still rolled up in my garret; but the boat, after passing from hand to hand, has gone down the stream of time. With this more substantial shelter about me, I had made some progress toward settling in the world. This frame[③], so slightly clad, was a sort of crystallization around me, and reacted on the builder. It was suggestive somewhat as a picture in outlines. I did not need to go out doors to take the air, for the atmosphere within had lost none of its freshness. It was not so much within doors as behind a door where I sat, even in the rainiest weather, The Harivansa[④] says, "An abode without birds is like a meat without seasoning." Such was not my abode, for I found myself suddenly neighbor to the birds; not by having imprisoned one, but having caged myself near them. I was not only nearer to some of those which commonly frequent the garden and the orchard, but to those wilder and more thrilling songsters of the forest which never, or rarely, serenade a villager—the wood-thrush, the veery, the scarlet tanager, the field-sparrow, the whippoorwill[⑤], and many others.

I was seated by the shore of a small pond, about a mile and a half south of the

---

① auroral character: the atmosphere at the dawn time(黎明的情调).
② Olympus is but the outside of the earth every where: 奥林匹斯山就在大地的外表，随处可见。奥林匹斯山位于希腊东北部，传说在希腊神话中是诸神的居住地，常被用来喻指天堂乐园。这里的意思是，乐园到处皆是，但能领略其中奥妙之人却屈指可数。
③ this frame: small hut.
④ The Harivansa: an India's long narrative poem in the fifth century.
⑤ the wood-thrush, the veery, the scarlet tanager, the field-sparrow, the whippoorwill: wood-thrush 和 veery 是北美东北部林中的两种画眉鸟；scarlet tanager 红莺；field-sparrow 田雀；whippoorwill 北美夜鹰。

village of Concord and somewhat higher than it, in the midst of an extensive wood between that town and Lincoln, and about two miles south of that our only field known to fame, Concord Battle Ground①; but I was so low in the woods that the opposite shore, half a mile off, like the rest, covered with wood, was my most distant horizon. For the first week, whenever I looked out on the pond it impressed me like a tarn high up on the side of a mountain, its bottom far above the surface of other lakes, and, as the sun arose, I saw it throwing off its nightly clothing of mist, and here and there, by degrees, its soft ripples or its smooth reflecting surface was revealed, while the mists, like ghosts, were stealthily withdrawing in every direction into the woods, as at the breaking up of some nocturnal conventicle. The very dew seemed to hang upon the trees later into the day than usual, as on the sides of mountains.

  This small lake was of most value as a neighbor in the intervals of a gentle rain storm in August, when, both air and water being perfectly still, but the sky overcast, mid-afternoon had all the serenity of evening, and the wood-thrush sang around, and was heard from shore to shore. A lake like this is never smoother than at such a time; and the clear portion of the air above it being shallow and darkened by clouds, the water, full of light and reflections, becomes a lower heaven itself so much the more important.② From a hill-top nearby, where the wood had been recently cut off, there was a pleasing vista southward across the pond, through a wide indentation in the hills which form the shore there, where their opposite sides sloping toward each other suggested a stream flowing out in that direction through a wooded valley, but stream there was none. That way I looked between and over the near green hills to some distant and higher ones in the horizon, tinged with blue. Indeed, by standing on tiptoe I could catch a glimpse of some of the peaks of the still bluer and more distant mountain ranges in the north-west, those true-blue coins from heaven's own mint, and also of some portion of the village. But in other directions, even from this point, I could not see over or beyond the woods which surrounded me. It is well to have some water in your neighborhood, to give buoyancy to and float the earth. One value even of the smallest well is, that when you look into it you see that earth is not continent but insular. This is as important as that it keeps butter cool. When I looked across the pond from this peak toward the Sudbury meadows③, which in time of flood I distinguished elevated perhaps by a mirage in their seething valley, like a coin in a basin, all the earth beyond the pond appeared like a thin crust insulated and floated even by this small sheet of intervening water, and I was reminded that this on which I dwelt was

---

① Concord Battle Ground: the site of the American Revolutionary War battle which happened in April 19, 1775.
② the water... more important: 水中浮光闪闪，倒影绰绰，自成一片下界天国，更值得珍视。
③ Sudbury meadows: 萨德伯里草原。

but dry land.

Though the view from my door was still more contracted, I did not feel crowded or confined in the least. There was pasture enough for my imagination.① The low shrub-oak plateau to which the opposite shore arose, stretched away toward the prairies of the West and the steppes of Tartary②, affording ample room for all the roving families of men. "There are none happy in the world but beings who enjoy freely a vast horizon," said Damodara③, when his herds required new and larger pastures.

Both place and time were changed, and I dwelt nearer to those parts of the universe and to those eras in history which had most attracted me. Where I lived was as far off as many a region viewed nightly by astronomers. We are wont to imagine rare and delectable places in some remote and more celestial corner of the system, behind the constellation of Cassiopeia's Chair④, far from noise and disturbance, I discovered that my house actually had its site in such a withdrawn, but forever new and unprofaned, part of the universe. If it were worth the while to settle in those parts near to the Pleiades or the Hyades, to Aldebaran⑤ or Altair, then I was really there, or at an equal remoteness from the life which I had left behind, dwindled and twinkling with as fine a ray to my nearest neighbor, and to be seen only in moonless nights by him. Such was that part of creation where I had squatted;—

"There was a shepherd that did live,

And held his thoughts as high

As were the mounts whereon his flocks

Did hourly feed him by."⑥

What should we think of the shepherd's life if his flocks always wandered to higher pastures than his thoughts?

Every morning was a cheerful invitation to make my life of equal simplicity, and I may say innocence, with Nature herself. I have been as sincere a worshipper of Aurora as the Greeks. I got up early and bathed in the pond; that was a religious exercise⑦, and one of the best things which I did. They say that characters were

---

① There was...my imagination: 我想象的骏马仍有自由驰骋的天地。这里是说视野虽窄，但他想象的天地却非常宽广。
② Tartary: 泛指欧、亚两洲之间鞑靼人居住区，无固定区域，因为鞑靼人为游牧民族。
③ Damodara: Krishna, 印度神话中三大神之一，毗瑟拿(Vishnu) 的第八化身。梭罗的这段话引自长诗 Harivansa。
④ Cassiopeia's Chair: 仙后星座，椅子形状。
⑤ Aldebaran: 金牛星座中的一星，也是最明亮的星星之一。
⑥ "There was...by.": "从前住着个牧羊人，他的思想高过了山，山上有他的一群羊，时时将他来喂养。"
⑦ a religious exercise: 意指在湖中洗澡如同洗涤灵魂。

engraven on the bathing tub of King Tching-thang① to this effect: "Renew thyself completely each day; do it again, and again, and forever again."② I can understand that. Morning brings back the heroic ages. I was as much affected by the faint hum of a mosquito making its invisible and unimaginable tour through my apartment at earliest dawn, when I was sitting with door and windows open, as I could be by my trumpet that ever sang of fame. It was Homer's requiem; itself an Iliad and Odyssey in the air, singing its own wrath and wanderings. There was something cosmical about it; a standing advertisement, till forbidden③, of the everlasting vigor and fertility of the world. The morning, which is the most memorable season of the day, is the awakening hour. Then there is least somnolence in us; and for an hour, at least, some part of us awakes which slumbers all the rest of the day and night. Little is to be expected of that day, if it can be called a day, to which we are not awakened by our Genius, but by the mechanical nudgings of some servitor, ane not awakened by our own newly acquired force and aspirations from within, accompanied by the undulations of celestial music, instead of factory bells, and a fragrance filling the air—to a higher life than we fell asleep from④; and thus the darkness bear its fruit, and prove itself to be good, no less than the light. That man who does not believe that each day contains an earlier, more sacred, and auroral hour than he has yet profaned, has despaired of life, and is pursuing a descending and darkening way. After a partial cessation of his sensuous life, the soul of man, or its organs rather, are reinvigorated each day, and his Genius tries again what noble life it can make. All memorable events, I should say, transpire in morning time and in a morning atmosphere. The Vedas say, "All intelligences awake with the morning."⑤ Poetry and art, and the fairest and most memorable of the actions of men, date from such an hour. All poets and heroes, like Memnon⑥, are the children of Aurora, and emit their music at sunrise. To him whose elastic and vigorous thought keeps pace with the sun, the day is a perpetual morning.⑦ It matters not what the clocks say or the attitudes and labors of men. Morning is when I am awake and there is a dawn in me. Moral reform is the effort to throw off sleep. Why is it that men give so poor an account of their day if they have not been slumbering? They are not

---

① King Tching-thang: 商朝成汤王, 又称武汤, 商朝建立者。
② "Renew thyself...forever again": "苟日新, 日日新, 又日新。"据孔子《礼记·大学》记载, 商朝成汤王曾将上文刻于浴盆, 用于自戒。
③ till forbidden: 常写作 "TF", 一种符号, 意为广告需要连续登载, "直到最后被取消"。
④ a higher life than we fell asleep from: 一种比我们睡前生活更高尚的生活。
⑤ All intelligences awake with the morning: 万知醒于晨。意为 "一日之计在于晨"。
⑥ Memnon: 希腊神话中曙光女神奥罗拉(Aurora)的儿子, 在特洛伊战争中被浑身刀枪不入的阿基里斯所杀。
⑦ To him...a perpetual morning: 对那些与太阳同步的富有弹性和生机勃勃的思维来说, 一天的任何时候都是早晨。

such poor calculators. If they had not been overcome with drowsiness they would have performed something. The millions are awake enough for physical labor; but only one in a million is awake enough for effective intellectual exertion, only one in a hundred millions to a poetic or divine life.① To be awake is to be alive. I have never yet met a man who was quite awake. How could I have looked him in the face?

We must learn to reawaken and keep ourselves awake, not by mechanical aids, but by an infinite expectation of the dawn, which does not forsake us in our soundest sleep. I know of no more encouraging fact than the unquestionable ability of man to elevate his life by a conscious endeavor. It is something to be able to paint a particular picture, or to carve a statue, and so to make a few objects beautiful; but it is far more glorious to carve and paint the very atmosphere and medium through which we look, which morally we can do. To affect the quality of the day, that is the highest of arts. Every man is tasked to make his life, even in its details, worthy of the contemplation of his most elevated and critical hour. If we refused, or rather used up, such paltry information as we get, the oracles would distinctly inform us how this might be done.

I went to the woods because I wished to live deliberately, to front only the essential facts of life, and see if I could not learn what it had to teach, and not, when I came to die, discover that I had not lived. I did not wish to live what was not life, living is so dear; nor did I wish to practice resignation, unless it was quite necessary. I wanted to live deep and suck out all the marrow of life, to live so sturdily and Spartan-like as to put to rout all that was not life, to cut a broad swath and shave close, to drive life into a corner, and reduce it to its lowest terms, and, if it proved to be mean, why then to get the whole and genuine meanness of it, and publish its meanness to the world; or if it were sublime, to know it by experience, and be able to give a true account of it in my next excursion. For most men, it appears to me, are in a strange uncertainty about it, whether it is of the devil or of God, and have somewhat hastily concluded that it is the chief end of man here to "glorify God and enjoy him forever".②

Still we live meanly, like ants; though the fable tells us that we were long ago changed into men,③ like pygmies we fight with cranes④; it is error upon error, and clout upon clout, and our best virtue has for its occasion a superfluous and evitable wretchedness. Our life is frittered away by detail. An honest man has hardly need to

---

① only one...divine life: 一亿人中只有一人能尽享富有诗意或神圣的生活。
② glorify God and enjoy him forever: 永远崇拜上帝，热爱上帝。
③ We were long ago changed into men: 在希腊神话中，有个故事讲到冥界审判官阿依库斯曾劝他父亲天神宙斯把蚂蚁变成人。
④ cranes: 荷马在《伊利亚特》第三卷中，把特洛伊人比作作战的天鹅。

count more than his ten fingers, or in extreme cases he may add his ten toes, and lump the rest. Simplicity, simplicity, simplicity! I say, let your affairs be as two or three, and not a hundred or a thousand; instead of a million count half a dozen, and keep your accounts on your thumb nail. In the midst of this chopping sea of civilized life, such are the clouds and storms and quicksands and thousand-and-one items to be allowed for,① that a man has to live, if he would not founder and go to the bottom and not make his port at all, by dead reckoning, and he must be a great calculator indeed who succeeds. Simplify, simplify. Instead of three meals a day, if it be necessary eat but one; instead of a hundred dishes, five; and reduce other things in proportion. Our life is like a German Confederacy②, made up of petty states, with its boundary forever fluctuating, so that even a German cannot tell you how it is bounded at any moment. The nation itself, with all its so-called internal improvements, which, by the way, are all external and superficial, is just such an unwieldy and overgrown establishment, cluttered with furniture and tripped up by its own traps, ruined by luxury and heedless expense, by want of calculation and a worthy aim, as the million households in the land; and the only cure for it as for them is in a rigid economy, a stern and more than Spartan simplicity of life and elevation of purpose. It lives too fast. Men think that is essential that the Nation have commerce, and export ice, and talk through a telegraph, and ride thirty miles an hour, without a doubt, whether they do or not;③ but whether we should live like baboons or like men, is a little uncertain. If we do not get out sleepers④, and forge rails, and devote days and nights to the work, but go to tinkering upon our lives to improve them, who will build railroads? And if railroads are not built, how shall we get to heaven in season? But if we stay at home and mind our business, who will want railroads? We do not ride on the railroad; it rides upon us. Did you ever think what those sleepers are that underlie the railroad? Each one is a man, an Irish-man, or a Yankee man. The rails are laid on them, and they are covered with sand, and the cars run smoothly over them. They are sound sleepers, I assure you. And every few years a new lot is laid down and run over; so that, if some have the pleasure of riding on a rail, others have the misfortune to be ridden upon. And when they run over a man that is walking in his sleep, a supernumerary sleeper in the wrong position, and wake him up, they suddenly stop the cars, and make a hue and cry about it, as if this were an exception. I am glad to know that it takes a gang of men for every five miles to keep the sleepers down and level in their beds as it is, for this is a sign that

---

① thousand-and-one items to be allowed for: a lot of things to think about.
② German Confederacy: 德意志联邦。德意志直到 1871 年才得以统一，因此德意志联邦的边界不断在变。
③ whether they do or not: they=men.
④ sleeper: 枕木。

they may sometime get up again.①

Why should we live with such hurry and waste of life? We are determined to be starved before we are hungry. Men say that a stitch in time saves nine, and so they take a thousand stitches to-day to save nine to-morrow.② As for work, we haven't any of any consequence.③ We have the Saint Vitus' dance, and cannot possibly keep our heads still. If I should only give a few pulls at the parish bell-rope, as for a fire, that is, without setting the bell, there is hardly a man on his farm in the outskirts of Concord, notwithstanding that press of engagements which was his excuse so many times this morning, nor a boy, nor a woman, I might almost say, but would forsake all and follow that sound, not mainly to save property from the flames, but, if we will confess the truth, much more to see it burn, since burn it must, and we, be it known, did not set it on fire—or to see it put out, and have a hand in it, if that is done as handsomely;④ yes, even if it were the parish church itself. Hardly a man takes a half hour's nap after dinner but when he wakes he holds up his head and asks "What's the news?" as if the rest of mankind had stood his sentinels. Some give directions to be waked every half hour, doubtless for no other purpose; and then, to pay for it, they tell what they have dreamed. After a night's sleep the news is as indispensable as the breakfast. "Pray tell me any thing new that has happened to a man any where on this globe"—and he reads it over his coffee and rolls, that a man had had his eyes gouged out this morning on the Wachito River; never dreaming the while that he lives in the dark unfathomed mammoth cave⑤ of this world and has but the rudiment of an eye himself.

For my part, I could easily do without the post-office. I think that there are very few important communications made through it. To speak critically, I never received more than one or two letters in my life—I wrote this some years ago—that were worth the postage. The penny-post is, commonly, an institution through which you seriously offer a man that penny for his thoughts which is so often safely offered in jest. And I am sure that I never read any memorable news in a newspaper. If we read of one man robbed, or murdered, or killed by accident, or one house burned, or one vessel wrecked, or one steamboat blown up, or one cow run over on the Western Railroad, or one mad dog killed, or one lot of grasshoppers in the winter,—we never need read

---

① I am glad...get up again: 每 5 公里铁路就有一对养路工这个事实, 本身说明这些枕木(即昏睡不醒的人)终将松动, 并醒悟过来。Sleeper 是个双关语, 表面的意思为"枕木", 隐含的意思为"昏睡不醒的人", 即忙于名利的浑浑噩噩的人。
② take a thousand stitches...to save nine to-morrow: 事半功倍。
③ haven't any of any consequence: haven't any work of any consequence.
④ have a hand...handsomely: 如果不用费什么劲的话, 那就帮个忙救救火。
⑤ the dark unfathomed mammoth cave: 传说在美国肯塔基州的大山洞里发现过无视力的鱼类, 作者在此把世界比作这种尚未探明的黑暗山洞。

of another. One is enough. If you are acquainted with the principle, what do you care for a myriad instances and applications? To a philosopher all news, as it is called, is gossip, and they who edit and read it are old women over their tea. Yet not a few are greedy after this gossip. There was such a rush, as I hear, the other day at one of the offices to learn the foreign news by the last arrival, that several large squares of plate glass belonging to the establishment were broken by the pressure—news which I seriously think a ready wit might write twelve months or twelve years beforehand with sufficient accuracy. As for Spain, for instance, if you know how to throw in Don Carlos and the Infanta, and Don Pedro and Seville and Granada, from time to time in the right proportions—they may have changed the names a little since I saw the papers—and serve up a bull-fight when other entertainments fail, it will be true to the letter, and give us as good an idea of the exact state or ruin of things in Spain as the most succinct and lucid reports under this head in the newspapers: and as for England, almost the last significant scrap of news from that quarter was the revolution of 1649; and if you have learned the history of her crops for an average year, you never need attend to that thing again, unless your speculations are of a merely pecuniary character. If one may judge who rarely looks into the newspapers①, nothing new does ever happen in foreign parts, a French revolution not excepted.②

What news! How much more important to know what that is which was never old! "Kieou-pe-yu③ (great dignitary of the state of Wei) sent a man to Khoung-tseu④ to know his news. Khoung-tseu caused the messenger to be seated near him, and questioned him in these terms: What is your master doing? The messenger answered with respect: My master desires to diminish the number of his faults, but he cannot accomplish it. The messenger being gone, the philosopher remarked: What a worthy messenger! What a worthy messenger!⑤ The preacher, instead of vexing the ears of drowsy farmers on their day of rest at the end of the week—for Sunday is the fit conclusion of an ill-spent week, and not the fresh and brave beginning of a new one—with this one other draggle-tail of a sermon, should shout with thundering voice, "Pause! Avast! Why so seeming fast, but deadly slow?"

Shams and delusion are esteemed for the soundest truths, while reality is fabulous. If men would steadily observe realities only, and not allow themselves to

---

① If one may judge...who rarely looks into...: If one who rarely looks into...may judge...
② a French revolution not excepted: 法国革命也不例外。意为：对一个不看报的人来说，国外并没有什么新闻，连法国革命也等于没发生一般。
③ Kieou-pe-yu: 蘧伯玉，名瑗，孔子弟子，春秋卫国大夫。
④ Khoung-tseu: 孔丘。
⑤ Kieou-pe-yu...messager: 中文原文："蘧伯玉使人于孔子；子与之坐而问焉，曰：'夫子何为？'对曰：'夫子欲寡其过，而未能也。'子曰：'使呼，使呼！'"出自《论语·宪问》第十四章。

be deluded, life, to compare it with such things as we know, would be like a fairy tale and the Arabian Nights' Entertainments.① If we respected only what is inevitable and has a right to be, music and poetry would resound along the streets. When we are unhurried and wise, we perceive that only great and worthy things have any permanent and absolute existence, that petty fears and petty pleasures are but the shadow of the reality. This is always exhilarating and sublime. By closing the eyes and slumbering, and consenting to be deceived by shows, men establish and confirm their daily life of routine and habit every where, which still is built on purely illusory foundations. Children, who play life, discern its true law and relations more clearly than men, who fail to live it worthily, but who think that they are wiser by experience, that is, by failure. I have read in a Hindoo book, that "there was a king's son, who, being expelled in infancy from his native city, was brought up by a forester, and, growing up to maturity in that state, imagined himself to belong to the barbarous race with which he lived. One of his father's ministers having discovered him, revealed to him what he was, and the misconception of his character was removed, and he knew himself to be a prince. So soul," continues the Hindoo philosopher, "from the circumstances in which it is placed, mistakes its own character, until the truth is revealed to it by some holy teacher, and then it knows itself to be Brahme②." I perceive that we inhabitants of New England live this mean life that we do because our vision does not penetrate the surface of things. We think that that is which appears to be.③ If a man should walk through this town and see only the reality, where, think you, would the "Mill-dam" go to? If he should give us an account of the realities he beheld there, we should not recognize the place in his description. Look at a meeting-house, or a court-house, or a jail, or a shop, or a dwelling-house and say what that thing really is before a true gaze, and they would all go to pieces in your account of them. Men esteem truth remote, in the outskirts of the system, behind the farthest star, before Adam and after the last man.④ In eternity there is indeed something true and sublime. But all these times and places and occasions are now and here. God himself culminates in the present moment, and will never be more divine in the lapse of all the ages. And we are enabled to apprehend at all what is sublime and noble only by the perpetual instilling and

---

① If men would...the Arabian Nights' Entertainments: 如果人们脚踏实地观察现实，不让自己受到欺骗，那么用我们所知道的来譬喻，生活将好像一篇童话，犹如"天方夜谭"。

② Brahme: Brahma. 印度教有三位主神：梵或梵天(Brahma)是创造之神，亦指众生之本，或智慧的象征；毗瑟拿(Vishnu)是保护之神；湿婆(Siva)是毁灭之神。

③ We think that that is which appears to be: 我们把似是而非的东西当作真实的东西。

④ Before Adam and after the last man: 上帝创造了亚当和夏娃之后，才开始有了人类，因此亚当是人类的先祖。before Adam 指人类诞生之前，after the last man 指人类消亡之后，旨在说明现今人们只重视远古和遥远的将来，而不重视眼前。

drenching of the reality which surrounds us. The universe constantly and obediently answers to our conceptions; whether we travel fast or slow, the track is laid for us. Let us spend our lives in conceiving then. The poet or the artist never yet had so fair and noble a design but some of his posterity at least could accomplish it.

Let us spend one day as deliberately as Nature, and not be thrown off the track by every nutshell and mosquito's wing that falls on the rails. Let us rise early and fast, or break fast, gently and without perturbation; let company come and let company go, let the bells ring and the children cry—determined to make a day of it. Why should we knock under and go with the stream? Let us not be upset and overwhelmed in that terrible rapid and whirlpool called a dinner, situated in the meridian shallows.① Weather this danger and you are safe, for the rest of the way is down hill. With unrelaxed nerves, with morning vigor, sail by it, looking another way, tied to the mast like Ulysses. If the engine whistles, let it whistle till it is hoarse for its pains. If the bell rings, why should we run? We will consider what kind of music they are like. Let us settle ourselves, and work and wedge our feet downward through the mud and slush of opinion, and prejudice, and tradition, and delusion, and appearance, that alluvion which covers the globe, through Paris and London, through New York and Boston and Concord, through church and state, through poetry and philosophy and religion, till we come to a hard bottom and rocks in place, which we can call reality and say, This is, and no mistake; and then begin, having a point d'appui, below freshet and frost and fire, a place where you might found a wall or a state, or set a lamp-post safely, or perhaps a gauge, not a Nilometer②, but a Realometer③, that future ages might know how deep a freshet of shams and appearances had gathered from time to time. If you stand right fronting and face to face to a fact, you will see the sun glimmer on both its surfaces, as if it were a cimeter, and feel its sweet edge dividing you through the heart and marrow, and so you will happily conclude your mortal career.④ Be it life or death, we crave only reality. If we are really dying, let us hear the rattle in our throats and feel cold in the extremities; if we are alive, let us go about our business.

Time is but the stream I go a-fishing in. I drink at it; but while I drink I see the sandy bottom and detect how shallow it is. Its thin current slides away, but eternity remains. I would drink deeper; fish in the sky, whose bottom is pebbly with stars. I cannot count one. I know not the first letter of the alphabet. I have always been

---

① Let us not be upset and overwhelmed...in the meridian shallows: 大意是不要饮食无度。佳肴珍膳就像浅滩，有着可怕的激流和漩涡（有潜在的危险）。
② Nilometer: 古时埃及孟菲斯城里用来测定尼罗河水位的仪器。
③ Realometer: 真实测量计。
④ conclude your mortal career: 告别人生。意为一旦真理在握，死也甘心。

regretting that I was not as wise as the day I was born. The intellect is a cleaver; it discerns and rifts its way into the secret of things. I do not wish to be any more busy with my hands than is necessary. My head is hands and feet. I feel all my best faculties concentrated in it. My instinct tells me that my head is an organ for burrowing, as some creatures use their snout and fore-paws, and with it I would mine and burrow my way through these hills. I think that the richest vein is somewhere hereabouts; so by the divining rod and thin rising vapors I judge; and here I will begin to mine.

译文链接：https://www.kanunu8.com/files/world/201106/2870/67608.html

Questions for Understanding

1. How does Thoreau describe the atmosphere of his house?
2. What is the best part of the day according to Thoreau?
3. What did Thoreau endeavor to learn by going to live in the woods?
4. What opinion does he express about railroads?
5. Why does Thoreau feel that newspapers are not essential?
6. What is the one-word formula Thoreau gives us to help us arrange our lives more satisfyingly and effectively?

Aspects of Appreciation

1. The title of this chapter combines a practical topic of residence ("Where I Lived") with what is probably the most profound philosophical topic of all, the meaning of life ("What I Lived For"). Thoreau thus reminds us again that he is neither a practical do-it-yourself aficionado nor an erudite philosopher, but a mixture of both, attending to matters of everyday existence and questioning its final meaning and purpose. This chapter pulls away from the bookkeeping lists and details about expenditures on nails and door hinges, and opens up onto the more transcendent vista of how it all matters, containing less how-to advice and much more philosophical meditation and grandiose universalizing assertion. It is here that we see the full influence of Ralph Waldo Emerson on Thoreau's project. Emersonian self-reliance is not just a matter of supporting oneself materially (as many people believe) but a much loftier doctrine about the active role that every soul plays in its experience of reality. The reality for Emerson is not a set of objective facts in which we are plunked down, but rather an emanation of our minds and souls that create the world around ourselves every day.

2. Thoreau's building of a house on Walden Pond is, for him, a miniature re-enactment of God's creation of the world. He describes its placement in the cosmos, in a region viewed by astronomers, just as God created a world within the void of space. He says outright that he resides in his home as if on Mount Olympus, home of the gods. He claims a divine freedom from the flow of time, describing himself as fishing in its river. Thoreau's point in all this divine talk is not to inflate his own personality to godlike heights but rather to insist on everyone's divine ability to create a world of his own. Our capacity to choose reality is evident in his metaphor of the "Realometer", a spin-off of the Nilometer, a device used to measure the depth of the Nile River. Thoreau urges us to wade through the muck that constitutes our everyday lives until we come to a firm place "which we can call Reality, and say, This is". The stamp of existence we give to our vision of reality—"This is"—evokes God's simple language in the creation story of Genesis, "Let there be..." And the mere fact that Thoreau imagines that one can choose to call one thing reality and another thing not provides the spiritual freedom that is central to Emerson's Transcendentalist thought. When we create and claim this reality, all the "news" of the world shrinks immediately to insignificance, as Thoreau illustrates in his mocking parody of newspapers reporting a cow run over on the Western Railway. He opines that the last important bit of news to come out of England was about the revolution of 1649, almost two centuries earlier. The only current events that matter to the transcendent mind are itself and its place in the cosmos.

Suggested Further Reading

"Civil Disobedience" (1849); *A Week on the Concord and Merrimack River* (1849).

Topics for Further Study

1. Thoreau's advice—to simplify—applies only to those who, like him, want to live the life of a thinker. Discuss the statement.

2. It is foolish to suppose that a modern nation like ours would prosper very long if it were to adopt the kind of "rigid economy" and "Spartan simplicity" that Thoreau recommends. Discuss the statement.

3. A civilization necessarily "pays for" every technological advance it makes; in a real sense there has been no progress since the beginning of recorded time. Discuss the statement.

4. Times have changed to such an extent that many things Thoreau considered

nonessential for his time are essential for us. Discuss the statement.

Knowledge of Literature

Ecocriticism(生态批评)

Ecocriticism is the study of literature and the environment from an interdisciplinary point of view. The term "ecocriticism" was coined in 1978 by William Rueckert in his essay " Literature and Ecology: An Experiment in Ecocriticism".

Ecocriticism is a criticism that explores the relationship between literature and the natural environment. The main tasks of ecocriticism are to review human culture and carry out cultural criticism through literature. In other words, it explores how human thoughts, culture and patterns of social development affect and determine human attitudes and behaviors toward nature, and how they lead to environmental deterioration and ecological crisis. As a method of literary criticism, ecocriticism should not only explore the relationship between man and nature in literature, but also reveal the enquiry of literature into the root of ecological crisis.

Ecocriticism can also be called "green (cultural) studies", "ecopoetics" and "environmental literary criticism", and is often informed by other fields such as ecology, sustainable design, biopolitics, environmental history, environmentalism, and social ecology, among others.

推荐阅读的论文：
[1] 赵莹，张建国. 物质生态批评视角下《瓦尔登湖》再解读 [J]. 井冈山大学学报（社会科学版），2017(2).
[2] 刘霞. 从人类中心主义到地球中心主义 [J]. 河南师范大学学报（哲学社会科学版），2016(5)

Edgar Allen Poe (1809~1849)

About the Author

Edgar Allan Poe's whole life could be summed up in two words, that is, gifted and tragic. The first word is quite easy to understand. When we mention Poe today, we automatically confer him a series of titles, such as one of the most outstanding American poets, a great short story writer, the father of American detective stories as well as the first conscious modern literary theorist in America.

However, in order to understand the latter modifier, we need to examine Poe's whole life. Compared with his contemporaries, Poe suffered a lot in life as well as in literary career. Ever since he was a small child, he had undergone great misfortunes. As a toddler, he lost both of his parents. Though later he was adopted by John Allan, from whom he got the middle name, Poe shared a rather unpleasant relation with his adopter. At 27, he married his 13-year-old cousin Virginia Clemm over a public protest. But unfortunately, his beloved wife died soon, which left an indelible influence on his life and his writings. He became more and more depressed, and kept using the death of a beautiful lady as a theme of his works, including "Ligeia" (1845), "The Raven" (1845), "Annabel Lee" (1849) and so forth. At forty, he died in poverty and illness. Until his death, he had not been received by the American critics and the public, remaining the most controversial and most misunderstood literary figure. His odd style, his tendency to write about the dark side of life, especially his unusual preference to gothic themes, expelled him from the mainstream of the literary circle. Emerson once called Poe "a jingle man", meaning he was only good at making pleasant sounds in poems. He was even reduced to "a sham artist, his works being more redolent of the carnival house of horrors than of the salons of serious art". Ironically, it was outside of his motherland, especially in France that Poe enjoyed great respect and acclaim, and was highly praised as the pioneer in poetic and fictional techniques. In America, it was not until the late 19th century that Poe was well recognized by critics. Today, Poe has been universally acclaimed as a great writer of the first rank in the world and parallelized with some top men of letters including Hawthorne, Mark Twain and Hemingway.

Given the brevity of his life, lasting only forty years, Poe was really prolific. Despite the desperate living, he managed to create fifty-some poems, a short novel, two novellas, about seventy short stories and a more or less equal volume of essays. His works can be generally classified into three groups, including the poems, best represented by "To Helen" (1831), and "The City in the Sea" (1831); the horror and detective stories, such as "The Fall of the House of Usher" (1839), and "The Purloined Letter" (1842); and three important critical essays "The Review of Hawthorne's Twice-told Tales" (1840), "The Philosophy of Composition" (1846) and "The Poetic Principle" (1850).

As the first major American critic, Poe spared no efforts to apply his writing theories to the writing practice. He insisted that a literary work should strive for a single effect, that is, the creation of beauty, and the immediate object of the writing is pleasure, not truth, which highly resounds with the key notion of the Aesthetic Movement, namely, "art for art's sake". In order to achieve this end, Poe formulated several principles of writing. In terms of length, novels and poems should be of such length as to be read at one sitting in order to ensure that the readers can be well engaged without any interruption. As for the theme, Poe argued that the highest form of beauty is a young lady and the highest degree of melancholy is death; therefore, the death of a beautiful young lady, which he sees as "the most poetical topic in the world", frequently appears in his writings. What's more, as Poe defines true poetry as "the rhythmical creation of beauty" and declares that "music is the perfection of the soul, or idea of poetry", he attaches much importance to the rhythm, making full use of various poetic devices to create a mood appropriate to the themes of his poems.

What's more, Poe's prominence in American literature also lies in his unique theme. Unlike the mainstream in his contemporary literary circle permeated with optimistic and uprising spirits, Poe likes to treat such gloomy and dark themes as chaos, death, isolation and mental illness. His works, often characterized by Gothic elements, macabre factors and mostly neurotic protagonists, are fraught with dead or dying women, violence, perversity and madness. To some extent, Poe is far ahead of his age, for those themes concerning inner heart later become recurrent topics.

On a cold winter night in 1849, Poe died quietly in a street of Baltimore, leaving behind an obscure image for the world. However, as the dust of time settles down, his figure appears clearer and clearer. With the skillfully wrought stories and poems loaded with rich imagination, Poe has successfully cast a magic spell on generations of readers as well as critics, luring them into a mysterious and dreamlike world pervaded with shocking horror and impressive beauty.

The Raven

About the Poem

Written in 1844, "The Raven" is widely acclaimed as Poe's most famous composition. After its publication in the *New York Evening Mirror* in 1845, it won immediate success among critics and readers. Even Poe himself praised it as "most generally known". The poem is noted for its melancholy mood, supernatural atmosphere, and musical language.

The Raven

> Once upon a midnight dreary, while I pondered, weak and weary,
> Over many a quaint and curious volume of forgotten lore—
> While I nodded, nearly napping, suddenly there came a tapping,

As of some one gently rapping, rapping at my chamber door.
"'Tis some visitor," I muttered, "tapping at my chamber door—
Only this and nothing more."

Ah, distinctly I remember it was in the bleak December;
And each separate dying ember wrought its ghost upon the floor.
Eagerly I wished the morrow;—vainly I had sought to borrow
From my books surcease① of sorrow—sorrow for the lost Lenore②—
For the rare and radiant maiden whom the angels name Lenore—
Nameless here for evermore.

And the silken, sad, uncertain rustling of each purple curtain
Thrilled me—filled me with fantastic terrors never felt before;
So that now, to still the beating of my heart, I stood repeating
"'Tis③ some visitor entreating entrance at my chamber door—
Some late visitor entreating entrance at my chamber door;—
This it is and nothing more."

Presently my soul grew stronger; hesitating then no longer,
"Sir," said I, "or Madam, truly your forgiveness I implore;
But the fact is I was napping, and so gently you came rapping,
And so faintly you came tapping, tapping at my chamber door,
That I scarce was sure I heard you"—here I opened wide the door;—
Darkness there and nothing more.

Deep into that darkness peering, long I stood there wondering, fearing,
Doubting, dreaming dreams no mortal ever dared to dream before;
But the silence was unbroken, and the stillness gave no token,
And the only word there spoken was the whispered word, "Lenore?"
This I whispered, and an echo murmured back the word, "Lenore!"—
Merely this and nothing more.

Back into the chamber turning, all my soul within me burning,
Soon again I heard a tapping somewhat louder than before.

---

① surcease: (archaic) cease; to put an end to.
② Lenore: the speaker's dead lover. 诗中说话者已逝情人的名字。
③ 'Tis: 等同于 It is。

"Surely," said I, "surely that is something at my window lattice;
Let me see, then, what thereat is, and this mystery explore—
Let my heart be still a moment and this mystery explore;—
'Tis the wind and nothing more!"

Open here I flung the shutter, when, with many a flirt and flutter,
In there stepped a stately Raven of the saintly days of yore①;
Not the least obeisance② made he; not a minute stopped or stayed he;
But, with mien of lord or lady, perched above my chamber door—
Perched upon a bust of Pallas③ just above my chamber door—
Perched, and sat, and nothing more.

Then this ebony bird beguiling my sad fancy④ into smiling,
By the grave and stern decorum of the countenance it wore,
"Though thy crest be shorn and shaven, thou," I said, "art sure no craven,
Ghastly grim and ancient Raven wandering from the Nightly shore⑤—
Tell me what thy lordly name is on the Night's Plutonian shore!"
Quoth the Raven "Nevermore."

Much I marvelled this ungainly fowl to hear discourse so plainly,
Though its answer little meaning—little relevancy bore;
For we cannot help agreeing that no living human being
Ever yet was blessed with seeing bird above his chamber door—
Bird or beast upon the sculptured bust above his chamber door,
With such name as "Nevermore."

But the Raven, sitting lonely on the placid bust, spoke only
That one word, as if his soul in that one word he did outpour.
Nothing farther then he uttered—not a feather then he fluttered—
Till I scarcely more than muttered "Other friends have flown before—
On the morrow he will leave me, as my Hopes have flown before."
Then the bird said "Nevermore."

---

① days of yore: days of long ago（往昔）.
② obeisance: a gesture expressing deferential respect, such as a bow or curtsy. 敬礼（指鞠躬、屈膝礼等）。
③ Pallas: Pallas Athene, one of the names of ATHEN. 希腊神话中智慧与技艺女神雅典娜的名字之一。
④ my sad fancy: 等同于 my mad soul。
⑤ the Nightly shore: the hell. 指地狱，意同下行中的 the Night's Plutonian shore. "Plutonian" refers to "to or relating to Pluto (the god of the underworld)". 根据希腊神话，冥王普鲁托统治的地府中有五条河流。

Startled at the stillness broken by reply so aptly spoken,
"Doubtless," said I, "what it utters is its only stock and store
Caught from some unhappy master whom unmerciful Disaster
Followed fast and followed faster till his songs one burden bore—
Till the dirges of his Hope that melancholy burden bore
Of 'Never—nevermore'."

But the Raven still beguiling all my fancy into smiling,
Straight I wheeled a cushioned seat in front of bird, and bust and door;
Then, upon the velvet sinking, I betook myself to linking
Fancy unto fancy, thinking what this ominous bird of yore—
What this grim, ungainly, ghastly, gaunt, and ominous bird of yore
Meant in croaking "Nevermore."

This I sat engaged in guessing, but no syllable expressing
To the fowl whose fiery eyes now burned into my bosom's core;
This and more I sat divining, with my head at ease reclining
On the cushion's velvet lining that the lamp-light gloated o'er,
But whose velvet-violet lining with the lamp-light gloating o'er,
She shall press, ah, nevermore!

Then, methought, the air grew denser, perfumed from an unseen censer
Swung by Seraphim whose foot-falls tinkled[①] on the tufted floor.
"Wretch," I cried, "thy God hath lent thee—by these angels he hath sent thee
Respite—respite and Nepenthe[②] from thy memories of Lenore;
Quaff, oh quaff this kind nepenthe and forget this lost Lenore!"
Quoth the Raven "Nevermore."

"Prophet!" said I, "thing of evil!—prophet still, if bird or devil![③]—
Whether Tempter[④] sent, or whether tempest tossed thee here ashore,
Desolate yet all undaunted, on this desert land enchanted—
On this home by Horror haunted—tell me truly, I implore—

---

① tinkled: 坡将此拟声词比拟作天使的脚步声,让人产生一种奇妙的感觉。
② Nepenthe: drug or plant that induces oblivion. 忘忧草或忘忧药,据传能消解哀愁。
③ if bird or devil: whether you are a bird or a devil. 不管你是鸟还是魔鬼。
④ Tempter: Satan regarded as trying to lead men into sin. 撒旦;诱人犯罪的魔鬼。

Is there—is there balm in Gilead①?—tell me—tell me, I implore!"
Quoth the Raven "Nevermore."

"Prophet!" said I, "thing of evil!—prophet still, if bird or devil!
By that Heaven that bends above us—by that God we both adore—
Tell this soul with sorrow laden if, within the distant Aidenn②,
It shall clasp a sainted maiden whom the angels name Lenore—
Clasp a rare and radiant maiden whom the angels name Lenore."
Quoth the Raven "Nevermore."

"Be that word our sign of parting, bird or fiend!" I shrieked, upstarting—
"Get thee back into the tempest and the Night's Plutonian shore!
Leave no black plume as a token of that lie thy soul hath spoken!
Leave my loneliness unbroken!—quit the bust above my door!
Take thy beak from out my heart, and take thy form from off my door!"
Quoth the Raven "Nevermore."

And the Raven, never flitting, still is sitting, still is sitting
On the pallid bust of Pallas just above my chamber door;
And his eyes have all the seeming of a demon's that is dreaming,
And the lamp-light o'er him streaming throws his shadow on the floor;
And my soul from out that shadow that lies floating on the floor
Shall be lifted—nevermore!

译文链接：https://www.douban.com/event/31629696/discussion/615905750/?author=1

Questions for Understanding

1. Analyze the theme and the tone of the poem.
2. What is the symbolic meaning of the raven in the poem?
3. This poem is noted for its musical beauty. What devices are employed to produce such musical beauty?
4. Evaluate the speaker's emotional state at the beginning of the poem, in the

---

① is there balm in Gilead: "基列有香膏吗？" 语出《旧约·耶利米书》第 8 章第 22 节："难道基列没有镇痛香膏吗？难道那里没有治病的医生吗？我百姓为何不得痊愈呢？"（"Is there no balm in Gilead; is there no physician there? Why then is not the health of the daughter of my people recovered?"）据说基列（今约旦境内）的一种香脂树出产可治百病的香膏。
② Aidenn: 这是坡虚构的一个地方，暗指伊甸园。

penultimate stanza, and in the last stanza.

Aspects of Appreciation

1. This narrative poem describes a mysterious story about a sorrowful young scholar and a deathlike talking raven. On a stormy winter midnight, the young man is sitting in his well-decorated chamber and reading "quaint and curious" books as a way to forget the loss of his lover Lenore. A raven steps into the room and perches on a bust of the goddess Athena. Out of curiosity, the man asks it several questions, including whether he will be reunited with Lenore in another world. The raven says only one word "nevermore". Its insistent repetition finally drives the man into madness.

2. The poem is composed of 18 six-line stanzas. Generally, it is written in trochaic octameter, that is, eight trochaic feet per line, each foot having one stressed syllable followed by one unstressed syllable. Its rhyme scheme is abcbbb, and the b lines rhyme with "Lenore" and "Nevermore", which enhances the gloom of the whole poem.

3. In his follow-up essay "The Philosophy of Composition"(1846), Poe described his elaborate crafting of this poem as a case to illustrate his aesthetic and poetic principles. For instance, he considers beauty as "the sole legitimate province" of his work, and melancholy as "the most legitimate of all the poetical tones". Under such guidance, Poe's predominate theme, the death of a beautiful woman, recurs in the *The Raven*. And the repeated "nevermore" conveys a sense of melancholy and sadness.

Annabelle Lee

About the Poem

This poem, the last poetic work made by Poe, is acclaimed as "the culmination of Poe's lyric style in his recurrent theme of the loss of a beautiful and loved woman". It is generally believed to memorize his deceased wife Virginia Clemm, who died in 1847 at the age of 26.

Annabelle Lee

It was many and many a year ago,
In a kingdom by the sea,
That a maiden there lived whom you may know
By the name of ANNABLE LEE;
And this maiden she① lived with no other thought
Than to love and be loved by me.

I was a child and she was a child,
In this kingdom by the sea;
But we loved with a love that was more than love —
I and my ANNABLE LEE;
With a love that the winged seraphs② of heaven
Coveted her and me.

And this was the reason that, long ago,
In this kingdom by the sea,
A wind blew out of a cloud, chilling
My beautiful ANNABLE LEE;
So that her highborn kinsman③ came
And bore her away④ from me,
To shut her up in a sepulcher⑤
In this kingdom by the sea.

The angels, not half so happy in heaven,
Went envying her and me —
Yes! —that was the reason (as all men know,
In this kingdom by the sea)
That the wind came out of the cloud by night,
Chilling and killing my ANNABLE LEE.

---

① The word "she" is used here for the sake of rhythm, namely, to contribute an unstressed syllable to the anapestic foot. 为了押韵（抑抑扬格），坡有意添加了 she 一词。
② seraph: a celestial being having three pairs of wings. In Christian angelology, seraphim (the plural form of seraph) are the first of the nine orders of angels. 撒拉弗，六翼天使（九级天使中地位最高者）。
③ highborn kinsmen: the winged seraph mentioned above. 高贵的亲族，指上文出现的天使。
④ bore: brought back, took away. Poe implies that Annabel Lee is actually an angel from heaven, and she was taken back by other angels to heaven. 带走，此处坡暗示安娜贝尔是天使。
⑤ sepulchre: (archaic) tomb, grand grave.（古）坟墓。

But our love was stronger by far than the love
Of those who were older than we —
Of many far wiser than we —
And neither the angels in heaven above,
Nor the demons down under the sea,
Can ever dissever my soul from the soul
Of the beautiful ANNABLE LEE.

For the moon never beams without bringing me dreams
Of the beautiful ANNABLE LEE;
And the stars never rise but I feel the bright eyes
Of the beautiful ANNABLE LEE;
And so, all the night-tide①, I lie down by the side
Of my darling, my darling, my life and my bride,
In the sepulcher there by the sea—
In her tomb by the sounding sea.

译文链接：https://www.douban.com/note/669354984/?_i=5486236dDJIlWZ

Questions for Understanding

1. What happened to Annable Lee?
2. Why was Lee taken away according to the author?
3. What mood does the poem render you after you read it?
4. The long vowel /i:/ is repeated in the poem again and again. What does it stand for?
5. It is said that this poem coincides on every side with Poe's poetic theories. Could you find some examples to illustrate this point?
6. John Milton ("To his deceased wife"), and Su Shi ("Jiang Chengzi" 苏轼《江城子》) also wrote poems to memorize their deceased wives. Try to compare these three versions and find out which one you like best.

Aspects of Appreciation

1. Thematically speaking, this is not only a mourning song for his beloved wife, but also a love song celebrating the beauty and timelessness of their love, which is

---

①night-tide: night.

even envied by the angels and could not be dissevered by death. It is noted that Poe does not describe his life and death of his wife directly. Instead, he uses a fictional place (a kingdom by the sea) and an imagined figure (Annabel Lee), which produces a romantic and legendary quality for their love, and in the meanwhile eulogizes their true love, for it is as pure as crystal and could only exist nowhere but in a mythical kingdom.

2. This lyric is composed of six stanzas of alternating three and four stress lines, and the meter of each line is basically anapestic. It is generally acclaimed that the concept of "word music" is best exemplified in this lyric, in which Poe utilizes various poetic devices, such as alliteration (e.g. demon/ down), the feminine rhyme, the repetition of the long vowel /i:/ (me, sea, Lee, which suggests a sigh). All these together produce a melodious and dramatic effect. No wonder, Walt Whitman comments that Poe "carried the rhyming art to excess."

3. Several figures of speech are applied to this lyric which enhances its artistic charm and the melancholy tone. For instance, the girl's name and phrases like "in this kingdom by the sea" become refrains and are repeated like the insistent tolling of the bell. Besides, Poe also uses the hyperbole to idealize his wife and their love, which is even coveted by the angels. What's more, in order to arouse the feeling of sadness, he uses such images as kinesthetic image ("shuts her up") and visual image ("speculchre").

4. Acclaimed as the best of Poe's works, this last poem coincides on every side with Poe's poetic theories. In terms of the form, it consists of six stanzas, 41 lines, which is quite readable at one sitting. As for the theme, it repeats Poe's favorite topic of the loss of a beautiful and loved lady. The sense of melancholy runs through the whole poem. Besides, various poetic devices are skillfully adopted, which makes the whole poem gleam with perfection and beauty.

Suggested Further Reading

Poems: "The City in the Sea" (1831); "To Helen" (1831);"The Bells"(1849);

Short stories: "Ligeia"(1838); "The Fall of the House of Usher"(1839); "The Purloined Letter"(1842);"The Black Cat"(1843).

Topics for Further Study

1. Whitman once criticized Poe's verses as the lines "belong among the electric lights of imagination literature, brilliant and dazzling, but with no heat." Do you agree with his comment?

2. According to Poe, a literary work must strive for a single effect, that is, the creation of beauty and the immediate object of the writing is pleasure, not truth. Try to compare his view with some traditional ideas about the function of literature, for instance, Sidney's opinion.

3. Poe is considered as a special literary figure in American Romanticism. Try to compare him with his contemporary counterparts, such as Emerson and Hawthorne, and find their similarities and differences.

Knowledge of Literature

1. Feminine rhyme(阴韵)

Feminine rhyme refers to the rhyming sounds involving two or more syllables, and usually the final syllables are unstressed. For instance, wining and beginning. Its opposite is masculine rhyme (阳韵), referring to the rhyming sounds involving only one syllable. For instance, late and fate.

2. An Element of Poetry: Tone(语气)

The tone of a poem refers to the implied attitude of the poet or the speaker towards his subject, himself or his intended readers. When used as a literary device, it can be serious or satiric, formal or informal, optimistic or pessimistic, and so on. The tone of a poem can be revealed through the poet's choice of words and sentence patterns and his use of meter, rhyme, imagery and figures of speech. Take Poe's "Annabel Lee" for example. The repetition of the long vowel /i:/ at the end of each stanza suggests a sigh, which adds to a certain tone of sorrow and melancholy.

推荐阅读的论文：

[1] 高冬生. 永恒的美：爱伦·坡诗作艺术解读 [J]. 长江大学学报（社科版），2014(1).

[2] 朱振武，王二磊. 爱伦·坡诗歌的美学表征及诗学理念 [J]. 外语教学，2011(5).

Nathaniel Hawthorne (1804~1864)

About the Author

  Nathaniel Hawthorne is an American novelist and short-story writer who is a master of the allegorical and symbolic tale. One of the greatest fiction writers in American literature, he is best-known for *The Scarlet Letter* (1850) and *The House of the Seven Gables* (1851).

  Hawthorne's ancestors had lived in Salem since the 17th Century. His earliest American ancestor, William Hathorne (Nathaniel added the w to the name when he began to write), was a magistrate who sentenced a Quaker woman to public whipping. He acted as a staunch defender of Puritan orthodoxy, with its zealous advocacy of a "pure", unaffected form of religious worship, its rigid adherence to a simple, almost severe, mode of life, and its conviction of the "natural depravity" of "fallen" man. Hawthorne was later to wonder whether the decline of his family's prosperity and prominence during the 18th century, while other Salem families were growing wealthy from the lucrative shipping trade, might be a retribution for this act and for the role of William's son John as one of three judges in the Salem witchcraft trials of 1692. When Nathaniel's father—a ship captain—died during one of his voyages, he left his young widow without the means to care for her two girls and young Nathaniel, aged four. She moved in with her affluent brothers, the Mannings. Hawthorne grew up in their house in Salem and, for extensive periods during his teens, in Raymond, Maine, on the shores of Sebago Lake. He returned to Salem in 1825 after four years at Bowdoin College, in Brunswick, Maine. Hawthorne did not distinguish himself as a young man. Instead, he spent nearly a dozen years reading and trying to master the art of writing fiction.

  In college Hawthorne excelled only in composition anddetermined to become a writer. Upon graduation, he wrote an amateurish novel, *Fanshawe*, which he published at his own expense—only to decide that it was unworthy of him and to try to destroy all copies. Hawthorne, however, soon found his own voice, style, and subjects, and within five years of his graduation he published such impressive and distinctive stories as "The Hollow of the Three Hills" and "An Old Woman's Tale". By 1832, "My Kinsman, Major Molineux" and "Roger Malvin's Burial", two of his greatest tales—and among the finest in the language—had been published. "Young Goodman Brown", perhaps the greatest tale of witchcraft ever written, appeared in 1835.

  His increasing success in stories brought him a little fame. Unwilling to depend any longer on his uncles' generosity, he turned to a job in the Boston Custom House (1839~1840) and for six months in 1841 was a resident at the agricultural cooperative Brook Farm, in West Roxbury, Mass. Even when his first signed book, *Twice-Told Tales*, was published in 1837, the work brought gratifying recognition but no dependable income. By 1842, however, Hawthorne's writing had brought him a sufficient income to allow him to marry Sophia Peabody. The couple rented the Old Manse in Concord and began a happy three-year period that Hawthorne would later record in his essay "The Old Manse".

The presence of some of the leading social thinkers and philosophers of his day, such as Ralph Waldo Emerson, Henry Thoreau and Bronson Alcott in Concord made the village the center of the philosophy of Transcendentalism, which encouraged man to transcend the materialistic world of experience and facts and become conscious of the pervading spirit of the universe and the potentialities for human freedom. Hawthorne welcomed the companionship of his Transcendentalist neighbours, but he had little to say to them. Artists and intellectuals never inspired his full confidence, but he thoroughly enjoyed the visit of his old college friend and classmate Franklin Pierce, who later became president of the United States. At the Old Manse, Hawthorne continued to write stories, with the same result as before: literary success, and monetary failure. His new short-story collection, *Mosses from an Old Manse*, appeared in 1846.

A growing family and mounting debts compelled the Hawthornes' return in 1845 to Salem, where Nathaniel was appointed surveyor of the Custom House by the Polk administration (Hawthorne had always been a loyal Democrat and pulled all the political strings he could to get this appointment). Three years later the presidential election brought the Whigs into power under Zachary Taylor, and Hawthorne lost his job; but in a few months of concentrated effort, he produced his masterpiece *The Scarlet Letter*. The bitterness he felt over his dismissal is apparent in "The Custom House" essay prefixed to the novel. *The Scarlet Letter* tells the story of two lovers kept apart by the ironies of fate, their own mingled strengths and weaknesses, and the Puritan community's interpretation of moral law, until at last death unites them under a single headstone. The book made Hawthorne famous and was eventually recognized as one of the greatest of American novels.

Determined to leave Salem forever, Hawthorne moved to Lenox, located in the mountain scenery of the Berkshires in western Massachusetts. There he began work on *The House of the Seven Gables* (1851), the story of the Pyncheon family, who for generations had lived under a curse until it was removed at last by love.

At Lenox he enjoyed the stimulating friendship of Herman Melville, who lived in nearby Pittsfield. This friendship, although important for the younger writer and his work, was much less so for Hawthorne. Melville praised Hawthorne extravagantly in a review of his *Mosses from an Old Manse*, and he also dedicated *Moby Dick* to Hawthorne. But eventually Melville came to feel that the friendship he so ardently pursued was one-sided. Later he was to picture the relationship with disillusion in his introductory sketch to *The Piazza Tales* and depicted Hawthorne himself unflatteringly as "Vine" in his long poem *Clarel*.

In the autumn of 1851 Hawthorne moved his family to another temporary residence, this time in West Newton, near Boston. There he quickly wrote *The Blithedale Romance*, which was based on his disenchantment with Brook Farm. Then he purchased and redecorated Bronson Alcott's house in Concord, the Wayside. *Blithedale* was disappointingly received and did not produce the income Hawthorne had expected. He was hoping for a lucrative political appointment that would bolster his finances; in the meantime, he wrote a campaign biography of his old friend Franklin Pierce. When Pierce won the presidency, Hawthorne was in 1853 rewarded with the consulship in Liverpool, Lancashire, a position he hoped would enable him in a few years to leave his family financially secure.

The remaining 11 years of Hawthorne's life were, from a creative point of view, largely anticlimactic. He performed his consular duties faithfully and effectively until his position was terminated in 1857, and then he spent a year and a half sightseeing in Italy. Determined to produce yet another romance, he finally retreated to a seaside town in England and quickly produced *The Marble Faun*. In writing it, he drew heavily upon the experiences and impressions he had recorded in a notebook kept during his Italian tour to give substance to an allegory of the fall of man, a theme that had usually been assumed in his earlier works but that now received direct and philosophic treatment.

Back in the Wayside once more in 1860, Hawthorne devoted himself entirely to his writing but was unable to make any progress with his plans for a new novel. The drafts of unfinished works he left are mostly incoherent and show many signs of a psychic regression, already foreshadowed by his increasing restlessness and discontent of the preceding half dozen years. Some two years before his death he began to age very suddenly. His hair turned white, his handwriting changed, he suffered frequent nosebleeds, and he took to writing the figure "64" compulsively on scraps of paper. He died in his sleep on a trip in search of health with his friend Pierce.

Dr. Rappaccini's Daughter

About the Story

"Dr. Rappaccini's Daughter" is a short story by Nathaniel Hawthorne, published in 1844. The story is set in Padua, Italy, and revolves around a young man named Giovanni Guasconti, who falls in love with a beautiful and mysterious woman named Beatrice Rappaccini. Beatrice is the daughter of a brilliant but reclusive scientist, Dr. Rappaccini, who has been conducting experiments on plants to create deadly poisons. As Giovanni becomes more involved with Beatrice, he begins to suspect that her father has turned her into a poisonous creature. The story explores themes of obsession, love, and the dangers of scientific experimentation.

Dr. Rappaccini's Daughter

A YOUNG man, named Giovanni Guasconti, came, very long ago, from the more southern region of Italy, to pursue his studies at the University of Padua. Giovanni, who had but a scanty① supply of gold ducats② in his pocket, took lodgings in a high and gloomy chamber of an old edifice③, which looked not unworthy to have been the palace of a Paduan noble, and which, in fact, exhibited over its entrance the armorial④ bearings of a family long since extinct. The young stranger, who was not unstudied in the great poem of his country, recollected that one of the ancestors of this family, and perhaps an occupant of this very mansion, had been pictured by Dante as a partaker of the immortal agonies of his Inferno⑤. These reminiscences and associations, together with the tendency to heart-break natural to a young man for the first time out of his native sphere, caused Giovanni to sigh heavily, as he looked around the desolate and ill-furnished apartment.

"Holy Virgin⑥, signor⑦," cried old dame⑧ Lisabetta, who, won by the youth's remarkable beauty of person, was kindly endeavoring to give the chamber a habitable air, "what a sigh was that to come out of a young man's heart! Do you find this old

---

① scanty: too little in amount for what is needed(不足的).
② ducats: gold coins used in many European countries.
③ edifice: a large, impressive building.
④ armorial: connected with heraldry(纹章的).
⑤ Inferno: hell (with reference to Dante's Divine Comedy).
⑥ Holy Virgin: the mother of Jesus; the Virgin Mary.
⑦ Signor: a title or form of address used of or to an Italian-speaking man, corresponding to Mr or sir.
⑧ dame: a woman.

mansion gloomy? For the love of heaven, then, put your head out of the window, and you will see as bright sunshine as you have left in Naples."

Guasconti mechanically did as the old woman advised, but could not quite agree with her that the Lombard sunshine was as cheerful as that of southern Italy. Such as it was, however, it fell upon a garden beneath the window, and expended its fostering influences on a variety of plants, which seemed to have been cultivated with exceeding care.

"Does this garden belong to the house?" Asked Giovanni.

"Heaven forbid, signor!—Unless it were fruitful of better pot-herbs than any that grow there now," answered old Lisabetta. "No; that garden is cultivated by the own hands of Signor Giacomo Rappaccini, the famous Doctor, who, I warrant him, has been heard of as far as Naples. It is said he distills these plants into medicines that are as potent as a charm. Oftentimes you may see the Signor Doctor at work, and perchance the Signora his daughter, too, gathering the strange flowers that grow in the garden."

The old woman had now done what she could for the aspect of the chamber, and, commending① the young man to the protection of the saints, took her departure.

Giovanni still found no better occupation than to look down into the garden beneath his window. From its appearance, he judged it to be one of those botanic gardens, which were of earlier date in Padua than elsewhere in Italy, or in the world. Or, not improbably, it might once have been the pleasure-place of an opulent② family; for there was the ruin of a marble fountain in the centre, sculptured with rare art, but so woefully shattered that it was impossible to trace the original design from the chaos of remaining fragments. The water, however, continued to gush and sparkle into the sunbeams as cheerfully as ever. A little gurgling sound ascended to the young man's window, and made him feel as if a fountain were an immortal spirit, that sung its song unceasingly, and without heeding③ the vicissitudes④ around it; while one century embodied it in marble, and another scattered the perishable garniture⑤ on the soil. All about the pool into which the water subsided, grew various plants, that seemed to require a plentiful supply of moisture for the nourishment of gigantic leaves, and, in some instances, flowers gorgeously magnificent. There was one shrub in particular, set in a marble vase in the midst of the pool, that bore a profusion of purple blossoms,

---

① commend sb/sth to sb/sth: give somebody/something to somebody/something in order to be taken care of (把……托付给).
② opulent: (of people) extremely rich.
③ heed: to pay careful attention to.
④ vicissitude: one of the many changes and problems in a situation or in your life, that you have to deal with (变迁).
⑤ garniture: decoration (装饰品).

each of which had the lustre and richness of a gem; and the whole together made a show so resplendent① that it seemed enough to illuminate the garden, even had there been no sunshine. Every portion of the soil was peopled with plants and herbs, which, if less beautiful, still bore tokens of assiduous② care; as if all had their individual virtues, known to the scientific mind that fostered them. Some were placed in urns, rich with old carving, and others in common garden-pots; some crept serpent-like along the ground, or climbed on high, using whatever means of ascent was offered them. One plant had wreathed itself round a statue of Vertumnus③, which was thus quite veiled and shrouded in a drapery of hanging foliage, so happily arranged that it might have served a sculptor for a study.

While Giovanni stood at the window, he heard a rustling behind a screen of leaves, and became aware that a person was at work in the garden. His figure soon emerged into view, and showed itself to be that of no common laborer, but a tall, emaciated④, sallow⑤, and sickly looking man, dressed in a scholar's garb of black. He was beyond the middle term of life, with gray hair, a thin gray beard, and a face singularly marked with intellect and cultivation, but which could never, even in his more youthful days, have expressed much warmth of heart.

Nothing could exceed the intentness with which this scientific gardener examined every shrub which grew in his path; it seemed as if he was looking into their inmost nature, making observations in regard to their creative essence, and discovering why one leaf grew in this shape, and another in that, and wherefore such and such flowers differed among themselves in hue and perfume. Nevertheless, in spite of the deep intelligence on his part, there was no approach to intimacy between himself and these vegetable existences. On the contrary, he avoided their actual touch, or the direct inhaling of their odors, with a caution that impressed Giovanni most disagreeably; for the man's demeanor was that of one walking among malignant influences, such as savage beasts, or deadly snakes, or evil spirits, which, should he allow them one moment of license, would wreak upon him some terrible fatality. It was strangely frightful to the young man's imagination, to see this air of insecurity in a person cultivating a garden, that most simple and innocent of human toils, and which had been alike the joy and labor of the unfallen parents⑥ of the race. Was this garden, then, the Eden of the present world?—And this man, with such a perception of harm in what

---

① resplendent: brightly coloured in an impressive way(灿烂的，华丽的).
② assiduous: working very hard and taking great care that everything is done as well as it can be.
③ Vertumnus: 罗马神话中掌管庭园、果树和四季变化的神。
④ emaciated: thin and weak, usually because of illness or lack of food.
⑤ sallow: (of a person's skin or face) having a slightly yellow colour that does not look healthy.
⑥ unfallen parents: referring to unfallen Adam and Eve in the Garden of Eden.

his own hands caused to grow, was he the Adam?

The distrustful gardener, while plucking away the dead leaves or pruning the too-luxuriant-growth of the shrubs, defended his hands with a pair of thick gloves. Nor were these his only armor. When, in his walk through the garden, he came to the magnificent plant that hung its purple gems beside the marble fountain, he placed a kind of mask over his mouth and nostrils, as if all this beauty did but conceal a deadlier malice. But finding his task still too dangerous, he drew back, removed the mask, and called loudly, but in the infirm voice of a person affected with inward disease:

"Beatrice!—Beatrice!"

"Here am I, my father! What would you?" Cried a rich and youthful voice from the window of the opposite house; a voice as rich as a tropical sunset, and which made Giovanni, though he knew not why, think of deep hues of purple or crimson, and of perfumes heavily delectable①.—"Are you in the garden?"

"Yes, Beatrice," answered the gardener, "and I need your help."

Soon there emerged from under a sculptured portal the figure of a young girl, arrayed with as much richness of taste as the most splendid of the flowers, beautiful as the day, and with a bloom so deep and vivid that one shade more would have been too much. She looked redundant with life, health, and energy; all of which attributes were bound down and compressed, as it were, and girdled tensely, in their luxuriance, by her virgin zone. Yet Giovanni's fancy must have grown morbid②, while he looked down into the garden; for the impression which the fair stranger made upon him was as if here were another flower, the human sister of those vegetable ones, as beautiful as they—more beautiful than the richest of them—but still to be touched only with a glove, nor to be approached without a mask. As Beatrice came down the garden-path, it was observable that she handled and inhaled the odor of several of the plants, which her father had most sedulously③ avoided.

"Here, Beatrice," said the latter,—"see how many needful offices require to be done to our chief treasure. Yet, shattered as I am, my life might pay the penalty of approaching it so closely as circumstances demand. Henceforth, I fear, this plant must be consigned to your sole charge."

"And gladly will I undertake it," cried again the rich tones of the young lady, as she bent towards the magnificent plant, and opened her arms as if to embrace it. "Yes, my sister, my splendor, it shall be Beatrice's task to nurse and serve thee; and thou

---

① delectable: extremely pleasant to taste, smell or look at.
② morbid: having or expressing a strong interest in sad or unpleasant things, especially disease or death (病态的).
③ sedulously: in a way that shows great care and effort (小心周到地).

shalt reward her with thy kisses and perfume breath, which to her is as the breath of life!"

Then, with all the tenderness in her manner that was so strikingly expressed in her words, she busied herself with such attentions as the plant seemed to require; and Giovanni, at his lofty window, rubbed his eyes, and almost doubted whether it were a girl tending her favorite flower, or one sister performing the duties of affection to another. The scene soon terminated. Whether Doctor Rappaccini had finished his labors in the garden, or that his watchful eye had caught the stranger's face, he now took his daughter's arm and retired. Night was already closing in; oppressive exhalations seemed to proceed from the plants, and steal upward past the open window; and Giovanni, closing the lattice, went to his couch, and dreamed of a rich flower and beautiful girl. Flower and maiden were different and yet the same, and fraught with① some strange peril② in either shape.

But there is an influence in the light of morning that tends to rectify whatever errors of fancy, or even of judgment, we may have incurred during the sun's decline, or among the shadows of the night, or in the less wholesome glow of moonshine. Giovanni's first movement on starting from sleep, was to throw open the window, and gaze down into the garden which his dreams had made so fertile of mysteries. He was surprised, and a little ashamed, to find how real and matter-of-fact an affair it proved to be, in the first rays of the sun, which gilded the dew-drops that hung upon leaf and blossom, and, while giving a brighter beauty to each rare flower, brought everything within the limits of ordinary experience. The young man rejoiced, that, in the heart of the barren city, he had the privilege of overlooking this spot of lovely and luxuriant vegetation. It would serve, he said to himself, as a symbolic language, to keep him in communion with Nature. Neither the sickly and thought-worn Doctor Giacomo Rappaccini, it is true, nor his brilliant daughter, were now visible; so that Giovanni could not determine how much of the singularity which he attributed to both, was due to their own qualities, and how much to his wonder-working fancy. But he was inclined to take a most rational view of the whole matter.

In the course of the day, he paid his respects to Signor Pietro Baglioni, Professor of Medicine in the University, a physician of eminent repute, to whom Giovanni had brought a letter of introduction. The Professor was an elderly personage, apparently of genial nature, and habits that might almost be called jovial③; he kept the young man to dinner, and made himself very agreeable by the freedom and liveliness of his

---

① fraught with: filled with (something unpleasant).
② peril: serious danger.
③ jovial: very cheerful and friendly.

conversation, especially when warmed by a flask or two of Tuscan wine. Giovanni, conceiving that men of science, inhabitants of the same city, must needs be on familiar terms with one another, took an opportunity to mention the name of Doctor Rappaccini. But the Professor did not respond with so much cordiality as he had anticipated.

"I'll would it become a teacher of the divine art of medicine," said Professor Pietro Baglioni, in answer to a question of Giovanni, "to withhold due and well-considered praise of a physician so eminently skilled as Rappaccini. But, on the other hand, I should answer it but scantily to my conscience, were I to permit a worthy youth like yourself, Signor Giovanni, the son of an ancient friend, to imbibe① erroneous ideas respecting a man who might hereafter chance to hold your life and death in his hands. The truth is, our worshipful Doctor Rappaccini has as much science as any member of the faculty—with perhaps one single exception—in Padua, or all Italy. But there are certain grave objections to his professional character."

"And what are they?" Asked the young man.

"Has my friend Giovanni any disease of body or heart, that he is so inquisitive about physicians?" Said the Professor, with a smile. "But as for Rappaccini, it is said of him—and I, who know the man well, can answer for its truth—that he cares infinitely more for science than for mankind. His patients are interesting to him only as subjects for some new experiment. He would sacrifice human life, his own among the rest, or whatever else was dearest to him, for the sake of adding so much as a grain of mustard-seed② to the great heap of his accumulated knowledge."

"Me thinks he is an awful man, indeed," remarked Guasconti, mentally recalling the cold and purely intellectual aspect of Rappaccini. "And yet, worshipful Professor, is it not a noble spirit? Are there many men capable of so spiritual a love of science?"

"God forbid," answered the Professor, somewhat testily③—"at least, unless they take sounder views of the healing art than those adopted by Rappaccini. It is his theory, that all medicinal virtues are comprised within those substances which we term vegetable poisons. These he cultivates with his own hands, and is said even to have produced new varieties of poison, more horribly deleterious④ than Nature, without the assistance of this learned person, would ever have plagued the world withal. That the Signor Doctor does less mischief than might be expected, with such dangerous substances, is undeniable. Now and then, it must be owned, he has effected—

---

① imbibe: to absorb.
② a grain of mustard-seed: 一粒芥籽。
③ testily: irritably.
④ deleteious: harmful and damaging.

or seemed to effect—a marvellous cure. But, to tell you my private mind, Signor Giovanni, he should receive little credit for such instances of success—they being probably the work of chance—but should be held strictly accountable for his failures, which may justly be considered his own work."

The youth might have taken Baglioni's opinions with many grains of allowance, had he known that there was a professional warfare of long continuance between him and Doctor Rappaccini, in which the latter was generally thought to have gained the advantage. If the reader be inclined to judge for himself, we refer him to certain black-letter tracts on both sides, preserved in the medical department of the University of Padua.

"I know not, most learned Professor," returned Giovanni, after musing on what had been said of Rappaccini's exclusive zeal for science—"I know not how dearly this physician may love his art; but surely there is one object more dear to him. He has a daughter."

"Aha!" Cried the Professor with a laugh. "So now our friend Giovanni's secret is out. You have heard of this daughter, whom all the young men in Padua are wild about, though not half a dozen have ever had the good hap to see her face. I know little of the Signora Beatrice, save that Rappaccini is said to have instructed her deeply in his science, and that, young and beautiful as fame reports her, she is already qualified to fill a professor's chair. Perchance her father destines her for mine! Other absurd rumors there be, not worth talking about, or listening to. So now, Signor Giovanni, drink off your glass of Lacryma."

Guasconti returned to his lodgings somewhat heated with the wine he had quaffed, and which caused his brain to swim with strange fantasies in reference to Doctor Rappaccini and the beautiful Beatrice. On his way, happening to pass by a florist's, he bought a fresh bouquet of flowers.

Ascending to his chamber, he seated himself near the window, but within the shadow thrown by the depth of the wall, so that he could look down into the garden with little risk of being discovered. All beneath his eye was a solitude. The strange plants were basking in the sunshine, and now and then nodding gently to one another, as if in acknowledgment of sympathy and kindred. In the midst, by the shattered fountain, grew the magnificent shrub, with its purple gems clustering all over it; they glowed in the air, and gleamed back again out of the depths of the pool, which thus seemed to overflow with colored radiance from the rich reflection that was steeped in it. At first, as we have said, the garden was a solitude. Soon, however,—as Giovanni had half hoped, half feared, would be the case,—a figure appeared beneath the antique sculptured portal, and came down between the rows of plants, inhaling their various perfumes, as if she were one of those beings of old classic fable, that lived upon sweet odors. On again beholding Beatrice, the young man was even startled to perceive how much her beauty exceeded his recollection of it; so brilliant, so vivid in its character, that she glowed amid the sunlight, and, as Giovanni whispered to himself, positively illuminated the more shadowy intervals of the garden path. Her face being now more revealed than on the former occasion, he was struck by its expression of simplicity and sweetness; qualities that had not entered into his idea of her character, and which made him ask anew, what manner of mortal she might be. Nor did he fail again to observe, or imagine, an analogy between the beautiful girl and the gorgeous shrub that hung its gem-like flowers over the fountain; a resemblance which Beatrice seemed to have indulged a fantastic humor in heightening, both by the arrangement of her dress and the selection of its hues.

Approaching the shrub, she threw open her arms, as with a passionate ardor, and drew its branches into an intimate embrace; so intimate, that her features were hidden in its leafy bosom, and her glistening ringlets all intermingled with the flowers.

"Give me thy breath, my sister," exclaimed Beatrice; "for I am faint with common air! And give me this flower of thine, which I separate with gentlest fingers from the stem, and place it close beside my heart."

With these words, the beautiful daughter of Rappaccini plucked one of the richest blossoms of the shrub, and was about to fasten it in her bosom. But now, unless Giovanni's draughts of wine had bewildered his senses, a singular incident occurred. A small orange-colored reptile①, of the lizard or chameleon species, chanced to be creeping along the path, just at the feet of Beatrice. It appeared to Giovanni—but, at the distance from which he gazed, he could scarcely have seen anything so minute—it appeared to him, however, that a drop or two of moisture from the broken stem of the flower descended upon the lizard's head. For an instant, the reptile contorted itself violently, and then lay motionless in the sunshine. Beatrice observed this remarkable phenomenon, and crossed herself, sadly, but without surprise; nor did she therefore hesitate to arrange the fatal flower in her bosom. There it blushed, and almost glimmered with the dazzling effect of a precious stone, adding to her dress and aspect the one appropriate charm, which nothing else in the world could have supplied. But Giovanni, out of the shadow of his window, bent forward and shrank back, and murmured and trembled.

"Am I awake? Have I my senses?" Said he to himself. "What is this being?—Beautiful, shall I call her?—Or inexpressibly terrible?"

---

① reptile: 爬行动物。

Beatrice now strayed carelessly through the garden, approaching closer beneath Giovanni's window, so that he was compelled to thrust his head quite out of its concealment, in order to gratify the intense and painful curiosity which she excited. At this moment, there came a beautiful insect over the garden wall; it had perhaps wandered through the city and found no flowers nor verdure among those antique haunts of men, until the heavy perfumes of Doctor Rappaccini's shrubs had lured it from afar. Without alighting on the flowers, this winged brightness seemed to be attracted by Beatrice, and lingered in the air and fluttered about her head. Now here it could not be but that Giovanni Guasconti's eyes deceived him. Be that as it might, he fancied that while Beatrice was gazing at the insect with childish delight, it grew faint and fell at her feet; —its bright wings shivered; it was dead—from no cause that he could discern, unless it were the atmosphere of her breath. Again Beatrice crossed herself and sighed heavily, as she bent over the dead insect.

An impulsive movement of Giovanni drew her eyes to the window. There she beheld the beautiful head of the young man—rather a Grecian than an Italian head, with fair, regular features, and a glistening of gold among his ringlets—gazing down upon her like a being that hovered in mid-air. Scarcely knowing what he did, Giovanni threw down the bouquet which he had hitherto held in his hand.

"Signora," said he, "there are pure and healthful flowers. Wear them for the sake of Giovanni Guasconti!"

"Thanks, Signor," replied Beatrice, with her rich voice that came forth as it were like a gush of music; and with a mirthful expression half childish and half woman-like. "I accept your gift, and would fain recompense it with this precious purple flower; but if I toss it into the air, it will not reach you. So Signor Guasconti must even content himself with my thanks."

She lifted the bouquet from the ground, and then as if inwardly ashamed at having stepped aside from her maidenly reserve to respond to a stranger's greeting, passed swiftly homeward through the garden. But, few as the moments were, it seemed to Giovanni when she was on the point of vanishing beneath the sculptured portal, that his beautiful bouquet was already beginning to wither in her grasp. It was an idle thought; there could be no possibility of distinguishing a faded flower from a fresh one, at so great a distance.

For many days after this incident, the young man avoided the window that looked into Doctor Rappaccini's garden, as if something ugly and monstrous would have blasted his eye-sight, had he been betrayed into a glance. He felt conscious of having put himself, to a certain extent, within the influence of an unintelligible power, by the communication which he had opened with Beatrice. The wisest course would have been, if his heart were in any real danger, to quit his lodgings and Padua itself, at once; the next wiser, to have accustomed himself, as far as possible, to the familiar and daylight view of Beatrice; thus bringing her rigidly and systematically within the limits of ordinary experience. Least of all, while avoiding her sight, should Giovanni have remained so near this extraordinary being, that the proximity and possibility even of intercourse, should give a kind of substance and reality to the wild vagaries① which his imagination ran riot continually in producing. Guasconti had not a deep heart—or at all events, its depths were not sounded now—but he had a quick fancy, and an ardent southern temperament, which rose every instant to a higher fever-pitch. Whether or not Beatrice possessed those terrible attributes—that fatal breath—the affinity with those so beautiful and deadly flowers—which were indicated by what Giovanni had witnessed, she had at least instilled a fierce and subtle poison into his system. It was not love, although her rich beauty was a madness to him; nor horror, even while he fancied her spirit to be imbued with the same baneful② essence that seemed to pervade her physical frame; but a wild offspring of both love and horror that had each parent in it, and burned like one and shivered like the other. Giovanni knew not what to dread; still less did he know what to hope; yet hope and dread kept a continual warfare in his breast, alternately vanquishing one another and starting up afresh to renew the contest. Blessed are all simple emotions, be they dark or bright! It is the lurid intermixture of the two that produces the illuminating blaze of the infernal regions.

Sometimes he endeavored to assuage the fever of his spirit by a rapid walk through the streets of Padua, or beyond its gates; his footsteps kept time with the throbbings of his brain, so that the walk was apt to accelerate itself to a race. One day, he found himself arrested; his arm was seized by a portly personage who had turned back on recognizing the young man, and expended much breath in overtaking him.

"Signor Giovanni!—Stay, my young friend!" —Cried he. "Have you forgotten me? That might well be the case, if I were as much altered as yourself."

It was Baglioni, whom Giovanni had avoided, ever since their first meeting, from a doubt that the Professor's sagacity③ would look too deeply into his secrets. Endeavoring to recover himself, he stared forth wildly from his inner world into the outer one, and spoke like a man in a dream.

"Yes; I am Giovanni Guasconti. You are Professor Pietro Baglioni. Now let me pass!"

"Not yet—not yet, Signor Giovanni Guasconti," said the Professor, smiling, but

---

① vagaries: changes in somebody/something that are difficult to predict or control (漫无边际的幻想).
② baneful: evil or causing evil.
③ sagacity: good judgement and understanding.

at the same time scrutinizing the youth with an earnest glance. "What, did I grow up side by side with your father, and shall his son pass me like a stranger, in these old streets of Padua? Stand still, Signor Giovanni; for we must have a word or two before we part."

"Speedily, then, most worshipful Professor, speedily!" Said Giovanni, with feverish impatience. "Does not your worship see that I am in haste?"

Now, while he was speaking, there came a man in black along the street, stooping and moving feebly, like a person in inferior health. His face was all overspread with a most sickly and sallow hue, but yet so pervaded with an expression of piercing and active intellect, that an observer might easily have overlooked the merely physical attributes, and have seen only this wonderful energy. As he passed, this person exchanged a cold and distant salutation with Baglioni, but fixed his eyes upon Giovanni with an intentness that seemed to bring out whatever was within him worthy of notice. Nevertheless, there was a peculiar quietness in the look, as if taking merely a speculative, not a human interest, in the young man.

"It is Doctor Rappaccini!" Whispered the Professor, when the stranger had passed.—"Has he ever seen your face before?"

"Not that I know," answered Giovanni, starting at the name.

"He *has* seen you!—He must have seen you!" Said Baglioni, hastily. "For some purpose or other, this man of science is making a study of you. I know that look of his! It is the same that coldly illuminates his face, as he bends over a bird, a mouse, or a butterfly, which, in pursuance of some experiment, he has killed by the perfume of a flower;—a look as deep as Nature itself, but without Nature's warmth of love. Signor Giovanni, I will stake my life upon it, you are the subject of one of Rappaccini's experiments!"

"Will you make a fool of me?" Cried Giovanni, passionately. "*That,* Signor Professor, were an untoward① experiment."

"Patience, patience!" Replied the imperturbable Professor. "I tell thee, my poor Giovanni, that Rappaccini has a scientific interest in thee. Thou hast fallen into fearful hands! And the Signora Beatrice? What part does she act in this mystery?"

But Guasconti, finding Baglioni's pertinacity intolerable, here broke away, and was gone before the Professor could again seize his arm. He looked after the young man intently, and shook his head.

"This must not be," said Baglioni to himself. "The youth is the son of my old friend, and shall not come to any harm from which the arcana② of medical science

---

① untoward: unusual and unexpected, and usually unpleasant(异常的, 棘手的).
② arcana: 秘方。

can preserve him. Besides, it is too insufferable an impertinence in Rappaccini thus to snatch the lad out of my own hands, as I may say, and make use of him for his infernal experiments. This daughter of his! It shall be looked to. Perchance, most learned Rappaccini, I may foil you where you little dream of it!"

Meanwhile, Giovanni had pursued a circuitous route, and at length found himself at the door of his lodgings. As he crossed the threshold, he was met by old Lisabetta, who smirked and smiled, and was evidently desirous to attract his attention; vainly, however, as the ebullition of his feelings had momentarily subsided into a cold and dull vacuity. He turned his eyes full upon the withered face that was puckering itself into a smile, but seemed to behold it not. The old dame, therefore, laid her grasp upon his cloak.

"Signor!—Signor!" Whispered she, still with a smile over the whole breadth of her visage, so that it looked not unlike a grotesque carving in wood, darkened by centuries—"Listen, Signor! There is a private entrance into the garden!"

"What do you say?" Exclaimed Giovanni, turning quickly about, as if an inanimate thing should start into feverish life.—"A private entrance into Doctor Rappaccini's garden!"

"Hush! Hush!—Not so loud!" Whispered Lisabetta, putting her hand over his mouth. "Yes; into the worshipful Doctor's garden, where you may see all his fine shrubbery. Many a young man in Padua would give gold to be admitted among those flowers." Giovanni put a piece of gold into her hand.

"Show me the way," said he.

A surmise[①], probably excited by his conversation with Baglioni, crossed his mind, that this interposition of old Lisabetta might perchance be connected with the intrigue, whatever were its nature, in which the Professor seemed to suppose that Doctor Rappaccini was involving him. But such a suspicion, though it disturbed Giovanni, was inadequate to restrain him. The instant he was aware of the possibility of approaching Beatrice, it seemed an absolute necessity of his existence to do so. It mattered not whether she were angel or demon; he was irrevocably within her sphere, and must obey the law that whirled him onward, in ever lessening circles, towards a result which he did not attempt to foreshadow. And yet, strange to say, there came across him a sudden doubt, whether this intense interest on his part were not delusory—whether it were really of so deep and positive a nature as to justify him in now thrusting himself into an incalculable position-whether it were not merely the fantasy of a young man's brain, only slightly, or not at all, connected with his heart!

---

① surmise: a guess.

He paused—hesitated—turned half about—but again went on. His withered guide led him along several obscure passages, and finally undid a door, through which, as it was opened, there came the sight and sound of rustling leaves, with the broken sunshine glimmering among them. Giovanni stepped forth, and forcing himself through the entanglement of a shrub that wreathed its tendrils① over the hidden entrance, he stood beneath his own window, in the open area of Doctor Rappaccini's garden.

How often is it the case, that, when impossibilities have come to pass, and dreams have condensed their misty substance into tangible realities, we find ourselves calm, and even coldly self-possessed, amid circumstances which it would have been a delirium② of joy or agony to anticipate! Fate delights to thwart us thus. Passion will choose his own time to rush upon the scene, and lingers sluggishly behind, when an appropriate adjustment of events would seem to summon his appearance. So was it now with Giovanni. Day after day, his pulses had throbbed with feverish blood, at the improbable idea of an interview with Beatrice, and of standing with her, face to face, in this very garden, basking in the oriental sunshine of her beauty, and snatching from her full gaze the mystery which he deemed the riddle of his own existence. But now there was a singular and untimely equanimity③ within his breast. He threw a glance around the garden to discover if Beatrice or her father were present, and perceiving that he was alone, began a critical observation of the plants.

The aspect of one and all of them dissatisfied him; their gorgeousness seemed fierce, passionate, and even unnatural. There was hardly an individual shrub which a wanderer, straying by himself through a forest, would not have been startled to find growing wild, as if an unearthly face had glared at him out of the thicket. Several, also, would have shocked a delicate instinct by an appearance of artificialness, indicating that there had been such commixture④, and, as it were, adultery of various vegetable species, that the production was no longer of God's making, but the monstrous offspring of man's depraved fancy, glowing with only an evil mockery of beauty. They were probably the result of experiment, which, in one or two cases, had succeeded in mingling plants individually lovely into a compound possessing the questionable and ominous character that distinguished the whole growth of the garden. In fine, Giovanni recognized but two or three plants in the collection, and those of a kind that he well

---

① tendril:（攀缘植物的）卷须。
② delirium: state of violent mental agitation（发狂，狂热）.
③ equanimity: a calm state of mind which means that you do not become angry or upset, especially in difficult situations（镇静，沉着）.
④ commixture: the act of mixing together（混合）.

knew to be poisonous. While busy with these contemplations, he heard the rustling of a silken garment, and turning, beheld Beatrice emerging from beneath the sculptured portal.

Giovanni had not considered with himself what should be his deportment[①]; whether he should apologize for his intrusion into the garden, or assume that he was there with the privity, at least, if not by the desire, of Doctor Rappaccini or his daughter. But Beatrice's manner placed him at his ease, though leaving him still in doubt by what agency he had gained admittance. She came lightly along the path, and met him near the broken fountain. There was surprise in her face, but brightened by a simple and kind expression of pleasure.

"You are a connoisseur[②] in flowers, Signor," said Beatrice with a smile, alluding to the bouquet which he had flung her from the window. "It is no marvel, therefore, if the sight of my father's rare collection has tempted you to take a nearer view. If he were here, he could tell you many strange and interesting facts as to the nature and habits of these shrubs, for he has spent a life time in such studies, and this garden is his world."

"And yourself, lady"—observed Giovanni—"if fame says true—you, likewise, are deeply skilled in the virtues indicated by these rich blossoms, and these spicy perfumes. Would you deign to be my instructress, I should prove an apter scholar than under Signor Rappaccini himself."

"Are there such idle rumors?" asked Beatrice, with the music of a pleasant laugh. "Do people say that I am skilled in my father's science of plants? What a jest is there! No; though I have grown up among these flowers, I know no more of them than their hues and perfume; and sometimes, methinks I would fain rid myself of even that small knowledge. There are many flowers here, and those not the least brilliant, that shock and offend me, when they meet my eye. But, pray, Signor, do not believe these stories about my science. Believe nothing of me save what you see with your own eyes."

"And must I believe all that I have seen with my own eyes?" asked Giovanni pointedly, while the recollection of former scenes made him shrink. "No, Signora, you demand too little of me. Bid me believe nothing, save what comes from your own lips."

It would appear that Beatrice understood him. There came a deep flush to her cheek; but she looked full into Giovanni's eyes, and responded to his gaze of uneasy suspicion with a queen-like haughtiness.

---

① deportment: the way in which a person behaves(行为, 举止).
② connoisseur: an expert on matters involving the judgement of beauty, quality or skill in art, food or music(鉴赏家; 鉴定家).

"I do so bid you, Signor!" She replied. "Forget whatever you may have fancied in regard to me. If true to the outward senses, still it may be false in its essence. But the words of Beatrice Rappaccini's lips are true from the heart outward. Those you may believe!"

A fervor glowed in her whole aspect, and beamed upon Giovanni's consciousness like the light of truth itself. But while she spoke, there was a fragrance in the atmosphere around her rich and delightful, though evanescent①, yet which the young man, from an indefinable reluctance, scarcely dared to draw into his lungs. It might be the odor of the flowers. Could it be Beatrice's breath, which thus embalmed her words with a strange richness, as if by steeping them in her heart? A faintness passed like a shadow over Giovanni, and flitted away; he seemed to gaze through the beautiful girl's eyes into her transparent soul, and felt no more doubt or fear.

The tinge② of passion that had colored Beatrice's manner vanished; she became gay, and appeared to derive a pure delight from her communion with the youth, not unlike what the maiden of a lonely island might have felt, conversing with a voyager from the civilized world. Evidently her experience of life had been confined within the limits of that garden. She talked now about matters as simple as the day-light or summer-clouds, and now asked questions in reference to the city, or Giovanni's distant home, his friends, his mother, and his sisters; questions indicating such seclusion, and such lack of familiarity with modes and forms, that Giovanni responded as if to an infant. Her spirit gushed out before him like a freshrill③, that was just catching its first glimpse of the sunlight, and wondering, at the reflections of earth and sky which were flung into its bosom. There came thoughts, too, from a deep source, and fantasies of a gem-like brilliancy, as if diamonds and rubies sparkled upward among the bubbles of the fountain. Ever and anon, there gleamed across the young man's mind a sense of wonder, that he should be walking side by side with the being who had so wrought upon his imagination-whom he had idealized in such hues of terror—in whom he had positively witnessed such manifestations of dreadful attributes—that he should be conversing with Beatrice like a brother, and should find her so human and so maiden-like. But such reflections were only momentary; the effect of her character was too real, not to make itself familiar at once.

In this free intercourse, they had strayed through the garden, and now, after many turns among its avenues, were come to the shattered fountain, beside which grew the magnificent shrub with its treasury of glowing blossoms. A fragrance was diffused

---

① evanescent: disappearing quickly from sight or memory(转瞬即逝的).
② tinge: a small amount of a colour, feeling or quality.
③ rill: a shallow channel cut by water flowing over rock or soil(小溪).

from it, which Giovanni recognized as identical with that which he had attributed to Beatrice's breath, but incomparably more powerful. As her eyes fell upon it, Giovanni beheld her press her hand to her bosom, as if her heart were throbbing suddenly and painfully.

"For the first time in my life," murmured she, addressing the shrub, "I had forgotten thee!"

"I remember, Signora," said Giovanni, "that you once promised to reward me with one of these living gems for the bouquet, which I had the happy boldness to fling to your feet. Permit me now to pluck it as a memorial of this interview."

He made a step towards the shrub, with extended hand. But Beatrice darted forward, uttering a shriek that went through his heart like a dagger. She caught his hand, and drew it back with the whole force of her slender figure. Giovanni felt her touch thrilling through his fibres.

"Touch it not!" Exclaimed she, in a voice of agony. "Not for thy life! It is fatal!"

Then, hiding her face, she fled from him, and vanished beneath the sculptured portal. As Giovanni followed her with his eyes, he beheld the emaciated figure and pale intelligence of Doctor Rappaccini, who had been watching the scene, he knew not how long, within the shadow of the entrance.

No sooner was Guasconti alone in his chamber, than the image of Beatrice came back to his passionate musings, invested with all the witchery that had been gathering around it ever since his first glimpse of her, and now likewise imbued with a tender warmth of girlish womanhood. She was human: her nature was endowed with all gentle and feminine qualities; she was worthiest to be worshipped; she was capable, surely, on her part, of the height and heroism of love. Those tokens, which he had hitherto considered as proofs of a frightful peculiarity in her physical and moral system, were now either forgotten, or, by the subtle sophistry of passion, transmuted into a golden crown of enchantment, rendering Beatrice the more admirable, by so much as she was the more unique. Whatever had looked ugly, was now beautiful; or, if incapable of such a change, it stole away and hid itself among those shapeless half-ideas, which throng the dim region beyond the daylight of our perfect consciousness. Thus did Giovanni spend the night, nor fell asleep, until the dawn had begun to awake the slumbering flowers in Doctor Rappaccini's garden, whither his dreams doubtless led him. Up rose the sun in his due season, and flinging his beams upon the young man's eyelids, awoke him to a sense of pain. When thoroughly aroused, he became sensible of a burning and tingling agony in his hand—in his right hand—the very hand which Beatrice had grasped in her own, when he was on the point of plucking one of the gem-like flowers. On the back of that hand there was now a purple print, like that of four small fingers, and the likeness of a slender thumb upon his wrist.

Oh, how stubbornly does love—or even that cunning semblance of love which flourishes in the imagination, but strikes no depth of root into the heart—how stubbornly does it hold its faith, until the moment comes, when it is doomed to vanish into thin mist! Giovanni wrapt a handkerchief about his hand, and wondered what evil thing had stung him, and soon forgot his pain in a reverie① of Beatrice.

After the first interview, a second was in the inevitable course of what we call fate. A third; a fourth; and a meeting with Beatrice in the garden was no longer an incident in Giovanni's daily life, but the whole space in which he might be said to live; for the anticipation and memory of that ecstatic hour made up the remainder. Nor was it otherwise with the daughter of Rappaccini. She watched for the youth's appearance, and flew to his side with confidence as unreserved as if they had been playmates from early infancy—as if they were such playmates still. If, by any unwonted chance, he failed to come at the appointed moment, she stood beneath the window, and sent up the rich sweetness of her tones to float around him in his chamber, and echo and reverberate throughout his heart—"Giovanni! Giovanni! Why tarriest thou? Come down!" And down he hastened into that Eden of poisonous flowers.

But, with all this intimate familiarity, there was still a reserve in Beatrice's demeanor, so rigidly and invariably sustained, that the idea of infringing it scarcely occurred to his imagination. By all appreciable signs, they loved; they had looked love, with eyes that conveyed the holy secret from the depths of one soul into the depths of the other, as if it were too sacred to be whispered by the way; they had even spoken love, in those gushes of passion when their spirits darted forth in articulated breath, like tongues of long-hidden flame; and yet there had been no seal of lips, no clasp of hands, nor any slightest caress, such as love claims and hallows. He had never touched one of the gleaming ringlets of her hair; her garment—so marked was the physical barrier between them—had never been waved against him by a breeze. On the few occasions when Giovanni had seemed tempted to overstep the limit, Beatrice grew so sad, so stern, and withal wore such a look of desolate separation, shuddering at itself, that not a spoken word was requisite to repel him. At such times, he was startled at the horrible suspicions that rose, monster-like, out of the caverns of his heart, and stared him in the face; his love grew thin and faint as the morning-mist; his doubts alone had substance. But when Beatrice's face brightened again, after the momentary shadow, she was transformed at once from the mysterious, questionable being, whom he had watched with so much awe and horror; she was now the beautiful

---

① reverie: a state of thinking about pleasant things, almost as though you are dreaming(幻想，白日梦)。

and unsophisticated girl, whom he felt that his spirit knew with a certainty beyond all other knowledge.

A considerable time had now passed since Giovanni's last meeting with Baglioni. One morning, however, he was disagreeably surprised by a visit from the Professor, whom he had scarcely thought of for whole weeks, and would willingly have forgotten still longer. Given up, as he had long been, to a pervading excitement, he could tolerate no companions, except upon condition of their perfect sympathy with his present state of feeling. Such sympathy was not to be expected from Professor Baglioni.

The visitor chatted carelessly, for a few moments, about the gossip of the city and the University, and then took up another topic.

"I have been reading an old classic author lately," said he, "and met with a story that strangely interested me. Possibly you may remember it. It is of an Indian prince, who sent a beautiful woman as a present to Alexander the Great. She was as lovely as the dawn, and gorgeous as the sunset; but what especially distinguished her was a certain rich perfume in her breath—richer than a garden of Persian roses. Alexander, as was natural to a youthful conqueror, fell in love at first sight with this magnificent stranger. But a certain sage physician, happening to be present, discovered a terrible secret in regard to her."

"And what was that?" asked Giovanni, turning his eyes downward to avoid those of the Professor.

"That this lovely woman," continued Baglioni, with emphasis, "had been nourished with poisons from her birth upward, until her whole nature was so imbued with them, that she herself had become the deadliest poison in existence. Poison was her element of life. With that rich perfume of her breath, she blasted the very air. Her love would have been poison!—her embrace death! Is not this a marvellous tale?"

"A childish fable," answered Giovanni, nervously starting from his chair. "I marvel how your worship finds time to read such nonsense, among your graver studies."

"By the bye," said the Professor, looking uneasily about him, "what singular fragrance is this in your apartment? Is it the perfume of your gloves? It is faint, but delicious, and yet, after all, by no means agreeable. Were I to breathe it long, methinks it would make me ill. It is like the breath of a flower—but I see no flowers in the chamber."

"Nor are there any," replied Giovanni, who had turned pale as the Professor spoke; "nor, I think, is there any fragrance, except in your worship's imagination. Odors, being a sort of element combined of the sensual and the spiritual, are apt to deceive us in this manner. The recollection of a perfume—the bare idea of it—may easily be mistaken for a present reality."

"Aye; but my sober imagination does not often play such tricks," said Baglioni; "and were I to fancy any kind of odor, it would be that of some vile apothecary① drug, wherewith my fingers are likely enough to be imbued. Our worshipful friend Rappaccini, as I have heard, tinctures his medicaments with odors richer than those of Araby. Doubtless, likewise, the fair and learned Signora Beatrice would minister to her patients with draughts as sweet as a maiden's breath. But wo to him that sips them!"

Giovanni's face evinced many contending emotions. The tone in which the Professor alluded to the pure and lovely daughter of Rappaccini was a torture to his soul; and yet, the intimation of a view of her character, opposite to his own, gave instantaneous distinctness to a thousand dim suspicions, which now grinned at him like so many demons. But he strove hard to quell them, and to respond to Baglioni with a true lover's perfect faith.

"Signor Professor," said he, "you were my father's friend—perchance, too, it is your purpose to act a friendly part towards his son. I would fain feel nothing towards you save respect and deference. But I pray you to observe, Signor, that there is one subject on which we must not speak. You know not the Signora Beatrice. You cannot, therefore, estimate the wrong—the blasphemy②, I may even say—that is offered to her character by a light or injurious word."

"Giovanni!—My poor Giovanni!" Answered the Professor, with a calm expression of pity, "I know this wretched girl far better than yourself. You shall hear the truth in respect to the poisoner Rappaccini, and his poisonous daughter. Yes; poisonous as she is beautiful! Listen; for even should you do violence to my gray hairs, it shall not silence me. That old fable of the Indian woman has become a truth, by the deep and deadly science of Rappaccini, and in the person of the lovely Beatrice!" Giovanni groaned and hid his face.

"Her father," continued Baglioni, "was not restrained by natural affection from offering up his child, in this horrible manner, as the victim of his insane zeal for science. For—let us do him justice—he is as true a man of science as ever distilled his own heart in an alembic. What, then, will be your fate? Beyond a doubt, you are selected as the material of some new experiment. Perhaps the result is to be death—perhaps a fate more awful still! Rappaccini, with what he calls the interest of science before his eyes, will hesitate at nothing."

"It is a dream!" Muttered Giovanni to himself, "surely it is a dream!"

---

① apothecary:(旧时制药兼售药的)药剂师,药商。
② blasphemy: profane talk(亵渎).

"But," resumed the Professor, "be of good cheer, son of my friend! It is not yet too late for the rescue. Possibly, we may even succeed in bringing back this miserable child within the limits of ordinary nature, from which her father's madness has estranged her. Behold this little silver vase! It was wrought by the hands of the renowned Benvenuto Cellini, and is well worthy to be a love-gift to the fairest dame in Italy. But its contents are invaluable. One little sip of this antidote would have rendered the most virulent poisons of the Borgiasinnocuous[①]. Doubt not that it will be as efficacious against those of Rappaccini. Bestow the vase, and the precious liquid within it, on your Beatrice, and hopefully await the result."

Baglioni laid a small, exquisitely wrought silver phial on the table, and withdrew, leaving what he had said to produce its effect upon the young man's mind.

"We will thwart Rappaccini yet!" Thought he, chuckling to himself, as he descended the stairs. "But, let us confess the truth of him, he is a wonderful man! — A wonderful man indeed! A vile empiric, however, in his practice, and therefore not to be tolerated by those who respect the good old rules of the medical profession!"

Throughout Giovanni's whole acquaintance with Beatrice, he had occasionally, as we have said, been haunted by dark surmises as to her character. Yet, so thoroughly had she made herself felt by him as a simple, natural, most affectionate and guileless creature, that the image now held up by Professor Baglioni, looked as strange and incredible, as if it were not in accordance with his own original conception. True, there were ugly recollections connected with his first glimpses of the beautiful girl; he could not quite forget the bouquet that withered in her grasp, and the insect that perished amid the sunny air, by no ostensible agency save the fragrance of her breath. These incidents, however, dissolving in the pure light of her character, had no longer the efficacy of facts, but were acknowledged as mistaken fantasies, by whatever testimony of the senses they might appear to be substantiated. There is something truer and more real, than what we can see with the eyes, and touch with the finger. On such better evidence, had Giovanni founded his confidence in Beatrice, though rather by the necessary force of her high attributes, than by any deep and generous faith on his part. But, now, his spirit was incapable of sustaining itself at the height to which the early enthusiasm of passion had exalted it; he fell down, grovelling among earthly doubts, and defiled therewith the pure whiteness of Beatrice's image. Not that he gave her up; he did but distrust. He resolved to institute some decisive test that should satisfy him, once for all, whether there were those dreadful peculiarities in her physical nature, which could not be supposed to exist without some corresponding monstrosity of

---

① innocuous: not harmful.

soul. His eyes, gazing down afar, might have deceived him as to the lizard, the insect, and the flowers. But if he could witness, at the distance of a few paces, the sudden blight of one fresh and healthful flower in Beatrice's hand, there would be room for no further question. With this idea, he hastened to the florist's, and purchased a bouquet that was still gemmed with the morning dew-drops.

It was now the customary hour of his daily interview with Beatrice. Before descending into the garden, Giovanni failed not to look at his figure in the mirror; a vanity to be expected in a beautiful young man, yet, as displaying itself at that troubled and feverish moment, the token of a certain shallowness of feeling and insincerity of character. He did gaze, however, and said to himself, that his features had never before possessed so rich a grace, nor his eyes such vivacity, nor his cheeks so warm a hue of superabundant life.

"At least," thought he, "her poison has not yet insinuated itself into my system. I am no flower to perish in her grasp!"

With that thought, he turned his eyes on the bouquet, which he had never once laid aside from his hand. A thrill of indefinable horror shot through his frame, on perceiving that those dewy flowers were already beginning to droop; they wore the aspect of things that had been fresh and lovely, yesterday. Giovanni grew white as marble, and stood motionless before the mirror, staring at his own reflection there, as at the likeness of something frightful. He remembered Baglioni's remark about the fragrance that seemed to pervade the chamber. It must have been the poison in his breath! Then he shuddered-shuddered at himself! Recovering from his stupor, he began to watch, with curious eye, a spider that was busily at work, hanging its web from the antique cornice of the apartment, crossing and re-crossing the artful system of interwoven lines, as vigorous and active a spider as ever dangled from an old ceiling. Giovanni bent towards the insect, and emitted a deep, long breath. The spider suddenly ceased its toil; the web vibrated with a tremor originating in the body of the small artizan. Again Giovanni sent forth a breath, deeper, longer, and imbued with a venomous[①] feeling out of his heart; he knew not whether he were wicked or only desperate. The spider made a convulsive gripe with his limbs, and hung dead across the window.

"Accursed! Accursed!" Muttered Giovanni, addressing himself. "Hast thou grown so poisonous, that this deadly insect perishes by thy breath?"

At that moment, a rich, sweet voice came floating up from the garden: "Giovanni! Giovanni! It is past the hour! Why tarriest thou! Come down!"

---

① venomous: full of bitter feeling or hatred(恶毒的,恶意的).

"Yes," muttered Giovanni again. "She is the only being whom my breath may not slay! Would that it might!"

He rushed down, and in an instant, was standing before the bright and loving eyes of Beatrice. A moment ago, his wrath and despair had been so fierce that he could have desired nothing so much as to wither her by a glance. But, with her actual presence, there came influences which had too real an existence to be at once shaken off; recollections of the delicate and benign power of her feminine nature, which had so often enveloped him in a religious calm; recollections of many a holy and passionate outgush of her heart, when the pure fountain had been unsealed from its depths, and made visible in its transparency to his mental eye; recollections which, had Giovanni known how to estimate them, would have assured him that all this ugly mystery was but an earthly illusion, and that, whatever mist of evil might seem to have gathered over her, the real Beatrice was a heavenly angel. Incapable as he was of such high faith, still her presence had not utterly lost its magic. Giovanni's rage was quelled into an aspect of sullen insensibility. Beatrice, with a quick spiritual sense, immediately felt that there was a gulf of blackness between them, which neither he nor she could pass. They walked on together, sad and silent, and came thus to the marble fountain, and to its pool of water on the ground, in the midst of which grew the shrub that bore gem-like blossoms. Giovanni was affrighted at the eager enjoyment—the appetite, as it were—with which he found himself inhaling the fragrance of the flowers.

"Beatrice," asked he abruptly, "whence came this shrub!" "My father created it," answered she, with simplicity.

"Created it! Created it!" Repeated Giovanni. "What mean you, Beatrice?"

"He is a man fearfully acquainted with the secrets of nature," replied Beatrice; "and, at the hour when I first drew breath, this plant sprang from the soil, the offspring of his science, of his intellect, while I was but his earthly child. Approach it not!" Continued she, observing with terror that Giovanni was drawing nearer to the shrub. "It has qualities that you little dream of. But I, dearest Giovanni—I grew up and blossomed with the plant, and was nourished with its breath. It was my sister, and I loved it with a human affection: for—alas! Hast thou not suspected it? There was an awful doom."

Here Giovanni frowned so darkly upon her that Beatrice paused and trembled. But her faith in his tenderness reassured her, and made her blush that she had doubted for an instant.

"There was an awful doom," she continued, —"the effect of my father's fatal love of science—which estranged me from all society of my kind. Until Heaven sent thee, dearest Giovanni, oh! How lonely was thy poor Beatrice!"

"Was it a hard doom?" Asked Giovanni, fixing his eyes upon her.

"Only of late have I known how hard it was," answered she tenderly. "Oh, yes; but my heart was torpid①, and therefore quiet."

Giovanni's rage broke forth from his sullen gloom like a lightning-flash out of a dark cloud.

"Accursed one!" Cried he, with venomousscorn and anger. "And finding thy solitude wearisome, thou hast severed me, likewise, from all the warmth of life, and enticed me into thy region of unspeakable horror!"

"Giovanni!" Exclaimed Beatrice, turning her large bright eyes upon his face. The force of his words had not found its way into her mind; she was merely thunder-struck.

"Yes, poisonous thing!" Repeated Giovanni, beside himself with passion. "Thou hast done it! Thou hast blasted me! Thou hast filled my veins with poison! Thou hast made me as hateful, as ugly, as loathsome and deadly a creature as thyself—a world's wonder of hideous monstrosity! Now—if our breath be happily as fatal to ourselves as to all others—let us join our lips in one kiss of unutterable hatred, and so die!"

"What has befallen me?" Murmured Beatrice, with a low moan out of her heart. "Holy Virgin pity me, a poor heartbroken child!"

"Thou! Dost thou pray?" Cried Giovanni, still with the same fiendish scorn. "Thy very prayers, as they come from thy lips, taint the atmosphere with death. Yes, yes; let us pray! Let us to church, and dip our fingers in the holy water at the portal! They that come after us will perish as by a pestilence. Let us sign crosses in the air! It will be scattering curses abroad in the likeness of holy symbols!"

"Giovanni," said Beatrice calmly, for her grief was beyond passion, "why dost thou join thyself with me thus in those terrible words? I, it is true, am the horrible thing thou namest me. But thou!—What hast thou to do, save with one other shudder at my hideous misery, to go forth out of the garden and mingle with thy race, and forget that there ever crawled on earth such a monster as poor Beatrice?"

"Dost thou pretend ignorance?" Asked Giovanni, scowling② upon her. "Behold! This power have I gained from the pure daughter of Rappaccini!"

There was a swarm of summer-insects flitting through the air, in search of the food promised by the flower-odors of the fatal garden. They circled round Giovanni's head, and were evidently attracted towards him by the same influence which had drawn them, for an instant, within the sphere of several of the shrubs. He sent forth a breath among them, and smiled bitterly at Beatrice, as at least a score of the insects

---

① torpid: mentally or physically inactive(不活泼的, 迟钝的).
② scowl: look at sb/sth in an angry or annoyed way(怒视).

fell dead upon the ground.

"I see it! I see it!" Shrieked Beatrice. "It is my father's fatal science? No, no, Giovanni; it was not I! Never, never! I dreamed only to love thee, and be with thee a little time, and so to let thee pass away, leaving but thine image in mine heart. For, Giovanni—believe it—though my body be nourished with poison, my spirit is God's creature, and craves love as its daily food. But my father!—He has united us in this fearful sympathy. Yes; spurn me!—Tread upon me!—Kill me! Oh, what is death, after such words as thine? But it was not I! Not for a world of bliss would I have done it!"

Giovanni's passion had exhausted itself in its outburst from his lips. There now came across him a sense, mournful, and not without tenderness, of the intimate and peculiar relationship between Beatrice and himself. They stood, as it were, in an utter solitude, which would be made none the less solitary by the densest throng of human life. Ought not, then, the desert of humanity around them to press this insulated pair closer together? If they should be cruel to one another, who was there to be kind to them? Besides, thought Giovanni, might there not still be a hope of his returning within the limits of ordinary nature, and leading Beatrice—the redeemed Beatrice—by the hand? Oh, weak, and selfish, and unworthy spirit, that could dream of an earthly union and earthly happiness as possible, after such deep love had been so bitterly wronged as was Beatrice's love by Giovanni's blighting words! No, no; there could be no such hope. She must pass heavily, with that broken heart, across the borders of Time—she must bathe her hurts in some fount of Paradise, and forget her grief in the light of immortality—and there be well!

But Giovanni did not know it.

"Dear Beatrice," said he, approaching her, while she shrank away, as always at his approach, but now with a different impulse—"dearest Beatrice, our fate is not yet so desperate. Behold! There is a medicine, potent, as a wise physician has assured me, and almost divine in its efficacy. It is composed of ingredients the most opposite to those by which thy awful father has brought this calamity upon thee and me. It is distilled of blessed herbs. Shall we not quaff it together, and thus be purified from evil?"

"Give it me!" Said Beatrice, extending her hand to receive the little silver phial which Giovanni took from his bosom. She added, with a peculiar emphasis: "I will drink—but do thou await the result."

She put Baglioni's antidote to her lips; and, at the same moment, the figure of Rappaccini emerged from the portal, and came slowly towards the marble fountain. As he drew near, the pale man of science seemed to gaze with a triumphant expression at the beautiful youth and maiden, as might an artist who should spend his life in achieving a picture or a group of statuary, and finally be satisfied with his success. He paused—his bent form grew erect with conscious power, he spread out his hand over them, in the attitude of a father imploring a blessing upon his children. But those were the same hands that had thrown poison into the stream of their lives! Giovanni trembled. Beatrice shuddered very nervously, and pressed her hand upon her heart.

"My daughter," said Rappaccini, "thou art no longer lonely in the world! Pluck one of those precious gems from thy sister shrub, and bid thy bridegroom wear it in his bosom. It will not harm him now! My science, and the sympathy between thee and him, have so wrought within his system, that he now stands apart from common men, as thou dost, daughter of my pride and triumph, from ordinary women. Pass on, then, through the world, most dear to one another, and dreadful to all besides!"

"My father," said Beatrice, feebly—and still, as she spoke, she kept her hand upon her heart—"wherefore didst thou inflict[①] this miserable doom upon thy child?"

"Miserable!" Exclaimed Rappaccini. "What mean you, foolish girl? Dost thou deem it misery to be endowed with marvellous gifts, against which no power nor strength could avail an enemy? Misery, to be able to quell the mightiest with a breath? Misery, to be as terrible as thou art beautiful? Wouldst thou, then, have preferred the condition of a weak woman, exposed to all evil, and capable of none?"

"I would fain have been loved, not feared," murmured Beatrice, sinking down upon the ground. —"But now it matters not; I am going, father, where the evil, which thou hast striven to mingle with my being, will pass away like a dream—like the fragrance of these poisonous flowers, which will no longer taint my breath among the flowers of Eden. Farewell, Giovanni! Thy words of hatred are like lead within my heart—but they, too, will fall away as I ascend. Oh, was there not, from the first, more poison in thy nature than in mine?"

To Beatrice—so radically had her earthly part been wrought upon by Rappaccini's skill—as poison had been life, so the powerful antidote was death. And thus the poor victim of man's ingenuity and of thwarted nature, and of the fatality that attends all such efforts of perverted wisdom, perished there, at the feet of her father and Giovanni. Just at that moment, Professor Pietro Baglioni looked forth from the window, and called loudly, in a tone of triumph mixed with horror, to the thunder-stricken man of science: "Rappaccini! Rappaccini! And is *this* the upshot[②] of your experiment?"

译文链接：https://www.docin.com/p-259177082.html

---

① inflict: cause (something unpleasant or painful) to be suffered by someone or something.
② upshot: the final result of a series of events(最后结果，结局).

Questions for Understanding

1. Who is Dr. Rappaccini? What is his relationship with his daughter, Beatrice?
2. What is the garden like where Beatrice spends most of her time? What does it symbolize?
3. What role does the experiment play in the story? How does it impact the characters?
4. What does the protagonist, Giovanni, think of Beatrice at the beginning of the story?
5. What is the theme of the story? What is the author's attitude toward science?

Aspects of Appreciation

1."Dr. Rappacini's Daughter" contains various Gothic elements, including a gloomy setting, mysterious characters, and a tragic ending. The story is set in a garden that is beautiful but deadly, representing the dangers of an extreme obsession with knowledge and one-sided pursuit of reason.

2. Hawthorne uses various symbols throughout the story to convey his ideas. The garden is a symbol of both beauty and danger. Beatrice, the daughter of Dr. Rappacini, symbolizes not only innocence and purity, but also the victim of the one-sided pursuit of reason.

3. Hawthorne uses irony to highlight the story's theme. For example, the very things that make Beatrice so alluring to Giovanni, her innocence and purity, are also what make her deadly.

Suggested Further Reading

Twice-Told Tales (1837); *Mosses from an Old Manse*(1846); *The Scarlet Letter* (1850); *The House of the Seven Gables* (1851); *The Blithedale Romance* (1852); *The Marble Faun* (1860)

Topics for Further Study

1. What is the significance of Beatrice's relationship with the poisonous plants in the story?
2. How does the setting of the story, especially the garden, contribute to the theme of the story?
3. How does the author create the atmosphere of the story?

4. What are the drawbacks of the modern Western view of science according to the author?

Knowledge of Literature

An Element of Fiction: Symbol（象征）

In fiction, a symbol is usually a thing, character, place, action, situation, or even thought. In other words, a symbol is something that is itself and yet stands for or suggests or means something else. A symbol might appear over and over again in the same story, yet it always maintains the same meaning. To determine whether something in a story is symbolic, we must decide if it consistently refers beyond itself to a significant idea, emotion, or quality.

There are two kinds of symbols: public (universal, cultural, traditional or conventional) and private (contextual, authorial or original). Public symbols are those that most people in a particular culture or community would recognize as meaning something fairly definite. Examples of public symbols are the cross, the American eagle, flags of countries, and the colors red (for "stop") and green(for "go"). Private symbols are unique to an individual or to a single work. Only from clues in the work itself can we learn the symbolic value of the object.

推荐阅读的论文：
[1] 王静. 霍桑的象征世界——读《拉帕西尼的女儿》[J]. 重庆工学院学报（社会科学版），2009，23(08).
[2] 郭爱平. 霍桑《红字》中红字A的象征意义[J]. 鄂州大学学报，2020，27(02).

Walt Whitman (1819~1892)

About the Author

Walt Whitman is an American poet, journalist and essayist whose verse collection *Leaves of Grass* is a landmark in the history of American literature.

Walt Whitman was born into a family that settled in North America in the first half of the 17th century. His ancestry was typical of the region: his mother, Louisa Van Velsor, was Dutch, and his father, Walter Whitman, was of English descent. They were simple farm people, with little formal education. The Whitman family had at one time owned a large tract of land, but it was so diminished by the time Walt was born that his father had taken up carpentering, though the family still lived on a small section of the ancestral estate. In 1823 Walter Whitman, Sr. moved his growing family to Brooklyn, which was enjoying a boom. There he speculated in real estate and built cheap houses for artisans, but he was a poor manager and had difficulty in providing for his family, which increased to nine children.

Walt, the second child, attended public school in Brooklyn, began working at the age of 12, and learned the printing trade. He was employed as a printer in Brooklyn and New York City, taught in country schools on Long Island from 1836~1841, and later became a journalist. At the age of 23, he edited a daily newspaper in New York, and in 1846 he became an editor of *the Brooklyn Daily Eagle*, a fairly important newspaper of the time. Discharged from *the Eagle* early in 1848 because of his support for the Free Soil faction of the Democratic Party, he went to New Orleans, La., where he worked for three months on *the Crescent* before returning to New York via the Mississippi River and the Great Lakes. After another abortive attempt at Free Soil journalism, he built houses and dabbled in real estate in New York from about 1850 until 1855.

Whitman had spent a great deal of his 36 years walking and observing in New York City and Long Island. He had visited the theatre frequently and seen many plays of William Shakespeare, and he had developed a strong love of music, especially opera. During these years he had also read extensively at home and in the New York libraries, and began experimenting with a new style of poetry. While he had been a schoolteacher, printer, and journalist, he had published sentimental stories and poems in newspapers and popular magazines, but they showed almost no literary promise.

By the spring of 1855 Whitman had written enough poems in his new style for a thin volume. Unable to find a publisher, he sold a house and printed the first edition of *Leaves of Grass* at his own expense. No publisher's name, and no author's name appeared on the first edition in 1855. But the cover had a portrait of Walt Whitman, "broad-shouldered, rouge fleshed, Bacchus-browed, bearded like a satyr". Though little appreciated upon its appearance, *Leaves of Grass* was warmly praised by the poet and essayist Ralph Waldo Emerson, who wrote to Whitman on receiving the poems that they were "the most extraordinary piece of wit and wisdom" America had yet contributed.

Whitman continued practicing his new style of writing in his private notebooks, and in 1856 the second edition of *Leaves of Grass* appeared. This collection contained revisions of the poems of the first edition and a new one, the "Sun-down Poem" (later to become "Crossing Brooklyn Ferry"). The second edition was also a financial failure, and once again Whitman edited a daily newspaper, *Brooklyn Times*, but was unemployed by the summer of 1859. In 1860 a Boston publisher brought out the third edition of *Leaves of Grass*, greatly enlarged and rearranged, but the outbreak of the American Civil War bankrupted the firm. The 1860 volume contained the "Calamus" poems, which record a personal crisis of some intensity in Whitman's life, an apparent homosexual love affair (whether imagined or real is unknown), and "Premonition" (later entitled "Starting from Paumanok"), which records the violent emotions that often drained the poet's strength. "A Word out of the Sea" (later entitled "Out of the Cradle Endlessly Rocking") evoked some sombre feelings, as did "As I Ebb'd with the Ocean of Life". "Chants Democratic", "Enfans d'Adam", "Messenger Leaves" and "Thoughts" were more in the poet's earlier vein.

After the outbreak of the Civil War in 1861, Whitman's brother was wounded at Fredericksburg, and Whitman went there in 1862, staying some time in the camp, then taking a temporary post in the paymaster's office in Washington. He spent his spare time visiting wounded and dying soldiers in the Washington hospitals, spending his scanty salary on small gifts for Confederate and Unionist soldiers alike and offering his usual "cheer and magnetism" to try to alleviate some of the mental depression and bodily suffering he saw in the wards.

In January 1865, he became a clerk in the Department of the Interior; in May he was promoted but was dismissed in June because the secretary of the Interior thought that *Leaves of Grass* was indecent. Whitman then obtained a post in the attorney general's office, largely through the efforts of his friend, the journalist William O'Connor, who wrote a vindication of Whitman in *The Good Gray Poet* (published in 1866), which aroused sympathy for the victim of injustice.

In May 1865, a collection of war poems entitled *Drum Taps* showed Whitman's readers a new kind of poetry, moving from the oratorical excitement with which he had greeted the falling-in and arming of the young men at the beginning of the Civil War to a disturbing awareness of what war really meant. "Beat! Beat! Drums!" echoed the bitterness of the Battle of Bull Run, and "Vigil Strange I Kept on the Field One Night" had a new awareness of suffering, no less effective for its quietly plangent quality. *The Sequel to Drum Taps,* published in the autumn of 1865, contained his great elegy for President Abraham Lincoln, "When Lilacs Last in the Dooryard Bloom'd". His horror at the death of democracy's first "great martyr chief" was matched by his revulsion from the barbarities of war. Whitman's prose descriptions of the Civil War, published later in *Specimen Days & Collect* (1882~1883), are no less effective in their direct, moving simplicity.

The fourth edition of *Leaves of Grass*, published in 1867, contained much revision and rearrangement. Apart from the poems collected in *Drum Taps*, it contained eight new poems, and some poems had been omitted. In the late 1860s, Whitman's work began to receive greater recognition. O'Connor's *The Good Gray Poet* and John Burroughs'*Notes on Walt Whitman as Poet and Person* (1867) were followed in 1868 by an expurgated English edition of Whitman's poems prepared by William Michael Rossetti, the English man of letters. During the remainder of his life Whitman received much encouragement from leading writers in England.

Whitman was ill in 1872, probably as a result of long-experienced emotional strains related to his sexual ambiguity; in January 1873 he suffered a stroke that left him partially paralyzed. By May he had recovered sufficiently to travel to his brother's home in Camden, N.J., where his mother was dying. Her subsequent death he called "the great cloud" of his life. He thereafter lived with his brother in Camden, and his post in the attorney general's office was terminated in 1874.

In 1881 James R. Osgood published a second Boston edition of *Leaves of Grass*, and the Society for the Suppression of Vice claimed it to be immoral. Because of a threatened prosecution, Osgood gave up and Whitman found a new publisher, Rees Welsh of Philadelphia, who was shortly succeeded by David McKay. *Leaves of Grass* had now reached the form in which it was henceforth to be published. Newspaper publicity had created interest in the book, and it sold better than any previous edition. As a result, Whitman was able to buy a modest little cottage in Camden, where he spent the rest of his life. He had many new friends, among them Horace Traubel, who recorded his talk and wrote his biography. *The Complete Poems and Prose* was published in 1888, along with the eighth edition of *Leaves of Grass*. The ninth or "authorized" edition appeared in 1892, the year of Whitman's death.

At the time of his death, Whitman was more respected in Europe than in his own country. It was not as a poet, indeed, but as a symbol of American democracy that he first won recognition. In the late 19th century his poems exercised a strong fascination on English readers who found his championing of the common man idealistic and prophetic.

Whitman's aim was to transcend traditional epics, to eschew normal aesthetic form, and yet by reflecting American society to enable the poet and his readers to realize themselves and the nature of their American experience. He has continued to hold the attention of very different generations because he offered the welcome conviction that "the crowning growth of the United States" was to be spiritual and heroic and because he was able to uncompromisingly express his own personality in poetic form. Modern readers can still share his preoccupation with the problem of preserving the individual's integrity amid the pressures of mass civilization. Scholars in the 20th century, however, found his social thought less important than his artistry.

T.S. Eliot said, "When Whitman speaks of the lilacs or the mockingbird his theories and beliefs drop away like a needless pretext." Whitman invigorated language; he could be strong yet sentimental; and he possessed scope and inventiveness. He portrayed the relationships of man's body and soul and the universe in a new way, often emancipating poetry from contemporary conventions. He had sufficient universality to be considered one of the greatest American poets.

I Sit and Look Out

About the Poem

"I Sit and Look Out" is a poem by Walt Whitman, written in free verse form. It presents a series of images that depict the harsh realities of life, including oppression, violence, and betrayal, while also expressing the poet's empathy and compassion for those who suffer. The poem is a powerful reflection of the social and moral corruption in America.

I Sit and Look Out

I sit and look out upon all the sorrows of the world, and
    upon all oppression and shame,
I hear secret convulsive① sobs from young men at anguish with themselves,
    remorseful after deeds done,
I see in low life the mother misused by her children, dying,
    neglected, gaunt②, desperate,
I see the wife misused by her husband, I see the treacherous
    seducer of young women,
I mark the ranklings③ of jealousy and unrequited④ love
    attempted to be hid, I see these sights on the earth,
I see the workings of battle, pestilence⑤, tyranny, I see
    martyrs and prisoners,
I observe a famine at sea, I observe the sailors casting
    lots who shall be kill'd to preserve the lives of the rest,

---

① convulsive: (of movements or actions) sudden and impossible to control(痉挛的，抽搐的).
② gaunt: (of a person) very thin, usually because of illness, not having enough food, or worry.
③ rankling: anger.
④ unrequited: (of love) not returned by the person that you love(单相思的).
⑤ pestilence: any disease that spreads quickly and kills a lot of people.

I observe the slights and degradations cast by arrogant persons upon laborers,
    the poor, and upon negroes, and the like;
All these—all the meanness and agony without end, I
    sitting, look out upon,
See, hear, and am silent.

译文链接：https://www.zhihu.com/question/502669962

Questions for Understanding

1. What is the theme of the poem?
2. What is the speaker's perspective on American society?
3. How does the imagery help produce the poem's central message?
4. What is the tone of the poem? Is it hopeful, angry, compassionate or pessimistic?

Aspects of Appreciation

1. The poem captures the corruption of American society. Walt Whitman, an influential American poet, lived in the 1800s, a time that saw such sorrows as mistreatment, seduction, jealousy, unrequited love, battles, pestilence, tyranny, famine, slights, degradation, arrogance and slavery. In this poem, the speaker is merely an onlooker, not someone to get involved in all these negative affairs of society. The poet is trying to tell us that one should do one's part to alleviate the suffering instead of just being an observer.

2. The poem is written in free verse. The use of parallelism in the poem creates a musical rhythm and reinforces the ideas. The repetition of the first word of a line and the direct speaking tone of the poem indicate that the poet was influenced by oratory, which was very popular at the beginning of the American democracy. The repetition makes the poem coherent and musical. The direct speaking tone can make the poet get his message across clearly.

One's-Self I Sing

About the Poem

The poem was published as "Inscription" in *Leaves of Grass* (1867) and given its present title in 1871. According to Whitman's plan, the poem is printed first in his book. It celebrates the "simple, separate Person" as a physical, moral, intellectual, emotional, and aesthetic being, but declares that when he sings of himself, he uses the word "En-masse" to show that he represents the modern democratic man.

One's-Self I Sing

One's-self I sing, a simple separate person,
Yet utter the word Democratic, the word En-Masse①.

Of physiology from top to toe I sing,
Not physiognomy② alone nor brain alone is worthy for the Muse, I
Say the Form complete is worthier far,
The Female equality with the Male I sing.
Of Life immense in passion, pulse, and power,
Cheerful, for freest action form'd under the laws divine,
The Modern Man I sing.

译文链接：https://book.douban.com/review/13024334/

Questions for Understanding

1. Is this "I" in the poem the poet himself?
2. What is the democratic thought expressed in the poem?
3. What does Whitman's Muse sing highly of?
4. What features of the Modern Mancan you summarize from this poem?
5. Do you think all Americans are free to make their own decisions?
6. What is the function of capitalizing the first letter of one word in the middle of one poetic line?

Aspects of Appreciation

1. The poem, as the first poem in *Leaves of Grass*, sets the tone for the whole book. It eulogizes the Modern American man, being blessed with the features of free

---

① En-Masse: (French) in a body, all together （全体，一起）.
② physiognomy: facial features, especially as supposedly indicative of character （面相，相貌，揭示性格特征的面容特点）.

will, democratic thought, individual freedom and the equality of man and woman and so on. In a word, it is the core of American culture, "individualism", that the poet sings about with great effort. "Individualism" is embodied in the relentless pursuit of a new Garden of Eden by all Americans since they set foot on the New Continent.

2. Whitman's "free verse" creates a cadence by natural speech. The natural speech in the poem is created by such techniques as the inverted syntactic patterns: "… I sing", "… I say…", and "Of … I sing", the capitalized first letters of keywords in the poem, the phonetic recurrence of "sing" and "the word", the alliteration of "s", "t", "p" and "physio-" and the use of a comma or commas in a line. The meaning of "One's self" in the first line is enriched in the following stanzas and "The Modern Man" in the last line can be viewed as a summary of what "one's self" is.

Suggested Further Reading

Poems: "Crossing Brooklyn Ferry" (1856); "Out of the Cradle Endlessly Rocking" (1860); "When Lilacs Last in the Dooryard Bloom'd" (1865); "Song of Myself" (1881).

Topics for Further Study

1. What kind of language does Whitman use? And why?
2. What was Whitman's attitude towards technological change? Does he praise the city in his poems?
3. What, in Whitman's view, is the function of poetry?
4. Why is the influence of oratory and opera on Whitman's poetry regarded as evident?

Knowledge of Literature

1. Free Verse（自由诗）

Free verse is sometimes referred to as "open form" verse. Its rhythmic pattern is not organized into a regular metrical form—that is, into feet, or recurrent units of weak- and strong-stressed syllables. Most free verse also has irregular line lengths, and either lacks rhyme or else uses it only sporadically.

2. Elements of Poetry: rhythm and meter（韵律和格律）

In poetry, rhythm is mainly produced by the recurrence of stressed and unstressed syllables. It is also produced by pauses. A pause in a line of verse dictated by sense or natural speech rhythm is called caesura. A caesura is often marked with " ‖ ". A likely place for a caesura is in the middle of the line. A caesura may also occur near the beginning of a line or near the end. Or there may be no caesuras in a line. Caesuras often emphasize meaning. Caesuras in the middle of lines can emphasize strong contrasts or close relationships between ideas. Pauses also occur at the end of each line. When a line ends in a full pause marked by some punctuation mark, it is called an end-stopped line. If a line does not end in punctuation, it is called a run-on line. In this case, there is no pause at the end of the line.

Meter refers to the regular pattern of stressed and unstressed syllables. There are five basic meters in English poetry. Names for them are iamb (iambic), anapest (anapestic), trochee (trochaic), dactyl (dactylic) and spondee (spondaic). A unit of poetic meter is called a foot. Usually a line has three, four, five or six feet, but it can have as few as one foot or as many as eight feet. Names for feet are monometer, dimeter, trimeter, tetrameter, pentameter, hexameter, heptameter and octameter. In English poetry the best-known metrical pattern is iambic pentameter, which consists of five iambs. Poets rarely stick to the predominate metrical pattern of a poem. They stray from the established meter to avoid a mechanical, sing-songy rhythm and to make the language sound more colloquial. Equally important, poets vary meter to emphasize ideas. By substituting feet, poets catch us by surprise and call attention to meanings.

Rhythm and meter have many uses in poetry. Rhythm can help convey meaning. It can imitate action. Two or more stresses used together can create emphasis. A line of few stresses and many unstressed syllables can give the impression of uncertainty or hesitation. Meter provides a method of ordering material. Like the beat of music, it is enjoyable for itself. The greatest value of meter is the insights it gives us to the meanings of poems. In a word, by using rhythm and meter, poets can create different moods, emphasize certain words or phrases, and evoke different emotions in the reader.

推荐阅读的论文：
[1] 丁墨翰. 现代诗歌的先驱者——浅谈惠特曼的《自我之歌》[J]. 名作欣赏, 2015(36).
[2] 罗淑君. 试析惠特曼诗歌的音乐性 [J]. 惠州学院学报 (社会科学版), 2013, 33(02).

Chapter 3
American Literature of the Realist and Naturalistic Periods

1865 年，历时 4 年的美国内战结束。随着北方工业文明的胜利，美国工业资本主义迅猛发展，社会面貌和经济生活也随之发生了翻天覆地的变化：工厂和城市拔地而起，铁路、公路遍布全国，海外移民大量涌入。然而，这一派欣欣向荣的景象背后却隐藏着众多令人担忧的社会问题：贫富差距日益扩大，罢工此起彼伏，政治腐败屡见报端，社会不公比比皆是。

美国文学也参与并见证了这一社会巨变。新时期的美国作家深切感受到现实和理想之间的巨大鸿沟，开始摒弃浪漫主义时期那种过于乐观自信、超脱现实的写作基调，尝试以一种更为理性客观的角度来审视这个物质富足、矛盾滋生的"镀金时代"(The Gilded Age)，揭露和批判繁华背后的黑暗和弊端，展现社会各阶层的生活状态和精神面貌。自此，美国文学进入一个新阶段——现实主义文学时期。这一时期涌现出一大批优秀作家，其中最为引入瞩目的是豪威尔斯(William Dean Howells)、马克·吐温(Mark Twain)和亨利·詹姆斯(Henry James)。被誉为"现实主义文学奠基人"的豪威尔斯率先将欧洲现实主义理念引入美国本土，并在此基础上提出了一系列现实主义的创作原则和方法。在其近 60 年的文学生涯中，他始终身体力行地用现实主义手法描述中产阶级的生活方式和价值观。由于他侧重展现生活"微笑的一面"(the smiling aspect of life)，其作品大多触及生活表层，缺乏深度。相比之下，马克·吐温对现实的批判更为犀利深刻。这位出生于社会底层的文学巨擘以幽默讽刺的笔触、充满生活气息的语言淋漓尽致地揭露了社会的种种弊端，抨击所谓的民族平等、社会的不公和腐败。与之齐名的亨利·詹姆斯则开启了现实主义文学的新天地：将现实主义从对外部世界的刻画引入对人们内心的关注，生动细致地展现了人物纷繁复杂的心理活动和精神动机。

19 世纪末至 20 世纪初，随着垄断资本主义的发展，社会矛盾进一步激化：两极分化日趋加大，弊端和腐败不断滋生。越来越多的美国人意识到前辈们孜孜不倦追寻的民主平等的自由国度已是无法企及的镜花水月；惠特曼等浪漫主义作家笔下的美好新大陆已然成为绝望丛生、哀鸿遍野的人间地狱。受社会达尔文主义和欧洲自然主义的影响，以德莱塞（Theodore Dreiser）、杰克·伦敦（Jack London）和诺里斯（Frank Norris）为代表的年轻一代作家以更为激进的态度、更科学精准的手法和更悲观绝望的基调描述处于社会底层的小人物的苦难生活，揭示弱肉强食的冷酷现实和困苦绝望的人生，以及遗传因素和社会环境对命运的无情支配。

这一时期，现实主义和自然主义宛如两颗闪亮的明星，交相辉映，为美国现代主义文学奠定了良好的基础。

Mark Twain (1835~1910)

About the Author

Born Samuel Langhorne Clemens in Florida, Missouri, Mark Twain was the penname Clemens assumed when he began writing. Twain, the third of five children, was raised in the river town of Hanniba, Missouri. Twain went to work at twelve to help support his family after the death of his father. As a young man, following several years of restless travel, Twain fulfilled his boyhood dream of becoming a steamboat pilot. After a brief service for the Confederate militia in the Civil War, he traveled westward and began writing articles for newspapers, gradually building his reputation as a lively, at times wild, humorist and storyteller and adopting the penname Mark Twain, a navigation term meaning "safe water".

In his mid-thirties, Twain began drawing from his childhood and steamboat experiences on the Mississippi to write several of his best books, including the beloved American classics *The Adventures of Tom Sawyer* (1876) and *The Adventures of Huckleberry Finn* (1884). The latter took him eight years to complete. Twain's novels and short stories brought him wealth and international fame, and he and his family enjoyed a long period of prosperity. Twain's later years were beset with difficulties because of the bankruptcy and the death of his wife. Despite the grief and anger of his later years, Twain continued to write and lecture, often visiting friends and enjoying his revered status as one of the world's finest writers.

Shortly after Clemens's death, Howells published *My Mark Twain* (1910), in which he pronounced Samuel Clemens "sole, incomparable, the Lincoln of our literature". Twenty-five years later Ernest Hemingway wrote in *The Green Hills of Africa* (1935), saying that "All modern American literature comes from one book by Mark Twain called *Huckleberry Finn*". Both compliments are grandiose and a bit obscure. For Howells, Twain's significance was apparently social—the humorist, Howells wrote, spoke to and for the common American man and woman;

he emancipated and dignified the speech and manners of a class of people largely neglected by writers (except as objects of fun or disapproval) and largely ignored by genteel America. For Hemingway, Twain's achievement was evidently an aesthetic one principally located in one novel. For later generations, however, the reputation of and controversy surrounding *Huckleberry Finn* largely eclipsed the vast body of Clemens's substantial literary corpus: the novel has been dropped from some American schools' curricula on the basis of its characterization of the slave Jim, which some regard as demeaning, and its repeated use of an offensive racial epithet.

As a humorist and as a moralist, Twain worked best in short pieces. *Roughing It* is a rollicking account of his adventures in the American West, but it is also seasoned with such exquisite yarns as "Buck Fanshaw's Funeral" and "The Story of the Old Ram"; *A Tramp Abroad* is for many readers a disappointment, but it does contain the nearly perfect "Jim Baker's Blue-Jay Yarn". In "A True Story", told in an African American dialect, Twain transformed the resources of the typically American humorous story into something serious and profoundly moving. "The Man That Corrupted Hadleyburg" is relentless social satire; it is also the most formally controlled piece Twain ever wrote. The originality of the longer works is often to be found more in their conception than in their sustained execution. *The Innocents Abroad* is perhaps the funniest of all of Twain's books, but it also redefined the genre of the travel narrative by attempting to suggest to the reader, as Twain wrote, "how he would be likely to see Europe and the East if he looked at them with his own eyes." Similarly, in *Tom Sawyer*, he treated childhood not as the years of adjusting to adult authority but as a period of mischief-making and good-natured affection.

Twain was not the first Anglo-American to treat the problems of race and racism in all their complexity, but his treatment remains of vital interest more than a hundred years later. His ability to swiftly and convincingly create a variety of fictional characters rivals that of Charles Dickens. Twain's scalawags, dreamers, stalwarts, and toughs, his solicitous aunts, ambitious politicians, carping widows, false aristocrats, canny but generous slaves, sententious moralists, brave but misguided children, and decent but complicitous bystanders, his loyal lovers and friends, and his fractious rivals—these and many more constitute a virtual census of American types. And his mastery of spoken language, of slang and argot and dialect, gave these figures a voice. Howells, who had known most of the important American literary figures of the 19th century and thought them to be more or less like one another, believed that Twain was unique. Twain will always be remembered first and foremost as a humorist, but he was a great deal more—a public moralist, popular entertainer, political philosopher, travel writer and novelist. Perhaps it is too much to claim, as some have, that Twain invented the American point of view in fiction, but that such a notion might be entertained indicates that his place in American literary culture is secure.

The Adventures of Huckleberry Finn

About the Novel

This novel is written by Samuel Langhorne Clemens, under his pseudonym Mark Twain. A sequel to *Tom Sawyer*, it was begun in 1876 and published in 1884. Although it carries on the picaresque story of the characters in *Tom Sawyer*, the sequel is a more accomplished and more serious work of art, as well as a keen realistic portrayal of regional characters and frontier experience on the Mississippi.

The foursome travels downstream on the raft for several days without stopping, trying to outdistance any rumors of the scams of the duke and the dauphin. The con men try several schemes on various towns, without success. Then, the two start to have secret discussions, worrying Jim and Huck, who resolve to ditch them at the first opportunity. Finally, the duke, the dauphin, and Huck go ashore in one town to feel out the situation. The con men get into a fight at a tavern, and Huck takes the chance to escape. Back at the raft, however, there is no sign of Jim. A boy explains that a man recognized Jim as a runaway from a handbill that offered $200 for Jim's capture in New Orleans—the same fraudulent handbill that the duke had printed earlier. The boy says that the man who captured Jim had to leave suddenly and sold his interest in the captured runaway for forty dollars to a farmer named Silas Phelps.

Based on the boy's description, Huck realizes that it was the dauphin himself who captured and quickly sold Jim. Huck decides to write to Tom Sawyer to tell Miss Watson where Jim is. But Huck soon realizes that Miss Watson would sell Jim anyway. Furthermore, as soon as Huck's part in the story got out, he would be ashamed of having helped a slave, a black man, escape. Overwhelmed by his predicament, Huck suddenly realizes that this quandary must be God's punishment for the sin of helping Jim. Huck tries to pray for forgiveness but finds he cannot because his heart is not in it. Huck writes the letter to Miss Watson. Before he starts to pray, though, he thinks of the time he spent with Jim on the river, of Jim's kind heart, and of their friendship. Huck trembles. After a minute, he decides, "All right then, I'll go to hell!" And resolves to "steal Jim out of slavery".

Huckleberry Finn is regarded as Twain's greatest achievement. Hemingway once commented, "All modern American literature came from one book called *Huckleberry*

Finn. There was nothing before. There has been nothing as good since." The following is the 31st chapter of this novel.

Chapter 31

We dasn't stop again at any town, for days and days; kept right along down the river. We was down south in the warm weather, now, and a mighty long ways from home. We begun to come to trees with Spanish moss① on them, hanging down from the limbs like long gray beards. It was the first I ever see it growing, and it made the woods look solemn and dismal. So now the frauds reckoned they was out of danger, and they begun to work the villages again.

First they done a lecture on temperance; but they didn't make enough for them both to get drunk on. Then in another village they started a dancing school; but they didn't know no more how to dance than a kangaroo does; so the first prance they made, the general public jumped in and pranced them out of town. Another time they tried a go at yellocution②; but they didn't yellocute long till the audience got up and give them a solid good cussing and made them skip out. They tackled missionarying, and mesmerizing, and doctoring, and telling fortunes, and a little of everything; but they couldn't seem to have no luck. So at last they got just about dead broke, and laid around the raft, as she floated along, thinking, and thinking, and never saying nothing, but the half a day at a time, and dreadful blue and desperate.

And at last they took a change, and begun to lay their heads together in the wigwam and talk low and confidential two or three hours at a time. Jim and me got uneasy. We didn't like the look of it. We judged they was studying up some kind of worse deviltry than ever. We turned it over and over, and at last we made up our minds they was going to break into somebody's house or store, or was going into the counterfeit-money business, or something. So then we was pretty scared, and made up an agreement that we wouldn't have nothing in the world to do with such actions, and if we ever got the least show③ we would give them the cold shake④, and clear out and leave them behind. Well, early one morning we hid the raft in a good safe place about two mile below a little bit of a shabby village, named Pikesville, and the king he went ashore, and told us to stay hid whilst he went up to town and smelt around to see if anybody had got any wind of the Royal Nonesuch there yet. ("House to rob,

---

① Spanish moss: a tropical American plant that has long thin grey leaves and that grows over trees（铁兰）.
② yellocution: 这个词是哈克编造的，由 yell 和 elocution（演说术）构成。哈克使用这个词意在表明，这两个骗子的演讲主要是大喊大叫。
③ show: chance.
④ give them the shake:（俚语）摆脱他们。

you mean," says I to myself; "and when you get through robbing it you'll come back here and wonder what's become of me and Jim and the raft—and you'll have to take it out in wondering.") And he said if he warn't back by midday the duke and me would know it was all right, and we was to come along.

So we staid where we was. The duke he fretted and sweated around, and was in a mighty sour way. He scolded us for everything, and we couldn't seem to do nothing right; he found fault with every little thing. Something was a-brewing, sure. I was good and glad when midday come and no king; we could have a change, anyway—and maybe a chance for the change, on top of it. So me and the duke went up to the village, and hunted around there for the king, and by-and-by we found him in the back room of a little low doggery①, very tight②, and a lot of loafers bullyragging him for sport③, and he a cussing and threatening with all his might, and so tight he couldn't do nothing to them. The duke he began to abuse him for an old fool, and the king begun to sass④ back; and they minute they was fairly at it, I lit out⑤, and shook the reefs out of my hind legs⑥, and spun down the river road like a deer—for I see out chance; and I made up my mind that it would be a long day before they ever see me and Jim again. I got down there all out of breath but loaded up with joy, and sung out—

"Set her loose, Jim, we're all right, now!"

But there warn't no answer, and nobody come out of the wigwam. Jim was gone! I set up a shout—and then another—and then another one; and run this way and that in the woods, whooping and screeching; but it warn't no use, old Jim was gone. Then I set down and cried; I couldn't help it. But I couldn't set still long. Pretty soon I went out on the road, trying to think what I better do, and I run across a boy walking, and asked him if he'd seen a strange nigger, dressed so and so, and he says:

"Yes."

"Whereabouts?" Says I.

"Down to Silas Phelps's place, two mile below here. He's a runaway nigger, and they've got him. Was you looking for him?"

"You bet I ain't! I run across him in the woods about an hour to two ago, and he said if I hollered he'd cut my livers out—and told me to lay down and stay where I was; and I done it. Been there ever since; afeard to come out."

"Well," he says, "you needn't be afraid no more, becuz they've got him. He run

---

① doggery: a cheap bar or saloon(下等酒吧间,小酒馆).
② tight: drunk.
③ for sport: for fun.
④ sass: speak rudely.
⑤ lit out: left, departed.
⑥ shook the reefs out of my hind legs: 撒开腿拼命跑。

off f'm down South, som'ers."

"It's a good job they got him."

"Well, I reckon! There's two hundred dollars reward on him. It's like picking up money out'n the road."

"Yes, it is—and I could a had it if I'd been big enough; I see him first. Who nailed him?"

"It was an old fellow—a stranger—and he sold out his chance in him for forty dollars. Becuz he's got to go up the river and can't wait. Think o'that, now! You bet I'd wait, if it was seven year."

"That's me, every time." Say I. But maybe his chance ain't worth no more than that, if he'll sell it so cheap. Maybe there's something ain't straight about it."

"But it is, though—straight as a string. I see the handbill myself. It tells all about him, to a dot①—paints him like a picture, and tells the plantation he's frum, below Newrleans. No-siree-bob②, they ain't no trouble 'bout *that* speculation, you bet you. Say, gimme a chaw tobacker③, won't ye?"

I did't have none, so he left. I went to the raft, and set down in the wigwam to think. But I couldn't come to nothing. I thought till I wore my head sore, but I couldn't see no way out of the trouble. After all this long journey, and after all we'd done for them scoundrels, here was it all come to nothing, everything all busted up and ruined, because they could have the heart to serve Jim such a trick as that, and make him a slave again all his life, an amongst strangers, too, for forty dirty dollars.

Once I said to myself it would be a thousand times better for Jim to be a slave at home where his family was, as long as he'd got to be a slave, and so I'd better write a letter to Tom Sawyer and tell him to tell Miss Watson where he was. But I soon give up that notion, for two things: she'd be mad and disgusted at his rascality and ungratefulness for leaving her, and so she'd sell him straight down the river again; and if she didn't, everybody naturally despises an ungrateful nigger, and they'd make Jim feel it all the time, and so he'd feel ornery and disgraced. And then think of me! It would get all around, that Huck Finn helped a nigger to get his freedom; and if I was to ever see anybody from that town again, I'd be ready to get down and lick his boots for shame. That's just the way: a person does a low-down thing, and then he don't want to take no consequence of it. Thinks as long as he can hide it, it ain't no disgrace. That was my fix④ exactly. The more I studied about this, the more my conscience went

---

① to a dot: 丝毫不差地。
② No-siree-bob: no, sir.
③ a chaw tobacker: a chew of tobacco.
④ fix: a difficult situation.

to grinding me, and the more wicked and low-down and ornery I got to feeling. And at last, when it hit me all of a sudden that here was the plain hand of Providence① slapping me in the face and letting me know my wickedness was being watched all the time from up there in heaven, whilst I was stealing a poor old woman's nigger that hadn't ever down me no harm, and now was showing me there's One that's always on the lookout, and ain't agoing to allow no such miserable doings to go only just so fur and no further, I most dropped in my tracks② I was so scared. Well, I tried the best I could to kinder soften it up somehow for myself, by saying I was brung up wicked, and so I warn't so much to blame; but something inside of me kept saying, "There was the Sunday school; you could a gone to it; and if you'd a gone it they'd a learnt you, there, that people that acts as I'd been acting about that nigger goes to everlasting fire."

It made me shiver. And I about made up my mind to pray; and see if I couldn't try to quit being the kind of a boy I was, and be better. So I kneeled down. But the words wouldn't come. Why wouldn't they? It warn't no use to try and hide it from Him. Nor from me, neither. I knowed very well why they wouldn't come. It was because my heart warn't right; it was because I warn't square; it was because I was playing double. I was letting on③ to give up sin, but away inside of me I was holding on to the biggest one of all. I was trying to make my mouth say I would do the right thing and the clean thing, and go and write to that nigger's owner and tell where he was; but deep down in me I knowed it was a lie—and He knowed it. You can't pray a lie—I found that out.

So I was full of trouble, full as I could be; and didn't know what to do. At last I had an idea; and I says, I'll go and write the letter—and then see if I can pray. Why, it was astonishing, the way I felt as light as a feather, right straight off, and my troubles all gone. So I got a piece of paper and a pencil, all glad and excited, and set down and wrote:

Miss Watson your runaway nigger Jim is down here two mile between Pikesville and Mr Phelps has got him and he will give him up to the reward if you send.

Huck Finn

I felt good and all washed clean of sin for the first time I had ever felt so in my life, and I knowed I could pray now. But I didn't do it straight off, but laid the paper down and set there thinking—thinking how good it was all this happened so, and how near I come to being lost and going to hell. And went on thinking. And got to thinking over our trip down the river; and I see Jim before me, all the time, in the day, and in

---

① Providence: God.
② in my tracks: then and there(当即，立刻，当场).
③ letting on: pretending.

the night-time, sometimes moonlight, sometimes storms, and we a floating along, talking, and singing, and laughing. But somehow I couldn't seem to strike① no places to harden me against him, but only the other kind. I'd see him standing my watch on top of his'n, stead of calling me, so I could go on sleeping; and see him how glad he was when I come back out of the fog; and when I come to him again in the swamp, up there where the feud was; and such-like times; and would always call me honey, and pet me, and do everything he could think of for me, and how good he always was; and at last I struck the time I saved him by telling the men we had small-pox aboard, and he was so grateful, and said I was the best friend old Jim ever had in the world, and the *only* one he's got now; and then I happened to look around, and see that paper.

It was a close place. I took it up, and held it in my hand. I was a trembling, because I'd got to decide, forever, betwixt two things, and I knowed it. I studied a minute, sort of holding my breath, and then says to myself:

"All right, then, I'll *go* to hell"—and tore it up.

It was awful thoughts, and awful words, but they was said. And I let them stay said; and never thought no more about reforming. I shoved the whole thing out of my head; and said I would take up wickedness again, which was in my line, being brung up to it, and the other warn't. And for a starter, I would go to work and steal Jim out of slavery again; and if I could think up anything worse, I would do that, too; because as long as I was in, and in for good, I might as well go the whole hog②.

Then I set to thinking over how to get at it, and turned over considerable many ways in my mind; and at last fixed up a plan that suited me. So then I took the bearings of a woody island③ that was down the river a piece, and as soon as it was fairly dark I crept out with my raft and went for it, and hid it there, and then turned in④. I slept the night through, and got up before it was light, and had my breakfast, and put on my store clothes, and tied up some others and one thing or another in a bundle, and took the canoe and cleared for shore. I landed below where I judged was Phelps's place, and hid my bundle in the woods , and then filled up the canoe with water, and loaded rocks into her and sunk her where I could find her again when I wanted her, about a quarter of a mile below a little stream sawmill that was on the bank.

Then I stuck up the road, and when I passed the mill I see a sign on it, "Phelps's Sawmill," and when I come to the farmhouses, two or three hundred yards further

---

① strike: find.
② go the whole hog: 全力以赴，做个彻底。
③ I took the bearings of a woody island: 我认清了一个树林茂盛的岛的位置。
④ turned in: went to bed.

along, I kept my eyes peeled①, but didn't see nobody around, though it was good daylight, now. But I didn't mind, because I didn't want to see nobody just yet—I only wanted to get the lay of the land②. According to my plan, I was going to turn up there from the village, not from below. So I just took a look, and shoved along, straight for town. He was sticking up a bill for the Royal Nonesuch—three-night performance—like that other time. They had the check, then frauds! I was right on him, before I could shirk③. He looked astonished, and says:

"Hel-lo! Where'd *you* come from?" Then he says, kind of glad and eager, "Where's the raft?—got her in a good place?"

I says:

"Why, that's just what I was a going to ask your grace."

Then he didn't look so joyful—and says:

"What was your idea for asking *me*?" He says.

"Well," I says, "When I see the king in that doggery yesterday, I says to myself, we can't get him home for hours, till he's soberer; so I went a loafing around town to put in the time, and wait. A man up and offered me ten cents to help him pull a skiff over the river and back to fetch a sheep, and so I sent along; but when we was dragging him to the boat, and the man left me aholt of the rope and went behind him to shove him along, he was too strong for me, and jerked loose and run, and we after him. We didn't have no dog, and so we had to chase him all over the country till we tired him out. We never got him till dark, then we fetched him over, and I started down for the raft. When I got there and see it was gone, I says to myself, "they've got into trouble and had to leave; and they've took my nigger, which is the only nigger I've got in the world, and now I'm in a strange country, and ain't got no property no more, nor nothing, and no way to make my living"; so I set down and cried. I slept in the woods all night. But what *did* become of the raft then? —And Jim, poor Jim!"

"Blamed if I know—that is, what's become of the raft. That old fool had made a trade and got forty dollars, and when we found him in the doggery the loafers had matched④ half dollars with him and got every cent but what he'd spent for whisky; and when I got him home late last night and found the raft gone," we said, " That little rascal has stole our raft and shook us, and run off down the river."

"I wouldn't shake my *nigger*, would I?—The only nigger I had in the world, and the only property."

---

① kept my eyes peeled: kept my eyes open.
② the lay of the land: 地形。
③ shirk: 逃避。
④ matched: gambled by flipping coins.

"We never thought of that. Fact is, I reckon we'd come to consider him our nigger; yes, we did consider him so—goodness knows we had trouble enough for him. So when we see the raft was gone, and we flat broke, there warn't anything for it but to try the Royal Nonesuch another shake. And I've pegged along ever since, dry as a powderhorn. Where's that ten cents? Give it here."

I had considerable money, so I give him ten cents, but begged him to spend it for something to eat since yesterday. He never said nothing. The next minute he whirls on me and says:

"Do you reckon that nigger would blow① on us? We'd skin him if he done that!"

"How can he blow? Hain't he run off?"

"No! That old fool sold him, and never divided with me, and the money's gone."

"Sold him?" I say, and begun to cry: "Why, he was *my* nigger."

"Well, you can't *get* your nigger, that's all—so dry up your blubbering. Looky here—do you think *you'd* venture to blow on us? Blamed if I think I'd trust you. Why, if you was to blow on us—"

He stopped, but I never see the duke look so ugly out of his eyes before. I went on a-whimpering, and says:

"I don't want to blow on nobody; and I ain't got no time to blow, nohow. I got to turn out and find my nigger."

He looked kinder bothered, and stood there with his bills fluttering on his arm, thinking, and wrinkling up his forehead. At last he says:

"I'll tell you something. We got to be here three days. If you'll promise you won't blow, and won't let the nigger blow, I'll tell you where to find him."

So I promised, and he says:

"A farmer by the name of Silas Ph—" and then he stopped. You see he started to tell me the truth; but when he stopped, that way, and begun to study and think again, I reckoned he was changing his mind. And so he was. He wouldn't trust me; he wanted to make sure of having me out of the way the whole three days. So pretty soon he says: "The man that bought him is named Abram Foster—Abram G. Forster—and he lived mile back here in the country, on the road to Lafayette."

"All right," I says, "I can walk it in three days. And I'll start this very afternoon."

"No you won't, you'll start now; and don't you lose any time about it, neither, nor do any gabbling by the way. Just keep a tight tongue in your head and move right along, and then you won't get into trouble with *us*, d'ye hear?"

That was the order I wanted, and that was the one I prayed for. I wanted to be left

---

① blow on: 告发。

free to work my plans.

"So clear out," he says: "and you can tell Mr Foster whatever you want to. Maybe you can get him to believe that Jim is your nigger—some idiots don't require documents—leastways I've heard there's such down South here. And when you tell him the handbill and the reward's bogus, maybe he'll believe you when you explain to him what the idea was for getting' em out. Go 'long, now, and tell him anything you want to; but mind you don't work your jaw① any between here and there."

So I left, and struck for the back country. I didn't lock around, but I kinder felt like he was watching me. But I knowed I could tire him out at that. I went straight out in the country as much as a mile, before I stopped; then I doubled back through the woods towards Phelps's. I reckoned I better start in on my plan straight off, without fooling around, because I wanted to stop Jim's mouth till these fellows could get away. I didn't want to trouble with their kind. I'd seen all I wanted to of them and wanted to get entirely shut of② them.

译文链接：https://www.thn21.com/Article/chang/youji/1976236.html

Questions for Understanding

1. Huck Finn is a thirteen-year-old boy. Why does Twain use a child as the center of consciousness in this book?
2. Discuss Twain's use of dialects in the novel. What effect does this usage have on the reader? Does it make the novel less of an artistic achievement?
3. Discuss the use of the river as a symbol in the novel.
4. Is Huck's moral conflict reasonable? Why?
5. Elaborate on Mark Twain's use of language in the story.

Aspects of Appreciation

1. What distinguishes *The Adventures of Huckleberry Finn* from the others is the moral dilemma Huck faces in aiding the runaway slave Jim while at the same time escaping from the unwanted influences of so-called civilization. Through Huck, the novel's narrator, Twainis able to address the shameful legacy of chattel slavery prior to the Civil War and the persistent racial discrimination and violence afterwards. That he did so in the voice and consciousness of a 13-year-old boy, a character who

---

① work your jaw: 乱说。
② get shut of: get rid of.

shows the signs of having been trained to accept the cruel and indifferent attitudes of a slaveholding culture, gives the novel its affecting power, which can elicit genuine sympathies in readers but can also generate controversy and debate and can affront those who find the book patronizing toward African Americans, if not perhaps much worse. If *Huckleberry Finn* is a great book of American literature, its greatness may lie in its continuing ability to touch a nerve in the American national consciousness that is still raw and troubling.

2. In the selected chapter, Huck and Jim are with the frauds. Later Huck learns that Jim has been sold by the "King" to Mrs. Phelps. There is a very important description here of Huck's inner conflict about whether or not he should write a letter to tell Miss Watson where Jim is.

3. "It was a close place. I took it up… And I let them stay said; and never thought no more about reforming.":These lines from the selected chapter describe the moral climax of the novel. The duke and the dauphin have sold Jim, who is being held in the Phelps' shed pending his return to his rightful owner. Thinking that life at home in St. Petersburg—even if it means Jim will still be a slave and Huck will be a captive of the Widow— would be better than his current state of peril far from home, Huck composes a letter to Miss Watson, telling her where Jim is. When Huck thinks of his friendship with Jim, however, and realizes that Jim will be sold down the river anyway, he decides to tear up the letter. The logical consequences of Huck's action, rather than the lessons society has taught him, drive Huck. He decides that going to "hell", if it means following his gut and not society's hypocritical and cruel principles, is a better option than going to everyone else's heaven. This moment of decision represents Huck's true break with the world around him. At this point, Huck decides to help Jim escape slavery once and for all. Huck also realizes that he does not want to reenter the "civilized" world: after all his experiences and moral development on the river, he wants to move on to the freedom of the West instead.

Suggestions for Further Reading

The Gilded Age (1873); *The Adventures of Tom Sawyer* (1876); *Life on the Mississippi* (1883); *The Man That Corrupted Hadleyburg* (1900).

Topics for Further Study

1. Lying occurs frequently in this novel. Curiously, some lies, like those Huck tells to save Jim, seem to be "good" lies, while others, like the cons of the duke and the dauphin, seem to be "bad". What is the difference? Are both "wrong"? Why does so much lying go on in *Huckleberry Finn*?

2. The revelation at the novel's end that Tom has known all along that Jim is a free man is startling. Is Tom inexcusably cruel? Or is he just being a normal thirteen-year-old boy?

3. What techniques does Twain use to create sympathy for his characters, in particular, Jim? Are these techniques effective?

4. Why did Twain decide to set the novel in a time before the abolition of slavery, despite the fact that he published it in 1885, two decades after the end of the Civil War?

Knowledge of Literature

One Element of Fiction: Setting（背景）

Setting refers to the natural and artificial scenery or environment in which characters in fiction live and move, together with the things they use. In other words, setting includes the time, place and environment in a story. Setting is an important element of fiction. A setting may or may not be symbolic. In fiction, setting can perform some functions. It can figure as a background for action. It can also be used to establish credibility, evoke an appropriate atmosphere, reveal characters and reinforce themes. Overall, an understanding of the significance of the setting can illuminate much of the meaning of the story.

推荐阅读的论文：
[1] 董金平. 从马克·吐温的小说看美国本土色彩文学 [J]. 戏剧之家, 2015(21).
[2] 笪立. 从《镀金时代》看马克·吐温的写作背景 [J]. 山东农业工程学院学报, 2014, 31(01).

Henry James (1843~1916)

About the Author

Henry James was born in New York City on April 15, 1843. His father was an eccentric, independently wealthy philosopher and religious visionary. Henry James was educated chiefly in Europe by tutors in several countries, and his foreign education was culminated by his acquaintance with several European writers. The direction of his career as a man of letters was clearly marked in his early manhood. His familiarity with life on both sides of the Atlantic led him, in much of his writing, to contrast European and American cultures and, above all, to show the effects of their mingling. In 1876 he took up permanent residence in England, and became a naturalized citizen of that country in 1915 in protest against the initial neutrality of the United States in World War I.

Leon Edel, James's biographer, divides the writer's mature career into three stages. In the first, James felt his way toward the so-called international theme—the theme of innocence versus experience. He seems to value both the sophistication of Europe and the idealism of America. Examples are *The American* (1877), *Daisy Miller* (1878), and *The Portrait of a Lady* (1881). In the second stage, he experimented with various themes and forms—initially with novels dealing explicitly with the social and political currents of the 1870s and 1880s—as in *The Bostonians* (1886), then with writing for the theater, and finally with shorter fictions that explore the relationship of artists to society—as in *The Great Good Place* (1900)—and the troubled psychology of oppressed children and haunted or obsessed men and women such as those depicted in *The Turn of the Screw* (1898), *The Jolly Corner* (1908). In the last stage, James returned to international or cosmopolitan subjects in an extraordinary series of elaborately developed novels, shorter fiction, and criticism. He increasingly removed himself as controlling narrator and became invisible in his work. Novels such as *The Wings of the Dove* (1902), *The Ambassadors* (1903), and *The Golden Bowl* (1904) are characterized by an extraordinary richness of syntax, characterization, point of view, symbolic resonance, metaphor, and organizing rhythms.

During his lifetime Henry James's reputation prospered and declined, but today he is highly respected as an early master of psychological realism, formal structure, and narrative ambiguity, as well as for his ability to convey the nuances of human emotion and human consciousness. He changed the realist's focus from external expression to the human soul, and also created a limited third-person point of view out of an omniscient perspective.

Daisy Miller

About the Novel

Frederick Winterbourne, an American expatriate visiting at Vevay, Switzerland, meets commonplace, newly rich Mrs. Miller, from Schenectady, N.Y., her mischievous small son Randolph, and her daughter Daisy, an "inscrutable combination of audacity and innocence". The Millers have no perception of the complex code that underlies behavior in European society, and Winterbourne is astonished at the girl's innocence and her mother's unconcern. Some months later he meets the family in Rome, where Daisy has aroused suspicion among the American people living there by being seen constantly with Giovanelli, a third-rate Italian. Ostracized by former friends, who think her "intrigue" has gone too far, Daisy denies to Winterbourne that she is engaged to Giovanelli. A few days later she falls ill with fever, and a week afterward dies. At her funeral Giovanelli tells Winterbourne that Daisy was "the most beautiful young lady I ever saw, and the most amiable…and the most innocent".

First published in 1878, *Daisy Miller* brought Henry James, then living in London, his first international success, and established one of his primary leitmotifs: American innocence and looseness of manner in conflict with the complex social organization of sophisticated European societies. The following selection is the third part of it.

Daisy Miller (III)

Winterbourne, who had returned to Geneva the day after his excursion to Chillon,① went to Rome toward the end of January. His aunt had been established there a considerable time and he had received from her a couple of characteristic letters. "Those people you were so devoted to last summer at Vevay have turned up here, courier and all," she wrote. "They seem to have made several acquaintances, but the courier continues to be the most *intime*. The young lady, however, is also very intimate with various third-rate Italians, with whom she rackets about in a way that makes much talk. Bring me that pretty novel of Cherbuliez's②—*Paule Méré*—and don't come later than the 23rd."

In the natural course of events, Winterbourne, on arriving in Rome, would

---

① Chillon: 夏兰（瑞士古堡）。
② Cherbuliez: Victor Cherbuliez (1829~1899), a minor French novelist of Swiss origin.

presently have ascertained Mrs. Miller's address at the American banker's and have gone to pay his compliments to Miss Daisy. "After what happened at Vevay I certainly think I may call upon them," he said to Mrs. Costello.

"If, after what happens—at Vevay and everywhere—you desire to keep up the acquaintance, you're very welcome. Of course a man may know every one. Men are welcome to the privilege!"

"Pray what is it that happens—here, for instance?" Winterbourne demanded.

"The girl goes about alone with her foreigners. As to what happens further, you must apply elsewhere for information. She has picked up half a dozen of the regular Roman fortune-hunters, and she takes them about to people's houses. When she comes to a party she brings with her a gentleman with a good deal of manner and a wonderful moustache."

"And where's the mother?"

"I haven't the least idea. They are very dreadful people."

Winterbourne meditated a moment. "They are very ignorant—very innocent only. Depend upon it they are not bad."

"They are hopelessly vulgar," said Mrs. Costello. "Whether or no being hopelessly vulgar is being 'bad' is a question for the metaphysicians. They are bad enough to dislike, at any rate; and for this short life that is quite enough."

The news that Daisy Miller was surrounded by half a dozen wonderful moustaches checked Winterbourne's impulse to go straightway to see her. He had, perhaps, not definitely flattered himself that he had made an ineffaceable impression upon her heart, but he was annoyed at hearing of a state of affairs so little in harmony with an image that had lately flitted in and out of his own meditations; the image of a very pretty girl looking out of an old Roman window and asking herself urgently when Mr. Winterbourne would arrive. If, however, he determined to wait a little before reminding Miss Miller of his claims to her consideration, he went very soon to call upon two or three other friends. One of these friends was an American lady who had spent several winters at Geneva, where she had placed her children at school. She was a very accomplished woman and she lived in Via Gregoriana. Winterbourne found her in a little crimson drawing-room on a third floor; the room was filled with southern sunshine. He had not been there ten minutes when the servant came in, announced "Madame Mila!" This announcement was presently followed by the entrance of little Randolph Miller, who stopped in the middle of the room and stood staring at Winterbourne. An instant later his pretty sister crossed the threshold; and then, after a considerable interval, Mrs. Miller slowly advanced.

"I know you!" Said Randolph.

"I'm sure you know a great many things," exclaimed Winterbourne, taking him by the hand. "How's your education coming on?"

Daisy was exchanging greetings very prettily with her hostess; but when she heard Winterbourne's voice she quickly turned her head. "Well, I declare!" She said.

"I told you I should come, you know." Winterbourne rejoined, smiling.

"Well, I didn't believe it," said Miss Daisy.

"I am much obliged to you," laughed the young man.

"You might have come to see me," said Daisy.

"I arrived only yesterday."

"I don't believe that!" The young girl declared.

Winterbourne turned with a protesting smile to her mother; but this lady evaded his glance, and, seating herself, fixed her eyes upon her son. "We've got a bigger place than this," said Randolph. "It's all gold on the walls."

Mrs. Miller turned uneasily in her chair. "I told you if I were to bring you, you would say something!" She murmured.

"I told *you*!" Randolph exclaimed. "I tell *you*, sir!" He added, jocosely, giving Winterbourne a thump on the knee. "It *is* bigger, too!"

Daisy had entered upon a lively conversation with her hostess, and Winterbourne judged it becoming to address a few words to her mother. "I hope you have been well since we parted at Vevay," he said.

Mrs. Miller now certainly looked at him—at his chin. "Not very well, sir," she answered.

"She's got the dyspepsia," said Randolph. "I've got it, too. Father's got it. I've got it worst!"

This announcement, instead of embarrassing Mrs. Miller, seemed to relieve her. "I suffer from the liver," she said. "I think it's this climate; it's less bracing than Schenectady, especially in the winter season. I don't know whether you know we reside at Schenectady. I was saying to Daisy that I certainly hadn't found any one like Dr. Davis, and I didn't believe I should. Oh, at Schenectady he stands first; they think everything of him. He has so much to do, and yet there was nothing he wouldn't do for me. He said he never saw anything like my dyspepsia, but he was bound to cure it. I'm sure there was nothing he wouldn't try. He was just going to try something new when we came off. Mr. Miller wanted Daisy to see Europe for herself. But I wrote to Mr. Miller that it seems as if I couldn't get on without Dr. Davis. At Schenectady he stands at the very top; and there's a great deal of sickness there, too. It affects my sleep."

Winterbourne had a good deal of pathological gossip with Dr. Davis's patient, during which Daisy chattered unremittingly to her own companion. The young man asked Mrs. Miller how she was pleased with Rome. "Well, I must say I'm disappointed," she answered. "We had heard so much about it; I suppose we had heard too much. But we couldn't help that. We had been led to expect something different."

"Ah, wait a little, and you'll become very fond of it," said Winterbourne.

"I hate it worse and worse every day!" Cried Randolph.

"You're like the infant Hannibal,"① his friend laughed.

"No I ain't!" Randolph declared, at a venture.

"You are not much like an infant," said his mother. "But we have seen places," she resumed, "that I should put a long way before Rome." And in reply to Winterbourne's interrogation, "There's Zürich," she concluded; "I think Zürich is lovely; and we hadn't heard half so much about it."

"The best place we've seen is the City of Richmond!" Said Randolph.

"He means the ship," his mother explained. "We crossed in that ship. Randolph had a good time on the *City of Richmond*."

"It's the best place I've seen," the child repeated. "Only it was turned the wrong way."

"Well, we've got to turn the right way some time," said Mrs. Miller, with a little laugh. Winterbourne expressed the hope that her daughter at least found some gratification in Rome, and she declared that Daisy was quite carried away. "It's on account of the society—the society's splendid. She goes round everywhere; she has made a great number of acquaintances. Of course she goes round more than I do. I must say they have all been very sociable; they have taken her right in. And then she knows a great many gentlemen. Oh, she thinks there's nothing like Rome. Of course, it's a great deal pleasanter for a young lady if she knows plenty of gentlemen."

By this time Daisy had turned her attention again to Winterbourne. "I've been telling Mrs. Walker how mean you were!" The young girl announced.

"And what is the evidence you have offered?" Asked Winterbourne, rather annoyed at Miss Miller's want of appreciation of the zeal of an admirer who on his way down to Rome had stopped neither at Bologna nor at Florence, simply because of a certain sentimental impatience. He remembered that a cynical compatriot had once told him that American women—the pretty ones, and this gave a largeness to the axiom—were at once the most exacting in the world and the least endowed with a sense of indebtedness.

"Why, you were awfully mean up at Vevay," said Daisy. "You wouldn't do anything. You wouldn't stay there when I asked you."

---

① Hannibal: (247BC~183BC), a general who led the army of Carthage in its war against the Romans between 218 and 201BC. He was sworn at his birth to an eternal hatred of Rome.

"My dearest young lady," cried Winterbourne, with eloquence, "have I come all the way to Rome to encounter your reproaches?"

"Just hear him say that!" Said Daisy to her hostess, giving a twist to a bow on this lady's dress. "Did you ever hear anything so quaint?"

"So quaint, my dear?" Murmured Mrs. Walker, in the tone of a partisan of Winterbourne.

"Well, I don't know," said Daisy, fingering Mrs. Walker's ribbons. "Mrs. Walker, I want to tell you something."

"Mother-r," interposed Randolph, with his rough ends to his words, "I tell you you've got to go. Eugenio'll raise—something!"

"I'm not afraid of Eugenio," said Daisy, with a toss of her head. "Look here, Mrs. Walker," she went on, "you know I'm coming to your party."

"I'm delighted to hear it."

"I've got a lovely dress."

"I am very sure of that."

"But I want to ask a favor—permission to bring a friend."

"I shall be happy to see any of your friends," said Mrs. Walker, turning with a smile to Mrs. Miller.

"Oh, they are not my friends," answered Daisy's mamma, smiling shyly, in her own fashion. "I never spoke to them."

"It's an intimate friend of mine—Mr. Giovanelli," said Daisy, without a tremor in her clear little voice, or a shadow on her brilliant little face.

Mrs. Walker was silent a moment; she gave a rapid glance at Winterbourne. "I shall be glad to see Mr. Giovanelli," she then said.

"He is an Italian," Daisy pursued, with the prettiest serenity. "He's a great friend of mine; he's the handsomest man in the world—except Mr. Winterbourne! He knows plenty of Italians, but he wants to know some Americans. He thinks ever so much of Americans. He's tremendously clever. He's perfectly lovely!"

It was settled that this brilliant personage should be brought to Mrs. Walker's party, and then Mrs. Miller prepared to take her leave. "I guess we'll go back to the hotel," she said.

"You may go back to the hotel, mother, but I'm going to take a walk," said Daisy.

"She's going to walk with Mr. Giovanelli," Randolph proclaimed.

"I am going to the Pincio," said Daisy, smiling.

"Alone, my dear—at this hour?" Mrs. Walker asked. The afternoon was drawing to a close—it was the hour for the throng of carriages and of contemplative pedestrians. "I don't thinkit's safe, my dear," said Mrs. Walker.

"Neither do I," subjoined Mrs. Miller. "You'll get the fever, as sure as you live. Remember what Dr. Davis told you!"

"Give her some medicine before she goes," said Randolph.

The company had risen to its feet; Daisy, still showing her pretty teeth, bent over and kissed her hostess. "Mrs. Walker, you are too perfect," she said. "I'm not going alone; I am going to meet a friend."

"Your friend won't keep you from getting the fever," Mrs. Miller observed.

"Is it Mr. Giovanelli?" asked the hostess.

Winterbourne was watching the young girl; at this question his attention quickened. She stood there smiling and smoothing her bonnetribbons; she glanced at Winterbourne. Then, while she glanced and smiled, she answered, without a shade of hesitation, "Mr. Giovanelli—the beautiful Giovanelli."

"My dear young friend," said Mrs. Walker, taking her hand, pleading, "don't walk off to the Pincio at this unhealthy hour to meet a beautiful Italian."

"Well, he speaks English," said Mrs. Miller.

"Gracious me!" Daisy exclaimed, "I don't want to do anything improper. There's an easy way to settle it." She continued to glance at Winterbourne. "The Pincio is only a hundred yards distant; and if Mr. Winterbourne were as polite as he pretends, he would offer to walk with me!"

Winterbourne's politeness hastened to affirm itself, and the young girl gave him gracious leave to accompany her. They passed downstairs before her mother, and at the door Winterbourne perceived Mrs. Miller's carriage drawn up, with the ornamental courier whose acquaintance he had made at Vevay, seated within. "Good-bye, Eugenio!" cried Daisy; "I'm going to take a walk." The distance from the Via Gregoriana to the beautiful garden at the other end of the Pincian Hill is, in fact, rapidly traversed. As the day was splendid, however, and the concourse of vehicles, walkers, and loungers numerous, the young Americans found their progress much delayed. This fact was highly agreeable to Winterbourne, in spite of his consciousness of his singular situation. The slow-moving, idly-gazing Roman crowd bestowed much attention upon the extremely pretty young foreign lady who was passing through it upon his arm; and he wondered what on earth had been in Daisy's mind when she proposed to expose herself, unattended, to its appreciation. His own mission, to her sense, apparently, was to consign her to the hands of Mr. Giovanelli; but Winterbourne, at once annoyed and gratified, resolved that he would do no such thing.

"Why haven't you been to see me?" Asked Daisy. "You can't get out of that."

"I have had the honor of telling you that I have only just stepped out of the train."

"You must have stayed in the train a good while after it stopped!" cried the young girl, with her little laugh. "I suppose you were asleep. You have had time to go to see Mrs. Walker."

"I knew Mrs. Walker—" Winterbourne began to explain.

"I know where you knew her. You knew her at Geneva. She told me so. Well, you knew me at Vevay. That's just as good. So you ought to have come." She asked him no other question than this; she began to prattle about her own affairs. "We've got splendid rooms at the hotel; Eugenio says they're the best rooms in Rome. We are going to stay all winter—if we don't die of the fever; and I guess we'll stay then. It's a great deal nicer than I thought; I thought it would be fearfully quiet; I was sure it would be awfully poky. I was sure we should be going round all the time with one of those dreadful old men that explain about the pictures and things. But we only had about a week of that, and now I'm enjoying myself. I know ever so many people, and they're all so charming. The society's extremely select. There are all kinds—English and Germans and Italians. I think I like the English best. I like their style of conversation. But there are some lovely Americans. I never saw anything so hospitable. There's something or other every day. There's not much dancing; but I must say I never thought dancing was everything. I was always fond of conversation. I guess I shall have plenty at Mrs. Walker's, her rooms are so small." When they had passed the gate of the Pincian Gardens, Miss Miller began to wonder where Mr. Giovanelli might be. "We had better go straight to that place in front," she said, "where you look at the view."

"I certainly shall not help you to find him." Winterbourne declared.

"Then I shall find him without you," said Miss Daisy.

"You certainly won't leave me!" cried Winterbourne.

She burst into her little laugh. "Are you afraid you'll get lost—or run over? But there's Giovanelli leaning against that tree. He's staring at the women in the carriages; did you ever see anything so cool?"

Winterbourne perceived at some distance a little man standing with folded arms and nursing its cane. He had a handsome face, an artfully poised hat, a glass in one eye, and a nosegay in his buttonhole. Winterbourne looked at him a moment, and then said, "Do you mean to speak to that man?"

"Do I mean to speak to him? Why, you don't suppose I mean to communicate by signs!"

"Pray understand, then," said Winterbourne, "that I intend to remain with you."

Daisy stopped and looked at him, without a sign of troubled consciousness in her face; with nothing but the presence of her charming eyes and her happy dimples. "Well, she's a cool one!" thought the young man.

"I don't like the way you say that," said Daisy. "It's too imperious."

"I beg your pardon if I say it wrong. The main point is to give you an idea of my meaning."

The young girl looked at him more gravely, but with eyes that were prettier than ever. "I have never allowed a gentleman to dictate to me, or to interfere with anything I do."

"I think you have made a mistake," said Winterbourne. "You should sometimes listen to a gentleman—the right one."

Daisy began to laugh again. "I do nothing but listen to gentlemen!" she exclaimed. "Tell me if Mr. Giovanelli is the right one."

The gentleman with the nosegay in his bosom had now perceived our two friends, and was approaching the young girl with obsequious rapidity. He bowed to Winterbourne as well as to the latter's companion; he had a brilliant smile, an intelligent eye; Winterbourne thought him not a bad-looking fellow. But he nevertheless said to Daisy, "No, he's not the right one."

She evidently had a natural talent for performing introductions; she mentioned the name of each of her companions to the other. She strolled along with one of them on each side of her; Mr. Giovanelli, who spoke English very cleverly—Winterbourne afterwards learned that he had practised the idiom upon a great many American heiresses—addressed to her a great deal of very polite nonsense; he was extremely urbane, and the young American, who said nothing, reflected upon that profundity of Italian cleverness which enables people to appear more gracious in proportion as they are more acutely disappointed. Giovanelli, of course, had counted upon something more intimate; he had not bargained for a party of three. But he kept his temper in a manner that suggested far-stretching intentions. Winterbourne flattered himself that he had taken his measure. "He is not a gentleman," said the young American; "he is only a clever imitation of one. He is a music-master or a penny-a-liner,① or a third-rate artist. D—n② his good looks!" Mr. Giovanelli had certainly a very pretty face; but Winterbourne felt a superior indignation at his own lovely fellow-countrywoman's not knowing the difference between a spurious gentleman and a real one. Giovanelli chattered and jested, and made himself wonderfully agreeable. It was true that, if he was an imitation, the imitation was brilliant. "Nevertheless," Winterbourne said to himself, "a nice girl ought to know!" And then he came back to the question whether this was, in fact, a nice girl. Would a nice girl, even allowing for her being a little American flirt, make a rendezvous with a presumably low-lived foreigner? The

---

① penny-a-liner: 穷文人，低级文人。
② D—n: damn.

rendezvous in this case, indeed, had been in broad daylight, and in the most crowded corner of Rome; but was it not impossible to regard the choice of these circumstances as a proof extreme cynicism? Singular though it may seem, Winterbourne was vexed that the young girl, in joining her *amoroso*,① shouldnot appear more impatient of his own company, and he was vexed because of his inclination. It was impossible to regard her as a perfectly well-conducted young lady; she was wanting in a certain indispensable delicacy. It would therefore simplify matters greatly to be able to treat her as the object of one of those sentiments which are called by romancers "lawless passions." That she should seem to wish to get rid of him would help him to think more lightly of her, and to be able to think more lightly of her would make her much less perplexing. But Daisy, on this occasion, continued to present herself as an inscrutable combination of audacity and innocence.

She had been walking some quarter of an hour, attended by her two cavaliers, and responding in a tone of very childish gayety, as it seemed to Winterbourne, to the pretty speeches of Mr. Giovanelli, when a carriage that had detached itself from the revolving train drew up beside the path. At the same moment Winterbourne perceived that his friend Mrs. Walker—the lady whose house he had lately left—was seated in the vehicle, and was beckoning to him. Leaving Miss Miller's side, he hastened to obey her summons. Mrs. Walker was flushed; she wore an excited air. "It is really too dreadful," she said. "That girl must not do this sort of thing. She mustnot walk here with you two men. Fifty people have noticed her."

Winterbourne raised his eyebrows. "I think it's a pity to make too much fuss about it."

"It's a pity to let the girl ruin herself!"

"She is very innocent," said Winterbourne.

"She's very crazy!" cried Mrs. Walker. "Did you ever see anything so imbecile as her mother? After you had all left me just now I couldnot sit still for thinking of it. It seemed too pitiful not even to attempt to save her. I ordered the carriage and put on my bonnet, and came here as quickly as possible. Thank heaven I have found you!"

"What do you propose to do with us?" asked Winterbourne, smiling.

"To ask her to get in, to drive her about here for half an hour, so that the world may see that she is not running absolutely wild, and then take her safely home."

"I don't think it's a very happy thought," said Winterbourne; "but you can try."

Mrs. Walker tried. The young man went in pursuit of Miss Miller, who had simply nodded and smiled at his interlocutor in the carriage, and had gone her way with her

---

① amoroso: lover (Italian).

companion. Daisy, on learning that Mrs. Walker wished to speak to her, retraced her steps with a perfect good grace and with Mr. Giovanelli at her side. She declared that she was delighted to have a chance to present this gentleman to Mrs. Walker. She immediately achieved the introduction, and declared that she had never in her life seen anything so lovely as Mrs. Walker's carriage-rug.

"I am glad you admire it," said this lady, smiling sweetly. "Will you get in and let me put it over you?"

"Oh no, thank you," said Daisy. "I shall admire it much more as I see you driving round with it."

"Do get in and drive with me!" said Mrs. Walker.

"That would be charming, but it's so enchanting just as I am!" and Daisy gave a brilliant glance at the gentlemen on either side of her.

"It may be enchanting, dear child, but it is not the custom here," urged Mrs. Walker, leaning forward in her victoria,① with her hands devoutly clasped.

"Well, it ought to be, then!" said Daisy. "If I didn't walk I should expire."

"You should walk with your mother, dear," cried the lady from Geneva, losing patience.

"With my mother, dear?" exclaimed the young girl. Winterbourne saw that she scented interference. "My mother never walked ten steps in her life. And then, you know," she added, with a laugh, "I am more than five years old."

"You are old enough to be more reasonable. You are old enough, dear Miss Miller, to be talked about."

Daisy looked at Mrs. Walker, smiling intensely. "Talked about? What do you mean?"

"Come into my carriage, and I will tell you."

Daisy turned her quickened glance again from one of the gentlemen beside her to the other. Mr. Giovanelli was bowing to and fro, rubbing down his gloves and laughing very agreeably; Winterbourne thought it a most unpleasant scene. "I don't think I want to know what you mean," said Daisy, presently. "I don't think I should like it."

Winterbourne wished that Mrs. Walker would tuck in her carriage-rug and drive away; but this lady did not enjoy being defied, as she afterwards told him. "Should you prefer being thought a very reckless girl?" she demanded.

"Gracious!" exclaimed Daisy. She looked again at Mr. Giovanelli, then she turned to Winterbourne. There was a little pink flush in her cheek; she was tremendously

---

① victoria: A horse-drawn carriage for two with a raised seat in front for the driver（维多利亚式马车）.

pretty. "Does Mr. Winterbourne think," she asked slowly, smiling, throwing back her head and glancing at him from head to foot, "that, to save my reputation, I ought to get into the carriage?"

Winterbourne colored; for an instant he hesitated greatly. It seemed so strange to hear her speak that way of her "reputation." But he himself, in fact, must speak in accordance with gallantry. The finest gallantry here was simply to tell her the truth, and the truth for Winterbourne—as the few indications I have been able to give have made him known to the reader—was that Daisy Miller should take Mrs. Walker's advice. He looked at her exquisite prettiness, and then said, very gently, "I think you should get into the carriage."

Daisy gave a violent laugh. "I never heard anything so stiff! If this is improper, Mrs. Walker," she pursued, "then I am all improper, and you must give me up. Good-bye; I hope you'll have a lovely ride!" and, with Mr. Giovanelli, who made a triumphantly obsequious salute, she turned away.

Mrs. Walker sat looking after her, and there were tears in Mrs. Walker's eyes. "Get in here, sir," she said to Winterbourne, indicating the place beside her. The young man answered that he felt bound to accompany Miss Miller; whereupon Mrs. Walker declared that if he refused her this favor she would never speak to him again. She was evidently in earnest. Winterbourne overtook Daisy and her companion, and, offering the young girl his hand told her that Mrs. Walker had made an imperious claim upon his society. He expected that in answer she would say something rather free, something to commit herself still further to that "recklessness" from which Mrs. Walker had so charitably endeavored to dissuade her. But she only shook his hand, hardly looking at him; while Mr. Giovanelli bade him farewell with a too emphatic flourish of the hat.

Winterbourne was not in the best possible humor as he took his seat in Mrs. Walker's victoria. "That was not clever of you," he said, candidly, while the vehicle mingled again with the throng of carriages.

"In such a case," his companion answered, "I don't wish to be clever; I wish to be *earnest*!"

"Well, your earnestness has only offended her and put her off."

"It has happened very well," said Mrs. Walker. "If she is so perfectly determined to compromise herself, the sooner one knows it the better; one can act accordingly."

"I suspect she meant no harm," Winterbourne rejoined.

"So I thought a month ago. But she has been going too far."

"What has she been doing?"

"Everything that is not done here. Flirting with any man she can pick up; sitting in corners with mysterious Italians; dancing all the evening with the same partners; receiving visits at eleven o'clock at night. Her mother goes away when visitors come."

"But her brother," said Winterbourne, laughing, "sits up till midnight."

"He must be edified by what he sees. I'm told that at their hotel every one is talking about her, and that a smile goes round among all the servants when a gentleman comes and asks for Miss Miller."

"The servantsbe hanged!" said Winterbourne, angrily. "The poor girl's only fault," he presently added, "is that she is very uncultivated."

"She is naturally indelicate," Mrs. Walker declared. "Take that example this morning. How long had you known her at Vevay?"

"A couple of days."

"Fancy, then, her making it a personal matter that you should have left the place!"

Winterbourne was silent for some moments; then he said, "I suspect, Mrs. Walker, that you and I have lived too long at Geneva!" And he added a request that she should inform him with what particular design she had made him enter her carriage.

"I wished to beg you to cease your relations with Miss Miller—not to flirt with her—to give her no further opportunity to expose herself—to let her alone, in short."

"I'm afraid I can't do that," said Winterbourne. "I like her extremely."

"All the more reason that you shouldn't help her to make a scandal."

"There shall be nothing scandalous in my attentions to her."

"There certainly will be in the way she takes them. But I have said what I had on my conscience," Mrs. Walker pursued. "If you wish to rejoin the young lady I'll put you down. Here, by-the-way, you have a chance."

The carriage was traversing that part of the Pincian Garden that overhangs the wall of Rome and overlooks the beautiful Villa Borghese. It is bordered by a large parapet, near which are several seats. One of the seats at a distance was occupied by a gentleman and a lady, toward whom Mrs. Walker gave a toss of her head. At the same moment these persons rose and walked towards the parapet. Winterbourne had asked the coachman to stop; he now descended from the carriage. His companion looked at him a moment in silence, then, while he raised his hat, she drove majestically away. Winterbourne stood there; he had turned his eyes towards Daisy and her cavalier. They evidently saw no one; they were too deeply occupied with each other. When they reached the low garden-wall they stood a moment looking off at the great flat-topped pine-clusters of the Villa Borghese; then Giovanelli seated himself familiarly upon the broad ledge of the wall. The western sun in the opposite sky sent out a brilliant shaft through a couple of cloud-bars; whereupon Daisy's companion took her parasol out of her hands and opened it. She came a little nearer, and he held the parasol over her; then, still holding it, he let it rest upon her shoulder, so that both of their heads were hidden from Winterbourne. This young man lingered a moment; then he began to walk. But he walked—not towards the couple with the parasol—towards the residence of his aunt, Mrs. Costello.

译文链接：https://book.qidian.com/info/1023604014/; https://i.unistudy.top/book/detail/15

Questions for Understanding

1. Does Winterbourne think Daisy is a flirt? Why or why not?
2. Why does Mrs. Walker want to save Daisy? What does Mrs. Walker represent as an American living in Europe?
3. What does Winterbourne imply when he says "I suspect, Mrs. Walker, that you and I have lived too long at Geneva!"?
4. Explain James's "international theme" by citing examples from the text above.

Aspects of Appreciation

  1. On the surface, *Daisy Miller* unfolds a simple story of a young American girl's willful yet innocent flirtation with a young Italian, and its unfortunate consequences. But throughout the narrative, James contrasts American and European customs and values in a tale rich in psychological and social insight. This is a vivid portrayal of Americans abroad and a telling encounter between the values of the Old and New Worlds.

  2. Daisy Miller, fresh from the high society of Schenectady, New York, neither knows nor cares about local notions of propriety, and the conflict between her free-spirited foolishness and the society she offends is at the heart of the novel. *Daisy Miller* has been hailed as the first "international novel", but it is also an early treatment of another theme that was to absorb James throughout his career: the phenomenon of the life unlived. In a novel incorporating this theme, the protagonist, owing to some aspect of his or her own character, such as an unconscious fear or a lack of passion or feeling, lets some opportunity for happiness go by and realizes it too late. In *Daisy Miller*, such a protagonist is Winterbourne, who spends the entire novel trying to figure out Daisy. In fact, it has been argued that *Daisy Miller* is not really so much about Daisy herself as it is about Winterbourne's wholesale failure to understand her.

3. Throughout *Daisy Miller*, Winterbourne is preoccupied with the question of whether Daisy is innocent. The word *innocent* appears repeatedly, always with a different shade of meaning. *Innocent* had three meanings in James's day. First, it could mean "ignorant" or "uninstructed". Daisy is "innocent" of the art of conversation, for example. It could also mean "naïve", as it does today. Mrs. Costello uses the word in this sense when she calls Winterbourne "too innocent" in Chapter 2. Finally, when Winterbourne protests, twirling his moustache in a sinister fashion, he invokes the third meaning, "not having done harm or wrong." This third sense is the one that preoccupies Winterbourne as he tries to come to a decision about Daisy. He initially judges the Millers to be merely "very ignorant" and "very innocent," and he assesses Daisy as a "harmless" flirt. As the novel progresses, he becomes increasingly absorbed in the question of her culpability. He fears she is guilty not of any particular sex act per se but merely of a vulgar mindset, a lack of concern for modesty and decency, which would put her beyond his interest or concern. One could argue that it is the way in which Daisy embodies all the different meanings of "innocence" that is her downfall.

Suggested Further Reading

Novels: *The American* (1877); *The Portrait of a Lady* (1881); *The Turn of the Screw* (1898); *The Ambassadors* (1903)

Topics for Further Study

1. Some of James's contemporaries thought his portrait of Daisy insulting to Americans. Can you suggest why?

2. Is *Daisy Miller* more about discovering what kind of person Daisy is or what kind of person Winterbourne is? Defend your answer.

3. How does health function differently for different characters in the novel? In the case of Daisy's illness, might any symbolism be at work?

4. The original meaning of the word "daisy" is "a very common flower, which is white around a yellow centre and grows among the grass. People think of daisies as simple and ordinary, but attractive and fresh". The name of the novel is *Daisy Miller*. The protagonist Daisy is buried "among the April daisies" after her death. Are all these sheer coincidences? Is there anything implied?

5. F. W. Dupee called Henry James "the great feminine novelist of a feminine age of letters." (Elliott, 271-272) Do you agree that Henry James is a "great feminine

novelist"? Why or why not?

Knowledge of Literature

An Element of Fiction: Tone（语气）

For literary study the word tone is borrowed from the phrase tone of voice in speech. Just as tone of voice reflects your attitude toward a particular thing or situation and also toward your listeners, so tone designates a writer's unstated attitude toward the subject, the characters or the reader. A work may have a tone that is intimate, solemn, sombre, playful, serious, ironic, or any of many other possible attitudes. The tone of a story or novel can be achieved through the words, sentences, setting, character, dialogue, narrator's direct comment and whole context.

推荐阅读的论文：

[1] 杜健伟，唐海东. AB 被车轮碾碎的蝴蝶——试析亨利·詹姆斯对黛西米勒的态度（英文）[J]. 语文学刊（外语教育教学），2013(06).

[2] 田俊武. 亨利·詹姆斯小说中的旅欧叙事与"国际主题"实质 [J]. 烟台大学学报（哲学社会科学版），2018, 31(05).

Theodore Dreiser (1871—1945)

About the Author

Theodore Dreiser, a pioneer of naturalism in American literature, wrote novels reflecting his mechanistic view of life, a concept that regards human beings as the victim of such ungovernable forces as economy, biology, society, and even chance. His novels depict real-life subjects in a harsh light, and in his works conventional morality is unimportant, consciously virtuous behavior having little to do with material success and happiness. While his style and language tend to be clumsy and plodding, he plays an important role in introducing a new realism and sexual candor into American fiction. Dreiser's principal concern is with the conflict between human needs and the demands of society for material success.

Theodore Dreiser was born in Terre Haute, Indiana, the ninth of ten children. His parents were poor. In the 1860s his father, a devout Catholic German immigrant, attempted to establish his own woolen mill, but after it was destroyed in a fire, the family lived in poverty. Dreiser's schooling was irregular, as the family moved from town to town. He left home when he was 16 and worked at whatever jobs he could find. With the help of his former teacher, he was able to study at Indiana University. Dreiser left after only a year. He was, however, a voracious reader, and the impact of such writers as Hawthorne, Poe, Balzac, Herbert Spencer, and Freud influenced his thought and his reaction against organized religion.

After working as a journalist in several midwestern newspapers, in 1894 he went to New York City, where he began a career in publishing, eventually rising to the presidency of Butterick Publications. During this period he wrote the short story "Nigger Jeff", probably based on a lynching he witnessed. The story was published in Ainslee, a small monthly journal, and collected in *Free and Other Stories* (1918).

In 1898, Dreiser married Sara White, a Missouri schoolteacher, but the marriage was unhappy. Dreiser separated permanently from her in 1909, but never earnestly sought a divorce. In his own life Dreiser practised his principle that man's greatest appetite is sexual—the desire for women led him to carry on several affairs at once. As insensitive in his treatment of the English language as he was of many women in his life, he seems destined to survive as a major American writer.

Dreiser's first novel, *Sister Carrie* (1900), is a work of pivotal importance in American literature despite its inauspicious launching. It became a beacon to subsequent American writers whose allegiance was to the realistic treatment of any and all subject matter. *Sister Carrie* tells the story of a rudderless but pretty small-town girl who comes to the big city filled with vague ambitions. She is used by men and uses them in turn to become a successful Broadway actress while George Hurstwood, the married man who has run away with her, loses his grip on life and descends into beggary and suicide. *Sister Carrie* was the first masterpiece of the American naturalistic movement in its grittily factual presentation of the vagaries of urban life and in its ingenuous heroine, who goes unpunished for her transgressions against conventional sexual morality. The book's strengths include a brooding but compassionate view of humanity, a memorable cast of characters, and a compelling narrative line. The emotional disintegration of Hurstwood is a much-praised triumph of psychological analysis.

Dreiser's second novel, *Jennie Gerhardt* (1911), is a lesser achievement than *Sister Carrie* owing to its heroine's comparative lack of credibility. Based on Dreiser's remembrance of his beloved mother, Jennie emerges as a plaster saint with whom most modern readers find it difficult to empathize. The novel's strengths include stinging characterizations of social snobs and narrow "religionists", as well as a deep sympathy for the poor.

The Financier (1912) and *The Titan* (1914) are the first two novels of a trilogy dealing with the career of the late-19th century American financier and traction tycoon Charles T. Yerkes, who is cast in fictionalized form as Frank Cowperwood. As Cowperwood successfully plots monopolistic business coups first in Philadelphia and then in Chicago, the focus of the novels alternates between his amoral business dealings and his marital and other erotic relations. *The Financier* and *The Titan* are important examples of the business novel and represent probably the most meticulously researched and documented studies of high finance in first-rate fiction. Cowperwood, like all of Dreiser's major characters, remains unfulfilled despite achieving most of his apparent wishes. The third novel in the trilogy, *The Stoic* (1947), is fatally weakened by Dreiser's diminished interest in his protagonist.

The "Genius" (1915) is artistically one of Dreiser's least successful novels but is nonetheless indispensable to an understanding of his psychology. This book chronicles its autobiographical hero's career as an artist and his unpredictable pursuit of the perfect woman as a source of ultimate fulfillment.

Dreiser's longest novel, *An American Tragedy* (1925), is a complex and compassionate account of the life and death of a young antihero named Clyde Griffiths. The novel begins with Clyde's blighted background, recounts his path to success, and culminates in his apprehension, trial, and execution for murder. The book was called by one influential critic as "the worst-written great novel in the world", but its questionable grammar and style are transcended by its narrative power. Dreiser's labyrinthine speculations on the extent of Clyde's guilt do not blunt his searing indictment of materialism and the American dream of success.

Dreiser's next-to-last novel, *The Bulwark* (1946), is the story of a Quaker father's unavailing struggle to shield his children from the materialism of modern American life. More intellectually consistent than Dreiser's earlier novels, this book also boasts some of his most polished prose.

Sister Carrie

About the Novel

The first edition of *Sister Carrie* by Dreiser was printed in 1900, but it is said to have been withheld from circulation by the publishers because of its supposed immorality. It was reissued in 1907.

Sister Carrie tells the story of two characters: Carrie Meeber, an ordinary girl who rises from a low-paid wage earner to a high-paid actress, and George Hurstwood, a member of the upper-middle class who falls from his comfortable lifestyle to a life on the streets. Neither Carrie nor Hurstwood earn their fates through virtue or vice, but rather through random circumstances. Their successes and failures have no moral value; this stance marks *Sister Carrie* as a departure from the conventional literature of the period. Dreiser touches upon a wide range of themes and experiences in *Sister Carrie*, from grinding poverty to upper-middle class comfort. The novel dwells on the moment as it is experienced; the characters are plunged into the narrative without the reader being told much, if any, of their histories. Their identities are constantly subject to change, reflecting the modern American experience that was ushered in by the developing capitalist economy. In the process of this development, thousands of rural Americans rushed to the cities to find jobs and to build themselves new lives and identities. *Sister Carrie* captures the excitement of that experience.

Chapter 1 The Magnet Attracting: A Waif Amid Forces

When Caroline Meeber boarded the afternoon train for Chicago, her total outfit consisted of a small trunk, a cheap imitation alligator-skin satchel, a small lunch in a paper box, and a yellow leather, snap purse, containing her ticket, a scrap of paper with her sister's address in Van Buren Street, and four dollars in money. It was in August, 1889. She was eighteen years of age, bright, timid, and full of the illusions of ignorance and youth[①]. Whatever touch of regret at parting characterized her thoughts, it was certainly not for advantages now being given up. A gush of tears at her mother's farewell kiss, a touch in her throat when the cars clacked by the flour mill where her father worked by the day, a pathetic sigh as the familiar green environs of the village passed in review, and the threads which bound her so lightly to girlhood and home were irretrievably broken.

To be sure there was always the next station, where one might descend and return. There was the great city, bound more closely by these very trains which came up daily. Columbia City was not so very far away, even once she was in Chicago. What, pray, is a few hours—a few hundred miles? She looked at the little slip bearing her sister's address and wondered. She gazed at the green landscape, now passing in swift review, until her swifter thoughts replaced its impression with vague conjectures of what Chicago might be.

When a girl leaves her home at eighteen, she does one of two things. Either she falls into saving hands and becomes better, or she rapidly assumes the cosmopolitan standard of virtue[②] and becomes worse. Of an intermediate balance, under the circumstances, there is no possibility. The city had its cunning wiles, no less than the

---

① illusions of ignorance and youth: illusions resulting from her ignorance and youth.
② the cosmopolitan standard of virtue: the moral standard of the big city that is low in virtue and value.

infinitely smaller and more human tempter. There are large forces which allure with all the soulfulness of expression① possible in the most cultured human. The gleam of a thousand lights is often as effective as the persuasive light in a wooing and fascinating eye. Half the undoing of the unsophisticated and natural mind is accomplished by forces wholly superhuman. A blare of sound, a roar of life, a vast array of human hives, appeal to the astonished senses in equivocal terms. Without a counselor at hand to whisper cautious interpretations, what falsehoods may not these things breathe into the unguarded ear! Unrecognised for what they are, their beauty, like music, too often relaxes, then weakens, then perverts the simpler human perceptions.

Caroline, or Sister Carrie, as she had been half affectionately termed by the family, was possessed of a mind rudimentary in its power of observation and analysis. Self-interest with her was high, but not strong. It was, nevertheless, her guiding characteristic. Warm with the fancies of youth, pretty with the insipid prettiness of the formative period, possessed of a figure promising eventual shapeliness and an eye alight with certain native intelligence, she was a fair example of the middle American class—two generations removed from the emigrant. Books were beyond her interest—knowledge a sealed book②. In the intuitive graces she was still crude. She could scarcely toss her head gracefully. Her hands were almost intellectual. The feet, though small, were set flatly. And yet she was interested in her charms, quick to understand the keener pleasures of life, ambitious to gain in material things. A half-equipped little knight she was, venturing to reconnoiter the mysterious city and dreaming wild dreams of some vague, far-off supremacy, which should make it③ prey and subject—the proper penitent, groveling at a woman's slipper.

"That," said a voice in her ear, "is one of the prettiest little resorts in Wisconsin."

"Is it?" she answered nervously.

The train was just pulling out of Waukesha. For some time she had been conscious of a man behind. She felt him observing her mass of hair. He had been fidgeting, and with natural intuition she felt certain interest growing in that quarter. Her maidenly reserve, and a certain sense of what was conventional under the circumstances, called her to forestall and deny this familiarity, but the daring and magnetism of the individual, born of past experiences and triumphs, prevailed. She answered.

He leaned forward to put his elbows upon the back of her seat and proceeded to make himself volubly agreeable.

"Yes, that is a great resort for Chicago people. The hotels are swell. You are not

---

① the soulfulness of expression: verbal tricks.
② knowledge a sealed book: She has acquired little knowledge.
③ it: referring to the penitent.

familiar with this part of the country, are you?"

"Oh, yes, I'm," answered Carrie, "That is, I live at Columbia City. I have never been through here, though."

"And so this your first visit to Chicago," he observed.

All the time she was conscious of certain features out of this side of her eye. Flush, colourful checks, a light moustache, a gray fedora① hat. She now turned and looked upon him in full, the instincts of self-protection and coquetry mingling confusedly in her brain.

"I didn't say that," she said.

"Oh," he answered, in a very pleasing way and with an assumed air of mistake, "I thought you did."

Here was a type of the travelling canvasser② for a manufacturing house—a class which at that time was first being dubbed by the slang of the day "drummers". He came within the meaning of a still newer term, which has sprung into general use among Americans in 1880, and which concisely expressed the thoughts of one whose dress or manners are calculated to elicit the admiration of susceptible young women—a "masher". His suit was of a striped and crossed pattern of brown wool, new at that time, but since become familiar as a business suit. The low crotch of the vest revealed a stiff shirt bosom of white and pink stripes. From his coat sleeves protruded a pair of linen cuffs of the same pattern, fastened with large, gold plate buttons, set with the common yellow agates known as "cat's-eyes". His fingers bore several rings—one, the ever-enduring heavy seal—and from his vest dangled a neat gold watch chain, from which was suspended the secret insignia of the Order of Elks③. The whole suit was rather tight-fitting, and was finished off with heavy-soled tan shoes, highly polished, and the gray fedora hat. He was, for the order of intellect represented, attractive, and whatever he had to recommend him, you may be sure was not lost upon Carrie, in this, her first glance.

Lest this order of individual should permanently pass④, let me put down some of the most striking characteristics of his most successful manner and method. Good clothes, of course, were the first essential, the things without which he was nothing. A strong physical nature, actuated by a keen desire for the feminine, was the next. A mind free of any consideration of the problem or forces of the world and actuated not by greed, but an insatiable love of variable-pleasure. His method was always

---

① fedora: 浅顶卷檐软呢帽。
② canvasser: salesman.
③ Order of Elks: 麋鹿会，1868 年于纽约市创立的一个以兴办慈善事业为主的同人组织。
④ pass: disappear.

simple. Its principal element was daring, backed, of course, by an intense desire and admiration for the sex[①]. Let him meet with a young woman once and he would approach her with an air of kindly familiarity, not unmixed with pleading, which would result in most cases in a tolerant acceptance. If she showed any tendency to coquetry he would be apt to straighten her tie, or if she "took up" with him at all, to call her by her first name. If he visited a department store it was to lounge familiarly over the counter and ask some leading questions[②]. In more exclusive circles, on the train or in waiting stations, he went slower. If some seemingly vulnerable object appeared he was all attention—to pass the compliments of the day to lead the way to the parlor car, carrying her grip, or court her to her destination. Pillows, books, a footstools, the shade lowered: all these figured in the things which he could do. If, when she reached her destination, he did not alight and attend her baggage for her, it was because, in his own estimation, he had signally failed.

A woman should some day write the complete philosophy of clothes. No matter how young, it is one of the things she wholly comprehends. There is an indescribably faint line in the matter of man's apparel which somehow divides for her those who are worth glancing at and those who are not. Once an individual has passed this faint line on the way downward he will get no glance from her. There is another line at which the dress of a man will cause her to study her own. This line the individual at her elbow now marked for Carrie. She became conscious of an inequality. Her own plain blue dress, with its black cotton tape trimmings, now seemed to her shabby. She felt the worn state of her shoes.

"Let's see," he went on, "I know quite a number of people in your town. Morgenroth the clothier and Gibson the dry goods[③] man…"

"Oh, do you?" She interrupted, aroused by memories of longings their show windows had cost her.

At last he had a clew[④] to her interest, and followed it deftly. In a few minutes he had come about into her seat. He talked of sales of clothing, his travels, Chicago, and the amusements of their city.

"If you are going there, you will enjoy it immensely. Have you relatives?"

"I am going to visit my sister," She explained.

"You want to[⑤] see Lincoln Park," he said, "and Michigan Boulevard. They are

---

① the sex: the women.
② leading questions: questions put in such a way as to suggest the desired answers(诱导性问题).
③ dry goods: drapery and the like(布匹).
④ a clew: a clue.
⑤ want to: ought to.

putting up great building there. It's a second New York—great. So much to see—theatres, crowds, fine houses—oh, you'll like that."

There was a little ache in her fancy of all he described. Her insignificance faintly affected her. She realized that hers[①] was not to be a round of pleasure, and yet there was something promising in all the material prospect he set forth. There was something satisfactory in the attention of this individual with his good clothes. She could not help smiling as he told her of some popular actress of whom she reminded him. She was not silly, and yet attention of this sort had its weight.

"You will be in Chicago some little time, won't you?" He observed at one turn of the now easy conversation.

"I don't know," said Carrie vaguely—a flash vision of the possibility of her not securing employment rising in her mind.

"Several weeks, anyhow," he said, looking steadily into her eyes.

There was much more passing now than the mere words indicated. He recognized the indescribable thing that made up for fascination and beauty in her. She realized that she was of interest and fears. Her manner was simple, though for the very reason that she had not yet learned the many little affectations with which women conceal their true feelings. Some things she did appeared bold. A clever companion—had she ever had one—would have warned her never to look a man in the eyes so steadily.

"Why do you ask?" she said.

"Well, I'm going to be there several weeks. I'm going to study stock at our place and get new samples. I might show you 'round."

"I don't know whether you can or not. I mean I don't know whether I can. I shall be living with my sister, and—?"

"Well, if she minds, we'll fix that." He took out his pencil and a little pocket notebook as if it were all settled. "What is your address there?"

She fumbled her purse which contained the address slip.

He reached down in his hip pocket and took out a fat purse. It was filled with slips of paper, some mileage books, a roll of greenbacks. It impressed her deeply. Such a purse had never been carried by any one attentive to her. Indeed an experienced traveler, a brisk man of the world, had never come within such close range before. The purse, the shiny tan shoes, the smart new suit, and the air with which he did things, built up for her a dim world of fortune, of which he was the centre. It disposed her pleasantly toward all he might do.

He took out a neat business card, on which was engraved Battlett, Caryoe &

---

① hers: her trip to Chicago.

Company, and down in the left-hand corner, Chas. H. Drouet.

"That's me," he said, putting the card in her hand and touching his name. "It's pronounced Drew-eh. Our family was French on my father's side."

She looked at it while he put up his purse. Then he got out a letter from a bunch in his coat pocket. "This is the house I travel for," he went on pointing to a picture on it, "corner of State and Lake." There was pride in his voice. He felt that it was something to be connected with such a place, and he made her feel the way.

"What is your address?" He began again, fixing his pencil to write.

She looked at his hand.

"Carrie Meeber," she said slowly. "Three hundred and fifty-four West Van Buren Street, care S.C. Hanson."

He wrote it carefully down and got out the purse again. "You'll be at home if I come around Monday night?" He said.

"I think so, " she answered.

How true it is that words are but the vague shadows of the volumes we mean. Little audible links, they are, chaining together great inaudible feelings and purposes. Here were these two, bandying little phrases, drawing purses, looking at cards, and both unconscious of how inarticulate all their real feelings were. Neither was wise enough to be sure of the working of the mind of the other. He could not tell how his luring succeeded. She could not realize that she was drifting, until he secured her address. Now she felt that she had yielded something—he that he had gained a victory. Already they felt that they were somehow associated. Already he took control in directing the conversation. His words were easy. Her manner was relaxed.

They were nearing Chicago. Sighs were everywhere numerous. Trains flashed by them. Across wide stretches of flat, open prairie they could see lines of telegraph poles stalking across toward the great city. Far away were indications of suburban towns, some big smokestacks towering high in the air.

Frequently there were two-story frame houses standing out in the open fields, without fence or trees, lone outposts of the approaching army of homes.

To the child, the genius with imagination, or the wholly untraveled, the approach to a great city for the first time is a wonderful thing. Particularly if it be evening—that mystic period between the glare and gloom of the world when life is changing from one sphere or condition to another. Ah, the promise of the night. What does it not hold for the weary! What old illusion of hope is not here forever repeated! Says the soul of the toiler to itself, "I shall soon be free. I shall be in the ways and the hosts of the merry. The streets, the lamps, the lighted chamber set for dining, are for me. The theatre, the halls, the parties, the ways of rest and the paths of song—these are mine in the night." Though all humanity be still enclosed in the shops, the thrill runs abroad. It is in the air. The dullest feel something which they may not always express or describe. It is the lifting of the burden of toil.

Sister Carrie gazed out of the window. Her companion, affected by her wonder, so contagious are all things, felt anew some interest in the city and pointed out its marvels.

"This is Northwest Chicago," said Drouet. "This is the Chicago River," and he pointed to little muddy creek, crowded with the huge masted wanderes from far-off waters nosing the black-posted banks. With a puff, a clang, and a clatter of rails it was gone. "Chicago is getting to be a great town," he went on. "It's a wonder. You'll find lots to see here."

She did not hear this very well. Her heart was troubled by a kind of terror. The fact that she was alone, away from home, rushing into a great sea of life and endeavour, began to tell. She could not help but feel a little choked for breath—a little sick as her heart beat so fast. She half closed her eyes and tried to think it was nothing, that Columbia City was only a little way off.

"Chicago! Chicago!" Called the brakeman, slamming open the door. They were rushing into a more crowded yard, alive with the clatter and clang of life. She began to gather up her poor little grip and closed her hand firmly upon her purse. Drouet arose, kicked his legs to straighten his trousers, and seized his clean yellow grip.

"I suppose your people will be here to meet you?" He said, "Let me carry your grip."

"Oh, no," she said, "I'd rather you wouldn't. I'd rather you wouldn't be with me when I meet my sister."

"All right," he said in all kindness. "I'll be near, thought in case she isn't here, and take you out there safely."

"You're so kind," said Carrie, feeling the goodness of such attention in her strange situation.

"Chicago!" Called the brakeman, drawing the word out long. They were under a great shadowy train shed, where the lamps were already beginning to shine out, with passenger cars all about and the train moving at a snail's pace. The people in the car were all up and crowding about the door.

"Well, here we are," said Drouet, leading the way to the door. "Good-bye, till I see you Monday."

"Good-bye," she answered, taking his proffered hand.

"Remember, I'll be looking till you find your sister."

She smiled into his eyes.

They filed out and he affected to take no notice of her. A lean-faced, rather commonplace woman recognized Carrie on the platform and hurried forward.

"Why, Sister Carrie!" She began, and there was a perfunctory embrace of welcome.

Carrie realized the change of affectional atmosphere at once. Amid all the maze, uproar, and novelty she felt cold reality taking her by the hand. No world of light and merriment. No round of amusement. Her sister carried with her most of the grimness of shift and toil.

"Why, how are all the folks at home?" she began; "how is father, and mother?"

Carrie answered, but was looking away. Down the aisle, toward the gate leading into the waiting room and the street, stood Drouet. He was looking back. When he saw that she saw him and was safe with her sister he turned to go, sending back the shadow of a smile, only Carrie saw it. She felt something lost to her when he moved away. When he disappeared she felt his absence thoroughly. With her sister she was much alone, alone figure in a tossing, thoughtless sea.

译文链接：https://max.book118.com/html/2017/1011/136779308.shtm

Questions for Understanding

1. Does Caroline appear to be the type of person you like or admire? What do you think of her?
2. What does the fourth paragraph tell about Sister Carrie?
3. "Clothes make the man" is an epigram often used in English. How does the author express this idea? In what way is it important to the development of the chapter?
4. Do you like Drouet the salesman? Why or why not?
5. Does the author feel sympathy for the salesman or Carrie? Give reasons for your answer. To whom does your sympathy go out?
6. Does the author capture your interest in the first chapter and make you want to read the rest of the novel?
7. In what way is Carrie representative of thousands of young people who leave a small town for life in a big city? Does this tendency exist here in China? What do you think about this situation?

Aspects of Appreciation

1. The plot of the novel *Sister Carrie*, and the personality of Carrie Meeber,

are guided and developed by "conspicuous consumption", which characterizes the booming capitalist economy after the Civil War. Except for a few sparse details, and a catalog of her belongings— "a small trunk, a cheap imitation alligator-skin satchel, a small lunch in a paper box, and a yellow leather, snap purse, containing her ticket, a scrap of paper with her sister's address in Van Buren Street, and four dollars in money", we know nothing about her in the beginning chapter of the novel when she boards the train for Chicago to seek her fortune. Money or material things are utilized by Dreiser to govern secretly Carrie Meeber's fate as soon as the novel starts.

Chicago is the setting of *Sister Carrie*, in which Carrie is a pretty young girl whom Dreiser uses to express his own longings for wealth and affection, for the glitter and excitement of the city which has come to symbolize the possibility for the realization of the American Dream. The opening chapter shows Carrie leaving home and taking the train to the city. The passage is typical Dreiser. He gives his thoughts about Carrie and the salesman she meets, and describes them minutely.

2. Dreiser's *Sister Carrie* is a typical naturalist novel. Carrie, according to Dreiser, becomes either someone under another's care and protection ("falls into saving hands and becomes better"), or the victim of a voracious city. There is no middle ground. In either case, it is apparent that Carrie has little control over her life. "There are large forces which allure with all the soulfulness of expression possible in the most cultured human." The mind, the soul and the body are taken in. The beauty of the city is an illusion and a trap, which, "like music, too often relaxes, then weakens, then perverts the simpler human perceptions."

3. Carrie, a "half-equipped little knight", is involved in the search for the American Dream. She is naïve, although filled with self-interest, "warm with the fancies of youth". She meets a man on the train, well-dressed and impressive. "… Whatever he had to recommend him, you may be sure was not lost upon Carrie, in this, her first glance." He is a superficial man whose mind was "free of any consideration of the problems or forces of the world". His suavity attracts her, and she feels inferior by comparison. Here is the success story, incarnate, she feels. "Her own plain blue dress, with its black cotton tape trimmings, now seemed shabby." His fat purse "impressed her deeply". It is evident, when he asks for her address, that Carrie has embarked upon the beginning of her end.

4. From this chapter, it can be discovered that Carrie, in spite of being shy and convention-restrained as a country girl just leaving for a big city, can not help being

guided and controlled by the materialistic environment of Chicago and such persons from big cities as Drouet. This shows the naturalistic view of such writers as Theodore Dreiser.

5. Dreiser's vague treatment of Carrie Meeber at the end of the novel through the image of "the rocking chair" poses a challenge to the traditional moral standard, but it can also be regarded, from the feminist perspective, as a response to the feminist movement at the turn of the century with the creation of the "New Woman" image.

Suggested Further Reading

Jannie Gerhardt (1911); *"Trilogy of Desire": The Financier* (1912)*, The Titan* (1914) *and The Stoic* (1947); *The "Genius"* (1915); *An American Tragedy* (1925).

Topics for Further Study

1. What role does imitation play in feminine identity in *Sister Carrie*? Consider Carrie's relationship with Drouet, her fascination with the theater, and the role of masculine sexual desire.

2. How does economic class govern the individual's relationship to money in *Sister Carrie*?

3. What role does Carrie's unsatisfied desire play in the novel? Consider the nature of consumer society, the distinction between imitation and the genuine, and the book's portrayal of conventional social attitudes toward women's sexual desire.

4. What is the relationship between money and sex in the novel? Consider Drouet's relationship with Carrie, Hurstwood's relationship with Carrie, and Julia's reaction to Hurstwood's affair.

5. What is the relationship between power and performance in the novel? How do the men of the novel—Hurstwood and Drouet in particular—gain power over Carrie by performing certain roles? How does playing a role allow Carrie to assert her own power?

6. What is the connection between role-playing and lying? How are they both connected to the satisfaction of desire? Consider Drouet's lie about his intent to marry Carrie, Hurstwood's lie to Carrie about his own intent to marry her, and Hurstwood's lie to Carrie about Drouet's "injury".

7. Why does Carrie like Hurstwood better than Drouet? Consider the difference between *gaudy* conspicuous consumption and *tasteful* conspicuous consumption.

Consider also the function of role-playing and the distinction between imitation and the genuine.

8. How is Carrie's identity developed over the course of the novel? Consider the role of masculine desire, the role of imitation, and Carrie's lack of history.

9. How does consumer society turn people into commodities or objects? Discuss the role of "the captain" as a symbol for the commodification of people.

10. Why does Hurstwood fail? Why does Carrie succeed? Can any moral lessons be drawn from either of their fates? Why or why not? Consider Carrie's skill at imitation and her strong consumer drive, and Hurstwood's failure to perform his role as Julia's husband.

Knowledge of Literature

1. Naturalism（自然主义）

Naturalism is an extreme form of realism or a harsher or a pessimistic realism. Naturalistic writers usually depict the sordid side of life and show characters who are severely, if not hopelessly, limited by their environment and heredity. If a person inherits compulsive instincts—especially the hunger to accumulate possessions, and sexuality, he is then subject to social and economic forces. The French novelist Emile Zola, beginning in the 1870s, did much to develop this theory. Zola and such American naturalistic writers as Frank Norris, Stephen Crane and Theodore Dreiser try to present their subjects with scientific objectivity and with elaborate documentation. They tend to choose characters who exhibit strong animal drives such as greed and sexual desire, and who are helpless victims both of glandular secretions within and of sociological pressures without. The end of the naturalistic novel is usually "tragic", but not, as in classical and Elizabethan tragedy, because of a heroic but losing struggle of the individual mind and will against gods, enemies, and circumstances. Instead the protagonist of the naturalistic plot, a pawn to multiple compulsions, usually disintegrates, or is wiped out.

2. Literary Criticism: Reception Aesthetics（接受美学）

Reception aesthetics, rising since the 1970s, studies the interaction of reader with text. Critics of reception aesthetics hold that the text is incomplete until it is read. Each reader brings something to the text that completes it and that makes each reading different. Works contain "gaps" because of their incompleteness. Authors always leave something unsaid or unexplained and thus invite readers to fill the resulting spaces with their own imaginative constructs. The response of a particular reader, which constitutes for that reader the meaning and aesthetic qualities of a text, is the joint product of the reader's own "horizon of expectations" and the confirmations, disappointments, refutations, and reformulations of these expectations when they are challenged by the features of the text itself. Since the linguistic and aesthetic expectations of the population of readers change over the course of time, and since later readers and critics have access not only to the literary text but also to the published responses of earlier readers, there develops an evolving historical tradition of critical interpretations and evaluations of a given literary work. So a literary text possesses no fixed and final meanings.

推荐阅读的论文：
[1] 赵冬梅. 传统命运的再定义——从接受美学的角度分析《嘉莉妹妹》[J]. 泰山学院学报，2007 (7).
[2] 张磊. 从接受美学视角解读《嘉莉妹妹》[J]. 文学教育（上），2014 (5).

Chapter 4
American Literature in the Modern Period

  两次世界大战期间,美国社会经历了翻天覆地的巨变。美国虽然作为战胜国在一战中获利颇丰,一跃成为世界首屈一指的经济政治强国,但同时也付出了惨痛的代价。残酷的战争摧毁了整整一代人的信仰和理想,鲜血和死亡让他们意识到传统价值观的虚幻和荒谬,所谓"民主""自由"等一切神圣字眼只不过是政客攫取利益的幌子。这群"迷惘的一代"(the Lost Generation)身心严重受挫,彷徨在精神的荒原上;信仰的缺失和精神的迷惘使他们化身为畸形的享乐主义者,通过酒精和舞会来麻痹神经、挥霍人生,美国社会由此进入无尽奢华、喧嚣躁动的"爵士时代"(the Jazz Age)。但是,随后爆发的经济大萧条(The Great Depression, 1929~1933)给沉溺于纸醉金迷中的美国人敲响了警钟,促使他们走出空虚和绝望,用清醒客观的眼光审视自我和社会,批判政治和经济制度存在的缺陷和不公。

  伴随着动荡不安的社会巨变,这一时期的美国文学进入现代主义阶段,以蔚为大观之势迎来了第二次繁荣,小说、诗歌、戏剧全面发展,呈现出一派勃勃生机。以艾略特(T.S. Eliot)、庞德(Ezra Pound)、海明威(Ernest Hemingway)、福克纳(William Faulkner)和奥尼尔(Eugene O'Neill)为代表的新生代作家纷纷摒弃传统写作手法,大胆实验和创新,寻求用新文体、新形式来展现错综复杂、分崩离析的社会现实和虚幻绝望的现代生活。

  这场变革始于诗歌领域。艾略特、庞德等意象派诗人(Imagists)冲破传统诗歌对格律的禁锢,积极倡导用自由诗体来塑造具体直观的意象,为美国诗歌这幅画卷增添了浓墨重彩的一笔。以桑德堡(Carl Sandburg)为代表的芝加哥派(the Chicago Poets)承袭惠特曼的创新之风,吸收俚语和民谣中的精髓,用生动自然的语言、火一般的热情、强有力的节奏描述人民大众的普通生活,歌颂充满活力和朝气的工业化大都市,为这幅画卷贡献了粗犷绚烂的一笔。以弗罗斯特(Robert Frost)为首的新英格兰派(the New England poets)留下的印记虽貌似简单直白,却意境深远、发人深省。

  这一时期的小说也呈现出一派繁荣景象。德莱塞等老一辈文学巨匠仍活跃在文坛上；而经历过战争洗礼的年轻一代作家，如海明威、福克纳、菲茨杰拉德（F.S. Fitzgerald）和安德森（Sherwood Anderson）等，逐渐成为文坛主力军，积极用各种新的创作形式从不同角度细致深刻地勾勒现代精神荒原上的芸芸众生："迷惘的一代"的精神迷失和悲观厌世、"爵士时代"纵情于声色犬马中的享乐主义者的躁动和空虚、南方和中西部小镇居民的精神危机和心理痼疾以及挣扎在社会底层的劳动人民的伤痛和苦难。虽然这幅小说画卷的主色调低沉暗淡，但细细看来，仍可以察觉许多蕴含希望的亮色笔墨：海明威坚信人类虽如西西弗斯一样深陷绝望困境，但仍可以"在重压下保持优雅"，通过与命运的不懈抗争赋予空虚无望的人生以新的意义；福克纳不遗余力地提醒人们重拾南方传统价值观的精髓，用爱、同情心、牺牲精神和荣誉感等品质化解隔阂、孤寂、迷惘和空虚。30年代大萧条的爆发和蔓延则促使大批有社会责任感和良知的作家，如斯坦贝克（John Steinbeck）等，以纸笔为刀枪抨击资本主义制度的黑暗，揭露社会的种种弊端。此外，少数族裔文学也崭露头角，有了一定的发展。20年代末到30年代初兴起的"哈莱姆文艺复兴"（the Harlem Renaissance）打破了白人文学一统天下的局面，为二战后少数族裔文学的蓬勃发展奠定了良好的基础。

值得一提的是，美国戏剧也在这一时期发生了质的飞跃。以奥尼尔为首的戏剧家在萃取传统戏剧手法精华的基础上，博采现实主义、自然主义、象征主义和表现主义等众家之所长，革新戏剧的表现形式，创作了众多脍炙人口的经典剧目，为美国戏剧的发展掀开了崭新的一页。

T. S. Eliot (1888~1965)

About the Author

Thomas Stearns Eliot, or T.S. Eliot was born in 1888 in St. Louis. He was the son of a prominent industrialist who came from a well-connected Boston family. Eliot always felt the loss of his family's New England roots and seemed to be somewhat ashamed of his father's business success; throughout his life he continually sought to return to the center of Anglo-Saxon culture, first by attending Harvard and then by emigrating to England, where he lived from 1914 until his death. Eliot began graduate study in philosophy at Harvard and completed his dissertation, although the outbreak of World War I prevented him from taking his examinations and receiving the degree. The War, which kept him in England, led him to decide to pursue poetry full-time.

Eliot's poetry was noted for its fresh visual imagery, flexible tone, and highly expressive rhythm. He had begun writing traditional poetry as a college student. In 1908, however, he read Arthur Symons's *The Symbolist Movement in Literature* and learned about Jules LaForgue and other French Symbolist poets. Symons's book altered Eliot's view of poetry, as "The Love Song of J. Alfred Prufrock" (published in *Poetry* in 1915) and "Preludes" (published in *Blast* in the same year) clearly showed. Ezra Pound helped Eliot over several years to get financially established. He settled down in England, marrying Vivian Haigh-Wood in 1915. Separated in 1932, they never divorced. Eliot began working on *The Waste Land* in 1921. This poem, heavily edited by Pound and perhaps also by his wife, addressed the fragmentation and alienation characteristic of modern culture. After *The Hollow Man* and the *Sweeney* poems, which continue *The Waste Land*'s critique of modern civilization, he turned increasingly to poems of religious doubt and reconciliation. *The Journey of the Magi* and *Ash Wednesday* are poems about the search for a faith that is desperately needed, yet difficult to sustain. *Four Quartets*, his last major poetic work, combines a Christian sensibility with a profound uncertainty resulting from the war's devastation of Europe.

Eliot was also a distinguished literary critic. His *Tradition and the Individual Talent* defines the Western poetic tradition as an organic whole, an elastic equilibrium that constantly reforms itself to accommodate new poets who, therefore, become part of this whole. This antipolitical approach to poetry had a major influence on the practices of the school of close-reading critics whose work is known collectively as the "New Criticism". In other connected literary essays, Eliot denigrated didactic, expository, or narrative poets like Milton and the Victorians while applauding the verbally complex, ironic, indirect, symbolic work of 17th-century Metaphysical poets like Donne and Herbert.

Eliot wrote some verse plays. *Murder in the Cathedral* (1935) was a church pageant. *The Family Reunion* (1939), *The Cocktail Party* (1949), *The Confidential Clerk* (1953), and *The Elder Statesman* (1959), all religious in theme, were successfully produced in London and Broadway.

The Love Song of J. Alfred Prufrock

About the Poem

This poem was first published in *Poetry* (June 1915) and collected in *Prufrock and Other Observations* (1917). In the form of a dramatic monologue it presents with irony and pathos the musings of a man, uncertain, uneasy, and unable to commit himself to the love he desires or to life at all, a figure representative of frustrations in modern life and of the aridity of a sterile upper-class culture.

The Love Song of J. Alfred Prufrock

S'io credessi che mia risposta fosse
a persona che mai tornasse al mondo,
questa fiamma staria senza più scosse.
Ma per ciò che giammai di questo fondo
non tornò vivo alcun, s'i'odo il vero,
senza tema d'infamia ti rispondo[①].

Let us go then, you and I,
When the evening is spread out against the sky
Like a patient etherised[②] upon a table;
Let us go, through certain half-deserted streets,
The muttering retreats
Of restless nights in one-night cheap hotels
And sawdust restaurants with oyster-shells:
Streets that follow like a tedious argument
Of insidious intent
To lead you to an overwhelming question...
Oh, do not ask, "What is it?"
Let us go and make our visit.

In the room the women come and go
Talking of Michelangelo.[③]

The yellow fog that rubs its back upon the window-panes,
The yellow smoke that rubs its muzzle on the window-panes,
Licked its tongue into the corners of the evening,
Lingered upon the pools that stand in drains,
Let fall upon its back the soot that falls from chimneys,
Slipped by the terrace, made a sudden leap,
And seeing that it was a soft October night,

---

① The epigraph, written in Italian, is taken from Dante's *Inferno*, 27, 61-66. It can be translated into English as follows: If I thought my reply were to one who could ever return to the world, this flame would shake no more; but since, if what I hear is true, none ever did return alive from this depth, I answer you without fear of infamy.
② etherized: anesthetized (使麻醉).
③ Michelangelo: Buonarroti Michelangelo (1475-1564), a great Italian sculptor, painter, and poet of the Renaissance.

Curled once about the house, and fell asleep.

And indeed there will be time①
For the yellow smoke that slides along the street
Rubbing its back upon the window-panes;
There will be time, there will be time
To prepare a face② to meet the faces that you meet;
There will be time to murder and create,
And time for all the works and days③ of hands
That lift and drop a question on your plate;
Time for you and time for me,
And time yet for a hundred indecisions,
And for a hundred visions and revisions,
Before the taking of a toast and tea.④

In the room the women come and go
Talking of Michelangelo.

And indeed there will be time
To wonder, "Do I dare?" and, "Do I dare?"
Time to turn back and descend the stair,⑤
With a bald spot in the middle of my hair—
(They will say: "How his hair is growing thin!")
My morning coat, my collar mounting firmly to the chin,
My necktie rich and modest, but asserted by a simple pin—
(They will say: "But how his arms and legs are thin!")
Do I dare
Disturb the universe?⑥
In a minute there is time

---

① there will be time: Here is an echo of Andrew Marvell (1621~1678)'s seductive plea in To His Coy Mistress (1681): "Had we but world enough and time…"
② To prepare a face: to do one's facial make-up (化妆).
③ works and days: A reference to "Works and Days", a didactic poem, by the Greek poet Hesiod (8th century BC), on the rural life and labors of a peasant.
④ the taking of a toast and tea: 饮酒与喝茶，指生活中必须要做的琐碎事情。
⑤ descend the stair: go down the stairs.
⑥ Do I dare/ Disturb the universe?: Prufrock thinks that his proposal to one of those genteel women will be so shocking that the universe will be disturbed by it.

For decisions and revisions which a minute will reverse.

For I have known them all already, known them all—
Have known the evenings, mornings, afternoons,
I have measured out my life with coffee spoons;
I know the voices dying with a dying fall①
Beneath the music from a farther room.
So how should I presume?

AndI have known the eyes already, known them all—
The eyes that fix you in a formulated phrase,②
And when I am formulated, sprawling on a pin,
When I am pinned and wriggling on the wall,
Then how should I begin
To spit out all the butt-ends of my days and ways?③
And how should I presume?

AndI have known the arms already, known them all—
Arms that are braceleted and white and bare
(But in the lamplight, downed with light brown hair!)
Is it perfume from a dress
That makes me so digress?
Arms that lie along a table, or wrap about a shawl.
And should I then presume?
And how should I begin?
...
Shall I say, I have gone at dusk through narrow streets
And watched the smoke that rises from the pipes
Of lonely men in shirt-sleeves, leaning out of windows?...

I should have been a pair of ragged claws④
Scuttling across the floors of silent seas.

---

① a dying fall: a sinking of tone (音调下降).
② The eyes that fix you in a formulated phrase: the eyes that make an estimate of you with aformula.
③ To spit out all the butt-ends of my days and ways: to express angrily all the deeply-embedded thoughts reflecting my life and ways of living
④ a pair of ragged claws: a pair of ragged claws (of a crab). Here the poet means that it would be better to lead a merely instinctual life such as that of a crab that involves no moral decisions and revisions.

...
And the afternoon, the evening, sleeps so peacefully!
Smoothed by long fingers,
Asleep…tired…or it malingers,①
Stretched on the floor, here beside you and me.
Should I, after tea and cakes and ices,
Have the strength to force the moment to its crisis?
But though I have wept and fasted, wept and prayed,
Though I have seen my head (grown slightly bald) brought in upon a platter,
I am no prophet—and here's no great matter;②
I have seen the moment of my greatness flicker,
And I have seen the eternal Footman hold my coat, and snicker,③
Andin short, I was afraid.

And would it have been worth it, after all,
After the cups, the marmalade, the tea,
Among the porcelain, among some talk of you and me,
Would it have been worth while,
To have bitten off the matter④ with a smile,
To have squeezed the universe into a ball
To roll it towards some overwhelming question,⑤
To say: "I am Lazarus,⑥ come from the dead,
Come back to tell you all, I shall tell you all" —
If one, settling a pillow by her head,
Should say: "That is not what I meant at all.
That is not it, at all."

And would it have been worth it, after all,
Would it have been worth while,

---

① malingers: pretends to be sick
② head... upon a platter: an allusion taken from The Bible. The head of the prophet John the Baptist, who was killed at the behest of Princess Salome, was brought to her on a platter (Matthew 14:1~11).
③ the eternal Footman: Death（死神）.
④ To have bitten off the matter: 解决这件事。
⑤ To have squeezed the universe into a ball/ To roll it towards some overwhelming question: Here is an allusion to Andrew Marvell's To His Coy Mistress: "Let us roll our strength and all/ Our sweetness up into one ball." The two lines indicate Prufrock's determination to gather enough courage to propose to a lady. 这两行意指鼓足勇气求婚。
⑥ Lazarus: a man who died but was then brought back to life by Jesus Christ (John 11: 1~44).

After the sunsets and dooryards and the sprinkled streets,
After the novels, after the teacups, after the skirts that trail along the floor—
And this, and so much more? —
It is impossible to say just what I mean!
But as if a magic lantern threw the nerves in patterns on a screen:①
Would it have been worth while
If one, settling a pillow or throwing off a shawl,
And turning toward the window, should say:
"That is not it at all,
That is not what I meant, at all."
...
No! I am not Prince Hamlet, nor was meant to be;②
Am an attendant lord, one that will do
To swell a progress,③ start a scene or two,
Advise the prince; no doubt, an easy tool,
Deferential, glad to be of use,
Politic, cautious, and meticulous;
Full of high sentence,④ but a bit obtuse;
At times, indeed, almost ridiculous—
Almost, at times, the Fool.⑤

I grow old...I grow old...
I shall wear the bottoms of my trousers rolled.

Shall I part my hair behind? Do I dare to eat a peach?
I shall wear white flannel trousers, and walk upon the beach.
I have heard the mermaids singing,⑥ each to each.

I do not think that they will sing to me.

---

① a magic lantern threw the nerves in patterns on a screen: 宛如有一盏幻灯把我的紧张像图案一般映射在银幕上。
② No! I am not Prince Hamlet, nor was meant to be: The speaker means that he is not and can not expect to be a great man like Hamlet.
③ To swell a progress: The speaker thinks of himself as an unimportant actor participating in a progress in a play. A progress: a ceremonial royal journey.
④ high sentence: worthy opinions（宏词博论）.
⑤ the Fool: referring to the fool as a character in Elizabethan drama, who is a clown.
⑥ I have heard the mermaids singing: 我曾听到美人鱼在歌唱。"the mermaids singing" 可能暗指希腊神话中的海妖塞壬（the sirens），据说塞壬们以美妙歌声诱使航海者驶向礁石或进入危险水域。塞壬是爱和恐惧相结合的象征。

I have seen them riding seaward on the waves
Combing the white hair of the waves blown back
When the wind blows the water white and black.
We have lingered in the chambers of the sea
By sea-girls wreathed with seaweed red and brown
Till human voices wake us, and we drown.[①]

1915, 1917

译文链接：https://qb.zuoyebang.com/xfe-question/question/91bfbbe13a18efd95b2ae07864466425.html

Questions for Understanding

1. The opening line of this poem goes like this: "Let us go then, you and I." Who is "you"?
2. What is the problem the speaker faces now? How does he deal with it?
3. What are the natural and social environments of the poem? Describe them.
4. Describe Prufrock's personality by giving specific details from the poem.
5. How does Eliot use the relationships between men and women to comment on society and culture? Why is this poem a "love song"?

Aspects of Appreciation

  1. This poem is an examination of the tortured psyche of the prototypical modern man—overeducated, eloquent, neurotic, and emotionally stilted. Prufrock, the poem's speaker, seems to be addressing a potential lover, with whom he would like to "force the moment to its crisis" by somehow consummating their relationship. But Prufrock knows too much of life to "dare" an approach to the woman: In his mind he hears the comments others make about his inadequacies, and he chides himself for "presuming" emotional interaction could be possible at all. The poem moves from a series of fairly concrete (for Eliot) physical settings—a cityscape (the famous "patient etherised upon a table") and several interiors (women's arms in the lamplight, coffee spoons,

---

[①] Till human voices wake us, and we drown: Here the speaker means that he feels frustrated and is drowned when he is brought back to reality from his wandering thoughts and visions. 直到人声将我们唤醒，于是我们溺水而亡。

fireplaces)—to a series of vague ocean images conveying Prufrock's emotional distance from the world as he comes to recognize his second-rate status ("I am not Prince Hamlet").

2. The poem is a variation of the dramatic monologue, a type of poem popular with Eliot's predecessors. Eliot modernizes the form by removing the implied listeners and focusing on Prufrock's interiority and isolation. The epigraph to this poem, from Dante's *Inferno,* describes Prufrock's ideal listener: one who is as lost as the speaker and will never betray to the world the content of Prufrock's present confessions. In the world Prufrock describes, though, no such sympathetic figure exists, and he must, therefore, be content with silent reflection.

3. The rhyme scheme of this poem is irregular but not random. While sections of the poem may resemble free verse, in reality, "Prufrock" is a carefully structured amalgamation of poetic forms. The bits and pieces of rhyme become much more apparent when the poem is read aloud. One of the most prominent formal characteristics of this work is the use of refrains. Prufrock's continual return to the "women [who] come and go / Talking of Michelangelo" , his recurrent questionings ("how should I presume?") and pessimistic appraisals ("That is not it, at all.") reference an earlier poetic tradition and help Eliot describe the consciousness of a modern, neurotic individual. Prufrock's obsessiveness is aesthetic, but it is also a sign of compulsiveness and isolation. Another important formal feature is the use of fragments of sonnet form, particularly at the poem's conclusion. The three three-line stanzas are rhymed as the conclusion of a Petrarchan sonnet would be, but their pessimistic, anti-romantic content, coupled with the despairing interjection, "I do not think they (the mermaids) would sing to me," creates a contrast that comments bitterly on the bleakness of modernity.

4. Over the course of Eliot's life, gender roles and sexuality became increasingly flexible, and Eliot reflected those changes in his work. He simultaneously lauded the end of the Victorian era and expressed concern about the freedoms brought by the modern age. "The Love Song of J. Alfred Prufrock" reflects the feelings of emasculation experienced by many men as they returned home from World War I to find women empowered by their new role as wage earners. Prufrock, unable to make a decision, watches women wander in and out of a room, "talking of Michelangelo", and elsewhere admires their downy, bare arms.

Suggested Further Reading

Poems: *The Waste Land* (1922); *Four Quartets* (1943).
Plays: *Murder in the Cathedral* (1935); *The Cocktail Party* (1950).

Topics for Further Study

1. In Eliot's poetry, water symbolizes both life and death. Although water has the regenerative possibility of restoring life and fertility, it can also lead to drowning and death. Please cite some examples to illustrate.

2. Like most modernist writers, Eliot was interested in using music symbolically. Cite examples from "The Love Song of J. Alfred Prufrock" to prove this.

Knowledge of Literature

1. Dramatic Monologue（戏剧独白）

Dramatic monologues are similar to soliloquies in plays. Three things characterize the dramatic monologue, according to M.H. Abrams. First, they are the utterances of a specific individual (not the poet) at a specific moment in time. Secondly, the monologue is specifically directed at a listener or listeners whose presence is not directly referenced but is merely suggested in the speaker's words. Third, the primary focus is the development and revelation of the speaker's character. Dramatic monologue was perfected by Robert Browning (1812~1889) as represented in his "My Last Duchess". The best-known modern instance is T. S. Eliot's "The Love Song of J. Alfred Prufrock".

2. Refrain（叠句）

A repeated word, phrase, line, or group of lines, normally at some fixed position in a poem written in a stanzaic form.

3. Petrarchan Sonnet（彼特拉克十四行诗）

The Petrarchan sonnet (named after the fourteenth-century Italian poet Petrarch) falls into two main parts: an octave (eight lines) rhyming *abbaabba* followed by a sestet (six lines) rhyming *cdecde* or some variant, such as *cdccdc*. Petrarch's sonnets were first imitated in England, both in their stanza form and their subjects—the hopes and pains of an adoring male lover—by Sir Thomas Wyatt in the early sixteenth century. The Petrarchan form was later used, and for a variety of subjects, by Milton, Wordsworth, Christina Rossetti, D. G. Rossetti, and other sonneteers, who sometimes made it technically easier in English by introducing a new pair of rhymes in the second lines of the octave.

4. Elements of Poetry: Theme and Diction（主旨与措辞）

Theme

The theme of a poem is its total meaning, which is nothing less than the total experience the reader gets from reading the poem. It is embodied and dramatized in the evolving meanings and imagery.

Diction

Diction refers to the poet's choice of words. Poets like words, sometimes unusual words—slang, profanity, archaisms, foreign language words, made-up words, which can add different qualities and meanings to poems. They are sensitive to the subtle shades and levels of meanings of words, to the possible double or multiple meanings of words, and to the denotative and connotative meanings of words. They like to choose words that contribute to poems' meanings.

推荐阅读的论文：

[1] 凌越，许庆红. 艾略特的诗歌创作与批评理论的互动——论《J·阿尔弗雷德·普罗弗洛克的情歌》[J]. 安徽理工大学学报(社会科学版)，2015, 17(02).

[2] 赵平，丁建江. 英语诗的遣词探究 [J]. 淮海工学院学报（人文社会科学版），2004(03).

Robert Frost (1874~1963)

About the Author

Robert Frost is considered the quintessential New England poet, but he spent the first eleven years of his life in San Francisco. Only upon the death of Frost's father did the family go to live with relatives in Lawrence, Massachusetts. There, Frost excelled in high school. Occasional attendance at Dartmouth College and Harvard, and a variety of different jobs including an attempt to run a farm in Derry, New Hampshire, marked the next twenty years. Frost and his fanily moved to England in 1912. There he worked on his poetry and found a publisher for his first book, *A Boy's Will* (1913). Pound recommended Frost's poems to American editors and helped get his second book, *North of Boston,* published in 1914. The favorable reception persuaded Frost to return home. He bought another farm in New Hampshire and prospered financially through sales of his books and papers, along with teaching and lecturing at various colleges. His later books include *Mountain Interval* (1916), *New Hampshire* (1923), and *West-Running Brook* (1928).

The clarity of Frost's diction, the colloquial rhythms, the simplicity of his images, and above all the folksy speaker—these are intended to make the poems look natural and unplanned. He achieved an internal dynamic in his poems by employing the rhythms of ordinary speech to replace formal patterns of line and verse and containing them within traditional forms. The interaction of colloquial diction with blank verse is especially central to his dramatic monologue. Most of his poems fall into a few types—nature lyrics describing and commenting on a scene or event, dramatic narratives in blank verse about the grieves of country people, and humorous or sardonic poems.

Frost was the most widely admired and highly honoured American poet of the 20th century. Amy Lowell thought he had over-stressed the dark aspects of New England life, but Frost's later flood of more uniformly optimistic verses made that view seem antiquated. Louis Untermeyer's judgment that the dramatic poems in *North of Boston* were the most authentic and powerful of their kind ever produced by an American has only been confirmed by later opinions. Gradually, Frost's name ceased to be linked solely with New England, and he gained broad acceptance as a national poet.

It is true that certain criticisms of Frost have never been wholly refuted, one being that he is overly interested in the past, and another that he is too little concerned with the present and future of American society. Those who criticize Frost's detachment from the "modern" emphasize the undeniable absence in his poems of meaningful references to the modern realities of industrialization, urbanization and the concentration of wealth, or to such familiar items as radios, motion pictures, automobiles, factories or skyscrapers. The poet has been viewed as a singer of sweet nostalgia and a social and political conservative who was content to sigh for the good things of the past.

Such views have failed to gain general acceptance, however, in the face of the universality of Frost's themes, the emotional authenticity of his voice, and the austere technical brilliance of his verse. Frost was often able to endow his rural imagery with a larger symbolic or metaphysical significance, and his best poems transcend the immediate realities of their subject matter to illuminate the unique blend of tragic endurance, stoicism, and tenacious affirmation that marked his outlook on life. Over his long career Frost succeeded in lodging more than a few poems where, as he put it, they would be "hard to get rid of", and he can be said to have lodged himself just as solidly in the affections of his fellow Americans. For thousands he remains the only recent poet worth reading and the only one who matters.

The Road Not Taken

About the Poem

This poem was written in 1915 and first appeared in *Mountain Interval* in 1916. By then, Frost had established his reputation as a poet in Britain. The poem is set in the forest but it really can be anywhere and anytime. When one faces two roads, one must make a choice: which way to go. Frost turned this universal dilemma into a poem of a conventional style: classic five-line stanzas with the rhyme scheme of *abaab*.

The Road Not Taken

Two roads diverged in a yellow wood,
And sorry I could not travel both
And be one traveler, long I stood
And looked down one as far as I could
To where it bent in the undergrowth;

Then took the other, as just as fair,[①]
And having perhaps the better claim,
Because it was grassy and wanted wear;[②]
Though as for that, the passing there
Had worn[③] them really about the same,

And both[④] that morning equally lay
In leaves no step had trodden black.
Oh, I kept the first for another day!
Yet knowing how way leads on to way,[⑤]
I doubted if I should ever come back.

I shall be telling this with a sigh
Somewhere ages and ages hence:
Two roads diverged in a wood, and I—

---

① as just as fair: 既合适又平坦。
② wanted wear: 踩踏得较少。want 的意思相当于 lack。
③ Had worn: would have worn.
④ both: the two roads mentioned above.
⑤ way leads on to way: there is no end in one's way of pursuit.

I took the one less traveled by,
And that has made all the difference.

译文链接: https://www.douban.com/group/topic/90477394/?i=6776344-3lxHou

Questions for Understanding

1. What is the theme of the poem?
2. The speaker says "I shall be telling this with a sigh." Why with "a sigh?"
3. Laurence Perrine sees the poem as "an expression of regret that one's ability to explore different life possibilities is so limited. It comes from a man who loves life and thirsts after more of it". What details in the poem support such an interpretation?

Aspects of Appreciation

1. "The Road Not Taken" consists of four stanzas of five lines. The rhyme scheme is *abaab*; the rhymes are strict and masculine, with the notable exception of the last line (usually we do not stress the *-ence* of *difference*). There are four stressed syllables per line, varying on an iambic tetrameter base.

2. One of the attractions of the poem is its archetypal dilemma, one that we instantly recognize because each of us encounters it innumerable times, both literally and figuratively. Paths in the woods and forks in roads are ancient and deep-seated metaphors for the lifeline, its crises and decisions. Identical forks, in particular, symbolize for us the nexus of free will and fate: We are free to choose, but we do not really know beforehand what we are choosing between. Our route is, thus, determined by an accretion of choice and chance, and it is impossible to separate the two.

3. This poem does not advise. It does not say, "When you come to a fork in the road, study the footprints and take the road less traveled by". Frost's focus is more complicated. First, there is no less-traveled road in this poem; it isn't even an option. Next, the poem seems more concerned with the question of how the concrete present (yellow woods, grassy roads covered in fallen leaves) will look from a future vantage point.

Mending Wall

About the Poem

This poem describes the scene of two neighbors mending the wall in spring that separates their farms. The speaker is open-minded and dislikes walls. But his neighbor follows the conventional concept: Good fences make good neighbors. In fact, the wall stands for everything that alienates one person from another. This poem is written in blank verse, with five beats to a line, and the stress falls on every second syllable. And the lines do not rhyme.

Mending Wall

Something① there is that doesn't love a wall,
That sends the frozen-ground-swell② under it,
And spills the upper boulders③ in the sun,
And makes gaps even two can pass abreast.
The work of hunters is another thing:
I have come after them and made repair
Where they have left not one stone on a stone,④
But they would have the rabbit out of hiding,
To please the yelping dogs. The gaps I mean,
No one has seen them made or heard them made,
But at spring mending-time we find them there.
I let my neighbor know beyond the hill;
And on a day we meet to walk the line⑤
And set the wall between us once again.
We keep the wall between us as we go.⑥
To each the boulders that have fallen to each.⑦
And some are loaves and some so nearly balls⑧

---

① Something: referring to Nature or "Elves"(line 36).
② frozen-ground-swell: 冻地膨胀。
③ spills the upper boulders: makes the upper stones fall down.
④ left not one stone on a stone: 把石头掀得乱七八糟。
⑤ walk the line: walk along the boundary.
⑥ We keep the wall between us as we go: We go on either side of the wall.
⑦ To each the boulders that have fallen to each: Each person must deal with the stones that have fallen on his side.
⑧ some are loaves and some so nearly balls: 有些石头像长面包，有些似球状。

We have to use a spell① to make them balance:
"Stay where you are until our backs are turned!"
We wear our fingers rough with handling them.
Oh, just another kind of outdoor game,
One on a side. It comes to little more:
There where it is we do not need the wall:
He is all pine and I am apple orchard.②
My apple trees will never get across
And eat the cones under his pines, I tell him.
He only says, "Good fences make good neighbors."
Spring is the mischief in me, and I wonder
If I could put a notion in his head:
"*Why* do they make good neighbors? Isn't it
Where there are cows? But here there are no cows.
Before I built a wall I'd ask to know
What I was walling in or walling out,
And to whom I was like③ to give offense.
Something there is that doesn't love a wall,
That wants it down." I could say "Elves" to him,④
But it's not elves exactly, and I'd rather
He said it for himself. I see him there
Bringing a stone grasped firmly by the top
In each hand, like an old-stone savage⑤ armed.
He moves in darkness as it seems to me,
Not of woods only and the shade of trees.
He will not go behind his father's saying,
And he likes having thought of it so well
He says again, "Good fences make good neighbors."

译文链接：https://www.51test.net/show/2628168.html

---

① spell: 可以理解为"a period of time"，即把石头重新垒好需要一段时间；也可以理解为"magical power"或"magic words"，即这些石头什么形状的都有，很难垒，需要施某种魔力或念咒语才能完成。是一种诙谐的说法。
② He is all pine and I am apple orchard: He grows pine trees and I apple trees.
③ like: likely.
④ I could say "Elves" to him: I could tell him that it must be the "Elves" who had damaged the wall.
⑤ an old-stone savage: an uncivilized man of the Old Stone Age.

Questions for Understanding

1. What is the speaker's attitude towards the wall? And what is his neighbor's?
2. What does the speaker think of the neighbor? In what sense does he "move in darkness"?
3. What is the tone of the poem? How is it achieved?

Aspects of Appreciation

1. Blank verse is the baseline meter of this poem, but few of the lines march along in blank verse's characteristic lock-step iambs, five abreast. Frost maintains five stressed syllables per line, but he varies the feet extensively to sustain the natural speech-like quality of the verse. There are no stanza breaks, obvious end-rhymes, or rhyming patterns, but many of the end-words share an assonance. Internal rhymes, too, are subtle, slant, and conceivably coincidental. The vocabulary is all of a piece—no fancy words, all short (only one word, *another*, has three syllables), all conversational—and this is perhaps why the words resonate so consummately with each other in sound and feel.

2. The image at the heart of "Mending Wall" is arresting: two men meeting in terms of civility and neighborliness to build a barrier between them. They do so out of tradition, or out of habit. Yet the very earth conspires against them and makes their task Sisyphean. Sisyphus, you may recall, is the figure in Greek mythology condemned perpetually to push a boulder up a hill, only to have the boulder roll down again. These men push boulders back on top of the wall; yet just as inevitably, whether at the hand of hunters or sprites, or because of the frost and thaw of nature the boulders tumble down again. Still, the neighbors persist. The poem, thus, seems to meditate conventionally on three grand themes: barrier-building (segregation, in the broadest sense of the word), the doomed nature of this enterprise, and our persistence in this activity regardless.

Suggested Further Reading

"Mowing" (1913); "After Apple-picking" (1915); "Stopping by Woods on a Snowy Evening" (1923); "Fire and Ice" (1923); "Design" (1936); "Birches" (1916).

Topics for Further Study

1. Pressed in an interview to say where he stood on the issue of fences, Frost once said, "Maybe I was both fellows in the poem." What do you think he meant? Can you find any evidence from the poem?

2. Many of Frost's poems can be reasonably interpreted as commenting on the creative process; "Mending Wall" is no exception. On the basic level, we can find here a discussion of the construction-disruption duality of creativity. Creation is a positive act—a mending or a building. Even the most destructive-seeming creativity results in a change, the building of some new state of being: If you tear down an edifice, you create a new view for the folks living in the house across the way. Yet creation is also disruptive: If nothing else, it disrupts the status quo. Stated another way, disruption is creative: It is the impetus that leads directly and mysteriously (as with the groundswells) to creation. Does the stone wall embody this duality? In any case, there is something about "walking the line"—and building it, mending it, balancing each stone with equal skill and spell—that evokes the mysterious and laborious act of making poetry. Give some other examples to further illustrate this point.

Knowledge of Literature

1. Blank verse（无韵诗 / 素体诗）

Blank verse consists of lines of iambic pentameter (five-stress iambic verse) which are unrhymed—hence the term "blank." Of all English metrical forms it is closest to the natural rhythms of English speech, and at the same time flexible and adaptive to diverse levels of discourse. As a result, it has been more frequently and variously used than any other type of versification.

2. An Element of Poetry: Figures of Speech（修辞手法）

Figures of speech, widely used in poetry, are the various uses of language that depart from customary construction, order, or significance in order to achieve special effects or meanings. The most commonly employed figures of speech include simile, metaphor, metonymy, synecdoche, personification, apostrophe, hyperbole(overstatement), understatement, paradox, pun, irony, oxymoron, synesthesia, empathy, transferred epithet, rhetorical repetition, climax, anticlimax, euphemism and antithesis.

推荐阅读的论文：
[1] 娄崇《未选择的路》的艺术特色解读 [J]. 忻州师范学院学报，2012 (6).
[2] 戴新蕾. 始于欢愉，止于智慧——罗伯特·佛洛斯特诗歌语言艺术之探究 [J].

长沙大学学报，2010 (4).

F. Scott Fitzgerald (1896~1940)

About the Author

Best known for his celebrated novel *The Great Gatsby* (1925), F. Scott Fitzgerald wrote over 150 short stories, some of which are among the finest of the 20th century. Born in St. Paul, Minnesota, Fitzgerald was the only child in a financially unstable family. Though he attended private high school with the help of his aunt, he always felt like an outsider, excluded from the elite society to which he aspired. At Princeton University, he received encouragement as a writer, producing several stories that earned him critical attention. At twenty-two, he met the popular and glamorous Zelda Sayre, about whom he wrote in his journal, "Fell in love on the 7th". Motivated by Zelda's refusal to marry him because he lacked money, Fitzgerald sold his first novel, *This Side of Paradise* (1920), and several stories. With his sudden literary success, he and Zelda married in 1920 and embarked on the extravagant, high-profile lifestyle that made them one of America's most famous couples. For several years Scott and Zelda Fitzgerald were the darlings of the "Jazz Age"—the name that he gave to the 1920s. During the twenties, his stories appeared in the *Saturday Evening Post* and *Scribner's*, and were collected in *Flappers and Philosophers* (1920), *Tales of the Jazz Age* (1922), and *All the Sad Young Men* (1926). Fitzgerald's masterpiece, *The Great Gatsby*, was published in 1925, but from that point on his life and career became increasingly troubled. *Tender Is the Night* (1934) reflects the tragedy of Zelda's breakdown. During this time, Fitzgerald worked to support her and their daughter Scottie, though he suffered from alcoholism and breakdowns of his own. His experiences as a Hollywood screenwriter were the source materials for *The Last Tycoon,* which, though unfinished at Fitzgerald's death, was published posthumously in 1941. He died of a heart attack at forty-four.

The 1920s proved the most influential decade of Fitzgerald's development. Fitzgerald made several excursions to Europe, notably Paris and the French Riviera, and became friends with many members of the American expatriate community in Paris, notably Ernest Hemingway.

Fitzgerald's friendship with Hemingway was quite vigorous, as many of Fitzgerald's relationships would prove to be. Hemingway did not get on well with Zelda. In addition to describing her as "insane", he claimed that she "encouraged her husband to drink so as to distract Scott from his 'real' work on his novel". Fitzgerald claimed that he would first write his stories in an authentic manner but then put in "twists that made them into saleable magazine stories".

The Great Gatsby

About the novel

This novel tells of Gatsby, who tries to recapture his lost love but in vain and is finally ruined by the wealthy people around him. The story deals symbolically with the failure of the American dream as personified in the beautiful and rich woman Daisy who belongs to a corrupt society. The author mainly uses the first-person narrator Nick Carraway to observe and comment on what goes on in the novel, and his responses form a sort of subplot because he is a participant and an observer as well. The following selection is the last chapter of the novel. Nick stages a small funeral for Gatsby, ends his relationship with Jordan, moves back to the Midwest, and reflects on Gatsby's dream as well as the American dream.

Chapter 9

After two years I[①] remember the rest of that day, and that night and the next day, only as an endless drill of police and photographers and newspaper men in and out of Gatsby's front door. A rope stretched across the main gate and a policeman by it kept out the curious, but little boys soon discovered that they could enter through my yard, and there were always a few of them clustered open-mouthed about the pool. Someone with a positive manner, perhaps a detective, used the expression "madman" as he bent over Wilson's[②] body that afternoon, and the adventitious authority of his voice set the key for the newspaper reports next morning.

Most of those reports were a nightmare—grotesque, circumstantial, eager, and untrue. When Michaelis's[③] testimony at the inquest brought to light Wilson's suspicions of his wife I thought the whole tale would shortly be served up in racy pasquinade—but Catherine,[④] who might have said anything, didn't say a word. She showed a surprising amount of character about it too—looked at the coroner with determined eyes under that corrected brow of hers, and swore that her sister had never

---

① I: referring to the story's narrator Nick Caraway.
② Wilson: George Wilson. 此人经营一家汽车修理铺。其妻默特尔（Myrtle）因车祸丧生后，他听信妻子的情人汤姆（Tom）的谎言，以为盖茨比（Gatsby）是肇事者。杀死盖茨比后，他自尽了。
③ Michaelis: the neighbor of George Wilson. 此人目睹了威尔逊的妻子被汽车碾死的情景。
④ Catherine: Myrtle's younger sister.

seen Gatsby, that her sister was completely happy with her husband, that her sister had been into no mischief whatever. She convinced herself of it, and cried into her handkerchief, as if the very suggestion was more than she could endure. So Wilson was reduced to a man "deranged by grief" in order that the case might remain in its simplest form. And it rested there.

But all this part of it seemed remote and unessential. I found myself on Gatsby's side, and alone. From the moment I telephoned news of the catastrophe to West Egg village,① every surmise about him, and every practical question, was referred to me. At first I was surprised and confused; then, as he lay in his house and didn't move or breathe or speak, hour upon hour, it grew upon me that I was responsible, because no one else was interested—interested, I mean, with that intense personal interest to which every one has some vague right at the end.

I called up Daisy② half an hour after we found him, called her instinctively and without hesitation. But she and Tom③ had gone away early that afternoon, and taken baggage with them.

"Left no address?"

"No."

"Say when they'd be back?"

"No."

"Any idea where they are? How I could reach them?"

"I don't know. Can't say."

I wanted to get somebody for him. I wanted to go into the room where he lay and reassure him: "I'll get somebody for you, Gatsby. Don't worry. Just trust me and I'll get somebody for you—"

Meyer Wolfshiem's④ name wasn't in the phone book. The butler gave me his office address on Broadway, and I called Information,⑤ but by the time I had the number it was long after five, and no one answered the phone.

"Will you ring again?"

"I've rung them three times."

"It's very important."

"Sorry. I'm afraid no one's there."

I went back to the drawing-room and thought for an instant that they were chance

---

① West Egg village: 西卵村，虚构的地名，是 Gatsby 和 Nick Carraway 居住的地方。
② Daisy: 黛西，汤姆的妻子，曾经是盖茨比的恋人。
③ Tom: 即汤姆·布坎南（Tom Buchanan），黛西的丈夫。
④ Meyer Wolfshiem: 梅耶·沃夫希姆，盖茨比做非法生意的伙伴。
⑤ Information: an information desk（问讯处）。

visitors, all these official people who suddenly filled it. But, though they drew back the sheet and looked at Gatsby with shocked eyes, his protest continued in my brain:

"Look here, old sport, you've got to get somebody for me. You've got to try hard. I can't go through this alone."

Someone started to ask me questions, but I broke away and going upstairs looked hastily through the unlocked parts of his desk—he'd never told me definitely that his parents were dead. But there was nothing—only the picture of Dan Cody,① a token of forgotten violence, staring down from the wall.

Next morning I sent the butler to New York with a letter to Wolfshiem, which asked for information and urged him to come out on the next train. That request seemed superfluous when I wrote it. I was sure he'd start when he saw the newspapers, just as I was sure there'd be a wire from Daisy before noon—but neither a wire nor Mr. Wolfshiem arrived; no one arrived except more police and photographers and newspaper men. When the butler brought back Wolfshiem's answer I began to have a feeling of defiance, of scornful solidarity between Gatsby and me against them all.

DEAR MR. CARRAWAY
This has been one of the most terrible shocks of my life to me I hardly can believe it that it is true at all. Such a mad act as that man did should make us all think. I cannot come down now as I am tied up in some very important business and cannot get mixed up in this thing now. If there is anything I can do a little later let me know in a letter by Edgar. I hardly know where I am when I hear about a thing like this and am completely knocked down and out.
Yours truly
MEYER WOLFSHIEM

and then hasty addenda beneath:
Let me know about the funeral etc. do not know his family at all.

When the phone rang that afternoon and Long Distance said Chicago was calling I thought this would be Daisy at last. But the connection came through as a man's voice, very thin and far away.

"This is Slagle② speaking…"

"Yes?" The name was unfamiliar.

---

① Dan Cody: 丹·科迪，小说中一个从未露面的人，靠开发金矿起家。盖茨比年轻时曾在他手下工作过。
② Slagle: 斯莱格，盖茨比做非法生意的伙伴。

"Hell of[①] a note, isn't it? Get my wire?"

"There haven't been any wires."

"Young Parke's[②] in trouble," he said rapidly. "They picked him up when he handed the bonds over the counter. They got a circular from New York giving 'em the numbers just five minutes before. What d'you know about that, hey? You never can tell in these hick towns—"

"Hello!" I interrupted breathlessly. "Look here—this isn't Mr. Gatsby. Mr. Gatsby's dead."

There was a long silence on the other end of the wire, followed by an exclamation…then a quick squawk as the connection was broken.

I think it was on the third day that a telegram signed Henry C. Gatz arrived from a town in Minnesota. It said only that the sender was leaving immediately and to postpone the funeral until he came.

It was Gatsby's father, a solemn old man, very helpless and dismayed, bundled up in a long cheap ulster[③] against the warm September day. His eyes leaked continuously with excitement, and when I took the bag and umbrella from his hands he began to pull so incessantly at his sparse grey beard that I had difficulty in getting off his coat. He was on the point of collapse, so I took him into the music room and made him sit down while I sent for something to eat. But he wouldn't eat, and the glass of milk spilled from his trembling hand.

"I saw it in the Chicago newspaper," he said. "It was all in the Chicago newspaper. I started right away."

"I didn't know how to reach you."

His eyes, seeing nothing, moved ceaselessly about the room.

"It was a madman," he said. "He must have been mad."

"Wouldn't you like some coffee?" I urged him.

"I don't want anything. I'm all right now, Mr.—"

"Carraway."

"Well, I'm all right now. Where have they got Jimmy?"

I took him into the drawing-room, where his son lay, and left him there. Some little boys had come up on the steps and were looking into the hall; when I told them who had arrived, they went reluctantly away.

After a little while Mr. Gatz opened the door and came out, his mouth ajar, his

---

① Hell of: 用于口语中，表示强调。
② Parke: 帕克，盖茨比做非法生意的伙伴。
③ ulster: 有腰带、厚重的男士大衣。

face flushed slightly, his eyes leaking isolated and unpunctual tears. He had reached an age where death no longer has the quality of ghastly surprise, and when he looked around him now for the first time and saw the height and splendor of the hall and the great rooms opening out from it into other rooms, his grief began to be mixed with an awed pride. I helped him to a bedroom upstairs; while he took off his coat and vest I told him that all arrangements had been deferred until he came.

"I didn't know what you'd want, Mr. Gatsby—"

"Gatz is my name."

"—Mr. Gatz. I thought you might want to take the body West."

He shook his head.

"Jimmy always liked it better down East. He rose up to his position in the East. Were you a friend of my boy's, Mr.—?"

"We were close friends."

"He had a big future before him, you know. He was only a young man, but he had a lot of brain power here."

He touched his head impressively, and I nodded.

"If he'd of lived, he'd of been a great man.[①] A man like James J. Hill.[②] He'd of helped build up the country."

"That's true," I said, uncomfortably.

He fumbled at the embroidered coverlet, trying to take it from the bed, and lay down stiffly—was instantly asleep.

That night an obviously frightened person called up, and demanded to know who I was before he would give his name.

"This is Mr. Carraway," I said.

"Oh!" He sounded relieved. "This is Klipspringer."[③]

I was relieved too, for that seemed to promise another friend at Gatsby's grave. I didn't want it to be in the papers and draw a sightseeing crowd, so I'd been calling up a few people myself. They were hard to find.

"The funeral's tomorrow," I said. "Three o'clock, here at the house. I wish you'd tell anybody who'd be interested."

"Oh, I will," he broke out hastily. "Of course I'm not likely to see anybody, but if I do."

His tone made me suspicious.

---

① If he'd of lived, he'd of been a great man: If he'd lived, he'd have been a great man. 不合语法的语句，说话人可能受教育程度不高。
② James J. Hill: 詹姆斯·J·希尔（1838-1916），白手起家的铁路大王，14岁就投身商海，成为亿万富翁。
③ Klipspringer: 一个经常到盖茨比家长住的寄宿者。

"Of course you'll be there yourself."

"Well, I'll certainly try. What I called up about is—"

"Wait a minute," I interrupted. "How about saying you'll come?"

"Well, the fact is—the truth of the matter is that I'm staying with some people up here in Greenwich,① and they rather expect me to be with them tomorrow. In fact, there's a sort of picnic or something. Of course I'll do my very best to get away."

I ejaculated an unrestrained "Huh!" and he must have heard me, for he went on nervously:

"What I called up about was a pair of shoes I left there. I wonder if it'd be too much trouble to have the butler send them on. You see, they're tennis shoes, and I'm sort of helpless without them. My address is care of B. F.—"

I didn't hear the rest of the name, because I hung up the receiver.

After that I felt a certain shame for Gatsby—one gentleman to whom I telephoned implied that he had got what he deserved. However, that was my fault, for he was one of those who used to sneer most bitterly at Gatsby on the courage of Gatsby's liquor, and I should have known better than to call him.

The morning of the funeral I went up to New York to see Meyer Wolfshiem; I couldn't seem to reach him any other way. The door that I pushed open, on the advice of an elevator boy, was marked "The Swastika Holding Company", and at first there didn't seem to be anyone inside. But when I'd shouted "hello" several times in vain, an argument broke out behind a partition, and presently a lovely Jewess appeared at an interior door and scrutinized me with black hostile eyes.

"Nobody's in," she said. "Mr. Wolfshiem's gone to Chicago."

The first part of this was obviously untrue, for someone had begun to whistle "The Rosary", tunelessly, inside.

"Please say that Mr. Carraway wants to see him."

"I can't get him back from Chicago, can I?"

At this moment a voice, unmistakably Wolfshiem's, called "Stella!" from the other side of the door.

"Leave your name on the desk," she said quickly. "I'll give it to him when he gets back."

"But I know he's there."

She took a step toward me and began to slide her hands indignantly up and down her hips.

"You young men think you can force your way in here any time," she scolded.

---

① Greenwich: 格林尼治市，位于美国康涅狄格州西南部。

"We're getting sickantired[①] of it. When I say he's in Chicago, he's in Chicago."

I mentioned Gatsby.

"Oh—h!" She looked at me over again. "Will you just—What was your name?"

She vanished. In a moment Meyer Wolfshiem stood solemnly in the doorway, holding out both hands. He drew me into his office, remarking in a reverent voice that it was a sad time for all of us, and offered me a cigar.

"My memory goes back to when first I met him," he said. "A young major just out of the army and covered over with medals he got in the war. He was so hard up he had to keep on wearing his uniform because he couldn't buy some regular clothes. First time I saw him was when he came into Winebrenner's poolroom at Forty-third Street and asked for a job. He hadn't eat[②] anything for a couple of days. 'Come on have some lunch with me,' I said. He ate more than four dollars' worth of food in half an hour."

"Did you start him in business?" I inquired.

"Start him! I made him."

"Oh."

"I raised him up out of nothing, right out of the gutter. I saw right away he was a fine-appearing, gentlemanly young man, and when he told me he was an Oggsford[③] I knew I could use him good. I got him to join up in the American Legion[④] and he used to stand high there. Right off he did some work for a client of mine up to Albany. We were so thick like that in everything"—he held up two bulbous fingers—"always together."

I wondered if this partnership had included the World's Series transaction in 1919[⑤].

"Now he's dead," I said after a moment. "You were his closest friend, so I know you'll want to come to his funeral this afternoon."

"I'd like to come."

"Well, come then."

The hair in his nostrils quivered slightly, and as he shook his head his eyes filled with tears.

"I can't do it—I can't get mixed up in it," he said.

"There's nothing to get mixed up in. It's all over now."

---

① sickantired: 口语中 sick and tired 的缩写。sick and tired of(口): 腻味透了。
② He hadn't eat…: =He hadn't eaten… 沃夫希姆是欧洲移民，说话时常有语言错误。
③ an Oggsford: 应为 an Oxford。沃夫希姆不会发 x 的音。
④ American Legion: 美国退伍军人协会。
⑤ the World's Series transaction in 1919: 1919 年世界棒球赛的那项交易。在小说的第四章中，盖茨比曾对尼克说，沃夫希姆操纵过 1919 年的世界棒球赛。

"When a man gets killed I never like to get mixed up in it in any way. I keep out. When I was a young man it was different—if a friend of mine died, no matter how, I stuck with them to the end. You may think that's sentimental, but I mean it—to the bitter end."

I saw that for some reason of his own he was determined not to come, so I stood up.

"Are you a college man?" He inquired suddenly.

For a moment I thought he was going to suggest a "gonnegtion"①, but he only nodded and shook my hand.

"Let us learn to show our friendship for a man when he is alive and not after he is dead," he suggested. "After that my own rule is to let everything alone."

When I left his office the sky had turned dark and I got back to West Egg in a drizzle. After changing my clothes I went next door and found Mr. Gatz walking up and down excitedly in the hall. His pride in his son and in his son's possessions was continually increasing and now he had something to show me.

"Jimmy sent me this picture." He took out his wallet with trembling fingers. "Look there."

It was a photograph of the house, cracked in the corners and dirty with many hands. He pointed out every detail to me eagerly. "Look there!" and then sought admiration from my eyes. He had shown it so often that I think it was more real to him now than the house itself.

"Jimmy sent it to me. I think it's a very pretty picture. It shows up well."

"Very well. Had you seen him lately?"

"He come out② to see me two years ago and bought me the house I live in now. Of course we was broke up when he run off from home,③ but I see now there was a reason for it. He knew he had a big future in front of him. And ever since he made a success he was very generous with me."

He seemed reluctant to put away the picture, held it for another minute, lingeringly, before my eyes. Then he returned the wallet and pulled from his pocket a ragged old copy of a book called *Hopalong Cassidy*④.

"Look here, this is a book he had when he was a boy. It just shows you."

He opened it at the back cover and turned it around for me to see. On the last

---

① gonnegtion:（应为）connection.
② He come out…:（应为）He came out…
③ Of course we was broke up when he run off from home:（应为）Of course we were broken up when he ran off from home.
④ Hopalong Cassidy: 一部反映美国西部牛仔生活的小说，作者是 Clarence E. Mulford, 此小说的主人公就叫 Hopalong Cassidy。

fly-leaf was printed the word SCHEDULE①, and the date September 12, 1906. And underneath:

Rise from bed	6:00	A.M.
Dumbbell exercise and wall-scaling	6:15-6:30	..
Study electricity, etc.	7:15-8:15	..
Work	8:30-4:30	P.M.
Baseball and sports	4:30-5:00	..
Practice elocution, poise and how to attain it	5:00-6:00	..
Study needed inventions	7:00-9:00	..

GENERAL RESOLVES
No wasting time at Shafters or [a name, indecipherable]
No more smokeing② or chewing
Bath every other day
Read one improving book or magazine per week
Save $5.00 [crossed out] $3.00 per week
Be better to parents

"I come across③ this book by accident," said the old man. "It just shows you, don't it?"

"It just shows you."

"Jimmy was bound to get ahead. He always had some resolves like this or something. Do you notice what he's got about improving his mind? He was always great for that. He told me I et④ like a hog once, and I beat him for it."

He was reluctant to close the book, reading each item aloud and then looking eagerly at me. I think he rather expected me to copy down the list for my own use.

A little before three the Lutheran⑤ minister arrived from Flushing, and I began to look involuntarily out the windows for other cars. So did Gatsby's father. And as the time passed and the servants came in and stood waiting in the hall, his eyes began to blink anxiously, and he spoke of the rain in a worried, uncertain way. The minister glanced several times at his watch, so I took him aside and asked him to wait for half

---

① SCHEDULE: 作息时间表。它很像本杰明·富兰克林《自传》中的作息时间表。盖茨比的故事表明，富兰克林一生所体现的美国梦在盖茨比时代已不可能实现。
② smokeing:（应为）smoking.
③ come across:（应为）came across.
④ et:（应为）ate.
⑤ Lutheran: 路德教派的。

an hour. But it wasn't any use. Nobody came.

About five o'clock our procession of three cars reached the cemetery and stopped in a thick drizzle beside the gate—first a motor hearse, horribly black and wet, then Mr. Gatz and the minister and I in the limousine, and a little later four or five servants and the postman from West Egg in Gatsby's station wagon, all wet to the skin. As we started through the gate into the cemetery I heard a car stop and then the sound of someone splashing after us over the soggy ground. I looked around. It was the man with owl-eyed glasses① whom I had found marvelling over Gatsby's books in the library one night three months before.

I'd never seen him since then. I don't know how he knew about the funeral, or even his name. The rain poured down his thick glasses, and he took them off and wiped them to see the protecting canvas unrolled from Gatsby's grave.

I tried to think about Gatsby then for a moment, but he was already too far away, and I could only remember, without resentment, that Daisy hadn't sent a message or a flower. Dimly I heard someone murmur, "Blessed are the dead that the rain falls on," and then the owl-eyed man said "Amen to that", in a brave voice.

We straggled down quickly through the rain to the cars. Owl-eyes spoke to me by the gate.

"I couldn't get to the house," he remarked.

"Neither could anybody else."

"Go on!" He started. "Why, my God! They used to go there by the hundreds."

He took off his glasses and wiped them again, outside and in.

"The poor son-of-a-bitch," he said.

One of my most vivid memories is of coming back West from prep school and later from college at Christmas time. Those who went farther than Chicago would gather in the old dim Union Station at six o'clock of a December evening, with a few Chicago friends, already caught up into their own holiday gaieties, to bid them a hasty good-bye. I remember the fur coats of the girls returning from Miss This-or-That's② and the chatter of frozen breath and the hands waving overhead as we caught sight of old acquaintances, and the matchings of invitations: "Are you going to the Ordways'? The Herseys'? The Schultzes'?" And the long green tickets clasped tight in our gloved hands. And last the murky yellow cars of the Chicago, Milwaukee and St. Paul

---

① the man with owl-eyed glasses: the eccentric, bespectacled drunk whom Nick met at the first party he attended at Gatsby's mansion.
② Miss This-or-That's: 指当时以某某小姐为名字的女子学校。

railroad looking cheerful as Christmas itself on the tracks beside the gate.

When we pulled out into the winter night and the real snow, our snow, began to stretch out beside us and twinkle against the windows, and the dim lights of small Wisconsin stations moved by, a sharp wild brace came suddenly into the air. We drew in deep breaths of it as we walked back from dinner through the cold vestibules, unutterably aware of our identity with this country for one strange hour, before we melted indistinguishably into it again.

That's my Middle West—not the wheat or the prairies or the lost Swede towns, but the thrilling returning trains of my youth, and the street lamps and sleigh bells in the frosty dark and the shadows of holly wreaths thrown by lighted windows on the snow. I am part of that, a little solemn with the feel of those long winters, a little complacent from growing up in the Carraway house in a city where dwellings are still called through decades by a family's name. I see now that this has been a story of the West, after all—Tom and Gatsby, Daisy and Jordan and I, were all Westerners, and perhaps we possessed some deficiency in common which made us subtly unadaptable to Eastern life.

Even when the East excited me most, even when I was most keenly aware of its superiority to the bored, sprawling, swollen towns beyond the Ohio,[①] with their interminable inquisitions which spared only the children and the very old—even then it had always for me a quality of distortion. West Egg, especially, still figures in my more fantastic dreams. I see it as a night scene by El Greco:[②] a hundred houses, at once conventional and grotesque, crouching under a sullen, overhanging sky and a lustreless moon. In the foreground four solemn men in dress suits are walking along the sidewalk with a stretcher on which lies a drunken woman in a white evening dress. Her hand, which dangles over the side, sparkles cold with jewels. Gravely the men turn in at a house—the wrong house. But no one knows the woman's name, and no one cares.

After Gatsby's death the East was haunted for me like that, distorted beyond my eyes' power of correction. So when the blue smoke of brittle leaves was in the air and the wind blew the wet laundry stiff on the line I decided to come back home.

There was one thing to be done before I left, an awkward, unpleasant thing that perhaps had better have been let alone. But I wanted to leave things in order and not just trust that obliging and indifferent sea to sweep my refuse away. I saw Jordan Baker[③] and talked over and around what had happened to us together, and what had

---

① the Ohio: the Ohio River.
② El Greco: 埃尔·格列柯 (1541~1614), 西班牙画家, 作品多为宗教题材, 用阴冷色调渲染超现实的气氛。
③ Jordan Baker: 乔丹·贝克, 黛西的女友。她与故事的叙述者尼克·卡拉威曾一度保持若即若离的爱情关系。

happened afterward to me, and she lay perfectly still, listening, in a big chair.

She was dressed to play golf, and I remember thinking she looked like a good illustration, her chin raised a little jauntily, her hair the color of an autumn leaf, her face the same brown tint as the fingerless glove on her knee. When I had finished she told me without comment that she was engaged to another man. I doubted that, though there were several she could have married at a nod of her head, but I pretended to be surprised. For just a minute I wondered if I wasn't making a mistake, then I thought it all over again quickly and got up to say goodbye.

"Nevertheless you did throw me over," said Jordan suddenly. "You threw me over on the telephone. I don't give a damn about you now, but it was a new experience for me, and I felt a little dizzy for a while."

We shook hands.

"Oh, and do you remember"—she added—"a conversation we had once about driving a car?"

"Why—not exactly."

"You said a bad driver was only safe until she met another bad driver? Well, I met another bad driver, didn't I? I mean it was careless of me to make such a wrong guess. I thought you were rather an honest, straightforward person. I thought it was your secret pride."

"I'm thirty," I said. "I'm five years too old to lie to myself and call it honor."

She didn't answer. Angry, and half in love with her, and tremendously sorry, I turned away.

One afternoon late in October I saw Tom Buchanan. He was walking ahead of me along Fifth Avenue in his alert, aggressive way, his hands out a little from his body as if to fight off interference, his head moving sharply here and there, adapting itself to his restless eyes. Just as I slowed up to avoid overtaking him he stopped and began frowning into the windows of a jewellery store. Suddenly he saw me and walked back, holding out his hand.

"What's the matter, Nick? Do you object to shaking hands with me?"

"Yes. You know what I think of you."

"You're crazy, Nick," he said quickly. "Crazy as hell. I don't know what's the matter with you."

"Tom," I inquired, "what did you say to Wilson that afternoon?"

He stared at me without a word, and I knew I had guessed right about those missing hours. I started to turn away, but he took a step after me and grabbed my arm.

"I told him the truth," he said. "He came to the door while we were getting ready to leave, and when I sent down word that we weren't in he tried to force his way upstairs. He was crazy enough to kill me if I hadn't told him who owned the car. His hand was on a revolver in his pocket every minute he was in the house—" He broke off defiantly. "What if I did tell him? That fellow had it coming to him.① He threw dust into your eyes② just like he did in Daisy's, but he was a tough one. He ran over Myrtle like you'd run over a dog and never even stopped his car."

There was nothing I could say, except the one unutterable fact that it wasn't true.

"And if you think I didn't have my share of suffering—look here, when I went to give up that flat and saw that damn box of dog biscuits sitting there on the sideboard, I sat down and cried like a baby. By God it was awful—"

I couldn't forgive him or like him, but I saw that what he had done was, to him, entirely justified. It was all very careless and confused. They were careless people, Tom and Daisy—they smashed up things and creatures and then retreated back into their money or their vast carelessness, or whatever it was that kept them together, and let other people clean up the mess they had made…

I shook hands with him; it seemed silly not to, for I felt suddenly as though I were talking to a child. Then he went into the jewellery store to buy a pearl necklace—or perhaps only a pair of cuff buttons—rid of my provincial squeamishness forever.

Gatsby's house was still empty when I left—the grass on his lawn had grown as long as mine. One of the taxi drivers in the village never took a fare past the entrance gate without stopping for a minute and pointing inside; perhaps it was he who drove Daisy and Gatsby over to East Egg③ the night of the accident, and perhaps he had made a story about it all his own. I didn't want to hear it and I avoided him when I got off the train.

I spent my Saturday nights in New York because those gleaming, dazzling parties of his were with me so vividly that I could still hear the music and the laughter, faint and incessant, from his garden, and the cars going up and down his drive. One night I did hear a material car④ there, and saw its lights stop at his front steps. But I didn't investigate. Probably it was some final guest who had been away at the ends of the earth and didn't know that the party was over.⑤

On the last night, with my trunk packed and my car sold to the grocer, I went

---

① That fellow had it coming to him.: 那家伙(盖茨比)是咎由自取。
② He threw dust into your eyes…: He cheated you…
③ East Egg: 东卵村，汤姆和黛西居住过的地方。
④ a material car: 真真切切的一辆车。
⑤ the party was over: 与第三章的 "The party has begun" 相呼应，充分表达了卡拉威对人生浮沉的无限感叹。

over and looked at that huge incoherent failure of a house once more. On the white steps an obscene word, scrawled by some boy with a piece of brick, stood out clearly in the moonlight, and I erased it, drawing my shoe raspingly along the stone. Then I wandered down to the beach and sprawled out on the sand.

Most of the big shore places were closed now and there were hardly any lights except the shadowy, moving glow of a ferryboat across the Sound.① And as the moon rose higher the inessential houses began to melt away until gradually I became aware of the old island here that flowered once for Dutch sailors' eyes—a fresh, green breast of the new world. Its vanished trees, the trees that had made way for Gatsby's house, had once pandered in whispers to the last and greatest of all human dreams; for a transitory enchanted moment man must have held his breath in the presence of this continent, compelled into an aesthetic contemplation he neither understood nor desired, face to face for the last time in history with something commensurate to his capacity for wonder.

And as I sat there brooding on the old, unknown world, I thought of Gatsby's wonder when he first picked out the green light at the end of Daisy's dock.② He had come a long way to this blue lawn, and his dream must have seemed so close that he could hardly fail to grasp it. He did not know that it was already behind him, somewhere back in that vast obscurity beyond the city, where the dark fields of the republic rolled on under the night.

Gatsby believed in the green light, the orgiastic future that year by year recedes before us. It eluded us then, but that's no matter—tomorrow we will run faster, stretch out our arms farther… And one fine morning—

So we beat on, boats against the current, borne back ceaselessly into the past.

译文链接：https://www.docin.com/p-514061689.html

Questions for Understanding

1. Those former party-goers are not willing to either give a wire or come to Gatsby's funeral. Why?
2. What do you know about young Gatsby's character according to the SCHEDULE and GENERAL RESOLVES?

---

① the Sound: Long Island Sound（长岛海峡）.
② the green light at the end of Daisy's dock: 东卵村海岸边的码头尽头整夜亮着一盏灯。盖茨比经常夜里独自从西卵村向黛西居住的东卵村眺望，但看到的只是一盏闪着绿光的灯。很显然，the green light 是盖茨比梦想的象征。

3. How does Henry Gatz feel about his son?
4. What is the symbolic meaning of "green light"?

Aspects of Appreciation

1. On the surface, *The Great Gatsby* is a story of the thwarted love between a man and a woman. The main theme of the novel, however, encompasses a much larger, less romantic scope. Though all of its action takes place over a mere few months during the summer of 1922 and is set in a circumscribed geographical area in the vicinity of Long Island, New York, *The Great Gatsby* is a highly symbolic meditation on 1920s America as a whole, in particular the disillusionment of the American dream in an era of unprecedented prosperity and material excess. Fitzgerald portrays the 1920s as an era of decayed social and moral values, evidenced by its overarching cynicism, greed, and empty pursuit of pleasure. The reckless jubilance that led to decadent parties and wild jazz music—epitomized in *The Great Gatsby* by the opulent parties that Gatsby throws every Saturday night—resulted ultimately in the corruption of the American dream, as the unrestrained desire for money and pleasure surpassed more noble goals.

2. Nick Carraway narrates in both first and third person, presenting only what he himself observes. Nick alternates sections where he presents events objectively, as they appeared to him at the time, with sections where he gives his own interpretations of the story's meaning and of the motivations of the other characters.

3. Throughout the novel, places and settings epitomize the various aspects of the 1920s American society that Fitzgerald depicts. East Egg represents the old aristocracy, West Egg the newly rich, the valley of ashes the moral and social decay of America, and New York City the uninhibited, amoral quest for money and pleasure. Additionally, the East is connected to the moral decay and social cynicism of New York, while the West (including Midwestern and northern areas such as Minnesota) is connected to more traditional social values and ideals. Nick's analysis in Chapter IX of the story he has related reveals his sensitivity to this dichotomy: though it is set in the East, the story is really one of the West, as it tells how people originally from west of the Appalachians (as all of the main characters are) react to the pace and style of life on the East Coast.

Suggested Further Reading

Tales of the Jazz Age (1922): *Tender Is the Night* (1934).

Topics for Further Study

1. What are the differences among the American dreams embodied by Benjamin Franklin, Sister Carrie and Gatsby?

2. Discuss Gatsby's character as Nick perceives him throughout the novel. What makes Gatsby "great"?

3. In what sense is *The Great Gatsby* an autobiographical novel? Does Fitzgerald write more of himself into the character of Nick or the character of Gatsby, or are the author's qualities found in both characters?

4. Compare and contrast Gatsby and Tom. How are they alike? How are they different? Why does Daisy choose to remain with Tom instead of leaving him for Gatsby?

Knowledge of Literature

1. Lost Generation（迷惘的一代）

It is the name applied to the disillusioned intellectuals and aesthetes of the years following World War I. A number of them became expatriates, moving to London or Paris in their quest for a richer literary and artistic milieu and a freer way of life. The remark of Gertrude Stein, "You are all a lost generation," addressed to Hemingway, was used as a preface to the latter's novel *The Sun Also Rises*, which brilliantly describes an expatriate group typical of the "Lost Generation".

2. Literary Criticism: Western Marxist Criticism（西方马克思主义批评）

Western Marxist Criticism, which is different from classical Marxist Criticism, appeared in the 1920s. It has turned Marxist Criticism into a cultural critique from the philosophical perspective. The first major branch of Western Marxist criticism was developed by the Hungarian Georg Lukács who emphasizes the negative effects of capitalism such as alienation. He thinks that a great literary work not only reproduces the then leading ideology but also contains the criticism of the leading ideology. Another group of theorists emerged in Germany known as the Frankfurt School. Included in this group are Theodor Adorno, Walter Benjamin, Max Horkheimer, Herbert Marcuse and Erich Fromm. They lauded modernist writers, proposing that their experiments, by the very fact that they fragment and disrupt the life they reflect, effect a distance and detachment that serve as an implicit critique of mass society. Antonio Gramsci, an Italian communist, formulated the concept of hegemony: that a social class achieves a predominant influence and power, not by direct and overt means, but by succeeding in making its ideological view of society so pervasive that the subordinate classes unwittingly accept and participate in their own oppression. According to Gramsci, capitalism will not be overcome until the working class develops its counter-hegemony. In Louis Althusser's view, the dominant class's hegemony is never complete. Through artistic expression of their own cultural activities, the working classes can successfully revolt and usurp the hegemony of the dominant class.

Since the 1960s, Fredric Jameson in the United States and Terry Eagleton in Britain have dominated Western Marxist Criticism. Borrowing Freud's idea of a repressed unconscious, Jameson discovers a political unconscious, the repressed conditions of exploitation and oppression. The function of literary analysis, is to uncover the political unconscious present in a text. Terry Eagleton holds that literature is a product of an ideology which is itself a product of history. This ideology is a result of the actual social interactions that occur between people in definite times and locations. One of the critic's tasks, then, is to reconstruct an author's ideology or the author's ideological milieu. Throughout his career, he attacks the bourgeois dominance of the hegemony and advocates revolution against such values.

推荐阅读的论文：
[1] 陈晦. 透过"美国梦"看菲茨杰拉德的现实主义思想——以卢卡契的文艺理论解读《了不起的盖茨比》[J]. 湖北第二师范学院学报，2008(06)
[2] 陈梅. 从西方马克思主义批评视角解析《了不起的盖茨比》的悲剧主题 [J]. 开封教育学院学报，2017, 37(02).

Ernest Hemingway (1899~1961)

About the Author

Probably no other American writers enjoyed such flamboyant and legendary life as Hemingway did. He is deeply fixed in American minds in a series of images: a tough hero who courageously fought in the two World Wars and went through numerous dangers including three bad automobile accidents and two air crashes; an enthusiastic bullfight fan, deep-sea fisherman, amateur boxer, war correspondent and big-game hunter who incorporated such splendid personal exploits into the writing; a first-class novelist well embraced by generations of readers throughout the world with his unique telegraph-like prose style and strikingly impressive Code Heroes whose indomitable spirit remains inspiring all the time; the spokesman for the "Lost Generation" vividly describing pains and sorrows of the whole postwar American generation disillusioned and cast adrift by the war experiences; "Papa Hemingway" affectionately called and highly praised by many men of letters including J.D. Salinger, Jack Kerouac and so on.

Born in Oak Park, Illinois in 1899, Hemingway enjoyed a happy boyhood on the whole. Influenced by his father, a highly respected doctor who was fond of hunting and fishing, young Hemingway developed an enduring enthusiasm for the outdoor life, which later became one of his favorite topics in the writing. After graduation from a high school, Hemingway worked briefly as a reporter in Kansas City. When the United States joined WWI in 1917, inspired by the ideas, together with other passionate young men, that this "just" war could end all the wars, he was eager to enlist in the army. However, an eye problem barred him from the army, so he joined the ambulance corps. Shortly after he arrived at the front, he was seriously wounded by shrapnel and sent to the hospital. Though he recovered soon, the nightmarish war experience left an indelible influence on his life and writing.

In 1920 he married Hadley Richardson and moved to Paris, where he took up work as a journalist for the *Toronto Star* and came to know some famous expatriate artistic and literary Americans including Gertrude Stein, Sherwood Anderson, Ezra Pound, F. Scott Fitzgerald. Under their influence and encouragement, he completed his literary debut *Three Stories and Ten Poems*(1923), borrowing the style of simplicity from Anderson and Stein. Two years later, his first collection of short stories *In Our Times*(1925) came out, centering on the initiation into the world of adulthood filled with pain and violence of an adolescent boy Nick Adams, a prototype for later Hemingway heroes.

By then, Hemingway had finished his apprenticeship and began to develop his own distinctive style. In 1926, he published his first novel *The Torrents of Spring* which won immediate public attention. In the same year, with the publication of *The Sun Also Rises,* Hemingway was regarded as the spokesman of the "Lost Generation". Set in the postwar years in Spain and Paris, the novel concerns a group of expatriates, mainly represented by the protagonist Jake Barns, who has suffered physically and emotionally from the war, and seeks psychic refuge in a hedonistic and nihilistic lifestyle. Equally successful was *A Farewell to Arms* (1929), a tragic romance between an American solider Frederic Henry and an English nurse Catharine Barkley. Modeled on Hemingway's own wartime experiences, it mainly centers on Henry's painful disillusionment of the war as well as the life. Infested with the prevailing fever of joining the so-called "glorious and sacred" war, Henry volunteers to go to battlefields, but soon he is greatly shocked by its violence and brutality, and runs away with his beloved girl Catherine with the intention of making "a separate peace". However, the threat of death and danger still hovers over their lives. In the end Catherine dies in childbirth, which makes Henry realize that the very texture of life involves violence and death.

To some extent, the period from 1926 up to 1936 seemed to be one of the golden ages of Hemingway's literary career. Besides the novels mentioned above, Hemingway also published three collections of short stories including *Men without Women* (1927), *Winner Take Nothing* (1933) and the *First Forty-Nine Stories*(1938), the last of which contains such famous short stories as "The Killers", "The Undefeated" and "The Snows of Kilimanjaro", and two nonfiction works *Death in the Afternoon* (1932) and *Green Hills of Africa* (1935), which interweave his favorite sports, big-game hunting and bullfighting, with acute observations on virility, death, modern literature and the essence of life.

In 1936 when the Spanish Civil War broke out, Hemingway threw himself into supporting the Republican side against Fascist Fransco. Later he used this experience to create two excellent works including *The Fifth Column* (1938), his only play with the setting of the siege of Madrid, and *For Whom the Bell Tolls* (1940), arguably his most ambitious novel, telling the story of an American teacher Robert Jordan fighting with Spanish soldiers on the Republican side.

Following the great success of *For Whom the Bell Tolls*, Hemingway lapsed into a literary silence lasting a full decade, largely due to his active and courageous participation in WWII. When the war ended, Hemingway settled down in Cuba, where he accomplished the novel *Across the River and Into the Trees*(1950) concerning an aging colonel's trip to revisit the place where he was wounded in WWI, and his last published work *The Old Man and the Sea* (1952) which positioned him for the Pulitzer Prize in 1953 and the Nobel Prize in Literature in 1954. Centering on an aged Cuban fisherman Santiago's futile struggle to save his catch of a giant marlin from fierce sharks, this novella celebrates the theme that a man can be destroyed but not defeated.

Thereafter, Hemingway's productivity declined dramatically because of the failing health and an increasingly severe psychological disturbance, and finally he committed suicide with a gunshot on July 2, 1961. Shortly after his death, people found voluminous unfinished manuscripts at his home, some of which were later edited and published. Those posthumous works include *A Moveable Feast* (1964), his memoir of Paris in the 1920s, *Islands in the Stream* (1970) concerning some recollections of a lonely painter who bears much resemblance to Hemingway, and *The Garden of Eden* (1986) exploring the relation between men and women.

As a witness and a participant of the two historic catastrophes in human history, Hemingway was permanently affected by the terrible war experience. In a sense, his whole life could be viewed as one of struggling with its influence, and using his pen to relive it and forget about it. While denying the glory and justice of the war, Hemingway revealed its brutality and violence in details, and discussed its lingering psychological effects on those who survived but still suffered the mental trauma from it. What's more, the wartime experience also influenced his attitude towards the world and life to a great extent. His works are permeated with the bleak and nihilistic vision of failure, violence and death. However, such negative visions are in the meanwhile modified by his affirmative assertion of the possibility of living with grace and courage, which is best exemplified by his stoical Code Heroes who always face various tribulations, even sometimes the threat of death, in the hostile world yet still "keep grace under pressure".

Hemingway's greatness does not just lie in his impressive heroes and thought-provoking themes, but also in his contribution to the development of the colloquial style in American literature. Following the example of his predecessor Mark Twain, Hemingway went on to refine this style and presented it at its finest. His writings abound in simple and concrete words, short and uncomplicated sentences, causal and plain conversations. However, such language is never natural and simple as it seems to be. Bearing the Iceberg theory in his mind, Hemingway labored to hide certain profound meanings between the textual lines, and thus his language is highly symbolic and suggestive. No wonder he is generally hailed as a great stylist with "powerful style-forming mastery of the art".

A Clean Well-lighted House

About the Story

First published in *Scribner's Magazine*(1933), "A Clean Well-lighted House" is one of Hemingway's most anthologized short stories. Set in a small Spanish café at midnight, this masterpiece mainly presents a conversation between two waiters when they wait for the leave of their last lingering customer, an old man who has recently attempted to commit suicide.

A Clean Well-lighted House

It was very late and everyone had left the café except an old man who sat in the shadow the leaves of the tree made against the electric light. In the day time the street was dusty, but at night the dew settled the dust and the old man liked to sit late because he was deaf and now at night it was quiet and he felt the difference. The two waiters inside the café knew that the old man was a little drunk, and while he was a good client they knew that if he became too drunk he would leave without paying, so they kept watch on him.

"Last week he tried to commit suicide," one waiter said.

"Why?"

"He was in despair."

"What about?"

"Nothing."

"How do you know it was nothing?"

"He has plenty of money."

They sat together at a table that was close against the wall near the door of the café and looked at the terrace where the tables were all empty except where the old man sat in the shadow of the leaves of the tree that moved slightly in the wind. A girl and a soldier went by in the street. The street light shone on the brass number on his collar. The girl wore no head covering and hurried beside him.

"The guard will pick him up[①]," one waiter said.

"What does it matter if he gets what he's after?"

"He had better get off the street now. The guard will get him. They went by five minutes ago."

The old man sitting in the shadow rapped on his saucer with his glass. The younger waiter went over to him.

"What do you want?"

The old man looked at him. "Another brandy," he said.

"You'll be drunk," the waiter said. The old man looked at him. The waiter went away.

"He'll stay all night," he said to his colleague. "I'm sleepy now. I never get into bed before three o'clock. He should have killed himself last week."

The waiter took the brandy bottle and another saucer from the counter inside the café and marched out to the old man's table. He put down the saucer and poured the glass full of brandy.

"You should have killed yourself last week," he said to the deaf man. The old man motioned with his finger. "A little more," he said. The waiter poured on into the glass

---

① The guard will pick him up: 卫兵会逮捕他。

so that the brandy slopped[①] over and ran down the stem into the top saucer of the pile. "Thank you," the old man said. The waiter took the bottle back inside the café. He sat down at the table with his colleague again.

"He's drunk now," he said.

"He's drunk every night."

"What did he want to kill himself for?"

"How should I know."

"How did he do it?"

"He hung himself with a rope."

"Who cut him down?"

"His niece."

"Why did they do it?"

"Fear for his soul.[②]"

"How much money has he got?"

"He's got plenty."

"He must be eighty years old."

"Anyway I should say he was eighty."

"I wish he would go home. I never get to bed before three o'clock. What kind of hour is that to go to bed?"

"He stays up because he likes it."

"He's lonely. I'm not lonely. I have a wife waiting in bed for me."

"He had a wife once too."

"A wife would be no good to him now."

"You can't tell. He might be better with a wife."

"His niece looks after him. You said she cut him down."

"I know."

"I wouldn't want to be that old. An old man is a nasty thing."

"Not always. This old man is clean. He drinks without spilling. Even now, drunk.

"Look at him."

"I don't want to look at him. I wish he would go home. He has no regard for those who must work."

The old man looked from his glass across the square, then over at the waiters.

"Another brandy," he said, pointing to his glass. The waiter who was in a hurry came over.

---

① slop: (of a liquid) spill or flow over the edge of a container, typically as a result of careless handling.

② Fear for his soul: 为他的灵魂不能被上帝拯救而感到害怕。According to Christianity, if people commit suicide, their souls will go to hell, for they have committed the unforgivable sin, self-murder.

"Finished," he said, speaking with that omission of syntax stupid people employ when talking to drunken people or foreigners. "No more tonight. Close now."

"Another," said the old man.

"No. Finished." The waiter wiped the edge of the table with a towel and shook his head.

The old man stood up, slowly counted the saucers[①], took a leather coin purse from his pocket and paid for the drinks, leaving half a peseta[②] tip. The waiter watched him go down the street, a very old man walking unsteadily but with dignity.

"Why didn't you let him stay and drink?" the unhurried waiter asked. They were putting up the shutters. "It is not half-past two."

"I want to go home to bed."

"What is an hour?"

"More to me than to him."

"An hour is the same."

"You talk like an old man yourself. He can buy a bottle and drink at home."

"It's not the same."

"No, it is not," agreed the waiter with a wife. He did not wish to be unjust. He was only in a hurry.

"And you? You have no fear of going home before your usual hour?"

"Are you trying to insult me?"

"No, hombre[③], only to make a joke."

"No," the waiter who was in a hurry said, rising from pulling down the metal shutters. "I have confidence. I am all confidence."

"You have youth, confidence, and a job," the older waiter said. "You have everything."

"And what do you lack?"

"Everything but work."

"You have everything I have."

"No. I have never had confidence and I am not young."

"Come on. Stop talking nonsense and lock up."

"I am of those who like to stay late at the café," the older waiter said. "With all those who do not want to go to bed. With all those who need a light for the night."

"I want to go home and into bed."

"We are of two different kinds," the older waiter said. He was now dressed to

---

① count the saucers: 根据酒碟数计算点了多少杯酒。
② peseta: the unit of money that was used in Spain before it was replaced by the euro.
③ hombre: (Spanish) man.

go home. "It is not only a question of youth and confidence although those things are very beautiful. Each night I am reluctant to close up because there may be some one who needs the café."

"Hombre, there are bodegas open all night long.①"

"You do not understand. This is a clean and pleasant café. It is well lighted. The light is very good and also, now, there are shadows of the leaves."

"Good night," said the younger waiter.

"Good night," the other said. Turning off the electric light he continued the conversation with himself, It was the light of course but it is necessary that the place be clean and pleasant. You do not want music. Certainly you do not want music. Nor can you stand before a bar with dignity although that is all that is provided for these hours. What did he fear? It was not a fear or dread, It was a nothing that he knew too well. It was all a nothing and a man was a nothing too. It was only that and light was all it needed and a certain cleanness and order. Some lived in it and never felt it but he knew it all was nada② y③ pues④ nada y nada y pues nada. Our nada who art in nada, nada be thy name thy kingdom nada thy will be nada in nada as it is in nada. Give us this nada our daily nada and nada us our nada as we nada our nadas and nada us not into nada but deliver us from nada; pues nada. Hail nothing full of nothing, nothing is with thee⑤. He smiled and stood before a bar with a shining steam pressure coffee machine.

"What's yours?" asked the barman.

"Nada."

"Otro loco mas⑥," said the barman and turned away.

"A little cup," said the waiter.

The barman poured it for him.

"The light is very bright and pleasant but the bar is unpolished," the waiter said.

The barman looked at him but did not answer. It was too late at night for conversation.

"You want another copita⑦?" The barman asked.

"No, thank you," said the waiter and went out. He disliked bars and bodegas. A clean, well-lighted café was a very different thing. Now, without thinking further,

---

① bodega: a shop selling wine and sometimes groceries, especially in a Spanish-speaking country.
② nada: (Spanish) nothing.
③ y: (Spanish) and.
④ pues:（西班牙语）既然、那么。
⑤ Our nada who art...nothing is with thee: 在这里,海明威用西班牙语"虚无"替代了原主祷文中的大部分名词。
⑥ otro loco mas: (Spanish) another lunatic（西班牙语）又一个疯子。
⑦ copita: a tulip-shaped sherry glass（郁金香形状的）雪利酒杯。

he would go home to his room. He would lie in the bed and finally, with daylight, he would go to sleep. After all, he said to himself, it's probably only insomnia①. Many must have it.

译文链接：https://www.sohu.com/a/100806608_119656

Questions for Understanding

1. What's the implied meaning of the title of the story?
2. Why did the old man try to commit suicide?
3. Describe the different attitudes of the two waiters toward the old man. What does the difference imply?
4. Why did the older waiter emphasize that "this is necessary that the place be clean and pleasant, and well-lighted"?
5. Make a comment on the style of the story. Point out all the distinctive features of Hemingway's style shown in this story.

Aspects of Appreciation

1. The title of the story does have some significant meanings. A clean, well-lighted place refers to the café, the setting as well as the central symbol of the story, which stands for a temporary refuge from the absurd and meaningless modern life where men without the innocence of youth and the illusions of belief, like the old man and by extension, the older waiter, can preserve the dignity and get some comfort.

2. The younger waiter, eager to go home to meet his wife, keeps complaining and serves the old man impatiently, while the older waiter is much more sympathetic to the man and willing to keep the café open, for he shares the empathy for the old man's profound despair and loneliness, and understands his need for a clean, well-lighted place, a solace in the darkness.

3. After the young waiter's leaving, the old one continues to talk to himself. He recites the Lord's Prayer, but replaces most of the nouns in it with the Spanish word "nada", meaning "nothing". The change of the words in the Lord's Prayer reveals one important theme of the story that the essence of modern life is nothingness, meaninglessness and futility.

---

① insomnia: the condition of being unable to sleep 失眠。

Hemingway said that inhis stories he told the reader aslittle as possible but tried his best to reveal characters' motives and their conflicts. This story illustrates this principle well. Narrated in the objective third-person point of view, the story reveals very lettle information about the two waiters and the old man, only recording a brief conversation between two waiters in a small café. Fortunately, Hemingway intentionally leaves a few details to the sensibilities of the readers, allowing them to explore the characters' words and behaviors laboriously in an attempt to find the meanings submerged beneath the textual lines, and infer the theme and the relationships between characters.

Suggested Further Reading

"Hills like White Elephants"(1927); "The Snow of Kilimanjaro" (1936); "The Old Man and the Sea" (1952)

Topics for Further Study

1. In the latter portion of his life, Hemingway was affectionately called as "Papa Hemingway" and highly praised by many men of letters including J.D. Salinger, Jack Kerouac and so on. Try to find the reason why his shadow looms so large over the landscape of American literature.

2. The wartime experience left an indelible trauma on Hemingway. In a sense, throughout his life, he struggled with his pen to relive it and forget about it. Read some of his famous novels such as *The Sun Also Rises*, *A Farewell to Arms* and *For Whom the Bell Tolls,* and find his opinions of the war and its influences on men.

3. As a master of the language, Hemingway is very good at using symbolism, which adds profound meanings to his works. Select one of his works, for instance *The Old Man and the Sea* or "Hills like White Elephants", and try to analyze the symbols involved in it.

4. With most of his stories praising the male protagonists, Hemingway is often stereotyped as a masculine writer and has long been criticized to perpetuate sexual prejudices in his writings. However, the recent study on his short stories suggests that he is also concerned about the living and mental conditions of women. Choose one of his short stories, such as "The Short Happy Life of Francis Macomber", "Hills like White Elephants" and "Cat in the Rain" and try to find evidence to support this view.

Knowledge of Literature

An Element of Fiction: Style（风格）

As Jonathan Swift put it, "proper words in proper places make the true definition of a style". Style refers to the distinctive way in which a writer arranges words to achieve particular effects. The analysis and assessment of style involves the examination of a writer's choice of words, his figures of speech, the rhetorical devices, the shape of his sentences (whether they be loose or periodic) , the shape of his paragraphs—indeed, of every conceivable aspect of his language and the way in which he uses it.

Styles have been roughly classified and these crude categories are helpful: (a) according to period: Metaphysical, Augustan, Georgian, etc.; (b) according to individual authors: Chaucerian, Miltonic, Jamesian, etc.; (c) according to level: grand, plain, etc.; (d) and according to language: scientific, expository, poetic, emotive, journalistic, etc.

推荐阅读的论文：
[1] 杜寅寅. 海明威作品中文学极简主义的体现——以短篇小说《一个干净、明亮的地方》中对话部分为例 [J]. 广东外语外贸大学学报, 2006(1).
[2] 王茹. 论海明威小说《一个干净明亮的地方》的写作风格 [J]. 学术交流, 2012(08).

William Faulkner (1897~1962)

About the Author

The circumstances surrounding the birth of a male infant in New Albany, Mississippi on September 25, 1897, were not as promising as his forefathers. Like other prestigious old southern families, the one William Faulkner grew up in was reduced to "genteel" poverty by the Civil War. The wealth, fame and privilege they once enjoyed were deprived gradually with the encroaching industrialization. The values and traditions they had once highly respected and maintained were replaced little by little with the overwhelming spirits of modern industry. However, it turns out that his birth was an extremely eventful one, for it was this southern boy who used his pen to create a "cosmos of his own", chronicling the great changes of the South during its historic periods, and with imaginative power and psychological depth granted the American South a glamorous and impressive mark in the American literature.

With the help of Sherwood Anderson, Faulkner began his literary adventure.

However, his debut was not as successful as expected, because his poems and several novels attracted little attention either from the critics or from the public. It was in *Sartoris* (1929) that he found his most congenial and engaging subject for the rest of his literary career, that is, the Yoknapatawpha County, a mythical place modeling on the South, especially his native town. In this "little postage stamp of native soil", he accomplished a series of works for which he is now best renowned, including *The Sound and the Fury*(1929), *As I Lay Dying*(1930), *Light in August*(1932), *Absalom, Absalom!*(1936), *Go down, Moses*(1942) and so forth. All these stories are interwoven together to build a grand "dream kingdom" with specific size, population and classes, spanning almost one and a half century from the original days of Native Americans' possession to the pre-Civil War times when the white plantation owners such as the Compson, Sartoris, Benbow and McCaslin families settled down and flourished, and then on through reconstruction and rebellion to a modern era featured by the downfall of these prestigious families and the rise of the unscrupulous poor white family named Snopes. To some extent, Yoknapatawpha County is not merely an intricate and fantastic creation of imaginary land, it could be considered as an allegory or a parable of the South, the place where Faulkner was born, grew up, and devoted his whole life to paying tribute.

Of the Yoknapatawpha County saga, four novels are unanimously acclaimed as masterpieces: *The Sound and the Fury*, *As I Lay Dying*, *Light in August*, and *Absalom, Absalom!*. Taking its title from the lines in Shakespeare's *Macbeth*, "it (life) is a tale told by an idiot, full of sound and fury", *The Sound and the Fury* recounts the decline and degeneracy of an old southern family—the Compsons and, by implication, of the aristocratic south with the bold experiments in narrative skills. The novel consists of four parts, each with a different narrator, including the Compson brothers: Benjy, the youngest brother and also the idiot; Quentin, the eldest brother who commits suicide at last; Jason, the shrewdest and cruelest one, as well as Dilsey, an old Black housemaid of the family. Each of them provides a piece of the plot which together makes up the tragedy of the daughter, Caddie Compson, and in a broader sense the elegy for the deterioration and downfall of the South from the past to the present. With an even more intricate structure, *As I Lay Dying* describes the journey of a poor white family to the town of Jefferson to fulfill their mother's deathbed request for burial. The psychological states and relationship among the family members are elaborately revealed in the interior monologues of fifteen characters. By juxtaposing the grim tragedy of a social outcast Joe Christmas and a journey, filled with hope, of a pregnant girl Lena Grove searching for her lover, *Light in August* makes a profound discussion about the positive and negative human qualities mainly represented by Lena (innocence and endurance) and Joe (violence and loneliness), and advocates to adopt a tolerant and peaceful attitude towards the life despite all the tribulations and difficulties. *Absalom, Absalom!* adds another classic legend to the Yoknapatawpha County saga by detailing the rise and fall of the southern plantation culture with its representative Thomas Sutpen, a poor white man who spares no efforts to establish a wealthy family, but finally ends up in futility and desperation.

Sharing much affinity with his literary predecessor Hawthorne, Faulkner also places much emphasis on the heritage of his ancestors—the Southern culture, explores the relationship between the past and the present, and examines how the past events influence modern people and how these modern people, in turn, treat the past. Though deeply rooted in the South, he holds an ambivalent feeling towards it. He is nostalgic for the Old South, mourns for its decline and glorious past, and shows great respect to such precious traditional values as tolerance, serenity and compassion. On the other hand, he is critical about the negative side of southern morals and ethics, for instance, the slavery and the harsh suppression of human nature and so forth. Moreover, to some degree, he goes further than Hawthorne in exploring the innermost recess of the psyche of the characters, for he daringly employs several narrative techniques including the stream of consciousness, the interior monologue, the dislocation of narrative time, and multiple points of view. Though surely posing certain difficulty in comprehension, these skills do help Faulkner create a panoramic, fantastic yet intricate picture of the living and mental conditions of the southerners.

However, his greatness not merely rests on a complete body of works about the South, but also lies in his deep concern towards general human situation. The central theme throughout these southern sagas is, as he puts it, "the problem of the human heart in conflict with itself", transcending the boundaries of space and time. And although most of his novels abound in grim and sordid aspects of life, they are not pessimistic in general, for they are grounded in a profound and compassionate humanism that celebrates the joys and sorrows of the ordinary human life.

Near the end of his Nobel Prize Speech in 1949, Faulkner commented on the role of writers:

I believe that man will not merely endure, he will prevail. He is immortal, not because he alone among creatures has an inexhaustible voice, but because he has a soul, a spirit capable of compassion, and sacrifice, and endurance. The poets, the writers' duty is to write about these things. It's his privilege to help man endure, lifting his heart, by reminding him of the courage, and honor and hope and compassion and pity and sacrifice which have been the glory of his past. The poets' voice need not merely be the recall of man, it can be one of the props, the pillars to help him endure and prevail.

No doubt, with vivid panoramic descriptions of the South, innovative and bold experiments in narrative skills and deep concern for the human situation in general, he has successfully fulfilled this aim, touching the hearts from generation to generation and leaving each one uplifted with the precious spirits once lost.

A Rose for Emily

About the Story

"A Rose for Emily" is Faulkner's first short story published in a national magazine (April 30, 1930 issue of *Forum*). Set in the southern town of Jefferson in Faulkner's most favorite fictional land—Yoknapatawpha County, this masterpiece, full of gothic and grotesque color, centers on the tragic life of an aristocratic southern lady Emily Grierson. Owing to her secluded life and prestigious family background, Miss Emily, an eccentric, queer and inaccessible spinster, remains the focus of the townspeople in her lifetime. However, when she dies, they surprisingly find her dark secret that she has poisoned her lover Homer Barron and kept his rotten corpse in her bedroom and slept with it for many years.

I

When Miss Emily Grierson died, our whole town went to her funeral: the men through a sort of respectful affection for a fallen monument, the women mostly out of curiosity to see the inside of her house, which no one save an old man-servant—a combined gardener and cook—had seen in at least ten years.

It was a big, squarish frame house that had once been white, decorated with cupolas and spires and scrolled balconies in the heavily lightsome style of the seventies①, set on what had once been our most select street. But garages and cotton gins had encroached and obliterated even the august names of that neighborhood; only Miss Emily's house was left, lifting its stubborn and coquettish decay above the cotton wagons and the gasoline pumps—an eyesore among eyesores. And now Miss Emily had gone to join the representatives of those august names where they lay in the cedar-bemused cemetery② among the ranked and anonymous graves of Union and

---

① the seventies: the 1870s.
② cedar-bemused cemetery: 雪松环绕的墓园。

Confederate soldiers[①] who fell at the battle of Jefferson[②].

Alive, Miss Emily had been a tradition, a duty, and a care; a sort of hereditary obligation upon the town, dating from that day in 1894 when Colonel Sartoris[③], the mayor—he who fathered the edict that no Negro woman should appear on the streets without an apron—remitted her taxes, the dispensation dating from the death of her father on into perpetuity. Not that Miss Emily would have accepted charity. Colonel Sartoris invented an involved tale to the effect that Miss Emily's father had loaned money to the town, which the town, as a matter of business, preferred this way of repaying. Only a man of Colonel Sartoris' generation and thought could have invented it, and only a woman could have believed it.

When the next generation, with its more modern ideas, became mayors and aldermen[④], this arrangement created some little dissatisfaction. On the first of the year they mailed her a tax notice. February came, and there was no reply. They wrote her a formal letter, asking her to call at the sheriff's office at her convenience. A week later the mayor wrote her himself, offering to call or to send his car for her, and received in reply a note on paper of an archaic shape, in a thin, flowing calligraphy in faded ink, to the effect that she no longer went out at all. The tax notice was also enclosed, without comment.

They called a special meeting of the Board of Aldermen. A deputation waited upon her, knocked at the door through which no visitor had passed since she ceased giving china-painting lessons eight or ten years earlier. They were admitted by the old Negro into a dim hall from which a stairway mounted into still more shadow. It smelled of dust and disuse—a close, dank smell. The Negro led them into the parlor. It was furnished in heavy, leather-covered furniture. When the Negro opened the blinds of one window, they could see that the leather was cracked; and when they sat down, a faint dust rose sluggishly about their thighs, spinning with slow motes in the single sun-ray. On a tarnished gilt easel before the fireplace stood a crayon portrait of Miss Emily's father.

They rose when she entered—a small, fat woman in black, with a thin gold chain descending to her waist and vanishing into her belt, leaning on an ebony cane with a tarnished gold head. Her skeleton was small and spare; perhaps that was why what would have been merely plumpness in another was obesity in her[⑤]. She looked

---

① Union and Confederate soldiers: soldiers of the North and the South who fought in the American Civil War (1861~1865).
② Jefferson: the central town of Faulkner's mythical Yoknapatawpha County(杰弗逊镇).
③ Colonel Sartoris: Bayard Sartoris (1851~1919), the son of John Sartoris, the protagonist in Sartoris.
④ Alderman: 市政会的成员。
⑤ what would have been merely plumpness in another was obesity in her: 要是落在别的女人身上，那种胖就是

bloated, like a body long submerged in motionless water, and of that pallid hue. Her eyes, lost in the fatty ridges of her face, looked like two small pieces of coal pressed into a lump of dough as they moved from one face to another while the visitors stated their errand.

She did not ask them to sit. She just stood in the door and listened quietly until the spokesman came to a stumbling halt. Then they could hear the invisible watch ticking at the end of the gold chain.

Her voice was dry and cold. "I have no taxes in Jefferson. Colonel Sartoris explained it to me. Perhaps one of you can gain access to the city records and satisfy yourselves."

"But we have. We are the city authorities, Miss Emily. Didn't you get a notice from the sheriff, signed by him?"

"I received a paper, yes," Miss Emily said. "Perhaps he considers himself the sheriff... I have no taxes in Jefferson."

"But there is nothing on the books to show that, you see We must go by the—"

"See Colonel Sartoris. I have no taxes in Jefferson."

"But, Miss Emily—"

"See Colonel Sartoris." (Colonel Sartoris had been dead almost ten years.) "I have no taxes in Jefferson. Tobe!" The Negro appeared. "Show these gentlemen out."

II

So she vanquished them, horse and foot[①], just as she had vanquished their fathers thirty years before about the smell.

That was two years after her father's death and a short time after her sweetheart—the one we believed would marry her—had deserted her. After her father's death she went out very little; after her sweetheart went away, people hardly saw her at all. A few of the ladies had the temerity to call, but were not received, and the only sign of life about the place was the Negro man—a young man then—going in and out with a market basket.

"Just as if a man—any man—could keep a kitchen properly," the ladies said; so they were not surprised when the smell developed. It was another link between the gross, teeming world and the high and mighty Griersons.

A neighbor, a woman, complained to the mayor, Judge Stevens, eighty years old.

"But what will you have me do about it, madam?" He said.

"Why, send her word to stop it," the woman said. "Isn't there a law?"

丰满,而落在她身上,就显得臃肿。

① horse and foot: all of them.

"I'm sure that won't be necessary," Judge Stevens said. "It's probably just a snake or a rat that nigger of hers killed in the yard. I'll speak to him about it."

The next day he received two more complaints, one from a man who came in diffident deprecation. "We really must do something about it, Judge. I'd be the last one in the world to bother Miss Emily, but we've got to do something." That night the Board of Aldermen met—three graybeards and one younger man, a member of the rising generation.

"It's simple enough," he said. "Send her word to have her place cleaned up. Give her a certain time to do it in, and if she don't..."

"Dammit, sir," Judge Stevens said, "will you accuse a lady to her face of smelling bad?"

So the next night, after midnight, four men crossed Miss Emily's lawn and slunk about the house like burglars, sniffing along the base of the brickwork and at the cellar openings while one of them performed a regular sowing motion with his hand out of a sack slung from his shoulder. They broke open the cellar door and sprinkled lime there, and in all the outbuildings. As they recrossed the lawn, a window that had been dark was lighted and Miss Emily sat in it, the light behind her, and her upright torso motionless as that of an idol. They crept quietly across the lawn and into the shadow of the locusts that lined the street. After a week or two the smell went away.

That was when people had begun to feel really sorry for her. People in our town, remembering how old lady Wyatt, her great-aunt, had gone completely crazy at last, believed that the Griersons held themselves a little too high for what they really were. None of the young men were quite good enough for Miss Emily and such. We had long thought of them as a tableau, Miss Emily a slender figure in white in the background, her father a spraddled silhouette① in the foreground, his back to her and clutching a horsewhip②, the two of them framed by the back-flung front door. So when she got to be thirty and was still single, we were not pleased exactly, but vindicated; even with insanity in the family she wouldn't have turned down all of her chances if they had really materialized.

When her father died, it got about that the house was all that was left to her; and in a way, people were glad. At last they could pity Miss Emily. Being left alone, and a pauper, she had become humanized. Now she too would know the old thrill and the old despair of a penny more or less.

The day after his death all the ladies prepared to call at the house and offer condolence and aid, as is our custom Miss Emily met them at the door, dressed as

---

① her father a spraddled silhouette: 她父亲两腿叉开的身影。
② horsewhip: 马鞭。

usual and with no trace of grief on her face. She told them that her father was not dead. She did that for three days, with the ministers calling on her, and the doctors, trying to persuade her to let them dispose of the body. Just as they were about to resort to law and force, she broke down, and they buried her father quickly.

We did not say she was crazy then. We believed she had to do that. We remembered all the young men her father had driven away, and we knew that with nothing left, she would have to cling to that which had robbed her, as people will.

III

She was sick for a long time. When we saw her again, her hair was cut short, making her look like a girl, with a vague resemblance to those angels in colored church windows—sort of tragic and serene.

The town had just let the contracts for paving the sidewalks, and in the summer after her father's death they began the work. The construction company came with riggers and mules and machinery, and a foreman named Homer Barron, a Yankee[①]— a big, dark, ready man, with a big voice and eyes lighter than his face. The little boys would follow in groups to hear him cuss the riggers, and the riggers singing in time to the rise and fall of picks. Pretty soon he knew everybody in town. Whenever you heard a lot of laughing anywhere about the square, Homer Barron would be in the center of the group. Presently we began to see him and Miss Emily on Sunday afternoons driving in the yellow-wheeled buggy and the matched team of bays from the livery stable.

At first we were glad that Miss Emily would have an interest, because the ladies all said, "Of course a Grierson would not think seriously of a Northerner, a day laborer." But there were still others, older people, who said that even grief could not cause a real lady to forget noblesse oblige[②]—without calling it noblesse oblige. They just said, "Poor Emily. Her kinsfolk should come to her." She had some kin in Alabama; but years ago her father had fallen out with them over the estate of old lady Wyatt, the crazy woman, and there was no communication between the two families. They had not even been represented at the funeral.

And as soon as the old people said, "Poor Emily," the whispering began. "Do you suppose it's really so?" They said to one another. "Of course it is. What else could…" This behind their hands; rustling of craned silk and satin behind jalousies[③] closed

---

① Yankee: a person from a northern or northeastern state of the United States.
② noblesse oblige: (French) the idea that people who have special advantages of wealth, etc. should help other people who do not have these advantages(位高则任重；显贵者应有高尚品德；贵族义务).
③ This behind their hands; rustling of craned silk and satin behind jalousies: This behind their hands 这句话他们

upon the sun of Sunday afternoon as the thin, swift clop-clop-clop of the matched team passed: "Poor Emily."

She carried her head high enough—even when we believed that she was fallen. It was as if she demanded more than ever the recognition of her dignity as the last Grierson; as if it had wanted that touch of earthiness to reaffirm her imperviousness. Like when she bought the rat poison, the arsenic. That was over a year after they had begun to say "Poor Emily," and while the two female cousins were visiting her.

"I want some poison," she said to the druggist. She was over thirty then, still a slight woman, though thinner than usual, with cold, haughty black eyes in a face the flesh of which was strained across the temples and about the eyesockets as you imagine a lighthouse-keeper's face[①]ought to look. "I want some poison," she said.

"Yes, Miss Emily. What kind? For rats and such? I'd recom—"

"I want the best you have. I don't care what kind."

The druggist named several. "They'll kill anything up to an elephant. But what you want is—"

"Arsenic," Miss Emily said. "Is that a good one?"

"Is... arsenic? Yes, ma'am. But what you want—"

"I want arsenic."

The druggist looked down at her. She looked back at him, erect, her face like a strained flag. "Why, of course," the druggist said. "If that's what you want. But the law requires you to tell what you are going to use it for."

Miss Emily just stared at him, her head tilted back in order to look him eye for eye, until he looked away and went and got the arsenic and wrapped it up. The Negro delivery boy brought her the package; the druggist didn't come back. When she opened the package at home there was written on the box, under the skull and bones: "For rats."

IV

So the next day we all said, "She will kill herself"; and we said it would be the best thing. When she had first begun to be seen with Homer Barron, we had said, "She will marry him." Then we said, "She will persuade him yet," because Homer himself had remarked—he liked men, and it was known that he drank with the younger men in the Elks' Club—that he was not a marrying man. Later we said, "Poor Emily" behind

---

是用手捂住嘴轻轻地说的；rustling of silk and satin 绸缎衣服的窸窣声，此处指当艾米莉和伯顿驾马车经过时，镇上人伸长脖子透过自家的百叶窗注视他们的一举一动。这两个动作表现了镇上人十分好奇和关注艾米莉和伯顿的交往。

① a lighthouse-keeper's face: a face with a tense or nervous expression.

the jalousies as they passed on Sunday afternoon in the glittering buggy, Miss Emily with her head high and Homer Barron with his hat cocked and a cigar in his teeth, reins and whip in a yellow glove.

Then some of the ladies began to say that it was a disgrace to the town and a bad example to the young people. The men did not want to interfere, but at last the ladies forced the Baptist minister①—Miss Emily's people were Episcopalto call upon her. He would never divulge what happened during that interview, but he refused to go back again. The next Sunday they again drove about the streets, and the following day the minister's wife wrote to Miss Emily's relations in Alabama.

So she had blood-kin under her roof again and we sat back to watch developments. At first nothing happened. Then we were sure that they were to be married. We learned that Miss Emily had been to the jeweler's and ordered a man's toilet set in silver, with the letters H. B. on each piece. Two days later we learned that she had bought a complete outfit of men's clothing, including a nightshirt, and we said, "They are married." We were really glad. We were glad because the two female cousins were even more Grierson② than Miss Emily had ever been.

So we were not surprised when Homer Barron—the streets had been finished some time since—was gone. We were a little disappointed that there was not a public blowing-off, but we believed that he had gone on to prepare for Miss Emily's coming, or to give her a chance to get rid of the cousins. (By that time it was a cabal, and we were all Miss Emily's allies to help circumvent the cousins.) Sure enough, after another week they departed. And, as we had expected all along, within three days Homer Barron was back in town. A neighbor saw the Negro man admit him at the kitchen door at dusk one evening.

And that was the last we saw of Homer Barron. And of Miss Emily for some time. The Negro man went in and out with the market basket, but the front door remained closed. Now and then we would see her at a window for a moment, as the men did that night when they sprinkled the lime, but for almost six months she did not appear on the streets. Then we knew that this was to be expected too; as if that quality of her father which had thwarted her woman's life so many times had been too virulent and too furious to die.

When we next saw Miss Emily, she had grown fat and her hair was turning gray. During the next few years it grew grayer and grayer until it attained an even pepper-and-salt iron-gray, when it ceased turning. Up to the day of her death at seventy-four it was still that vigorous iron-gray, like the hair of an active man.

---

① the Baptist minister: 浸礼会牧师。
② Grierson: of the traits of the Griersons, such as pride, arrogance and self-importance.

From that time on her front door remained closed, save for a period of six or seven years, when she was about forty, during which she gave lessons in china-painting. She fitted up a studio in one of the downstairs rooms, where the daughters and granddaughters of Colonel Sartoris' contemporaries were sent to her with the same regularity and in the same spirit that they were sent to church on Sundays with a twenty-five-cent piece for the collection plate①. Meanwhile her taxes had been remitted.

Then the newer generation became the backbone and the spirit of the town, and the painting pupils grew up and fell away and did not send their children to her with boxes of color and tedious brushes and pictures cut from the ladies' magazines. The front door closed upon the last one and remained closed for good. When the town got free postal delivery, Miss Emily alone refused to let them fasten the metal numbers above her door and attach a mailbox to it. She would not listen to them.

Daily, monthly, yearly we watched the Negro grow grayer and more stooped, going in and out with the market basket. Each December we sent her a tax notice, which would be returned by the post office a week later, unclaimed. Now and then we would see her in one of the downstairs windows—she had evidently shut up the top floor of the house—like the carven torso of an idol in a niche, looking or not looking at us, we could never tell which. Thus she passed from generation to generation—dear, inescapable, impervious, tranquil, and perverse.

And so she died. Fell ill in the house filled with dust and shadows, with only a doddering Negro man to wait on her. We did not even know she was sick; we had long since given up trying to get any information from the Negro.

He talked to no one, probably not even to her, for his voice had grown harsh and rusty, as if from disuse.

She died in one of the downstairs rooms, in a heavy walnut bed with a curtain, her gray head propped on a pillow yellow and moldy with age and lack of sunlight.

V

The Negro met the first of the ladies at the front door and let them in, with their hushed, sibilant voices and their quick, curious glances, and then he disappeared. He walked right through the house and out the back and was not seen again.

The two female cousins came at once. They held the funeral on the second day, with the town coming to look at Miss Emily beneath a mass of bought flowers, with the crayon face of her father musing profoundly above the bier and the ladies sibilant

---

① the collection plate: the plate used to collect donations in the church(捐款盘).

and macabre; and the very old men—some in their brushed Confederate uniforms—on the porch and the lawn, talking of Miss Emily as if she had been a contemporary of theirs, believing that they had danced with her and courted her perhaps, confusing time with its mathematical progression, as the old do, to whom all the past is not a diminishing road but, instead, a huge meadow which no winter ever quite touches, divided from them now by the narrow bottle-neck of the most recent decade of years.

Already we knew that there was one room in that region above stairs which no one had seen in forty years, and which would have to be forced. They waited until Miss Emily was decently in the ground before they opened it.

The violence of breaking down the door seemed to fill this room with pervading dust. A thin, acrid pall as of the tomb seemed to lie everywhere upon this room decked and furnished as for a bridal: upon the valance curtains of faded rose color, upon the rose-shaded lights, upon the dressing table, upon the delicate array of crystal and the man's toilet things backed with tarnished silver, silver so tarnished that the monogram① was obscured. Among them lay a collar and tie, as if they had just been removed, which, lifted, left upon the surface a pale crescent in the dust. Upon a chair hung the suit, carefully folded; beneath it the two mute shoes and the discarded socks.

The man himself lay in the bed.

For a long while we just stood there, looking down at the profound and fleshless grin. The body had apparently once lain in the attitude of an embrace, but now the long sleep that outlasts love, that conquers even the grimace of love, had cuckolded him②. What was left of him, rotted beneath what was left of the nightshirt, had become inextricable from the bed in which he lay; and upon him and upon the pillow beside him lay that even coating of the patient and biding dust.

Then we noticed that in the second pillow was the indentation of a head. One of us lifted something from it, and leaning forward, that faint and invisible dust dry and acrid in the nostrils, we saw a long strand of iron-gray hair.

译文链接：https://vipreader.qidian.com/chapter/1016846967/503531684/

Questions for Understanding

1. Who is Miss Emily? What qualities does Miss Emily possess? What is the significance of her refusal to pay her taxes and bury her dead father?

---

① monogram: 由姓名首字母组成的图案。
② the long sleep that outlasts love, that conquers even the grimace of love, had cuckolded him: 比爱情更为持久、甚至战胜爱情煎熬的永恒的长眠已将他驯服了。

2. What do the people of the town think of Miss Emily? Why do the men in the town regard Miss Emily Grierson's death as a falling of the monument?
3. Who is Homer Baron? Why does the author give him such an identity? What happens to him? Why does Emily kill him?
4. What is the time sequence in the story? Try to outline the order of events as they happen in the story, and then contrast it with the order in which they are told. How does the construction of the plot create interest and suspense?
5. What is the meaning of the title of the story? What does the story imply about the relationship between past and present, permanence and change?

Aspects of Appreciation

1. "A Rose for Emily" has a symbolic title which involves several implications.

In one way, a rose is traditionally connected with the romantic love. However, the rose in this story bears the connotation of horror and death, as the room where the rotten corpse of Emily's lover lies is decorated with the color of roses, from the curtain to the lampshades. Therefore, in this sense, the title carries an ironic meaning, "a dead rotten love". For another, a rose also means a gift to a beloved one, a token in memory of somebody. In this story, Miss Emily is treated with a certain touch of compassion and pity by Faulkner. Though being eccentric, asocial, perverse, and even committing a murder, she is a tragic woman who invites sympathy. Though tortured by the forces beyond her control, she still struggles to assert her dignity and pride even in the form of madness. Thus, the whole story could be viewed as a rose — a salute given by Faulkner to Miss Emily as well as the Old South which she stands for.

2. The tragedy of Miss Emily could be attributed to both external and internal factors.

Born in an aristocratic southern family and dominated by a tyrannical father, she is seen as a figure to be highly admired but never approached. Her prestigious root makes the townspeople respect her as a symbol of the Old South and "an idol in the niche". However, on the other hand, this reputation and the strict domination of her father deprive her of any opportunities for a happy marriage and for a normal woman's life. After her father dies, she makes a certain attempt to break away from these restraints, but sadly ends up in failure. When she falls in love with Homer Barron, a Northern laborer, she is accused of being fallen and bringing a disgrace to the town. Though still carrying her head high "in her dignity as the last Grierson" and going out with her lover over the public's protest, the social and patriarchal pressure as well as the disloyalty of Homer Barron torture her so much that eventually she has no choice but to resort to the terrifying murder. What's more, her tragic life is partly due to her own faults. She puts herself into the prison of the past, which means privilege and glory to her, and thus refuses to adapt to the inevitable change and loss when time goes by. Just as the invisible watch under her clothes hints, she isolates herself in her own private and secret time despite the fast progression of the time and tremendous changes accompanying it. And this pathetic attempt to cling to the past gradually develops into a kind of unusual obsession, either for her father's memory or for her secluded life, and finally ends up in morbid insanity, which prompts her to poison her beloved one in order to keep him for good.

Though her mind is insane, her actions grotesque and horrible, Miss Emily is still a tragic woman who deserves certain respect and pity rather than disgust or fear. By presenting her tragedy, Faulkner not only expresses his mixed feelings of pity and criticism towards her, but also reveals his ambivalent attitude towards the Old South which she symbolizes, a feeling not altogether unfriendly and critical, one probably of pride and respect.

3. In terms of narrative skills, the story is narrated from a first-person plural perspective. Though in the whole story, the identity of the collective narrator is not specifically given, from the context we can infer that the narrator, "We" in the story, probably speaks for the whole town of Jefferson. As interested witnesses, or to some extent, crazy fans of Miss Emily, the collective narrator closely observes the life of the "celebrity" of their town. The narration of the collective narrator adds some factual and convincing elements to the story, and tempts us readers to speculate about why Miss Emily killed her lover.

The complexity and intricacy of this story depends much on the unique arrangement of the order of the events. Unlike his contemporaries, Faulkner does not present the story in a linear order, but rather moves back and forth between the past and the present frequently or rapidly to provide information that leads up to the final startling moment. This way of arranging events in a plot can be conducive to suspense, and cause the reader to be deeply immersed in the story.

4. This masterpiece bears many traits of Gothic novels. The atmosphere of gloom and depression hovers over the whole story from the very beginning to the end. The decrepit and desolate house decorated with cupolas and spires, the dim and disused room full of dank smell, the mysterious and speechless old servant, the lonely spinster with pallid face and eccentric behaviors, the strange and disgusting smell, and the

decayed corpse, all are interwoven together to create a gloomy and depressive scene, render the readers the impressive sensation of an impending horror, and dramatize Emily's distorted personality and life. However, despite all these Gothic elements, the feelings evoked by this story are not just as horrible and suffocating as those aroused by the traditional Gothic novels, for the Gothic elements also serve as a foil for the tragedy of Miss Emily. Alongside with the despair and gloom, the readers might in the meantime experience such strong emotions as sympathy and pity. Just like the title suggests, it is more than a horrible story involving desolation and blood, but also one with certain touch of "rose" color.

Suggested Further Reading

The Sound and the Fury (1929); *Absalom, Absalom!* (1936); "Barn Burning" (1939).

Topics for Further Study

1. John Donne once wrote, "No man is an island entire of itself; every man is a piece of the continent, a part of the main." Do you think it is reasonable? Try to use Miss Emily's tragedy to justify this point of view.

2. Faulkner is considered one of the most important Southern writers along with Mark Twain, Flannery O'Connor, Katherine Anne Porter, and Tennessee Williams. What do his works tell you about the culture and mores of the American South? Try to combine it with those reflected in the works of other southern men of letters to get more insights into the American South.

Knowledge of Literature

1. Stream of Consciousness（意识流）

The stream of consciousness is a narrative method of capturing and representing the inner thought of a character's mind. The technique was first employed by Édouard Dujardin in his novel *Les Lauriers sont coupés* (1888) and was subsequently used by such notable writers as James Joyce, Virginia Woolf, and William Faulkner. Usually, it is used to reflect all the forces, external and internal, influencing the psychology of a character at a single moment.

2. Gothic Novel（哥特式小说）

The Gothic novel was initiated by Horace Walpole's *The Castle of Otranto* in

1764, and has flourished since the early 19th century. Typically, Gothic novels are tales of horror and mystery, usually set in gloomy medieval castles or monasteries with a sinister, grotesque, or claustrophobic atmosphere. The principal aims of such novels are to evoke the feeling of terror and fear, forcibly expose the dark side of the society, and explore the darkness in humanity.

3. Unreliable Narrator（不可靠叙述者）

The unreliable narrator is one whose perception, interpretation, and evaluation of the matters he or she narrates do not coincide with the opinions and norms implied by the author, which the author expects the alert reader to share. You can almost always trust omniscient narrators. But be suspicious of first-person narrators and characters who serve as centers of consciousness. They may be self-deceived, untruthful, gullible, mentally troubled, innocent, inexperienced or self-serving. In the case of an unreliable narrator, the decreased credibility leaves space for the appreciation of dramatic irony and helps to develop both character and theme.

推荐阅读的论文：
[1] 任世芳. 韦恩·布斯的修辞伦理批评——从《小说修辞学》到《小说伦理学》[J]. 首都师范大学学报（社会科学版），2018（2）.
[2] 谭君强. 论叙事作品中叙述者的可靠与不可靠性 [J]. 思想战线，2005（6）.

Eugene O'Neill (1888~1953)

About the Author

Eugene O'Neill is universally acclaimed as America's greatest playwright of the 20th century, and is honored as "Father of Modern American Drama". He inaugurated modern American drama by making enormous contributions to its development and prosperity. Having dedicated his whole life to play writing, he won the Pulitzer Prize four times. In 1936, O'Neill was awarded the Nobel Prize for literature, as one of the Swiss critic commented on him, "there may be arguments about who is the greatest living American poet, or novelist, or essayist, but the position of O'Neill as the leading American dramatist has never been seriously questioned. This is an almost unique occurrence in modern criticism." His plays examined the coldness of an indifferent universe, the materialistic greed of human beings, the problems of discovering one's true identity, and the nature of fate.

Eugene O'Neill was born at a shabby hotel on Broadway in New York on October 16, 1888. His father was James O'Neill, an outstanding romantic actor. Also crucial to his development as a playwright was the nature of his family life. Guilt, betrayal and accusations, implicitly or explicitly, are found in most of his plays. Six years of Catholic schooling were succeeded by four at the Betts Academy, and Eugene's formal education ended with an unfinished year at Princeton University in 1907.

O'Neill began writing plays after being hospitalized for tuberculosis in 1912. On his release from the sanitarium, he enrolled in Professor George Pierce Baker's classes on playwriting at Harvard. In 1916, he joined the Provincetown Players, the ensemble with which his professional career began.

The Provincetown Players' production of *Bound East for Cardiff* (1916) signaled a new era in American drama. By the end of 1918, the players had produced 10 of O'Neill's plays. Combined with the support of the critic George Jean Nathan, it rocketed O'Neill into prominence. His plays of the sea were successful, particularly *Bound East for Cardiff* (1916), *In the Zone* (1917), *The Long Voyage Home* (1917), and *The Moon of the Caribbees* (1918), which were sometimes produced together under the title of *S.S. Glencairn* (1918).

In his early plays, O'Neill wrote mostly in short one-act form. His apprenticeship in this form culminated in great success with the production of his full-length *Beyond the Horizon* (1920), for which he won his first Pulitzer Prize. Although the play is essentially naturalistic, O'Neill elevates both characterization and dialogue, for the first time, by adding a poetic and articulate character.

In the 15 years following the appearance of *Beyond the Horizon*, 21 plays were produced. His many plays of the 1920s include *The Emperor Jones* (1921), *The Hairy Ape* (1922), *Anna Christie* (1922, Pulitzer Prize), *Desire Under the Elms* (1925), *The Great God Brown* (1926) and *Strange Interlude* (1928, Pulitzer Prize). *The Emperor Jones* (1920) is a theatrical piece in which Brutus Jones moves from reality, to conscious memories of his past, to subconscious roots of his ancient heritage, as he flees for his life. The play ends in the reality of his death. Another expressionistic piece, *The Hairy Ape* (1922), traces the path of a crude stoker shocked into self-awareness by a decadent lady, as he tries to find out where he belongs to in the world.

Among his later plays, *Mourning Becomes Electra* (1931), *Ah! Wilderness* (1933, his only comedy), *The Iceman Cometh* (1946), and the autobiographical *Long Day's Journey into Night* (produced in 1956, Pulitzer Prize) are considered his masterpieces.

In his later life, O'Neill's most ambitious project was a planned cycle of eleven plays tracing the history of a single American family for over a century. Before his death he destroyed most of the material for these plays, but two survived. Sickly, embittered, and overwhelmed with the despair that had long overshadowed his life, O'Neill died on November 27, 1953.

O'Neill's mastery of the form and his experiments with technique and theme earned heaps of critical praise. He has freed American plays from the mono-division of good and evil characters in the melodrama. Each of his plays is an exploration into and a deep concern for human nature as he introduces a wide range of new themes and styles to the American stage.

Long Day's Journey into Night

About the Play

Long Day's Journey into Night is a four-act tragic play created by O'Neill between 1939 and 1941. Chronicling a single day in the life of the Tyrone family, this masterpiece revolves around the heart-wrenching relationships between James Tyrone, his wife Mary and their two sons, Jamie and Edmund in a realistic and arresting style.

The father, James Tyrone, is a retired actor whose appalling miserliness has to some degree ruined his own talent and his relationship with his family members. In order to save pennies, he has chosen a quack doctor to treat his wife Mary when she gave birth to a child. The poor treatment has triggered Mary to get addicted to morphine for years. Though she loves her family much and has been institutionalized for the addiction, Mary resumes the habit soon and gradually retreats, via morphine, into memory from the unhappy married life. Their elder son Jamie is a cynical loser who idles away his life in chasing women and drinking, while the younger son Edmund, a sensitive and disillusioned young man, is greatly stricken with tuberculosis. Although they live under the same roof, they are constantly baffled, tormented and wounded by the war between love and hate. As the day turns into night, the whole family undergoes an inexorable descent into darkness as well as despair.

Because of its deeply personal nature, as much of it closely parallels O'Neill's own life, this play was not revealed to the public until 1956, three years after his death. Since its first world premiere on February 10th of that year in Stockholm, it has received enormous critical acclaim and garnered a fourth Pulitzer Prize for O'Neill.

Act Two, Scene Two

SCENE The same, about a half hour later[①]. The tray with the bottle of whiskey has been removed from the table. The family are returning from lunch as the curtain rises. Mary is the first to enter from the back parlor. Her husband follows. He is not

---

① The same, about a half hour later: the living room of the Tyrones' summer home, about 1:30 in the afternoon of one day in August, 1912.

with her as he was in the similar entrance after breakfast at the opening of Act One. He avoids touching her or looking at her. There is condemnation in his face[①], mingled now with the beginning of an old weary, helpless resignation. Jamie and Edmund follow their father. Jamie's face is hard with defensive cynicism. Edmund tries to copy this defense but without success. He plainly shows he is heartsick as well as physically ill.

Mary is terribly nervous again, as if the strain of sitting through lunch with them had been too much for her. Yet at the same time, in contrast to this, her expression shows more of that strange aloofness which seems to stand apart from her nerves and the anxieties which harry them.

She is talking as she enters—a stream of words that issues casually, in a routine of family conversation, from her mouth. She appears indifferent to the fact that their thoughts are not on what she is saying any more than her own are. As she talks, she comes to the left of the table and stands, facing front, one hand fumbling with the bosom of her dress, the other playing over the table top. Tyrone lights a cigar and goes to the screen door, staring out. Jamie fills a pipe from a jar on top of the bookcase at rear. He lights it as he goes to look out the window at right. Edmund sits in a chair by the table, turned half away from his mother so he does not have to watch her.

MARY

It's no use finding fault with Bridget[②]. She doesn't listen. I can't threaten her, or she'd threaten she'd leave. And she does do her best at times. It's too bad they seem to be just the times you're sure to be late, James. Well, there's this consolation: it's difficult to tell her cooking whether she's doing her best or her worst.

She gives a little laugh of detached amusement indifferently.

Never mind. The summer will soon be over, thank goodness. Your season will open again and we can go back to second-rate hotels and trains. I hate them, too, but at least I don't expect them to be like a home, and there's no housekeeping to worry about. It's unreasonable to expect Bridget or Cathleen[③] to act as if this was a home. They know it isn't as well as we know it. It never has been and it never will be.

TYRONE

Bitterly without turning around.

---

① There is condemnation in his face: At that time Tyrone has already found that Mary, who was recently discharged from a sanatorium as cured of morphine addiction, begins to take drugs again.
② Bridget: the cook of the Tyrones.
③ Cathleen: the housemaid of the Tyrones(蒂龙家的女佣).

No, it never can be now. But it was once, before you—①

MARY

Her face instantly set in blank denial.
Before I what?
There is a dead silence. She goes on with a return of her detached air.
No, no. whatever you mean, it isn't true, dear. It was never a home. You've always preferred the Club or a bathroom. And for me it's always as lonely as a dirty room in a one-night stand hotel. In a real home one is never lonely. You forget I know from experience what a home is like. I gave up to marry you—my father's home.
At once, through an association of ideas she turns to Edmund.
Her manner becomes tenderly solicitous, but there is the strange quality of detachment in it.
I'm worried about you, Edmund. You hardly touched a thing at lunch. That's no way to take care of yourself. It's all right for me not to have an appetite. I've been growing too fat. But you must eat.
Coaxingly maternal.
Promise me you will, dear, for my sake.

EDMUND

Dully.
Yes, Mama.

MARY

Pats his cheek as he tries not to shrink away.
That's a good boy.
There is another pause of dead silence. Then the telephone in the front hall rings and all of them stiffen startledly.

TYRONE

Hastily.
I'll answer. McGuire② said he'd call me.
He goes out through the front parlor.

---

① before you—: before you began to take drugs.
② McGuire: a real estate agent(房地产经纪人).

MARY

Indifferently.

McGuire. He must have another piece of property on his list that no one would think of buying except your father. It doesn't matter any more, but it's always seemed to me your father could afford to keep on buying property but never to give me a home.

She stops to listen as Tyrone's voice is heard from the hall.

TYRONE

Hello.

With forced heartiness.

Oh, how are you, Doctor?

Jamie turns from the window. Mary's fingers play more rapidly on the table top. Tyrone's voice, trying to conceal, reveals that he is hearing bad news.

I see—

Hurriedly.

Well, you'll explain all about it when you see him this afternoon. Yes, he'll be in without fall. Four o'clock. I'll drop in myself and have a talk with you before that. I have to go uptown on business, anyway. Goodbye, doctor.

EDMUND

Dully.

That didn't sound like glad tidings.

Jamie gives him a pitying glance—hen looks out the window again. Mary's face is terrified and her hands flutter distractedly. Tyrone comes in. The strain is obvious in his casualness as he addressed Edmund.

TYRONE

It was Doctor Hardy[①]. He wants you to be sure and see him at four.

EDMUND

Dully.

What did he say? Not that I give a damn now.

MARY

Bursts out excitedly.

---

① Doctor Hardy: the incompetent doctor who once treated Mary.

I wouldn't believe him if he swore on a stack of Bibles. You mustn't pay attention to a word he says, Edmund.

TYRONE

Sharply.
Mary!

MARY

More excitedly.
Oh, we all realize why you like him, James! Because he's cheap! But please don't try to tell me! I know all about Doctor Hardy. Heaven knows I ought to after all these years. He's ignorant fool! There should be a law to keep men like him from practicing. He hasn't the slightest idea—when you're in agony and half insane, he sits and holds your hand and delivers sermons on will power!

Her face is drawn in an expression of intense suffering by the memory. For the moment, she loses all caution. With bitter hatred.

He deliberately humiliates you! He makes you beg and plead! He treats you like a criminal! He understands nothing! And yet it was exactly the same type of cheap quack who first gave you the medicine—and you never knew what it was until too late!

Passionately.

I hate doctors! They'll do anything—anything to keep you coming to them. They'll sell their souls! What's worse, they'll sell yours and you never know it till one day you find yourself in hell!

EDMUND

Mama! For God's sake, stop talking.

TYRONE

Shakenly.
Yes, Mary, it's no time—

MARY

Suddenly is overcome by guilty confusion—stammers.
I—Forgive me, dear. You're right. It's useless to be angry now.

There is again a pause of dead silence. When she speaks again, her face has cleared and is calm, and the quality of uncanny detachment is in her voice and manner.

I'm going upstairs for a moment, if you'll excuse me. I have to fix my hair.
She adds smilingly.
That is if I can find my glasses. I'll be right down.

TYRONE

As she starts through the doorway—pleading and rebuking.
Mary!

MARY

Turns to stare at him calmly.
Yes, dear? What is it?

TYRONE

Helplessly.
Nothing.

MARY

With a strange derisive smile.
You're welcome to come up and watch me if you're so suspicious.

TYRONE

As if that could do any good! You'd only postpone it[①]. And I'm not your jailor. This isn't a prison.

MARY

No, I know you can't help thinking it's a home.
She adds quickly with a detached contrition.
I'm sorry, dear. I don't mean to be bitter. It's not your fault.
She turns and disappears through the back parlor. The three in the room remain silent. It is as if they were waiting until she got upstairs before speaking.

JAMIE

Cynically brutal.
Another shot in the arm!

---

① postpone it: postpone taking drugs.

EDMUND

Angrily.
Cut out that kind of talk!

TYRONE

Yes! Hold your foul tongue and your rotten Broadway loafer's lingo! Have you no pity or decency?

Losing his temper.

You ought to be kicked out in the gutter! But if I did it, you know damned well who'd weep and plead for you, and excuse you and complain till I let you come back.

JAMIE

A spasm of pain crossed his face.

Christ, don't I know that? No pity? I have all the pity in the world for her. I understand what a hard game to beat she's up against—which is more than you ever have! My lingo didn't mean I had no feeling. I was merely putting bluntly what we all know, and have to live with now, again.

Bitterly.

The cures are no damned good except for a while. The truth is there is no cure and we've been saps[①] to hope—

Cynically.

They never come back!

EDMUND

Scornfully parodying his brother's cynicism.

They never come back! Everything is in the bag! It's all a frame-up[②]! We're all fall guys and suckers and we can't beat the game!

Disdainfully.

Christ, if I felt the way you do—!

JAMIE

Stung for a moment—then shrugging his shoulders, dryly.

I thought you did. Your poetry isn't very cheery. Nor the stuff you read and claim you admire.

He indicates the small bookcase at rear.

---

① sap: vigor or energy.
② frame-up: (informal) a plot to bring about a dishonest result, as in a contest.

Your pet with the unpronounceable name, for example.

EDMUND
Nietzsche[1]. You don't know what you're talking about. You haven't read him.

JAMIE
Enough to know it's a lot of bunk[2]!

TYRONE
Shut up, both of you! There's little choice between the philosophy you learned from Broadway loafers, and the one Edmund got from his books. They're both rotten to the core. You've both flouted the faith you were born and brought up in—the one true faith of the Catholic Church—and your denial has brought nothing but self-destruction!

His two sons stare at him contemptuously. They forget their quarrel and are as one against him on this issue.

EDMUND
That's the bunk, Papa!

JAMIE
We don't pretend, at any rate.
Caustically.
I don't notice you've worn any holes in the knees of your pants going to Mass.

TYRONE
It's true I'm a bad Catholic in the observance, God forgive me. But I believe!
Angrily.
And you're a liar! I may not go to church but every night and morning of my life I get on my knees and pray!

EDMUND
Bitterly.

---

[1] Nietzsche: Friedrich Wilhelm Nietzsche (1844~1900), who was a German philosopher, poet, and critic, noted for his concept of superman and his rejection of traditional Christian values. His chief works are The Birth of Tragedy (1872), Thus Spake Zarathustra (1883-91), and Beyond Good and Evil (1886).

[2] bunk: (informal) bunkum, nonsense(胡说八道，无稽之谈).

Did you pray for Mama?

TYRONE

I did. I've prayed to God these many years for her.

EDMUND

Then Nietzsche must be right.
He quotes from Thus Spake Zarathustra.
"God is dead: of His pity for man hath God died."

TYRONE

Ignores this.
If your mother had prayed, too—She hasn't denied her faith, but she's forgotten it, until now there's no strength of the spirit left in her to fight against her curse.
Then dully resigned.
But what's the good of talk? We've lived with this before and now we must again. There's no help for it.
Bitterly.
Only I wish she hadn't led me to hope this time. By God, I never will again!

EDMUND

That's a rotten thing to say, Papa!
Defiantly.
Well, I'll hope! She's just started. It can't have got a hold on her yet! She can still stop. I'm going to talk to her.

JAMIE

Shrugs his shoulder.
You can't talk to her now. She'll listen but she won't listen. She'll be here but she won't be here. You know the way she gets.

TYRONE

Yes, that's the way the poison acts on her always. Every day from now on, there'll be the same drifting away from us until by the end of each night—

EDMUND

Miserably.

Cut it out, Papa!
He jumps up from his chair.
I'm going to get dressed.
Bitterly, as he goes.
I'll make so much noise she can't suspect I've come to spy on her.
He disappears through the front parlor and can be heard stamping noisily upstairs.

JAMIE
After a pause.
What did Doc Hardy say about the Kid?

TYRONE
Dully.
It's what you thought. He's got consumption.

JAMIE
God damn it!

TYRONE
There is no possible doubt, he said.

JAMIE
He'll have to go to a sanatorium.

TYRONE
Yes, and the sooner the better, Hardy said, for him and everyone around him. He claims that in six months to a year Edmund will be cured, if he obeys orders.
He sighs—gloomily and resentfully.
I never thought a child of mine—It doesn't come from my side of the family. There wasn't one of us that didn't have lungs as strong as an ox.

JAMIE
Who gives a damn about that part of it! Where does Hardy want to send him?

TYRONE
That's what I'm to see him about.

JAMIE
Well, for God's sake, pick out a good place and not some cheap dump!

TYRONE
Stung.
I'll send him wherever Hardy thinks best!

JAMIE
Well, don't give Hardy your old over-the-hills-to-the-poorhouse song[①] about taxes and mortgages.

TYRONE
I'm no millionaire who can throw money away! Why shouldn't I tell Hardy the truth?

JAMIE
Because he'll think you want him to pick a cheap dump, and because he'll know it isn't the truth—especially if he hears afterwards you've seen McGuire and let that flannel-mouth, gold-brick merchant sting you with another piece of bum property!

TYRONE
Furiously.
Keep your nose out of my business!

JAMIE
This is Edmund's business. What I'm afraid of is, with your Irish bogtrotter[②] idea that consumption is fatal, you'll figure it would be a waste of money to spend any more than you can help.

TYRONE
You liar!

JAMIE
All right. Prove I'm a liar. That's what I want. That's why I brought it up.

---

①. over-the-hills-to-the-poorhouse song: miserable life.
② Bogtrotter: 爱尔兰人(含冒犯意)。

TYRONE

His rage still smouldering.

I have every hope Edmund will be cured. And keep your dirty tongue off Ireland! You're a fine one to sneer, with the map of it on your face[①]!

JAMIE

Not after I wash my face.

Then before his father can react to this insult to the Old Sod[②], he adds dryly, shrugging his shoulders.

Well, I've said all I have to say. It's up to you.

Abruptly.

What do you want me to do this afternoon, now you're going uptown? I've done all I can do on the hedge until you cut more of it. You don't want me to go ahead with your clipping, Iknow that.

TYRONE

No. You'd get it crooked, as you get everything else.

JAMIE

Then I'd better go uptown with Edmund. The bad news coming on top of what's happened to Mama may hit him hard.

TYRONE

Forgetting his quarrel.

Yes, go with him, Jamie. Keep up his spirits, if you can.

He adds caustically.

If you can without making it an excuse to get drunk!

JAMIE

What would I use for money? The last I heard they still selling booze, not giving it way.

He starts for the front-parlor doorway.

I'll get dressed.

He stops in the doorway as he sees his mother approaching from the hall, and

---

① with the map of it on your face: here Tyrone indicates that Jamie bears great resemblance to the Irishman.
② Old Sod: (informal) one's native country.

moves aside to let her come in. Her eyes look brighter, and her manner is more detached. This change becomes more marked as the scene goes on.

MARY

Vaguely.

You haven't seen my glasses anywhere, have you, Jamie?

She doesn't look at him. He glances way, ignoring her question but she doesn't seem to expect an answer. She comes forward, addressing her husband without looking at him.

You haven't seen them, have you, James?

Behind her Jamie disappears through the front parlor.

TYRONE

Turns to look out the screen door.

No, Mary.

MARY

What's the matter with Jamie? Have you been nagging at him again? You shouldn't treat him with such contempt all the time. He's not to blame. If he'd been brought up in a real home, I'm sure he would have been different.

She comes to the windows at right—lightly.

You're not much of weather prophet, dear. See how hazy it's getting. I can hardly see the other shore.

TYRONE

Trying to speak naturally.

Yes, I spoke too soon. We're in for another night of fog, I'm afraid.

MARY

Oh, well, I won't mind it tonight.

TYRONE

No, I don't imagine you will, Mary.

MARY

Flashes a glance at him—after a pause.

I don't see Jamie going down to the hedge. Where did he go?

TYRONE

He's going with Edmund to the Doctor's. He went up to change his clothes.

Then, glad of an excuse to leave her.

I'd better do the same or I'll be late for my appointment at the Club.

He makes a move toward the front-parlor doorway, but with a swift impulsive movement she reaches out and clasps his arm.

MARY

A note of pleading in her voice.

Don't go yet, dear. I don't want to be alone.

Hastily.

I mean, you have plenty of time. You know you boast you can dress in one-tenth the time it takes the boys.

Vaguely.

There is something I wanted to say. What is it? I've forgotten. I'm glad Jamie is going uptown. You didn't give him any money, I hope.

TYRONE

I did not.

MARY

He'd only spend it on drink and you know what a vile, poisonous tongue he has when he's drunk. Not that I would mind anything he said tonight, but he always manages to drive you into a rage, especially if you're drunk, too, as you will be.

TYRONE

Resentfully.

I won't. I never get drunk.

MARY

Teasing indifferently.

Oh, I'm sure you'll hold it well. You always have. It's hard for a stranger to tell, but after thirty-five years of marriage—

TYRONE

I've never missed a performance in my life. That's the proof!

Then bitterly.

If I did get drunk it is not you who should blame me. No man has ever had a better reason.

MARY

Reason? What reason? You always drink too much when you go to the Club, don't you? Particularly when you meet McGuire. He sees to that. Don't think I'm finding fault, dear. You must do as you please. I won't mind.

TYRONE

I know you won't.
He turns toward the front parlor, anxious to escape.
I've got to get dressed.

MARY

Again she reached out and grasps his arm—pleadingly.

No, please wait a little while, dear. At least, until one the boys comes down. You will all be leaving me so soon.

TYRONE

With bitter sadness.
It's you who are leaving us, Mary.

MARY

I? That's silly thing to say, James. How could I leave? There is nowhere I could go. Who would I go to see? I have no friends.

TYRONE

It's your own fault—
He stops and sighs helplessly—persuasively.
There's surly one thing you can do this afternoon that will be good for you, May. Take a drive in the automobile. Get away from the house. Get a little sun and fresh air.
Injuredly.
I bought the automobile for you. You know I don't like the damned things. I'd rather walk any day, or take a trolley.
With growing resentment.
I had it here waiting for you when you came back from the sanatorium. I hoped it

would give you pleasure and distract your mind. You used to ride in it every day, but you've hardly used it at all lately. I paid a lot of money Icouldn't afford, and there's the chauffeur I have to board and lodge and pay high wages whether he drives you or not.

Bitterly.

Waste! The same old waste that will land me in the poorhouse in my old age! What good did it do you? I might as well have thrown the money out the window.

MARY

With detached calm.

Yes, it was a waste of money, James. You shouldn't have brought a secondhand automobile. You were swindled again as you always are, because you insist on secondhand bargains in everything.

TYRONE

It's one of the best makes! Everyone says it's better than any of the new one!

MARY

Ignoring this.

It was another waster to hire Smythe, who was only a helper in a garage and had never been a chauffeur. Oh, I realize his wages are less than a real chauffeur's but he more than makes up for that, I'm sure, by the graft he gets from the garage on repair bills. Something is always wrong. Smythe sees to that, I'm afraid.

TYRONE

I don't believe it! He may not be a fancy millionaire's flunky[①] but he's honest! You're as bad as Jamie, suspecting everyone!

MARY

You mustn't be offended, dear. I wasn't offended when you gave me the automobile. I knew you didn't mean to humiliate me. I knew that was the way you had to do everything. I was grateful and touched. I knew buying the car was a hard thing for you to do, and it proved how much you loved me, in your way, especially when you couldn't really believe it would do me any good.

---

① flunky: a liveried manservant(穿制服的男仆).

TYRONE

Mary!

He suddenly hugs her to him—brokenly.

Dear Mary! For the love of God, for my sake and the boys' sake and your own, won't you stop now?

MARY

Stammers in guilty confusion for a second.

I—James! Please!

Her strange, stubborn defense comes back instantly.

Stop what? What are you talking about?

He lets his arm fall to his side brokenly. She impulsively puts her arms around him.

James! We've loved each other! We always will! Let's remember only that, and not try to understand what we cannot understand, or help things that cannot be helped—the things life has done to us we cannot excuse or explain.

TYRONE

As if he hadn't heard—bitterly.

You won't even try?

MARY

Her arms drop hopelessly and she turns away—with detachment.

Try to go for a drive this afternoon, you mean? Why, yes, if you wish me to, although it makes me feel lonelier than if I stayed here. There is no one I can invite to drive with me, and I never know where to tell Smythe to go. If there was a friend's house where I could drop in and laugh and gossip a while. But, of course, there isn't. There never has been.

Her manner becoming more and more remote.

At the Convent I had so many friends. Girls whose families lived in lovely home. I used to visit them and they'd visit me in my father's home. But, naturally, after I married an actor—you know how actors were considered in those days—a lot of them gave me the cold shoulder. And then, right after we were married, there was the scandal of that women who had been your mistress, suing you. From then on, all my old friends either pitied me or cut me dead[①]. I hated the ones who cut me much less

---

[①] cut (sb.) dead: refuse to recognize sb. in public as if he were totally a stranger.

than the pitiers.

TYRONE

With guilty resentment.

For God's sake, don't dig up what's long forgotten. If you're that far gone in the past already, when it's only the beginning of the afternoon, what will you be tonight?

MARY

Stares at him defiantly now.

Come to think of it, I do have to drive uptown. There's something I must get at the drugstore.

TYRONE

Bitterly scornful.

Leave it to you to have some of the stuff hidden, and prescriptions for more! I hope you'll lay in a good stock ahead so we'll never have another night like the one when you screamed for it, and ran out of the house in your nightdress half crazy, to try and throw yourself off the dock!

MARY

Tries to ignore this.

I have to get tooth power and toilet soap and cold cream—
She breaks down pitiably.
James! You mustn't remember! You mustn't humiliate me so!

TYRONE

Ashamed.
I'm sorry. Forgive me, Mary!

MARY

Defensively detached again.

It doesn't matter. Nothing like that ever happened. You must have dreamed it.
He stares at her hopelessly. Her voice seems to drift farther and farther away.
I was so healthy before Edmund was born. You remember, James. There wasn't a nerve in my body. Even traveling with you season after season, with week after week of one-night stands, in trains without Pullmans, in dirty rooms of filthy hotels, eating bad food, bearing children in hotel rooms, I still kept healthy. But bearing Edmund

was the last straw. I was so sick afterwards, and that ignorant quack of a cheap hotel doctor—All he knew was I was in pain. It was easy for him to stop the pain.

TYRONE

Mary! For God's sake, forget the past!

MARY

With strange objective calm.

Why? How could I? The past is the present, isn't it? It's the future, too. We all try to lie out of that but life won't let us.

Going on.

I blame only myself. I swore after Eugene[①] died I would never have another baby. I was to blame for his death. If I hadn't left him with my mother to join you on the road, because you wrote telling me you missed me and were so lonely, Jamie would never have been allowed, when he still had measles, to go in the baby's room

Her face hardening.

I've always believed Jamie did it on purpose. He was jealous of the baby. He hated him.

As Tyrone starts to protest.

Oh, I know Jamie was only seven, but he was never stupid. He'd been warned it might kill the baby. He knew. I've never been able to forgive him for that.

TYRONE

With bitter sadness.

Are you back with Eugene now? Can't you let our dead baby rest in peace?

MARY

As if she hadn't heard him.

It was my fault. I should have insisted on staying with Eugene and not have let you persuade me to join you, just because I loved you. Above all, I shouldn't have you insist I have another baby to take Eugene's place, because you thought that would make me forget his death. I knew form experience buy then that children should have homes to be born in, if they are to be good children, and women need homes, if they are to be good mothers. I was afraid all the time I carried Edmund. I knew something terrible would happen. I knew I'd proved by the way I'd left Eugene that I wasn't

---

① Eugene: the second Tyrone's child who died in infancy.

worthy to have another baby, and that God would punish me if I did. I never should have born Edmund.

TYRONE

With an uneasy glance through the parlor.

Mary! Be careful with your talk. If he heard you he might think you never wanted him. He's feeling bad enough already without—

MARY

Violently.

It's a lie! I did want him! More than anything in the world! You don't understand! I meant, for his sake. He has never been happy. He never will be. Nor healthy. He was born nervous and too sensitive, and that's my fault. And now, ever since he's been so sick I've kept remembering Eugene and my father and I've been so frightened and guilty—

Then, catching herself, with an instant change to stubborn denial.

Oh, I know it's foolish to imagine dreadful things when there's no reason for it. After all, everyone has colds and gets over them.

Tyrone stares at her and sighs helplessly. He turns away toward the front parlor and sees Edmund coming down the stairs in the hall.

TYRONE

Sharply, in a low voice.

Here's Edmund. For God's sake try and be myself—at least until he goes! You can do that much for him!

He waits, forcing his face into a pleasantly paternal expression. She waits frightenedly, seized again by a nervous panic, her hands fluttering over the bosom of her dress, up to her throat and hair, with a distracted aimlessness. Then, as Edmund approaches the doorway, she cannot face him. She goes swiftly away to the windows at left and stares out with her back to the front parlor. Edmund enters. He has changed to a ready-made blue serge suit, high stiff collar and tie, black shoes.

TYRONE

With an actor's heartiness.

Well! You look spic and span[①]. I'm on my way up to change, too.

---

① spic and span: (also spick and span) completely neat and clean.

He starts to pass him.

EDMUND

Dryly.

Wait a minute, Papa. I hate to bring up disagreeable topics, but there's the matter of carfare. I'm broken.

TYRONE

Starts automatically on a customary lecture.

You'll always be broken until you learn the value—

Checks himself guiltily, looking at his son's sick face with worried pity.

But you've been learning, lad. You worked hard before you took ill. You've done splendidly. I'm proud of you.

He pulls out a small roll of bills from his pants pocket and carefully selects one. Edmund takes it. He glanced at it and his face expresses astonishment. His father again reacts customarily—sarcastically.

Thank you.

He quotes.

"How sharper than a serpent's tooth it is —"

EDMUND

"To have a thankless child.[①]" I know. Give me a change, Papa. I'm knocked speechless. This isn't a dollar. It's a ten spot[②].

TYRONE

Embarrassed by his generosity.

Put it in your pocket. You'll probably meet some of your friends uptown and you can't hold your end up and be sociable with nothing in your jeans.

EDMUND

You meant it? Gosh, thank you, Papa.

He is genuinely pleased and grateful for a moment—then he stares at his father's face with uneasy suspicion.

But why all of a sudden—?

---

① How sharper than a serpent's tooth it is/To have a thankless child: lines quoted from Shakespeare's King Lear (Act I, Scene IV).
② a ten spot: a ten-dollar bill(一张十美元的钞票).

Cynically.

Did Doc Hardy tell you I was going to die?

Then he sees his father is bitterly hurt.

NO! That's a rotten crack[①]. I was only kidding, Papa.

He puts an arm around his father impulsively and gives him an affectionate hug.

I'm very grateful. Honest, Papa.

TYRONE

Touched, returns his hug.

You're welcome, lad.

MARY

Suddenly turns to them in a confused panic of frightened anger.

I won't have it!

She stamps her foot.

Do you hear, Edmund! Such morbid nonsense! Saying you're going to die! It's the books you read! Nothing but sadness and death! Your father shouldn't allow you to have them. And some of the pomes you've written yourself are even worse! You'd think you didn't want to live! A boy of your age with everything before him! It's just a pose you get out of books! You're not really sick at all!

TYRONE

Mary! Hold your tongue!

MARY

Instantly changing to a detached tone.

But, James, it's absurd of Edmund to be so gloomy and make such a great to-do about nothing.

Turing to Edmund but avoiding his eyes— teasingly affectionate.

Never mind, dear. I'm on to you[②].

She comes to him.

You want to be petted and spoiled and made a fuss over, isn't that it? You're still such a baby.

She puts her arm around him and hugs him. He remains rigid and unyielding. Her voice begins to tremble.

---

① crack: a witty or sarcastic remark(诙谐或讽刺的话语).
② be on to: (slang) to be aware of or have information about.

But please don't carry it too far, dear. Don't say horrible thing. I know it's foolish to take them seriously but I can't help it. You've got me— so frightened.

She breaks and hides her face on his shoulder, sobbing. Edmund is moved in spite of himself. He pats her shoulder with an awkward tenderness.

EDMUND

Don't, mother.
His eyes meet his father's.

TYRONE

Huskily—clutching at hopeless hope.
Maybe if you asked your mother now what you said you were going to —
He fumbles with his watch.
By God, look at the time! I'll have to shake a leg.
He hurries away through the front parlor. Mary lifts her head. Her manner is again one of detached motherly solicitude. She seems to have forgotten the tears which are still in her eyes.

MARY

How do you feel, dear?
She feels his forehead.
Your head is a little hot, but that's just from going out in the sun. You look ever so much better than you did this morning.
Taking his head.
Come and sit down. You mustn't stand on your feet so much. You must learn to husband your strength.
She gets him to sit and she sits sideways on the arm of his chair, an arm around his shoulder, so he cannot meet her eyes.

EDMUND

Starts to blurt out the appeal he now feels is quite hopeless.
Listen, Mama—

MARY

Interrupting quickly.
Now, now! Don't talk. Lean back and rest.
Persuasively.

You know, I think it would be much better for you if you stayed home this afternoon and let me take care of you. It's such as a tiring trip uptown in the dirty old trolley on a hot day like this. I'm sure you'd be much better off here with me.

EDMUND
Dully.
You forget I have an appointment with Hardy.
Trying again to get his appeal started.
Listen, Mama—

MARY
Quickly.
You can telephone and say you don't feel well enough.
Excitedly.
It's simply a waste of time and money seeing him. He'll only tell you some lie. He'll pretend he's found something serious the matter because that's his bread and butter.
She gives a hard sneering little laugh.
The old idiot! All he knows about medicine is to look solemn and preach will power!

EDMUND
Trying to catch her eyes.
Mama! Please listen! I want to ask you something! You—you're only just started. You can still stop. You've got the will power! We'll all help you. I'll do anything! Won't you, Mama?

MARY
Stammers pleadingly.
Please don't—talk about things you don't understand!

EDMUND
Dully.
All right, I give up. I knew it was no use.

MARY
In blank denial now.

Anyway, I don't know what you're referring to. But I do know you should be the last one—Right after I returned from the sanatorium, you began to be ill. The doctor there had warned me I must have peace at home with nothing to upset me, and all I've done is worry about you.

Then distractedly.

But that's no excuse! I'm only trying to explain. It's not an excuse!

She hugs him to her—pleadingly.

Promise me, dear, you won't believe I made you an excuse.

EDMUND

Bitterly.

What else can I believe?

MARY

Slowly takes her arm away—her manner remote and objective again.

Yes, I suppose you can't help suspecting that.

MARY

Ashamed but still bitter.

What do you expect?

MARY

Nothing, I don't blame you. How could you believe me—when I can't believe myself? I've become such a liar. I never lied about anything once upon a time. Now I have to lie, especially to myself. But how can you understand, when I don't myself. I've never understood anything about it, except that one day long ago I found I could no longer call my soul my own.

She pauses—then lowering her voice to a strange tone of whispered confidence.

But someday, dear, I will find it again—some day when you're all well, and I see you healthy and happy and successful, and I don't have to feel guilty any more—some day when the Blessed Virgin Mary forgives me and gives me back the faith in Her love and pity I used to have in my convert days, and I can pray to Her again—when She sees no one in the world can believe in me even for a moment any more, then She will believe in me, and with Her help it will be so easy. I will hear myself scream with agony, and at the same time I will laugh because I will be so sure of myself.

Then as Edmund remains hopelessly silent, she adds sadly.

Of course, you can't believe that, either.

She rises from the arm of his chair and goes to stare out the windows at right with her back to him—casually.

Now I think of it, you might as well go uptown. I forgot I'm taking a drive. I have to go to the drugstore. You would hardly want to go there with me. You'd be so ashamed.

EDMUND
Brokenly.
Mama! Don't!

MARY
I suppose you'll divide that ten dollars your father gave you with Jamie. You always divide with each other, don't you? Like good sports. Well, I know what he'll do with his share. Get drunk someplace where he can be with the only kind of woman he understands or likes.
She turns to him, pleading frightenedly.
Edmund! Promise me you won't drink! It's so dangerous! You know Doctor Hardy told you—

EDMUND
Bitterly.
I thought he was an old idiot.

MARY
Painfully.
Edmund!

Jamie's voice is heard from the front hall.
"Come on, Kid, let's beat it."
Mary's manner at once becomes detached again.
Go on, Edmund. Jamie's waiting.
She goes to the front-parlor doorway.
There comes your father downstairs, too.
Tyrone's voice calls.
"Come on, Edmund."

MARY

Kisses him with detached affection.

Goodbye, dear. If you're coming home for dinner, try not to be late. And tell your father. You know what Bridget is.

He turns and hurries away. Tyrone calls from the hall, "Goodbye, Mary," and then Jamie, "Goodbye, Mama." She calls back.

Goodbye.

The front screen door is heard closing after them. She comes and stands by the table, one hand drumming on it, the other fluttering up to pat her hair. She stares about the room with frightened, forsaken eyes and whispers to herself.

It's so lonely here.

Then her face hardens into bitter self-contempt.

You're lying to yourself again. You wanted to get rid of them. Their contempt and disgust aren't pleasant company. You're glad they're gone.

She gives a little despairing laugh.

Then Mother of God, why do I feel so lonely?

Curtain

译文链接：https://book.douban.com/reading/44915376/

Questions for Understanding

1. Why does Mary refuse to consider their summer house as a home? What is her understanding of the nature of the "home"?
2. Why does Mary burst into rage when hearing that Doctor Hardy wants to make an appointment with Edmund?
3. What happens to Tyrone and his two sons when Mary goes upstairs? Do they keep a fairly harmonious relationship with each other?
4. What does Edmund think of life? Why does he hold such a pessimistic view?
5. What does Tyrone tell Jamie after Edmund left? What does Jamie ask Tyrone to do?
6. What led to Mary's addiction to morphine? Why does she blame Tyrone?
7. How does Mary react when Edmund pleads with her to stop using morphine?
8. Is Tyrone's family tragedy due to forces beyond the characters' control? What is the real cause of this tragedy?

Aspects of Appreciation

1. At the very beginning of this scene, Mary and Tyrone have a brief argument about the nature of the home. Mary keeps complaining that living with Tyrone, she has never had a real home. After marriage, she has spent most of her time following him on tour, from cheap hotel to cheap hotel or staying lonely in shabby and dirty rooms. Tyrone bitterly suggests that it is Mary's addiction that leads to the disintegration of the whole family. Both of they refuse to acknowledge their own faults. Instead, they choose to put the blame on each other. The same is true of their sons, Edmund and Jamie. The whole family is caught up in endless quarrels and disagreements.

2. When Tyrone asks Mary to forget the past, Mary replies, "Why? How can I? The past is the present, isn't it? It's the future too. We all try to lie out of that but life won't let us. " Her answer exactly reveals the overwhelming problem harassing the Tyrones. All the family members are to varying degrees mired in the pathos of the past. They can neither blot out the bitter memories, nor let go of the past pains and wrongs. Therefore, the past haunts the Tyrones continuously and has tremendously influenced their relationships with one another, making them hopelessly fall into a series of recriminations, self-justification and self-blame.

3. Although the play only covers a single day from morning to midnight, it does reveal a general picture of the Tyrones' life. Take the selected scene for example. The same arguments are heard again and again, and the Tyrones constantly dredge up the same bitter and troubled past. All these details, together with the impressive title of the play, suggest the repetitive nature of the Tyrones'life. This day is not really unique; instead, it is just one in a long string of similar days for the Tyrones, full of quarrels, bitterness and also an underlying love. All the family members are deeply stuck in such a desperate cycle till the very end of their lives.

Suggested Further Reading

The Hairy Ape (1921); *Desire under the Elms* (1924); *The Iceman Cometh*(1946)

Topics for Further Study

1. "A dysfunctional family is one in which denial, suspicion, and isolation characterize its members' behavior. Members of the family deny that they have problems. They feel people are watching their every move, and they tend to isolate

themselves." Does this description fit the Tyrones well? Try to find some examples in the play to support your view.

2. How does O'Neill make use of stage directions in the play?

3. Discuss the characterization in the play. Describe the ways O'Neill reveals the traits of one of his characters.

4. In the preface to the play, O'Neill wrote, "I mean it as a tribute to your (his third wife Carlotta) love and tenderness which gave me the faith in love that enabled me to face my dead at last and write this play—write it with deep pity and understanding and forgiveness for all the four haunted Tyrones". Does the play really show deep pity, understanding and forgiveness for the four characters?

Knowledge of Literature
Elements of Drama: Dialogue and Theme
1. Dialogue（对话）

In dramas dialogue is what the characters say to each other. A dramatist relies heavily on dialogue, for it serves many different functions in a play. It can reveal character, provide peripheral information—events which have occurred either previous to or separate from the main action of the play, develop thematic elements, control the pace and establish the tone of any one scene.

2. Theme（主题）

The theme of a dramatic work is its central idea which may be stated directly or indirectly. It is the abstract concept that is made concrete through the development and interrelationship of all the elements of drama (speeches, dialogue, actions, scenes, plot, images, etc.) However, three methods of developing a theme are especially worthy of note: repetitions (characters' actions and words, scenes, details of setting, etc.), symbols and contrasts (of characters, scenes, values, actions, etc).

推荐阅读的论文：

[1] 陈晶，王晓梅. 人性困境中的迷茫与彷徨——试析奥尼尔《长日入夜行》[J]. 延安大学学报（社会科学版），2012(6).

[2] 陈才忆. 分裂的双重性格，交织的爱恨之情——奥尼尔《长日入夜行》的人物性格 [J]. 四川师范学院学报（哲学社会科学版），2002(3).

Chapter 5
American Literature After World War II

　　二战后，美国已跻身世界政治经济强国。然而在经济高度繁荣和科技迅猛发展的同时，它也陷入了重重危机，社会局势动荡不安。50年代的美苏冷战和"麦卡锡主义"的盛行，让人们意识到战争的威胁并未消散，整个社会笼罩在恐惧不安的阴影之下。60年代相继发生的越南战争和肯尼迪被刺事件，引发了空前规模的国内运动，反战运动、民权运动、学生运动和妇女解放运动此起彼伏。70年代的"水门事件"和能源危机进一步加剧了民众的不安和恐慌。80年代以来，随着共和党的长期执政和冷战的结束，美国社会进入相对稳定的阶段。这一系列的社会巨变促使新一代的美国作家们积极寻找新的艺术形式和题材，以表现新时代的社会生活和个人经验。故此，战后的美国文学呈现多元化、多样性和多维度的新特质。各种文学思潮、流派相继涌现，争相斗妍；文学体裁、艺术风格千变万化，令人目不暇接。

　　这一时期的美国小说成果显著。大批重量级的作家相继出现，他们或承袭现实主义的传统，或大胆革新创作手法，扩展写作题材，多角度、多方位地展现错综复杂、动荡不定的现代社会，勾勒现代人的生活困境和精神危机。凯鲁亚克（Jack Kerouac）通过描述"垮掉的一代"（the Beat Generation）离经叛道的生活方式，抒发年轻一代对现实的不满和反叛；塞林格（J. D. Salinger）和厄普代克（John Updike）坚持现实主义传统，继续书写现代哈里贝里·费恩的传奇；麦卡勒斯（Carson McCullers）、奥康纳（Flannery O'Conner）等南方作家沿袭福克纳的风格，用更为冷峻的笔触描绘出美国南方独有的社会生活和精神风貌；品钦（Thomas Pynchon）、海勒（Joseph Heller）和冯内古特（Kurt Vonnegut）等后现代小说家以"黑色幽默"（the Black Humor）为载体酣畅淋漓地讽刺了现代社会的荒谬和混乱。

　　和小说一样，这一时期的诗歌也呈现出百家争鸣的繁荣景象。以金斯堡（Allen Ginsberg）为代表的垮掉派、黑山派（the Black Mountain poets）、自白派（the Confessional School）、纽约派（the New York School）等各种流派不断涌现。这些新派诗人，或发出振聋发聩的吼叫和呐喊，或谱写格律自由、形式开放的放射体诗歌，或进行赤裸裸的内心独白和自我审视，或建构杂糅现代绘画和音乐特征的抽象世界，用各种不同的艺术形式来描述自身对现代文明的独特感受和体验。

与此同时，战后的美国戏剧也大放异彩。以威廉斯（William Tennessee Williams）、米勒（Arthur Miller）和阿尔比（Edward Albee）为代表的新生代剧作家，用一幕幕震撼人心的悲剧和怪诞夸张的闹剧，淋漓尽致地展现出现代社会的混乱荒诞以及深陷其间的现代人的苦闷和绝望。

现当代美国文学的多元化不仅体现在各种文学思潮、流派和体裁的百花齐放，也反映在少数族裔文学的蓬勃发展。二战后，各少数族裔作家群体争相推陈出新，以强劲之势席卷美国文坛，成功地开辟出一条从沉默到喧哗、从边缘到中心的演变之路。以贝娄（Saul Bellow）、罗斯（Philip Roth）和辛格（Isaac Bashevis Singer）为首的犹太裔作家承袭犹太文学对精神世界探索的传统，用细腻的笔触和精湛的手法描述了现代社会中犹太人所面临的种族和社会问题。埃里森（Ralph Ellison）、莫里森（Toni Morrison）、沃克（Alice Walker）等非裔作家则突破战前黑人文学的传统，尝试运用各种新方法多角度地探讨处于社会边缘的美国黑人的生存困境以及他们寻求文化身份和精神归属的艰辛历程。以汤亭亭（Maxine Hong Kingston）、谭恩美（Amy Tan）和赵健秀（Frank Chin）为代表的华裔作家也开始崭露头角，打破华人文学在美国主流文坛的"沉默"状态，发出强劲有力的声音。

Tennessee Williams(1911~1983)

About the Author

Tennessee Williams was born in Columbus, Mississippi in 1911. His father, an alcoholic traveling salesman, was away from home more often than not; while his mother "Miss Edwina", the daughter of a minister, was better educated and genteel. From an early age, Williams was fully aware of the estrangement between his parents, and grew closely attached to his elder sister Rose. As a shy and fragile boy, little William was always ostracized and taunted at school. Luckily for him, from reading books and writing he found much solace to escape from the bitter and troubled reality. By the time he entered the University of Missouri, he had already won certain prizes and recognition by creating dozens of poems and short stories.

His road to a promising writer, however, was suspended by his father who forced him to withdraw from the school and take a job in a shoe-factory warehouse. Williams obeyed the instruction and worked there for almost two years, yet he never gave up his dream, always writing feverishly in his spare time. Hard work, coupled with the lack of enough rest, gradually took a heavy toll on his health, which eventually caused him to suffer a mental breakdown. After spending a pleasant time with his beloved grandparents, he recovered and returned to the school to continue the unfinished studies, where he exposed himself to a variety of literary theories and masterpieces of men of letters including Hart Crane, D.H. Lawrence and Anton Chekhov, and nurtured his style by writing a large amount of poems, sketches and plays. Meanwhile, misfortunes assaulted him again. His beloved sister Rose had a nervous breakdown and was sent to the sanatorium. This left an indelible pain to William which found its way into his impressive "mad heroines".

At the age of 27, he finally graduated from the University of Iowa. The life after graduation was filled with poverty and difficulty. Williams took up various kinds of menial jobs. Admirably, in such hard times, he still showed keen interest in writing. His passion for writing and hard work eventually paid off. With the release of his landmark play *The Glass Menagerie* (1945), a pathetic story about the Wingfields' futile attempts to escape from reality, he rose from obscurity to fame overnight. Three years later, his finest work *A Streetcar Named Desire* came out. Vividly delineating the fall of a frail southern lady Blanche DuBois, this tragedy received huge acclaim and recognition including a Pulitzer Prize and a Drama Critics' Circle award, which further cemented his reputation asone of the three greatest U.S. dramatists, along with Arthur Miller and Eugene O'Neill.

For more than a decade thereafter till his death, he worked laboriously and gave readers a rich and ample body of works, including dozens of full-length plays, the most famous ones of which are *The Rose Tattoo*(1950), the Pulitzer-winning *Cat on a Hot Tin Roof* (1955) and *The Night of the Iguana* (1960), hundreds of short stories and poems, as well as a memoir.

Following the steps of his predecessor Eugene O'Neill, Williams sought to continue the revolt against the realistic theater conventions. He moved seamlessly and freely from realism to surrealism, from reality to fantasy. However, his major contribution to American drama not only lies in this elaborate mixture of realism and fantasy, but, more importantly, lies in his blunt and explicit delineation of impressive characters struggling in the chaotic world full of violence, desire and loneliness, for which he is greatly admired by the public and critics, and highly ranked in the literary pantheon for good.

A Streetcar Named Desire

About the play

A Streetcar Named Desire, a Pulitzer-winning play, is widely acclaimed as one of the most splendid plays by Tennessee Williams. Set in a shabby apartment building in New Orleans in the 1940s, it starts with the unexpected visit of Blanche Du Bois, a fading southern belle, to her pregnant sister Stella and her crude working class husband Stanley Kowalski. Her visit turns out to be a longer stay, for later she admits that she lost the ancestral home and her job. During the stay, the animosity between Blanche and Stanley mounts. As a lady from an old southern family, Blanche feels rather bothered and disgusted by Stanley's roughness and lack of cultivation, while the latter is greatly infuriated by Blanche's pretentious airs and bitter criticism of his lifestyle. Later, Blanche starts to date Stanley's friend Mitch. However, Stanley breaks up the relationship by revealing to Mitch her disreputable past; that is, she was deeply involved into numerous amorous scandals which caused her to lose the decent job and be permanently expulsed from the native town. Hearing such a shocking fact, Mitch feels swindled by Blanche and leaves her for good. On the very night when Stella is giving birth to a child in the hospital, the tension between Blanche and Stanley reaches the climax, which leads to the most disastrous end that he rapes her. Unable to accept the harsh reality, Blanche breaks down and ends up in a lunatic asylum.

From *A Streetcar Named Desire*

And so it was I entered the broken world
To trace the visionary company of love, its voice
An instant in the wind (I know not whither hurled)
But not for long to hold each desperate choice.
— "The Broken Tower" by Hart Crane[①]

The Characters
BLANCHE	PABLO
STELLA	A NEGRO WOMAN
STANLEY	A DOCTOR

---

① Hart Crane: 哈特·克莱恩 (1899~1932), 20 世纪美国最重要的诗人之一。《断塔》是他自杀前写下的最后一首诗。

Chapter 5 American Literature After World War II

MITCH	A NURSE
EUNICE	A YOUNG COLLECTOR
STEVE	A MEXICAN WOMAN

SCENE ONE

The exterior of a two-story corner building on a street in New Orleans[①] which is named Elysian Fields and runs between the L & N tracks and the river. The section is poor but, unlike corresponding sections in other American cities, it has a raffish charm. The houses are mostly white frame, weathered grey, with rickety outside stairs and galleries and quaintly ornamented gables. This building contains two flats, upstairs and down. Faded white stairs ascend to the entrances of both.

It is first dark of an evening early in May. The sky that shows around the dim white building is a peculiarly tender blue, almost a turquoise, which invests the scene with a kind of lyricism and gracefully attenuates the atmosphere of decay. You can almost feel the warm breath of the brown river beyond the river warehouses with their faint redolences of bananas and coffee. A corresponding air is evoked by the music of Negro entertainers at a barroom around the corner. In this part of New Orleans you are practically always just around the corner, or a few doors down the street, from a tinny piano being played with the infatuated fluency of brown fingers. This "blue piano" expresses the spirit of the life which goes on here.

Two women, one white and one colored, are taking the air on the steps of the building. The white woman is **EUNICE**, who occupies the upstairs flat; the colored woman a neighbor, for New Orleans is a cosmopolitan city where there is a relatively warm and easy intermingling of races in the old part of town.

Above the music of the "blue piano" the voices of people on the street can be heard overlapping.

[*Two men come around the corner,* **STANLEY KOWALSKI** *and* **MITCH**. *They are about twenty-eight or thirty years old, roughly dressed in blue denim work clothes.* **STANLEY** *carries his bowling jacket and a red-stained package from a butcher's. They stop at the foot of the steps.*]

STANLEY [*bellowing*]: Hey, there! Stella, Baby!

[**STELLA** *comes out on the first floor landing, a gentle young woman, about twenty-five, and of a background obviously quite different from her husband's.*]

STELLA [*mildly*]: Don't holler at me like that. Hi, Mitch.

---

① New Orleans: 新奥尔良，美国路易斯安那州南部的一座城市，始建于 1718 年。

STANLEY: Catch!
STELLA: What?
STANLEY: Meat!

[*He heaves the package at her. She cries out in protest but manages to catch it: then she laughs breathlessly. Her husband and his companion have already started back around the corner.*]

STELLA [*calling after him*]: Stanley! Where are you going?
STANLEY: Bowling!
STELLA: Can I come watch?
STANLEY: Come on. [*He goes out.*]
STELLA: Be over soon. [*To the white woman*] Hello, Eunice. How are you?
EUNICE: I'm all right. Tell Steve to get him a poor boy's sandwich 'cause nothing's left here.

[*They all laugh; the colored woman does not stop. Stella goes out.*]

COLORED WOMAN: What was that package he th'ew at 'er' [*She rises from steps, laughing louder.*]
EUNICE: You hush, now!
NEGRO WOMAN: Catch what!

[*She continues to laugh.* **BLANCHE** *comes around the corner, carrying a valise. She looks at a slip of paper, then at the building, then again at the slip and again at the building. Her expression is one of shocked disbelief. Her appearance is incongruous to this setting. She is daintily dressed in a white suit with a fluffy bodice, necklace and earrings of pearl, white gloves and hat, looking as if she were arriving at a summer tea or cocktail party in the garden district. She is about five years older than Stella. Her delicate beauty must avoid a strong light. There is something about her uncertain manner, as well as her white clothes, that suggests a moth.*]

EUNICE [*finally*]: What's the matter, honey? Are you lost?
BLANCHE [*with faintly hysterical humor*]: They told me to take a street-car named Desire, and then transfer to one called Cemeteries[①] and ride six blocks and get off at—Elysian Fields!
EUNICE: That's where you are now.
BLANCHE: At Elysian Fields?
EUNICE: This here is Elysian Fields.
BLANCHE: They mustn't have—understood—what number I wanted...
EUNICE: What number you lookin' for?

---

① Cemeteries: "公墓号街车", 新奥尔良一路有轨电车的车名。

[*Blanche wearily refers to the slip of paper.*]

BLANCHE: Six thirty-two.

EUNICE: You don't have to look no further.

BLANCHE [*uncomprehendingly*]: I'm looking for my sister, Stella DuBois. I mean—Mrs. Stanley Kowalski.

EUNICE: That's the party. — You just did miss her, though.

BLANCHE: This—can this be—her home?

EUNICE: She's got the downstairs here and I got the up.

BLANCHE: Oh. She's—out?

EUNICE: You noticed that bowling alley around the corner?

BLANCHE: I'm—not sure I did.

EUNICE: Well, that's where she's at, watchin' her husband bowl. [*There is a pause*] You want to leave your suitcase here an' go find her?

BLANCHE: No.

NEGRO WOMAN: I'll go tell her you come.

BLANCHE: Thanks.

NEGRO WOMAN: You welcome. [*She goes out.*]

EUNICE: She wasn't expecting you?

BLANCHE: No. No, not tonight.

EUNICE: Well, why don't you just go in and make yourself at home till they get back.

BLANCHE: How could I—do that?

EUNICE: We own this place so I can let you in.

[*She gets up and opens the downstairs door. A light goes on behind the blind, turning it light blue.* **BLANCHE** *slowly follows her into the downstairs flat. The surrounding areas dim out as the interior is lighted. Two rooms can be seen, not too clearly defined. The one first entered is primarily a kitchen but contains a folding bed to be used by* **BLANCHE**. *The room beyond this is a bedroom. Off this room is a narrow door to a bathroom.*]

EUNICE [*defensively, noticing* **BLANCHE**'s *look*]: It's sort of messed up right now but when it's clean it's real sweet.

BLANCHE: Is it?

EUNICE: Uh-huh, I think so. So you're Stella's sister?

BLANCHE: Yes. [*Wanting to get rid of her*] Thanks for letting me in.

EUNICE: Por nada①, as the Mexicans say, por nada! Stella spoke of you.

---

① Por nada: (Spanish) It's nothing.(西班牙语)不客气。

BLANCHE: Yes?

EUNICE: I think she said you taught school.

BLANCHE: Yes.

EUNICE: And you're from Mississippi, huh?

BLANCHE: Yes.

EUNICE: She showed me a picture of your home-place, the plantation.

BLANCHE: Belle Reve[①]?

EUNICE: A great big place with white columns.

BLANCHE: Yes...

EUNICE: A place like that must be awful hard to keep up.

BLANCHE: If you will excuse me, I'm just about to drop.

EUNICE: Sure, honey. Why don't you set down?

BLANCHE: What I meant was I'd like to be left alone.

EUNICE [*offended*]: Aw. I'll make myself scarce, in that ease.

BLANCHE: I didn't mean to be rude, but—

EUNICE: I'll drop by the bowling alley an' hustle her up. [*She goes out the door.*]

[**BLANCHE** sits in a chair very stiffly with her shoulders slightly hunched and her legs pressed close together and her hands tightly clutching her purse as if she were quite cold. After a while the blind look goes out of her eyes and she begins to look slowly around. A cat screeches. She catches her breath with a startled gesture. Suddenly she notices something in a half opened closet. She springs up and crosses to it, and removes a whiskey bottle. She pours a half tumbler of whiskey and tosses it down. She carefully replaces the bottle and washes out the tumbler at the sink. Then she resumes her seat in front of the table.]

BLANCHE [*faintly to herself*]: I've got to keep hold of myself! [**STELLA** *comes quickly around the corner of the building and runs to the door of the downstairs flat.*]

STELLA [*calling out joyfully*]: Blanche!

[*For a moment they stare at each other. Then* **BLANCHE** *springs up and runs to her with a wild cry.*]

BLANCHE: Stella, oh, Stella, Stella! Stella for Star!

[She begins to speak with feverish vivacity as if she feared for either of them to stop and think. They catch each other in a spasmodic embrace.]

BLANCHE: Now, then, let me look at you. But don't you look at me, Stella, no, no, no, not till later, not till I've bathed and rested! And turn that over-light off! Turn that off! I won't be looked at in this merciless glare! [**STELLA** *laughs and complies*]

---

① Belle Reve:（法语）美梦。此处指美梦庄园，白兰琪家族在密西西比州的老宅。

Come back here now! Oh, my baby! Stella! Stella for Star! [*She embraces her again*] I thought you would never come back to this horrible place! What am I saying? I didn't mean to say that. I meant to be nice about it and say—Oh, what a convenient location and such—Ha-a-ha! Precious lamb! You haven't said a word to me.

STELLA: You haven't given me a chance to, honey! [*She laughs, but her glance at* **BLANCHE** *is a little anxious.*]

BLANCHE: Well, now you talk. Open your pretty mouth and talk while I look around for some liquor! I know you must have some liquor on the place! Where could it be, I wonder? Oh, I spy, I spy!

[*She rushes to the closet and removes the bottle; she is shaking all over and panting for breath as she tries to laugh. The bottle nearly slips from her grasp.*]

STELLA [*noticing*]: Blanche, you sit down and let me pour the drinks. I don't know what we've got to mix with. Maybe a coke's in the icebox. Look'n see, honey, while I'm—

BLANCHE: No coke, honey, not with my nerves tonight! Where—where—where is—?

STELLA: Stanley? Bowling! He loves it. They're having a—found some soda!—tournament...

BLANCHE: Just water, baby, to chase it! Now don't get worried, your sister hasn't turned into a drunkard, she's just all shaken up and hot and tired and dirty! You sit down, now, and explain this place to me! What are you doing in a place like this?

STELLA: Now, Blanche—

BLANCHE: Oh, I'm not going to be hypocritical, I'm going to be honestly critical about it! Never, never, never in my worst dreams could I picture—Only Poe! Only Mr. Edgar Allan Poe!—could do it justice! Out there I suppose is the ghoul-haunted woodland of Weir[①]! [*She laughs.*]

STELLA: No, honey, those are the L & N tracks.

BLANCHE: No, now seriously, putting joking aside. Why didn't you tell me, why didn't you write me, honey, why didn't you let me know?

STELLA [*carefully, pouring herself a drink*]: Tell you what, Blanche?

BLANCHE: Why, that you had to live in these conditions!

STELLA: Aren't you being a little intense about it? It's not that bad at all! New Orleans isn't like other cities.

BLANCHE: This has got nothing to do with New Orleans. You might as well say—forgive me, blessed baby! [*She suddenly stops short*] The subject is closed!

---

① Ghoul-haunted woodland of Weir: 这句诗出自爱伦·坡的诗歌《乌拉鲁姆》，诗中的叙述者难以摆脱爱人逝世的悲痛。威廉斯用这句诗暗指白兰琪仍未走出丈夫艾伦·格雷自杀的阴霾。

STELLA [*a little drily*]: Thanks.

[*During the pause,* **BLANCHE** *stares at her. She smiles at* **BLANCHE**.]

BLANCHE [*looking down at her glass, which shakes in her hand*]: You're all I've got in the world, and you're not glad to see me!

STELLA [*sincerely*]: Why, Blanche, you know that's not true.

BLANCHE: No?—I'd forgotten how quiet you were.

STELLA: You never did give me a chance to say much, Blanche. So I just got in the habit of being quiet around you.

BLANCHE [*vaguely*]: A good habit to get into... [*then, abruptly*] You haven't asked me how I happened to get away from the school before the spring term ended.

STELLA: Well, I thought you'd volunteer that information—if you wanted to tell me.

BLANCHE: You thought I'd been fired?

STELLA: No, I—thought you might have—resigned...

BLANCHE: I was so exhausted by all I'd been through my—nerves broke.

[*Nervously tamping cigarette*] I was on the verge of—lunacy, almost! So Mr. Graves—Mr. Graves is the high school superintendent—he suggested I take a leave of absence. I couldn't put all of those details into the wire... [*She drinks quickly*] Oh, this buzzes right through me and feels so good!

STELLA: Won't you have another?

BLANCHE: No, one's my limit.

STELLA: Sure?

BLANCHE: You haven't said a word about my appearance.

STELLA: You look just fine.

BLANCHE: God love you for a liar! Daylight never exposed so total a ruin! But you—you've put on some weight, yes, you're just as plump as a little partridge! And it's so becoming to you!

STELLA: Now, Blanche—

BLANCHE: Yes, it is, it is or I wouldn't say it! You just have to watch around the hips a little. Stand up.

STELLA: Not now.

BLANCHE: You hear me? I said stand up! [**STELLA** *complies reluctantly*] You messy child, you, you've spilt something on that pretty white lace collar! About your hair—you ought to have it cut in a feather bob with your dainty features. Stella, you have a maid, don't you?

STELLA: No. With only two rooms it's—

BLANCHE: What? Two rooms, did you say?

STELLA: This one and—[*She is embarrassed.*]

BLANCHE: The other one? [*She laughs sharply. There is an embarrassed silence.*]

BLANCHE: I am going to take just one little tiny nip more, sort of to put the stopper on, so to speak... Then put the bottle away so I won't be tempted. [*She rises*] I want you to look at my figure! [*She turns around*] You know I haven't put on one ounce in ten years, Stella? I weigh what I weighed the summer you left Belle Reve. The summer Dad died and you left us...

STELLA [*a little wearily*]: It's just incredible, Blanche, how well you're looking.

BLANCHE: [*They both laugh uncomfortably*] But, Stella, there's only two rooms, I don't see where you're going to put me!

STELLA: We're going to put you in here.

BLANCHE: What kind of bed's this—one of those collapsible things?

[*She sits on it.*]

STELLA: Does it feel all right?

BLANCHE [*dubiously*]: Wonderful, honey. I don't like a bed that gives much. But there's no door between the two rooms, and Stanley—will it be decent?

STELLA: Stanley is Polish, you know.

BLANCHE: Oh, yes. They're something like Irish, aren't they?

STELLA: Well—

BLANCHE: Only not so—highbrow? [*They both laugh again in the same way*] I brought some nice clothes to meet all your lovely friends in.

STELLA: I'm afraid you won't think they are lovely.

BLANCHE: What are they like?

STELLA: They're Stanley's friends.

BLANCHE: Polacks[①]?

STELLA: They're a mixed lot, Blanche.

BLANCHE: Heterogeneous—types?

STELLA: Oh, yes. Yes, types is right!

BLANCHE: Well—anyhow—I brought nice clothes and I'll wear them. I guess you're hoping I'll say I'll put up at a hotel, but I'm not going to put up at a hotel. I want be near you, got to be with somebody, I can't be alone! Because—as you must have noticed—I'm—not very well... [*Her voice drops and her look is frightened.*]

STELLA: You seem a little bit nervous or overwrought or something.

BLANCHE: Will Stanley like me, or will I be just a visiting in-law, Stella? I couldn't stand that.

STELLA: You'll get along fine together, if you'll just try not to—well—compare him

---

① Polacks: 波兰佬（含冒犯意，指波兰人或波兰后裔）。

with men that we went out with at home.

BLANCHE: Is he so—different?

STELLA: Yes. A different species.

BLANCHE: In what way; what's he like?

STELLA: Oh, you can't describe someone you're in love with! Here's a picture of him!

[*She hands a photograph to* **BLANCHE**]

BLANCHE: **An officer?**

STELLA: A Master Sergeant[①] in the Engineers' Corps. Those are decorations!

BLANCHE: He had those on when you met him?

STELLA: I assure you I wasn't just blinded by all the brass.

BLANCHE: That's not what I—

STELLA: But of course there were things to adjust myself to later on.

BLANCHE: Such as his civilian background!

[STELLA *laughs uncertainly.*] How did he take it when you said I was coming?

STELLA: Oh, Stanley doesn't know yet.

BLANCHE: [*frightened*] You—haven't told him?

STELLA: He's on the road a good deal.

BLANCHE: Oh. Travels?

STELLA: Yes.

BLANCHE: Good. I mean—isn't it?

STELLA [*half to herself*]: I can hardly stand it when he is away for a night…

BLANCHE: Why, Stella!

STELLA: When he's away for a week I nearly go wild!

BLANCHE: Gracious!

STELLA: And when he comes back I cry on his lap like a baby… [*She smiles to herself.*]

BLANCHE: I guess that is what is meant by being in love… [STELLA *looks up with a radiant smile.*] Stella —

STELLA: **What?**

BLANCHE: [*in an uneasy rush*] I haven't asked you the things you probably thought I was going to ask. And so I'll expect you to be understanding about what I have to tell you.

STELLA: What, Blanche? [*Her face turns anxious.*]

BLANCHE: Well, Stella—you are going to reproach me, I know that you're boung

---

① Master Sergeant:（美国军队的）军士长。

to reproach me—but before you do—take into consideration—you left! I stayed and struggled! You came to New Orleans and looked out for yourself! I stayed at Belle Reve and tried to hold it together! I'm not meaning this in any reproachful way, but all the burden descended on my shoulders.

STELLA: The best I could do was make my own living, Blanche.

[**BLANCHE** *begins to shake again with intensity.*]

BLANCHE: I know, I know. But you are the one that abandoned Belle Reve, not I. I stayed and fought for it, bled for it, almost dies for it!

STELLA: Stop this hysterical outburst and tell me what's happened? What do you mean fought and bled? What kind of—

BLANCHE: I knew you would, Stella. I knew you would take this attitude about it!

STELLA: About—what?—please!

BLANCHE[*slowly*]: The loss—the loss…

STELLA: Belle Reve? Lost, is it? No!

BLANCHE: Yes, Stella.

[*They stare at each other across the yellow-checked linoleum of the table.* **BLANCHE** *slowly nods her hand and* **STELLA** *looks slowly down at her hands folded on the table. The music of "Blue Piano" grows louder.* **BLANCHE** *touches her handkerchief to her forehead.*]

STELLA: But how did it go? What happened?

BLANCHE [*springing up*]: You're a fine one to ask me how it went!

STELLA: Blanche!

BLANCHE: You're a fine one to sit there accusing me of it!

STELLA: Blanche!

BLANCHE: I, I, I took the blows in my face and my body! All of those death! The lone parade to the graveyard! Father, mother! Margaret, that dreadful way! So big with it, it couldn't be put in a coffin! But had to be burned like rubbish! You just came home in time for the funeral, Stella. And funerals are pretty compared to deaths. Funerals are quiet, but deaths—not always. Sometimes their breathing is hoarse, and sometimes it rattles, and sometimes they even cry to you, "Don't let me go." As if you were able to stop them! But funerals are quiet, with pretty flowers. And, oh, what gorgeous boxes they pack them away in! Unless you were there at the bed when they cried out, "Hold me!" You'd never suspect there was the struggle for death and bleeding. You didn't dream, but I saw! Saw! Saw! And now you sit there telling me with your eyes that I let the place go! How in hell do you think all that sickness and dying was paid for? Death is expensive, Miss Stella! And old Cousin Jessie's right after Margaret's, hers!

Why, the Grim Reaper[①] had put up his tent on our doorstep...Stella. Belle Reve was his headquarters! Honey—that's how it slipped through my fingers! Which of them left us a fortune? Which of them left a cent of insurance even? Only poor Jessie—one hundred to pay for her coffin. That was all, Stella! And I with my pitiful salary at the school. Yes, accuse me! Sit there and stare at me, thinking I let the place go! I let the place go? Where were you! In bed with your— Polack!

STELLA: [*springing*] Blanche! You be still! That's enough! [*She starts out.*]

BLANCHE: Where are you going?

STELLA: I'm going into the bathroom to wash my face.

BLANCHE: Oh, Stella, Stella, you're crying!

STELLA: Does that surprise you?

BLANCHE: Forgive me—I didn't mean to—

[*The sound of men's voice is heard.* **STELLA** *goes into the bathroom, closing the door behind her. When the men appear, and* **BLANCHE** *realizes it must be* **STANLEY** *returning, she moves uncertainly from the bathroom door to the dressing table, looking apprehensively toward the front door.* **STANLEY** *enters, followed by* **STEVE** *and* **MITCH**. **STANLEY** *pauses near his door,* **STEVE** *by the foot of the spiral, and* **MITCH** *is slightly above and to the right of them, about to go out. As the men enter, we hear some of the following dialogue.*]

STANLEY: Is that how he got it?

STEVE: Sure that's how he got it. He hit the old weather-bird for 300 bucks on a six-number-ticket.

MITCH: Don't tell him those things; he'll believe it.

[**MITCH** *starts out.*]

STANLEY: [*restraining MITCH*] Hey, Mitch—come back here.

[**BLANCHE**, *at the sound of voices, retires in the bedroom. She picks up* **STANLEY**'*s photo from dressing table, looks at it, puts it down. When* **STANLEY** *enters the apartment, she darts and hides behind the screen at the head of bed.*]

STEVE [*to* **STANLEY** *and* **MITCH**] Hey, are we playin' poker tomorrow?

STANLEY: Sure— at Mitch's.

MITCH: [*hearing this, returns quickly to the stair rail*] No—not at my place. My mother's still sick!

STANLEY: Okay, at my place… [**MITCH** *starts out again.*] But you bring the beer!

[**MITCH** *pretends not to hear—calls out "Good night, all," and goes out, singing.* **EUNICE**'*s voice is heard, above.*]

---

① Grim Reaper: 狰狞的收割者（指骷髅形态的死神，身披斗篷，手持长柄大镰刀）。

Break it up down there! I made the spaghetti dish and ate it myself.
STEVE [*going upstairs*]: I told you and phoned you we was playing. [to the men] Jax beer[①]!
EUNICE: You never phoned me once.
STEVE: I told you at breakfast—and phoned you at lunch…
EUNICE: Well, never mind about that. You just get yourself home here once in a while.
STEVE: You want it in the papers?

[*More laughter and shouts of paring come from the men.* **STANLEY** *throws the screen door of the kitchen open and comes in. He is of medium height, about five feet eight or nine, and strongly, compactly built. Animal joy in his being is implicit in all his movements and attitudes. Since earliest manhood the center of his life has been pleasure with women, the giving and taking of it, not with weak indulgence, dependently, but with the power and pride of a richly feathered male bird among hens. Branching out from this complete and satisfying center are all the auxiliary channels of his life, such as his heartiness with men, his appreciation of rough humor, his love of good drink and food and games, his car, his radio, everything that is his, that bears his emblem of the gaudy seed-bearer. He seizes women up at a glance, with sexual classifications, crude images flashing into his mind and determining the way he smiles at them.*]

BLANCHE: [*drawing involuntarily back from his stare*] You must be Stanley. I'm Blanche.
STANLEY: Stella's sister?
BLANCHE: Yes.
STANLEY: H'lo. Where's the little woman?
BLANCHE: In the bathroom.
STANLEY: Oh. Didn't know you were coming in town.
BLANCHE: I—uh—
STANLEY: Where you from, Blanche?
BLANCHE: Why, I—live in Laurel. [*He has crossed to the closet and removed the whiskey bottle.*]
STANLEY: InLaurel, huh? Oh, yeah, in Laurel, that's right. Not in my territory. Liquor goes fast in hot weather. [*He holds the bottle to the light to observe its depletion.*] Have a shot?
BLANCHE: No, I—rarely touch it.

---

① Jax beer: a local brand of beer.

STANLEY: Some people rarely touch it, but it touches them often.

BLANCHE: [*faintly*] Ha-ha.

STANLEY: My clothes're stickin' to me. Do you mind if I make myself comfortable? [*He starts to removes his shirt.*]

BLANCHE: Please, please do.

STANLEY: Be comfortable is my motto.

BLANCHE: It's mine, too. It's hard to stay looking fresh. I haven't washed or even powdered my face and—here you are!

STANLEY: You know you can catch cold sitting around in damp things, especially when you been exercising hard like bowling is. You're a teacher, aren't you?

BLANCHE: Yes.

STANLEY: What do you teach, Blanche?

BLANCHE: English.

STANLEY: I never was a very good English student. How long you here for, Blanche?

BLANCHE: I— don't know yet.

STANLEY: You going to shack up① here?

BLANCHE: I thought I would if it's not inconvenient for you all.

STANLEY: Good.

BLANCHE: Traveling wears me out.

STANLEY: Well, take it easy.

[*A cat screeches near the window.* **BLANCHE** *springs up.*]

BLANCHE: What's that?

STANLEY: Cats… Hey, Stella!

STELLA [*faintly, form the bathroom*]: Yes, Stanley.

STANLEY: Haven't fallen in, have you? [*He grins at* **BLANCHE**. *She tried unsuccessfully to smile back. There is silence.*] I'm afraid I'll strike you as being the unrefined type. Stella's spoke of you a good deal. You were married once, weren't you?

[*The music of the polka rises up, faint in the distance.*]

BLANCHE: Yes. When I was quite young.

STANLEY: What happened?

BLANCHE: The boy—the boy died.[*She sinks back down.*] I'm afraid I'm—going to be sick! [*Her head falls on her arms.*]

---

① shack up: (slang) to live or take up residence(同住).

译文链接：https://www.docin.com/p-1985605328.html

Questions for Understanding

1. Williams quotes one stanza from Hart Crane's "The Broken Tower" as the epigraph to this play. What's the implication of these lines?
2. What do the opening stage directions reveal about the setting of the play?
3. What is the implied meaning of the scene in which Stanley hurls a package of meat to Stella? Does it simply show that Stanley is a powerful male who delivers what women want, or is there more to the scene?
4. What does Blanche look like? Is her appearance congruous with the setting? What does it imply?
5. In Scene One, Blanche describes her means of transportation from the train station to Stella's apartment, "They told me to take a street-car named Desire, and transfer to one called Cemeteries, and ride six blocks and get off at—Elysian Fields!" Does such description have certain symbolic meaning?
6. What happens to Blanche? Why does she come to New Orleans? What is her attitude towards Stella's apartment and her Polish working-class husband Stanley?
7. What do you learn about Stanley's character?

Aspects of Appreciation

    1. The poetic epigraph from Hart Crane holds certain explicit metaphorical value, suggesting Blanche's hopeless and doomed quest for love. Since the suicide of her beloved husband, she has entered the crumbling world full of desperation and loneliness. Longing for "the company of love, its voice", she indulges herself in various sexual affairs with casual acquaintances, and later tries to build a deep connection with Stella and Mitch. However, her pathetic attempt to recapture love is futile and only leads her to make many desperate choices.

    2. At the very beginning of the play, Stanley hurls a package of raw meat to Stella for her to catch. Such a meat-hurling episode is more than a simple action with sexual innuendo. It reveals Stanley's primitive qualities and his relationship with Stella. By tossing the meat at Stella, Stanley asserts his domination over his wife. Stella's delight in catching meat suggests her infatuation with Stanley and her willingness to obey him.

3. The journey Blanche makes from the railway station to Stella's apartment is an allegory about the trajectory of her life. The two streetcars named "Desire" and "Cemeteries" she takes symbolize her sexual desires and downfall respectively. Blanche's unbridled pursuit of carnal desires results in her dismissal from the teaching job and the final expulsion from her hometown Laurel. Blanche's arrival at Street Elysian Fields, which in Greek mythology refers to the blissful abode reserved for the great heroes after death, suggests her hope to leave behind the disgraced old self in Laurel and rejuvenate her life in New Orleans. However, it is quite ironic that the street, despite its wish-fulfilling name, turns out to be a shabby and filthy working-class district, which foreshadows Blanche's eventual tragedy.

Suggested Further Reading

The Glass Menagerie (1944), *Cat on a Hot Tin Roof* (1955)

Topics for Further Study

1. What do you think of Blanche? Is she a hypocritical fallen woman, or a pathetic and fragile woman who invites sympathy? What leads to her personal tragedy?

2. Compare Blanche with Miss Emily in "A Rose for Emily" and Scarlet O'Hara in *Gone with the Wind*, and try to explain the reasons for their different destinies.

3. This play is considered as an elegy for the Old South which declined and perished in the early 20th century. Do you agree with this view?

4. How does Williams use light as a dramatic device? What does its presence or absence indicate?

5. In the play, Williams describes an almost continuous soundscape, including the "blue piano", the polka music, the popular ballad "It's Only a Paper Moon", various noises from the street and so forth. How does such a soundscape contribute to the theme, characterization or dramatic intensity of the play?

6. It's said that the antagonism between Blanche and Stanley is a struggle between fantasy and reality, which propels the plot and creates an overarching tension. Expound on this opinion.

7. One particularly compelling aspect of the play is Williams' wide use of symbols, including names of characters and places, shadows and cries, paper lanterns, and Blanche's frequent baths. Find some instances and work out their meanings.

Knowledge of Literature

1. An Element of Drama: Plot(情节)

In terms of drama, the plot refers to a special arrangement of the dramatic action sharing cause-and-effect relationship. Regarded as "the soul of tragedy" by Aristotle in *Poetics*, the plot is an essential element of the drama, which helps to reveal themes and arouse the emotions of the audience.

According to the German playwright Gustav Freytag(1816~1895), a well-constructed dramatic plot commonly includes five stages of development, namely exposition, rising action, climax, falling action and denouement. The exposition presents the background information necessary for the development of the plot. The rising action consists of successive stages of conflict between the protagonist and the antagonist. This conflict builds up to the climax, the moment of the greatest dramatic tension. Then comes the falling action, where the tension subsides. Finally, the denouement comes as a natural outcome of the action. It should be noted that not all the plays strictly follow this plot development. The Theatre of the Absurd, for instance, rejects formulaic and coherent plots to show the irrationality and absurdity of life.

2. An Element of Drama: Character(人物)

As an important element of the drama, characters are the persons in a dramatic work. A character is endowed with particular qualities, which can be inferred from his or her appearance, speeches, actions and other characters' speeches. Like in fiction, characters in a dramatic work can be categorized as main characters and minor ones. The former ones play a significant role throughout the plot and are often round characters with various character traits, while the latter ones are less important and are often flat characters with a single quality.

推荐阅读的论文：

[1] 曾莉.《欲望号街车》人物塑造的文内互文性分析 [J]. 武汉理工大学学报（社会科学版），2006(3).

[2] 詹全旺. 心与物的对抗灵与肉的冲突——评精神悲剧《欲望号街车》[J]. 安徽大学学报，2002(1).

J. D. Salinger (1919~2010)

About the Author

Among all the important contemporary American writers, Jerome David Salingermight be the most enigmatic one. In his whole life, he attempted to evade the spotlights as much as possible. After stirring a sensation with the publication of his masterpiece *The Catcher in the Rye* (1951), he gradually retreated to near-total seclusion, steadfastly refusing interviews or any other forms of contact with the outside world, and in the meanwhile, leaving behind numerous speculations and rumors about his privacy and works.

Much like his renowned character Holden Caulfield, J. D. Salinger was born in a middle class family in New York City, and spent his youth in being shuttled between various prep schools. At the age of fifteen, he entered the Valley Forge Military Academy, which is generally considered to be the prototype of Pencey Prep, the high school in *The Catcher in the Rye*. After graduation, he attended a creative Columbia University writing course, from which he got tremendous confidence to take up a career as a writer. He began his literary debut with the publication of the short story "The Young Folks" in 1940, and continued to write even when he served in the army during the WWII.

After the war ended, Salinger's literary career took off, becoming one of the top contributors to the first-class magazines including *Collier's* and *The New Yorker*. And the appearance of *The Catcher in the Rye* in 1951 pushed his career to an unprecedented climax. Though sparking great controversy on its daring treatment of adolescent sexuality, liberal use of profanity and explicit portrayal of teenage angst, this soul-scarching novel of youthful alienation appealed to a great number of people, and won much critical and popular admiration. The proponents, especially those of postwar young generation felt great empathy with the protagonist Holden, deeming him as one of their peers who suffered the painful growth in a world laden with banalities and restricting conformity.

As the controversy of *The Catcher in the Rye* grew, Salinger was increasingly reclusive and his output declined. In the next decade, Salinger only published a collection of short stories *Nine Stories* (1953), a collection of a novella and a short story*Franny and Zooey* (1961), a collection of two novellas *Raise High the Roof Beam, Carpenters and Seymour: An Introduction* (1963), and a novella entitled *Hapworth 16, 1924*(1965). Most of these works centered on the Glass family and shared the common themes including teenagers' alienation, the corrupting influence of the adult world, and the innocence of the children.

Afterwards, Salinger lapsed into a literary silence until his death. He never gave up writing; instead, he continued his favorite job simply for his own satisfaction. Although he tried the utmost to escape public exposure, this elusiveness ironically drew even more public concern. Various rumors were swirling over his life and unpublished manuscripts. On January 27th, 2010, Salingerpassed away peacefully in his New Hampshire home, leaving permanently the world he once shocked and always contrived to shun.

The Catcher in the Rye

About the Novel

Set around the 1950s, Salinger's masterpiece *The Catcher in the Rye* centers on the disoriented three-day adventure of a troubled high-school boy Holden Caulfield. Expelled from Pencey prep school for poor academic performance, young Holden is so afraid to face the unpleasant confrontation with his parents that he chooses to hang out in New York City. During the three days, he spends most of his time wandering aimlessly from one brief encounter to another, and becomes increasingly disgusted with the adult world which he considers to be permeated with "phonies" and "jerks".

Even since its publication, the novel has been shrouded in controversy. Teachers and parents showed much concern about its liberal use of profanity, sexual references and the explicit portrayal of teenage angst, causing the work to be constantly challenged or even banned from schools and libraries. However, it is universally acknowledged as one of the best novels of the 20th century. Some readers even regard it as the testament to the honesty and innocence of the youth. By now, the whole sales of this novel are reported to have reached more than sixty-fivemillion copies.

The following selection, taken from Chapter 22, describes Holden sneaking back home to bid farewell to his little sister Phoebe, explaining why he was expelled from the school and telling her his great fantasy of being "the catcher in the rye".

The Catcher in the Rye (Chapter 22)

When I came back, she had the pillow off her head all right—I knew she would①—but she still wouldn't look at me, even though she was laying on her back and all. When I came around the side of the bed and sat down again, she turned her crazy face the other way. She was ostracizing② the hell out of me. Just like the fencing team at Pencey when I left all the goddam foils on the subway. "How's old Hazel Weatherfield?" I said. "You write any new stories about her? I got that one you sent me right in my suitcase. It's down at the station. It's very good."

---

① When Phoebe is afraid, she always covers her head with a pillow. In the former chapter (Chapter 21), when she realized that Holden must have been kicked out of school, she refused to listen to his explanation by covering her head with a pillow. Holden had to leave the room to get some cigarettes. This chapter just describes what happens later on.
② ostracize: 排挤；排斥。

"Daddy'll kill you."

Boy, she really gets something on her mind when she gets something on her mind. "No, he won't. The worst he'll do, he'll give me hell again, and then he'll send me to that goddam military school. That's all he'll do to me. And in the first place, I won't even be around. I'll be away. I'll be—I'll probably be in Colorado on this ranch①."

"Don't make me laugh. You can't even ride a horse."

"Who can't? Sure I can. Certainly I can. They can teach you in about two minutes," I said. "Stop picking at that." She was picking at that adhesive tape on her arm. "Who gave you that haircut?" I asked her. I just noticed what a stupid haircut somebody gave her. It was way too short.

"None of your business," she said. She can be very snotty sometimes. She can be quite snotty. "I suppose you failed in every single subject again," she said—very snotty. It was sort of funny, too, in a way. She sounds like a goddam schoolteacher sometimes, and she's only a little child.

"No, I didn't," I said. "I passed English." Then, just for the hell of it, I gave her a pinch on the behind②. It was sticking way out in the breeze, the way she was laying on her side. She has hardly any behind. I didn't do it hard, but she tried to hit my hand anyway, but she missed.

Then all of a sudden, she said, "Oh, why did you do it?" She meant why did I get the ax③ again. It made me sort of sad, the way she said it.

"Oh, God, Phoebe, don't ask me. I'm sick of everybody asking me that," I said. "A million reasons why. It was one of the worst schools I ever went to. It was full of phonies④. And mean guys. You never saw so many mean guys in your life. For instance, if you were having a bull session⑤ in somebody's room, and somebody wanted to come in, nobody'd let them in if they were some dopey⑥, pimply guy. Everybody was always locking their door when somebody wanted to come in. And they had this goddam secret fraternity⑦ that I was too yellow⑧ not to join. There was this one pimply, boring guy, Robert Ackley, that wanted to get in. He kept trying to

---

① ranch: a large farm, esp. in the US or Canada.
② behind: hip(臀部).
③ get the ax: (informal) be removed or dismissed(被开除).
④ phony: someone who is insincere, superficial or pretentious. Holden often uses this word to express his disgust towards the adult's world.
⑤ bull session: an informal conversation among a small group of people.
⑥ dopey: (slang) stupid, silly.
⑦ fraternity: a society joined by male students, usually functioning as a social club(兄弟会).
⑧ yellow: coward(懦夫).

join, and they wouldn't let him. Just because he was boring and pimply. I don't even feel like talking about it. It was a stinking school. Take my word."

Old Phoebe didn't say anything, but she was listening. I could tell by the back of her neck that she was listening. She always listens when you tell her something. And the funny part is she knows, half the time, what the hell you're talking about. She really does.

I kept talking about old Pencey. I sort of felt like it.

"Even the couple of nice teachers on the faculty, they were phonies, too," I said. "There was this one old guy, Mr. Spencer. His wife was always giving you hot chocolate and all that stuff, and they were really pretty nice. But you should've seen him when the headmaster, old Thurmer, came in the history class and sat down in the back of the room. He was always coming in and sitting down in the back of the room for about a half an hour. He was supposed to be incognito① or something. After a while, he'd be sitting back there and then he'd start interrupting what old Spencer was saying to crack a lot of corny jokes. Old Spencer'd practically kill himself chuckling and smiling and all, like as if Thurmer was a goddam prince or something."

"Don't swear so much."

"It would've made you puke, I swear it would," I said. "Then, on Veterans' Day②. They have this day, Veterans' Day, that all the jerks that graduated from Pencey around 1776③ come back and walk all over the place, with their wives and children and everybody. You should've seen this one old guy that was about fifty. What he did was, he came in our room and knocked on the door and asked us if we'd mind if he used the bathroom. The bathroom was at the end of the corridor—I don't know why the hell he asked us. You know what he said? He said he wanted to see if his initials were still in one of the can doors. What he did, he carved his goddam stupid sad old initials in one of the can doors about ninety years ago, and he wanted to see if they were still there. So my roommate and I walked him down to the bathroom and all, and we had to stand there while he looked for his initials in all the can doors. He kept talking to us the whole time, telling us how when he was at Pencey they were the happiest days of his life, and givingus a lot of advice for the future and all. Boy, did he depress me! I don't mean he was a bad guy—he wasn't. But you don't have to be a bad guy to depress somebody—you can be a good guy and do it. All you have to do to depress somebody is give them a lot of phony advice while you're looking for your initials in

---

① incognito: with one's true identity disguised or concealed(隐姓埋名地).
② Veterans' Day: an American holiday honoring military veterans which falls on the weekday closest to November 11th each year (退伍军人节).
③ around 1776: This is an exaggeration. A similar example is "ninety years ago" in the same paragraph.

some can door—that's all you have to do. I don't know. Maybe it wouldn't have been so bad if he hadn't been all out of breath. He was all out of breath from just climbing up the stairs, and the whole time he was looking for his initials he kept breathing hard, with his nostrils all funny and sad, while he kept telling Stradlater and I to get all we could out of Pencey. God, Phoebe! I can't explain. I just didn't like anything that was happening at Pencey. I can't explain."

Old Phoebe said something then, but I couldn't hear her. She had the side of her mouth right smack on the pillow, and I couldn't hear her.

"What?" I said. "Take your mouth away. I can't hear you with your mouth that way."

"You don't like anything that's happening."

It made me even more depressed when she said that.

"Yes I do. Yes I do. Sure I do. Don't say that. Why the hell do you say that?"

"Because you don't. You don't like any schools. You don't like a million things. You don't."

"I do! That's where you're wrong—that's exactly where you're wrong! Why the hell do you have to say that?" I said. Boy, was she depressing me.

"Because you don't," she said. "Name one thing."

"One thing? One thing I like?" I said. "Okay."

The trouble was, I couldn't concentrate too hot. Sometimes it's hard to concentrate.

"One thing I like a lot you mean?" I asked her.

She didn't answer me, though. She was in a cockeyed position way the hell over the other side of the bed. She was about a thousand miles away. "C'mon answer me," I said. "One thing I like a lot, or one thing I just like?"

"You like a lot."

"All right," I said. But the trouble was, I couldn't concentrate. About all I could think of were those two nuns that went around collecting dough[①] in those beatup old straw baskets. Especially the one with the glasses with those iron rims. And this boy I knew at Elkton Hills[②]. There was this one boy at Elkton Hills, named James Castle, that wouldn't take back something he said about this very conceited boy, Phil Stabile. James Castle called him a very conceited guy, and one of Stabile's lousy[③] friends went and squealed on him to Stabile. So Stabile, with about six other dirty bastards, went down to James Castle's room and went in and locked the goddam door and tried to make him take back what he said, but he wouldn't do it. So they started in on him. I won't even tell you what they did to him—it's too repulsive—but he still wouldn't

---

① dough: money.
② Elkton Hills: the name of a school.
③ lousy: (informal) very bad or unpleasant.

take it back, old James Castle. And you should've seen him. He was a skinny little weak-looking guy, with wrists about as big as pencils. Finally, what he did, instead of taking back what he said, he jumped out the window. I was in the shower and all, and even I could hear him land outside. But I just thought something fell out the window, a radio or a desk or something, not a boy or anything. Then I heard everybody running through the corridor and down the stairs, so I put on my bathrobe and I ran downstairs too, and there was old James Castle laying right on the stone steps and all. He was dead, and his teeth, and blood, were all over the place, and nobody would even go near him. He had on this turtleneck sweater I'd lent him. All they did with the guys that were in the room with him was expel them. They didn't even go to jail.

That was about all I could think of, though. Those two nuns I saw at breakfast and this boy James Castle I knew at Elkton Hills. The funny part is, I hardly even know James Castle, if you want to know the truth. He was one of these very quiet guys. He was in my math class, but he was way over on the other side of the room, and he hardly ever got up to recite or go to the blackboard or anything. Some guys in school hardly ever get up to recite or go to the blackboard. I think the only time I ever even had a conversation with him was that time he asked me if he could borrow this turtleneck sweater I had. I damn near dropped dead when he asked me, I was so surprised and all. I remember I was brushing my teeth, in the can, when he asked me. He said his cousin was coming in to take him for a drive and all. I didn't even know he knew I had a turtleneck sweater. All I knew about him was that his name was always right ahead of me at roll call. Cabel, R., Cabel, W., Castle, Caulfield—I can still remember it. If you want to know the truth, I almost didn't lend him my sweater. Just because I didn't know him too well.

"What?" I said to old Phoebe. She said something to me, but I didn't hear her.

"You can't even think of one thing."

"Yes, I can. Yes, I can."

"Well, do it, then."

"I like Allie[①]," I said. "And I like doing what I'm doing right now. Sitting here with you, and talking, and thinking about stuff, and—"

"Allie's dead—You always say that! If somebody's dead and everything, and in Heaven, then it isn't really—"

"I know he's dead! Don't you think I know that? I can still like him, though, can't I? Just because somebody's dead, you don't just stop liking them, for God's sake—especially if they were about a thousand times nicer than the people you know that're

---

① Allie: Holden's younger brother who died of leukemia three years before the beginning of the novel. Holden considers him as the smartest of the Caulfields and misses him very much.

alive and all."

Old Phoebe didn't say anything. When she can't think of anything to say, she doesn't say a goddam word.

"Anyway, I like it now," I said. "I mean right now. Sitting here with you and just chewing the fat① and horsing—"

"That isn't anything really!"

"It is so something really! Certainly it is! Why the hell isn't it? People never think anything is anything really. I'm getting goddam sick of it."

"Stop swearing. All right, name something else. Name something you'd like to be. Like a scientist. Or a lawyer or something."

"I couldn't be a scientist. I'm no good in science."

"Well, a lawyer—like Daddy and all."

"Lawyers are all right, I guess—but it doesn't appeal to me," I said. "I mean they're all right if they go around saving innocent guys' lives all the time, and like that, but you don't do that kind of stuff if you're a lawyer. All you do is make a lot of dough and play golf and play bridge and buy cars and drink Martinis and look like a hot-shot②. And besides. Even if you did go around saving guys' lives and all, how would you know if you did it because you really wanted to save guys' lives, or because you did it because what you really wanted to do was be a terrific lawyer, with everybody slapping you on the back and congratulating you in court when the goddam trial was over, the reporters and everybody, the way it is in the dirty movies? How would you know you weren't being a phony? The trouble is, you wouldn't."

I'm not too sure old Phoebe knew what the hell I was talking about. I mean she's only a little child and all. But she was listening, at least. If somebody at least listens, it's not too bad.

"Daddy's going to kill you. He's going to kill you," she said.

I wasn't listening, though. I was thinking about something else—something crazy. "You know what I'd like to be?" I said. "You know what I'd like to be? I mean if I had my goddam choice?"

"What? Stop swearing."

"You know that song 'If a body catch a body comin' through the rye'? I'd like—"

"It's 'If a body meet a body coming through the rye'!" old Phoebe said. "It's a poem. By Robert Burns③."

"I know it's a poem by Robert Burns."

---

① chew the fat: (informal, or "chew the rag") talk about sth. often in a grumbling or argumentative way.
② hot-shot: (informal) person who is skillful or talented in a showy or aggressive way.
③ Robert Burns: an outstanding Scottish poet (1759~1796).

She was right, though. It is "If a body meet a body coming through the rye." I didn't know it then, though.

"I thought it was 'if a body catch a body,'" I said. "Anyway, I keep picturing all these little kids playing some game in this big field of rye and all. Thousands of little kids, and nobody's around—nobody big, I mean—except me. And I'm standing on the edge of some crazy cliff. What I have to do, I have to catch everybody if they start to go over the cliff—I mean if they're running and they don't look where they're going I have to come out from somewhere and catch them. That's all I'd do all day. I'd just be the catcher in the rye and all. I know it's crazy, but that's the only thing I'd really like to be. I know it's crazy." Old Phoebe didn't say anything for a long time. Then, when she said something, all she said was, "Daddy's going to kill you."

"I don't give a damn if he does," I said. I got up from the bed then, because what I wanted to do, I wanted to phone up this guy that was my English teacher at Elkton Hills, Mr. Antolini. He lived in New York now. He quit Elkton Hills. He took this job teaching English at N.Y.U. "I have to make a phone call," I told Phoebe. "I'll be right back. Don't go to sleep." I didn't want her to go to sleep while I was in the living room. I knew she wouldn't but I said it anyway, just to make sure.

While I was walking toward the door, old Phoebe said, "Holden!" and I turned around.

She was sitting way up in bed. She looked so pretty. "I'm taking belching lessons from this girl, Phyllis Margulies," she said. "Listen."

I listened, and I heard something, but it wasn't much. "Good," I said. Then I went out in the living room and called up this teacher I had, Mr. Antolini.

译文链接：https://www.99csw.com/book/2430/72978.htm

Questions for Understanding

1. What does Holden say when Phoebe asks him why he "got the ax again"? What is his opinion of the school and adult world?
2. What does he say when Phoebe asks him to name one thing that he likes? Why does he say so?
3. Who is James Castle? What has happened to him?
4. What jobs does Holden refuse to do? Why?
5. Why does he want to be a catcher in the rye? What's his attitude towards the children like Phoebe and Allie?
6. What kind of person is Holden?

Aspects of Appreciation

1. When explaining why he is expelled from the school, Holden mentions that he hates mean classmates, the pretentious headmaster, the coward and humble teachers and the superficial alumni. To some extent, the school can be viewed as the microcosm of the adult world. Holden regards it as a world full of phoniness, hypocrisy and obscenity, which shows his great disappointment and disgust.

2. When Phoebe asks Holden to say what he wants to do, he shows his reluctance to fit into the roles his parents expect him to play, such as a scientist or a lawyer. Instead, he would like to be a catcher in the rye who stands on the edge of a cliff, guards thousands of children playing in a field of rye and protects them from falling off the cliff. This dream explains the novel's metaphoric title. The rye field actually stands for the innocent childhood; the cliff is a symbol of the dividing line between the rye field of childhood and the world of adulthood; and accordingly falling off the cliff symbolizes the progression from childhood to sophisticated and decadent adulthood. Holden views this change as a devastating one, just like the suicidal behavior of falling off the precipice. Therefore, he positions himself as a protector who stands on the edge of the cliff and saves the kids from losing their innocence and goodness. Though noble and good, this dream is only a fantasy hard to be fulfilled; even Holden himself realizes this, acknowledging that his idea is "crazy".

3. The whole book is narrated from the first-person point of view. The hero Holden Caulfield recounts his unusual experiences in New York, describing what he himself sees and thinks in the colloquial language of a contemporary teenager, full of slang, repetition, unconscious humor and etc., which easily creates a sense of reality that makes readers more inclined to trust the narrator andenter into Holden's experiences. More importantly, through this vantage point and interior monologue, the psychological state of Holden and most of his peers, full of adolescent angst, awkward sexual explorations, cynical attitudes toward the adult worldand the bitter struggle between the two worlds of childhood and adulthood, is brought to life, which finds an echo in the hearts of readers, especially the young generation.

Suggested Further Reading

Nine Stories (1953); *Raise High the Roofbeam, Carpenters*(1963); *Seymour: An*

Introduction (1963)

Topics for Further Study

1. Who is the narrator of the book? Is the narrator reliable? Why or why not? What would have changed if the story had been told from someone else's point of view, such as Holden's parents?

2. Holden often behaves like a prophet or a saint, pointing out the phoniness and ugliness in the world around him. Is Holden as perfect as he wants to be? Are there instances to show that he is phony and full of hypocrisy?

3. Besides the famous symbol of the catcher in the rye, the novel contains some other symbols, for instance, the carrousel, Holden's red hunting hat, the ducks in the Central Park lagoon and the Museum of Natural History. Try to work out the meanings of these symbols.

4. *The Catcher in the Rye and The Adventures of Huckleberry Finn* are Bildungsromans. Compare Holden and Huck and try to find out their similarities and differences.

Knowledge of Literature

1. Bildungsroman（成长小说）

Bildungsroman is a German term signifying "novel of formation" or "novel of education". The subject of these novels is the development of the protagonist's mind and character, in the passage from childhood through varied experiences— and often through a spiritual crisis—into maturity, which usually involves recognition of one's identity and role in the world. The mode was begun by Goethe's *WilhelmMeister'sApprenticeship*(1795-1796). In English literature famous examples are *David Copperfield* by Charles Dickens, and *A Portrait of the Artist as a Young Man* by James Joyce.

2. An Element of Fiction: Point of View（视角）

Point of view is the narrator's relationship to the world of the novel. Authors usually use four points of view. The first is the third-person omniscient point of view. A narrator from "outside" the story world tells the story. The narrator assumes complete knowledge of the characters' actions, thoughts, and locations. The second is the third-person limited point of view. A narrator, who is one character, tells the story. The author limits himself or herself to what is known by the narrator. The third is the third-person objective (dramatic) point of view. A narrator knows everything about places, times, and events. However, the narrator does not enter the mind of any character. Readers see the characters as they may observe them in a play. The key to the objective (dramatic) point of view is that the writer presents actions and dialogue, and leaves conclusions and interpretations to the readers. The fourth is the first-person point of view. One of the characters tells the story and uses the first-person pronoun, "I". First-person narrators report things that they see, hear, and think and, as they do, they convey not only the action of the work, but also some of their own background, thinking, attitudes, and prejudices.

To analyze the point of view of a novel, the reader should determine whether the narrator is reliable and explain how the point of view has contributed to making the work unique.

推荐阅读的论文：
[1] 张宝云. 浅谈《麦田里的守望者》中的叙事视角 [J]. 四川文理学院学报，2019(03).
[2] 胡铁生，赵远. 塞林格笔下青少年成长的艰难历程 [J]. 山东外语教学，2014(05).

Thomas Pynchon (1937~)

About the Author

Thomas Pynchon might be one of the most mysterious and elusive writers in the world, for so far only scanty information about him has ever been found. Born on Long Island, he studied engineering Physics at Cornell University, later transferred to the major of English, worked as a technical writer for Boeing Aircraft, and then has lived in hiding or incognito till now.

However, such silence did not deter him from becoming one of the best-known writer to emerge after World War II. Up to now, Pynchon has altogether created a number of short stories (most of which were published in a 1984 collection *Slow Learner*) as well as seven significant novels: *V.* (1963), *Crying of Lot 49* (1966), *Gravity's Rainbow* (1973), *Vineland* (1990), *Mason & Dixon* (1997), *Against the Day* (2006) and *Inherent Vice* (2009), which encompass a vast array of styles, subjects and themes covering such differing disciplines as science, sociology and anthropology, and are notable for the encyclopedic erudition, obscure language, absurd and labyrinthine plots, and elaborated application of scientific theories.

Although all these works received considerable critical and public attention, Pynchon's reputation rests largely on his third novel *Gravity's Rainbow*. Containing more than 400 characters, multiple threads of narrative, and profound specialist knowledge drawn from a wide range of disciplines, this masterpiece mainly recounts an offbeat quest undertaken by an American lieutenant Tyrone Slothrop. Due to his strange connection with the staging areas of the deadly weapon of Nazis, Rocket V-2, A4, Slothrop is assigned to uncover the mystery of the invention and deployment of the rocket. Though having traveled across most of Europe and encountered many people having to do either directly or tangentially with the rocket, he never discovers the weapon itself, and even he himself falls apart and vanishes into the air. Ever since its first printing, this encyclopedic fantasy has been canonized as a classic postmodern novel for its disruption of narrative conventions, the blurring of the traditional boundary between genres, and the ingenious employment of collage, pastiche and other postmodern skills, and what's more, has opened the minds of millions to the devastating effect of the war and technology on the civilization. Though frequently attached to such labels as "unreadable", "obscene" and "overwritten", this impressive fiction is unanimously recognized as Pynchon's magnum opus, together with *Moby Dick* ranking the first placein American novels.

Once as a student majoring in engineering Physics, Pynchon shows great interests in expounding the postwar world with some principal scientific theories, the most famous one being the theory of entropy. As a key notion in modern physics, it refers to a theory about energy in which the degradation of molecules makes the universe move into a state of increasing randomness, chaos and ultimately into the stasis of motion which will culminate in eventual heat-death. With these ideas in mind, Pynchon is sensitive enough to realize that the postbellum human world would probably face the ominous tendency of declining into the disorder and chaos. Such entropic vision prompts him to show great concern towards such problems existing in the contemporary world as mammon worship, decadent morality, the sterility of civilization and men's alienation, and more importantly, to spare no efforts to expose these alarming problems to the public by creating a labyrinthine fictional world haunted by entropic breakdown, ambiguity and indeterminacy.

Entropy

About the Story

Published first in *Kenyon Review* in 1960, "Entropy"[①] is acclaimed as Pynchon's most discussed and anthologized short story which introduces very directly his

---

① Entropy: 熵，指一切物体都将进入的混沌状态。

dominant metaphor, namely, the "entropy", for exploring the theme of decline. Entropy is often used by literary scholars as a metaphor for the forces that cause the decay of society and the demise of the world. The "entropy" described in the works of Thomas Pynchon reflects the individual's deep concern for the universal state of human existence and the constant vigilance against the dangers of scientific arbitrariness in modern society. The evolutionary trend of entropy in the context of informatics, in turn, is constantly decreasing. Therefore, in order to combat the entropy of information, Pynchon intentionally breaks the traditional narrative order and introduces a certain chaos to increase the uncertainty of the text. Since then, such metaphor has been frequently applied to most of his works including *V.* (1963), *The Crying of Lot 49* (1966) and *Gravity's Rainbow* (1973).

Boris has just given me a summary of his views. He is a weather prophet. The weather will continue bad, he says. There will be more calamities, more death, more despair. Not the slightest indication of a change anywhere...We must get into step, a lockstep toward the prison of death. There is no escape. The weather will not change.
—*Tropic of Cancer*[1]

Downstairs, Meatball Mulligan's lease-breaking party was moving into its 40th hour. On the kitchen floor, amid a litter of empty champagne fifths, were Sandor Rojas and three friends, playing spit in the ocean and staying on Heidseck[2] and benzedrine[3] pills. In the living room Duke, Vincent, Krinkles and Paco sat crouched over a 15-inch speaker which had been bolted into the top of a wastepaper basket, listening to 27 watts' worth of The Heroes' Gate at Kiev[4]. They all wore hornrimmed sunglasses and rapt expressions, and smoked funny-looking cigarettes which contained not, as you might expect, tobacco, but an adulterated form of cannabis sativa[5], This group was the Duke di Angelis quartet. They recorded for a local label called Tambu and had to their credit one ten 10" LP entitled Songs of Outer Space[6]. From time to time one of them would flick the ashes from his cigarette into the speaker cone to watch them dance around. Meatball himself was sleeping over by the window, holding an empty magnum to his chest as if it were a teddy bear. Several government girls, who worked

---

[1] Tropic of Cancer: a masterpiece written by American novelist Henry Miller (1891~1980). The selection here presents the terrible picture of the Doomsday.
[2] Heidseck: 法国香槟。
[3] Benzedrine: 苯丙胺，一种中枢兴奋药，可作毒品。
[4] The Heroes' Gate at Kiev: 这是俄罗斯作曲家穆索尔斯基的十五首古典乐曲组曲中的最佳乐章。
[5] cannabis sativa: 大麻。
[6] Songs of Outer Space: 该歌名含反讽意味，因为外层空间没有传递声波的空气，不可能有声音和歌曲。

for people like the State Department and NSA①, had passed out on couches, chairs and in one case the bathroom sink.

This was in early February of '57 and back then there were a lot of American expatriates around Washington, D.C., who would talk, every time they met you, about how someday they were going to go over to Europe for real but right now it seemed they were working for the government. Everyone saw a fine irony in this. They would stage, for instance, polyglot parties where the newcomer was sort of ignored if he couldn't carry on simultaneous conversations in three or four languages. They would haunt American delicatessens for weeks at a stretch and invite you over for bulghour and lamb② in tiny kitchens whose walls were covered with bullfight posters. They would have affairs with sultry girls from Audalucía or the Midi③ who studied economics at Georgetown. Their Dôme④ was a collegiate Rathskeller out on Wisconsin Avenue called the Old Heidelberg and they had to settle for cherry blossoms instead of lime trees when spring came, but in its lethargic way their life provided, as they said, kicks.

At the moment, Meatball's party seemed to be gathering its second wind. Outside there was rain. Rain splatted against the tar paper on the roof and was fractured into a fine spray off the noses, eyebrows and lips of wooden gargoyles under the eaves, and ran like drool down the windowpanes. The day before, it had snowed and the day before that there had been winds of gale force and before that the sun had made the city glitter bright as April, though the calendar read early February. It is a curious season in Washington, this false spring. Somewhere in it are Lincoln's Birthday and the Chinese New Year, and a forlornness in the streets because cherry blossoms are weeks away still and, as Sarah Vaughan⑤ has put it, spring will be a little late this year. Generally crowds like the one which would gather in the Old Heidelberg on weekday afternoons to drink Würtzburger⑥ and to sing Lili Marlene⑦(not to mention The Sweetheart of Sigma Chi⑧) are inevitably and incorrigibly Romantic. And as every

---

① the State Department and NSA: 美国国务院和美国国家安全局。
② bulghour and lamb: a delicious food in Middle East.
③ Andalucía: a region in southern Spain on the Atlantic and the Mediterranean; Midi: the south of France.
④ Le Dôme: a famous café in Montparnasse, Paris. 这是一家位于巴黎蒙巴纳斯的著名咖啡馆。从20世纪初开始，它就以知识分子聚集地而闻名，海明威和亨利·米勒等著名艺术家、作家和艺术鉴赏家都经常光顾这里。
⑤ Sarah Vaughan: American jazz and popular singer(1924~1990).
⑥ Würtzburger: 德国Würtzburger酿制的啤酒。
⑦ Lili Marlene: a famous German lyric song which gained wide popularity in Germany and the Allied Forces during the WWII.
⑧ The Sweetheart of Sigma Chi: an American love song which was popular in the universities in 1920s.

good Romantic knows, the soul (spiritus, ruach, pneuma①) is nothing, substantially, but air; it is only natural that warpings in the atmosphere should be recapitulated in those who breathe it. So that over and above the public components—holidays, tourist attractions—there are private meanderings, linked to the climate as if this spell were a stretto② passage in the year's fugue: haphazard weather, aimless loves, unpredicted commitments: months one can easily spend in fugue, because oddly enough, later on, winds, rains, passions of February and March are never remembered in that city, it is as if they had never been.

The last bass notes of the The Heroes' Gate boomed up through the floor and woke Callisto from an uneasy sleep. The first thing he became aware of was a small bird he has been holding gently between his hands, against his body. He turned his head sidewise on the pillow to smile down at it, at its blue hunched-down head and sick, lidded eyes, wondering how many more nights he would have to give it warmth before it was well again. He had been holding the bird like that for three days: it was the only way he knew to restore its health. Next to him the girl stirred and whimpered, her arm thrown across her face. Mingled with the sounds of the rain came the first tentative, querulous morning voices of the other birds, hidden in philodendrons③ and small fan palms: patches of scarlet, yellow and blue laced through this Rousseau④-like fantasy, this hothouse jungle it had taken him seven years to weave together. Hermetically sealed, it was a tiny enclave of regularity in the city's chaos, alien to the vagaries of the weather, of national politics, of any civil disorder. Through trial-and-error Callisto had perfected its ecological balance, with the help of the girl its artistic harmony, so that the swayings of its plant life, the stirrings of its birds and human inhabitants were all as integral as the rhythms of a perfectly-executed mobile. He and the girl could no longer, of course, be omitted from that sanctuary; they had become necessary to its unity. What they needed from outside was delivered. They did not go out.

"Is he all right," she whispered. She lay like a tawny question mark facing him, her eyes suddenly huge and dark and blinking slowly. Callisto ran a finger beneath the feathers at the base of the bird's neck; caressed it gently. "He's going to be well, I think. See: he hears his friends beginning to wake up." The girl had heard the rain and the birds even before she was fully awake. Her name was Aubade: she was part French

---

① spiritus, ruach, pneuma: the Latin, Hebrew and Greek name of "soul".
② stretto: （意大利语）狭窄。此处作为音乐术语，指赋格曲中紧密的合应或声音的重叠。
③ philodendrons: 喜林芋属植物（热带美洲产）。
④ Rousseau: French primitive painter（1844~1910）.

and part Annamese①, and she lived on her own curious and lonely planet, where the clouds and the odor of poincianas②, the bitterness of wine and the accidental fingers at the small of her back or feathery against her breasts came to her reduced inevitably to the terms of sound: of music which emerged at intervals from a howling darkness of discordancy. "Aubade," he said, "go see." Obedient, she arose; padded to the window, pulled aside the drapes and after a moment said: "It is 37. Still 37." Callisto frowned. "Since Tuesday, then," he said. "No change." Henry Adams③, three generations before his own, had stared aghast at Power; Callisto found himself now in much the same state over Thermodynamics④, the inner life of that power, realizing like his predecessor that the Virgin and the dynamo stand as much for love as for power; that the two are indeed identical; and that love therefore not only makes the world go round but also makes the boccie ball⑤ spin, the nebula precess⑥. It was this latter or sidereal element which disturbed him. The cosmologists had predicted an eventual heat-death for the universe (something like Limbo: form and motion abolished, heat-energy identical at every point in it); the meteorologists, day-to-day, staved it off by contradicting with a reassuring array of varied temperatures.

But for three days now, despite the changeful weather, the mercury had stayed at 37 degrees Fahrenheit. Leery at omens of apocalypse⑦, Callisto shifted beneath the covers. His fingers pressed the bird more firmly, as if needing some pulsing or suffering assurance of an early break in the temperature.

It was that last cymbal crash that did it. Meatball was hurled wincing into consciousness as the synchronized wagging of heads over the wastebasket stopped. The final hiss remained for an instant in the room, then melted into the whisper of rain outside. "Aarrgghh," announced Meatball in the silence, looking at the empty magnum. Krinkles, in slow motion, turned, smiled and held out a cigarette. "Tea time⑧, man," he said. "No, no," said Meatball. "How many times I got to tell you guys. Not at my place. You ought to know, Washington is lousy with Feds⑨." Krinkles looked wistful. "Jeez, Meatball," he said, "you don't want to do nothing no more." "Hair of dog," said Meatball. "Only hope. Any juice left?" He began to crawl toward

---

① Annamese: Vietnamese(越南人).
② Poincianas: 黄蝴蝶属植物。
③ Henry Adams: 亨利·亚当斯，美国著名历史学家。
④ Thermodynamics: 热力学第二定律, 即熵定律。
⑤ boccie ball: 室外地滚球。
⑥ the nebula precess: 星际中围绕一呈锥状自转的中轴旋转的气体或尘埃。
⑦ apocalypse: a situation causing very serious damage and destruction(大灾变)。
⑧ tea time: 下午茶时间。这里指抽大麻的时间。
⑨ Fed: (Slang) A federal agent or official.

the kitchen. "No champagne, I don't think," Duke said. "Case of tequila[①] behind the icebox." They put on an Earl Bostic[②] side. Meatball paused at the kitchen door, glowering at Sandor Rojas. "Lemons," he said after some thought. He crawled to the refrigerator and got out three lemons and some cubes, found the tequila and set about restoring order to his nervous system. He drew blood once cutting the lemons and had to use two hands squeezing them and his foot to crack the ice tray but after about ten minutes he found himself, through some miracle, beaming down into a monster tequila sour. "That looks yummy," Sandor Rojas said. "How about you make me one." Meatball blinked at him. "Kitchi lofass a shegibe[③]," he replied automatically, and wandered away into the bathroom." I say, "he called out a moment later to no one in particular. "I say, there seems to be a girl or something sleeping in the sink." He took her by the shoulder and shook. "Wha," she said. "You don't look too comfortable," Meatball said. "Well," she agreed. She stumbled to the shower, turned on the cold water and sat down crosslegged in the spray. "That's better," she smiled.

"Meatball," Sandor Rojas yelled from the kitchen. "Somebody is trying to come in the window. A burglar, 1 think. A second-story man." "What are you worrying about," Meatball said. "We're on the third floor." He loped back into the kitchen. A shaggy woebegone[④] figure stood out on the fire escape, raking his fingernails down the windowpane. Meatball opened the window. "Saul," he said.

"Sort of wet out," Saul said. He climbed in, dripping. "You heard, I guess."

"Miriam left you," Meatball said, "or something, is all I heard."

There was a sudden flurry of knocking at the front door. "Do come in," Sandor Rojas called. The door opened and there were three coeds[⑤] from George Washington, all of whom were majoring in philosophy. They were each holding a gallon of Chianti[⑥]. Sandor leaped up and dashed into the living room. "We heard there was a party," one blonde said. "Young blood," Sandor shouted. He was an ex-Hungarian freedomfighter who had easily the worst chronic case of what certain critics of the middleclass have called Don Giovannism[⑦] in the District of Columbia. Purche porti

---

① tequila: 龙舌兰酒。
② Earl Bostic: (1913~1965) an American jazz and rhythm and blues alto saxophonist, and a pioneer of the postwar American Rhythm and Blues style.
③ Kitchi lofass a shegibe: (Hungarian) Up yours. (匈牙利语) 去你的。
④ Woebegone: sorrowful or sad in appearance.
⑤ coed: (informal) a woman who attends a coeducational college or university.
⑥ Chianti: a dry red table wine made from a blend of different varieties of grapes, originally produced in northwest Italy.
⑦ Don Giovannism: 强行追求女人的做法,源自西班牙传奇人物唐璜(Don Juan,意大利语为 Don Giovanni)的名字。

la gonnella, voi sapete quel che fa①. Like Pavlov's② dog: a contralto③ voice or a whiff of Arpège④ and Sandor would begin to salivate. Meatball regarded the trio blearily as they filed into the kitchen; he shrugged. "Put the wine in the icebox," he said "and good morning."

Aubade's neck made a golden bow as she bent over the sheets of foolscap, scribbling away in the green murk of the room. "As a young man at Princeton," Callisto was dictating, nestling the bird against the gray hairs of his chest, "Callisto had learned a mnemonic device for remembering the Laws of Thermodynamics: you can't win, things are going to get worse before they get better, who says they're going to get better. At the age of 54, confronted with Gibbs'⑤ notion of the universe, he suddenly realized that undergraduate cant had been oracle, after all. That spindly maze of equations became, for him, a vision of ultimate, cosmic heat-death. He had known all along, of course, that nothing but a theoretical engine or system ever runs at 100% efficiency; and about the theorem of Clausius⑥, which states that the entropy of an isolated system always continually increases. It was not, however, until Gibbsand Boltzmann⑦ brought to this principle the methods of statistical mechanics that the horrible significance of it all dawned on him: only then did he realize that the isolated system—galaxy, engine, human being, culture, whatever—must evolve spontaneously toward the Condition of the More Probable. He was forced, therefore, in the sad dying fall of middle age, to a radical reevaluation of everything he had learned up to then; all the cities and seasons and casual passions of his days had now to be looked at in a new and elusive light. He did not know if he was equal to the task. He was aware of the dangers of the reductive fallacy⑧ and, he hoped, strong enough not to drift into the graceful decadence of an enervated fatalism. His had always been a vigorous, Italian

---

① Purche porti la gonnella, voi sapete quel che fa:（意大利语）如果她穿着裙子，你就知道他会干什么。出自莫扎特的歌剧《唐璜》（1787）第一幕中仆人 Leporello 描述唐璜风流轶事的台词。
② Pavlov:（1849~1936）an outstanding Russian physiologist who was noted for discovering the conditioned response（条件反射学说）based on the research on conditioned salivary responses in dogs. He won a 1904 Nobel Prize for physiology or medicine.
③ contralto: 最低的女低音。
④ Arpège: a perfume produced by Lanvin in 1927.
⑤ Josiah Willard Gibbs: 约西亚·威拉德·吉布斯（1839~1903），美国著名物理学家。他奠定了化学热力学的基础，创立了向量分析并将其引入数学物理之中。
⑥ Rudolph Clausius: 鲁道夫·克劳修斯（1822~1888），德国物理学家，于1852年首先提出熵的概念，把熵定义为不能再被转化做功的能量的总和的测量单位。
⑦ Ludwig Boltzman: 路德维格·波尔兹曼（1844~1906），奥地利最伟大的物理学家之一，曾提出关于分子温度与能量比例的定律，认为温度越高，能量越大。
⑧ reductive fallacy: 过度的简化，即对于某些复杂的事情，把成因简单地归结为只有一种。

sort of pessimism: like Machiavelli[①], he allowed the forces of virtù and fortuna[②] to be about 50/50; but the equations now introduced a random factor which he found himself afraid to calculate." Around him loomed vague hothouse shapes; the pitifully small heart fluttered against his own. Counterpointed against his words the girl heard the chatter of birds and fitful car honkings scattered along the wet morning and Earl Bostic's alto[③] rising in occasional wild peaks through the floor. The architectonic purity of her world was constantly threatened by such hints of anarchy: gaps and excrescences and skew lines, and a shifting or tilting of planes to which she had continually to readjust lest the whole structure shiver into a disarray of discrete and meaningless signals. Callisto had described the process once as a kind of "feedback": she crawled into dreams each night with a sense of exhaustion, and a desperate resolve never to relax that vigilance. Even in the brief periods when Callisto made love to her, soaring above the bowing of taut nerves in haphazard double-stops[④] would be the one singing string of her determination.

"Nevertheless," continued Callisto, "he found in entropy or the measure of disorganization for a closed system an adequate metaphor to apply to certain phenomena in his own world. He saw, for example, the younger generation responding to Madison Avenue with the same spleen his own had once reserved for Wall Street: and in American 'consumerism' discovered a similar tendency from the least to the most probable, from differentiation to sameness, from ordered individuality to a kind of chaos. He found himself, in short, restating Gibb's prediction in social terms, and envisioned a heat-death for his culture in which ideas, like heat-energy, would no longer be transferred, since each point in it would ultimately have the same quantity of energy, and intellectual motion would, accordingly, cease." He glanced up suddenly, "Check it now," he said. Again she rose and peered out at the thermometer. "37," she said. "The rain has stopped." He bent his head quickly and held his lips against a quivering wing. "Then it will change soon," he said, trying to keep his voice firm.

Sitting on the stove Saul was like any big rag doll that a kid has been taking out some incomprehensible rage on. "What happened," Meatball said. "If you feel like talking, I mean."

"Of course I feel like talking," Saul said. "One thing I did, I slugged her."

"Discipline must be maintained."

---

① Machiavelli: a famed Italian statesman and political philosopher. His most famous work is The Prince (1513).
② virtù and fortuna: (Italian) Virtue and fortune.
③ alto: 男高音。
④ double-stops: 双音。在音乐中，"双音"指的是在小提琴、中提琴、大提琴或低音提琴等弓弦乐器上同时演奏两个音符的技巧。

"Ha, ha. I wish you'd been there. Oh Meatball, it was a lovely fight. She ended up throwing a Handbook of Chemistry and Physics at me, only it missed and went through the window, and when the glass broke I reckon something in her broke too. She stormed out of house crying, out in the rain. No raincoat or anything."

"She'll be back."

"No."

"Well." Soon Meatball said: "It was something earth-shattering, no doubt. Like who is better, Sal Mineo① or Ricky Nelson②."

"What it was about," Saul said, "was communication theory. Which of course makes it very hilarious."

"I don't know anything about communication theory."

"Neither does my wife. Come right down to it, who does? That's a joke."

When Meatball saw the kind of smile Saul had on his face he said: "Maybe you would like tequila or something."

"No. I mean, I'm sorry. It's a field you can go off the deep end in, is all. You get where you're watching all the time for security cops: behind bushes, around corners. MUFFET is top secret."

"Wha."

"Multi-unit factorial field electronic tabulator."

"You were fighting about that."

"Miriam has been reading science fiction again. That and *Scientific American*. It seems she is, as we say, bugging at this idea of computers acting like people. I made the mistake of saying you can just as well turn that around, and talk about human behavior like a program fed into an IBM machine."

"Why not," Meatball said.

"Indeed, why not. In fact it is sort of crucial to communication, not to mention information theory. Only when I said that she hit the roof. Up went the balloon. And I can't figure out why. If anybody should know why, I should. I refuse to believe the government is wasting taxpayers' money on me, when it has so many bigger and better things to waste it on."

Meatball made a mouse③. "Maybe she thought you were acting like a cold, dehumanized amoral scientist type."

"My god," Saul flung up an arm. "Dehumanized. How much more human can I get? I worry, Meatball, I do. There are Europeans wandering around North Africa

---

① Sal Mineo: an American film and theatre actor(1939~1976).
② Ricky Nelson: American pop singer in 1960s(1940~1985).
③ make a mouse: make a face(做鬼脸).

these days with their tongues torn out of their heads because those tongues have spoken the wrong words. Only the Europeans thought they were the right words."

"Language barrier," Meatball suggested.

Saul jumped down off the stove. "That," he said, angrily, "is a good candidate for sick joke of the year. No, ace, it is not a barrier. If it is anything it's a kind of leakage. Tell a girl: 'I love you.' No trouble with two-thirds of that, it's a closed circuit. Just you and she. But that nasty four-letter word in the middle, that's the one you have to look out for. Ambiguity. Redundancy. Irrelevance, even. Leakage. All this is noise. Noise screws up your signal, makes for disorganization in the circuit."

Meatball shuffled around. "Well, now, Saul," he muttered, "you're sort of, I don't know, expecting a lot from people. I mean, you know. What it is, most of the things we say, I guess, are mostly noise."

"Ha! Half of what you just said, for example."

"Well, you do it too."

"I know." Saul smiled grimly. "It's a bitch, ain't it."

"I bet that's what keeps divorce lawyers in business. Whoops."

"Oh I'm not sensitive. Besides," frowning, "you're right. You find I think that most 'successful' marriages—Miriam and me, up to last night—are sort of founded on compromises. You never run at top efficiency, usually all you have is a minimum basis for a workable thing. I believe the phrase is Togetherness."

"Aarrgghh."

"Exactly. You find that one is a bit noisy, don't you. But the noise content is different for each of us because you're a bachelor and I'm not. Or wasn't. The hell with it."

"Well sure," Meatball said, trying to be helpful, "you were using different words. By 'human being' you meant something that you can look at like it was a computer. It helps you think better on the job or something. But Miriam meant something entirely—"

"The hell with it."

Meatball fell silent. "I'll take that drink," Saul said after a while.

The card game had been abandoned and Sandor's friends were slowly getting wasted on tequila. On the living room couch, one of the coeds and Krinkles were engaged in amorous conversation. "No," Krinkles was saying, "no, I can't put Dave down[①]. In fact I give Dave a lot of credit, man. Especially considering his accident

---

① Dave Brubeck: American Jazz pianist who once joined in WWII.

and all." The girl's smile faded. "How terrible," she said. "What accident?" "Hadn't you heard?" Krinkles said. "When Dave was in the army, just a private E-2, they sent him down to Oak Ridge① on special duty. Something to do with the Manhattan Project②. He was handling hot stuff one day and got an overdose of radiation. So now he's got to wear lead gloves all the time." She shook her head sympathetically. "What an awful break for a piano-player."

Meatball had abandoned Saul to a bottle of tequila and was about to go to sleep in a closet when the front door flew open and the place was invaded by five enlisted personnel of the U.S. Navy, all in varying stages of abomination. "This is the place," shouted a fat, pimply seaman apprentice who had lost his white hat. "This here is the hoorhouse that chief was telling us about." A stringy-looking 3rd class boatswain's mate pushed him aside and cased the living room. "You're right, Slab," he said. "But it don't look like much, even for Stateside. I seen better tail in Naples, Italy." "How much, hey," boomed a large seaman with adenoids, who was holding a Mason jar full of white lightning③. "Oh, my god," said Meatball.

Outside the temperature remained constant at 37 degrees Fahrenheit. In the hothouse Aubade stood absently caressing the branches of a young mimosa, hearing a motif of sap-rising, the rough and unresolved anticipatory theme of those fragile pink blossoms which, it is said, insure fertility. That music rose in a tangled tracery: arabesques of order competing fugally with the improvised discords of the party downstairs, which peaked sometimes in cusps and ogees of noise. That precious signal-to-noise ratio, whose delicate balance required every calorie of her strength, seesawed inside the small tenuous skull as she watched Callisto, sheltering the bird. Callisto was trying to confront any idea of the heat-death now, as he nuzzled the feathery lump in his hands. He sought correspondences. Sade④, of course. And *Temple Drake*⑤, gaunt and hopeless in her little park in Paris, at the end of Sanctuary. Final equilibrium. *Nightwood*⑥. And the tango. Any tango, but more than any perhaps the sad sick dance in Stravinsky's *L'Histoire du Soldat*⑦. He thought back: what had

---

① Oak Ridge: a city in East Tennessee, U.S., which was established in the early 1940s as a base for the Manhattan Project.
② the Manhattan Project: the massive U.S. government operation that developed the atomic bomb.
③ white lightning: 非法酿制的威士忌酒。
④ Sade: Marquis de Sade(1740~1814), a French writer famous for his libertine sexuality and lifestyle.
⑤ Temple Drake: the heroine in Faulkner's novel Sanctuary. She unwittingly falls into the hands of a bootlegger named Popeye who kidnaps her and carts her off to a Memphis whorehouse. At the end of the novel, Temple and her father make a final appearance in the Jardin du Luxembourg, Paris.
⑥ Nightwood: a modernist masterpiece written by American writer Djuna Barnes(1892~1982) which depicts the sexual and psychological agonies of a group of expatriates in Paris and Berlin during the 1920s.
⑦ Stravinsky's L'Histoire du Soldat: the music piece composed by Russian composer Stravinsky.

tango music been for them after the war, what meanings had he missed in all the stately coupled automatons in the cafés-dansants①, or in the metronomes which had ticked behind the eyes of his own partners? Not even the clean constant winds of Switzerland could cure the grippe espagnole②: Stravinsky had had it, they all had had it. And how many musicians were left after Passchendaele, after the Marne③? It came down in this case to seven: violin, double-bass. Clarinet, bassoon. Cornet, trombone. Tympani. Almost as if any tiny troupe of saltimbanques④ had set about conveying the same information as a full pit-orchestra⑤. There was hardly a full complement left in Europe. Yet with violin and tympani Stravinsky had managed to communicate in that tango the same exhaustion, the same airlessness one saw in the slicked-down youths who were trying to imitate Vernon Castle⑥, and in their mistresses, who simply did not care. Ma matresse⑦. Celeste. Returning to Nice after the second war he had found that café replaced by a perfume shop which catered to American tourists. And no secret vestige of her in the cobblestones or in the old pension⑧ next door; no perfume to match her breath heavy with the sweet Spanish wine she always drank. And so instead he had purchased a Henry Miller novel and left for Paris, and read the book on the train so that when he arrived he had been given at least a little forewarning. And saw that Celeste and the others and even Temple Drake were not all that had changed. "Aubade," he said, "my head aches." The sound of his voice generated in the girl an answering scrap of melody. Her movement towards the kitchen, the towel, the cold water, and his eyes following her formed a weird and intricate canon; as she placed the compress on his forehead his sigh of gratitude seemed to signal a new subject, another series of modulations⑨.

"No," Meatball was still saying, "no, I'm afraid not. This is not a house of ill repute. I'm sorry, really I am." Slab was adamant. "But the chief said," he kept repeating. The seaman offered to swap the moonshine for a good piece. Meatball looked around frantically, as if seeking assistance. In the middle of the room, the Duke di Angelis quartet were engaged in a historic moment. Vincent was seated and the others standing: they were going through the motions of a group having a

---

① cafés-dansants: (French) ballroom, dancing hall.
② grippe espagnole: 1918 年爆发的西班牙大流感。此处品钦误认为是一战后欧洲知识分子的某种忧郁症或厌倦症。
③ Passchendaele: 比利时的帕申代尔村。Marne: 马恩河流域。这两处都是一战的战场。
④ saltimbanques: (French) performer, clown.
⑤ pit-orchestra: 在乐池里演奏的管弦乐团。
⑥ Vernon Castle: famous dancer during the WWI.
⑦ Ma maîtresse: (French) my mistress or lover.
⑧ pension: 廉价小旅店。
⑨ modulation: 调音。

session, only without instruments. "I say," Meatball said. Duke moved his head a few times, smiled faintly, lit a cigarette, and eventually caught sight of Meatball. "Quiet, man," he whispered. Vincent began to fling his arms around, his fists clenched; then, abruptly, was still, then repeated the performance. This went on for a few minutes while Meatball sipped his drink moodily. The navy had withdrawn to the kitchen. Finally at some invisible signal the group stopped tapping their feet and Duke grinned and said, "At least we ended together."

Meatball glared at him. "I say," he said. "I have this new conception, man," Duke said. "You remember your namesake. You remember Gerry[①]."

"No," said Meatball. "I'll remember April, if that's any help."

"As a matter of fact," Duke said, "it was Love for Sale, which shows how much you know. The point is, it was Mulligan, Chet Baker and that crew, way back then, out yonder. You dig?"

"Baritone sax[②]," Meatball said. "Something about a baritone sax."

"But no piano, man. No guitar. Or accordion. You know what that means."

"Not exactly," Meatball said.

"Well first let me just say, that I am no Mingus[③], no John Lewis[④]. Theory was never my strong point. I mean things like reading were always difficult for me and all—"

"I know," Meatball said drily. "You got your card taken away because you changed key on Happy Birthday at a Kiwanis[⑤] Club picnic."

"Rotarian[⑥]. But it occurred to me, in one of these flashes of insight, that if that first quartet of Mulligan's had no piano, it could only mean one thing."

"No chords," said Paco, the baby-faced bass.

"What he is trying to say," Duke said, "is no root[⑦] chords. Nothing to listen to while you blow a horizontal line. What one does in such a case is, one thinks the roots."

A horrified awareness was dawning on Meatball. "And the next logical extension," he said.

"Is to think everything," Duke announced with simple dignity. "Roots, line, everything."

---

① Gerry Mulligan: an American jazz saxophonist and composer(1927~1996).
② Baritone sax: 上低音萨克斯管。
③ Charlie Mingus: an American composer(1929~1979).
④ John Lewis: an American Jazz musician and composer(1920~).
⑤ Kiwanis: 基瓦尼斯俱乐部, 由美国工商业人士等组成的旨在振兴商业道德的会社。
⑥ Rotarian:(美)扶轮社的会员。
⑦ root chord: 一首乐曲的和声基音。

Meatball looked at Duke, awed. "But," he said.

"Well," Duke said modestly, "there are a few bugs to work out."

"But," Meatball said.

"Just listen," Duke said. "You'll catch on." And off they went again into orbit, presumably somewhere around the asteroid belt. After a while Krinkles made an embouchure① and started moving his fingers and Duke clapped his hand to his forehead. "Oaf!" he roared. "The new head② we're using, you remember, I wrote last night?" "Sure," Krinkles said, "the new head. I come in on the bridge. All your heads I come in then." "Right," Duke said. "So why—" "Wha," said Krinkles, "16 bars, I wait, I come in—" "16?" Duke said. "No. No, Krinkles. Eight you waited. You want me to sing it? A cigarette that bears a lipstick's traces, an airline ticket to romantic places." Krinkles scratched his head. "These Foolish Things, you mean." "Yes," Duke said, "yes, Krinkles. Bravo." "Not I'll Remember April," Krinkles said. "Minghe morte③," said Duke. "I figured we were playing it a little slow," Krinkles said. Meatball chuckled. "Back to the old drawing board," he said. "No, man," Duke said, "back to the airless void." And they took off again, only it seemed Paco was playing in G sharp while the rest were in E flat, so they had to start all over.

In the kitchen two of the girls from George Washington and the sailors were singing Let's All Go Down and Piss on the Forrestal④. There was a two-handed, bilingual morra⑤ game on over by the icebox. Saul had filled several paper bags with water and was sitting on the fire escape, dropping them on passersby in the street. A fat government girl in a Bennington sweatshirt, recently engaged to an ensign attached to the Forrestal, came charging into the kitchen, head lowered, and butted Slab in the stomach. Figuring this was as good an excuse for a fight as any, Slab's buddies piled in. The morra players were nose-to-nose, screaming trois, sette⑥ at the tops of their lungs. From the shower the girl Meatball had taken out of the sink announced that she was drowning. She had apparently sat on the drain and the water was now up to her neck. The noise in Meatball's apartment had reached a sustained, ungodly crescendo⑦.

Meatball stood and watched, scratching his stomach lazily. The way he figured, there were only about two ways he could cope: (a) lock himself in the closet and maybe eventually they would all go away, or (b) try to calm everybody down, one

---

① embouchure: 吹奏管乐器时的口型。
② new head: 一首乐曲的开头部分。
③ Minghe morte: (Italian slang) dead prick.
④ Forrestal: an American aircraft carrier named after then-Secretary of Defense Forrestal (1892~1949).
⑤ morra: 一种意大利游戏。
⑥ trois, sette: (Italian) three, seven.
⑦ crescendo: 持续噪声的最高点。

by one. (a) was certainly the more attractive alternative. But then he started thinking about that closet. It was dark and stuffy and he would be alone. He did not feature being alone. And then this crew off the good ship Lollipop or whatever it was might take it upon themselves to kick down the closet door, for a lark①. And if that happened he would be, at the very least, embarrassed. The other way was more a pain in the neck, but probably better in the long run.

So he decided to try and keep his lease-breaking party from deteriorating into total chaos: he gave wine to the sailors and separated the morra players; he introduced the fat government girl to Sandor Rojas, who would keep her out of trouble; he helped the girl in the shower to dry off and get into bed; he had another talk with Saul; he called a repairman for the refrigerator, which someone had discovered was on the blink②. This is what he did until nightfall, when most of the revellers had passed out and the party trembled on the threshold of its third day.

Upstairs Callisto, helpless in the past, did not feel the faint rhythm inside the bird begin to slacken and fail. Aubade was by the window, wandering the ashes of her own lovely world; the temperature held steady, the sky had become a uniform darkening gray. Then something from downstairs—a girl's scream, an overturned chair, a glass dropped on the floor, he would never know what exactly—pierced that private time-warp and he became aware of the faltering, the constriction of muscles, the tiny tossings of the bird's head; and his own pulse began to pound more fiercely, as if trying to compensate. "Aubade," he called weakly, "he's dying." The girl, flowing and rapt, crossed the hothouse to gaze down at Callisto's hands. The two remained like that, poised, for one minute, and two, while the heartbeat ticked a graceful diminuendo③ down at last into stillness. Callisto raised his head slowly. "I held him," he protested, impotent with the wonder of it, "to give him the warmth of my body. Almost as if I were communicating life to him, or a sense of life. What has happened? Has the transfer of heat ceased to work? Is there no more..." He did not finish.

"I was just at the window," she said. He sank back, terrified. She stood a moment more, irresolute; she had sensed his obsession long ago, realized somehow that that constant 37 was now decisive. Suddenly then, as if seeing the single and unavoidable conclusion to all this she moved swiftly to the window before Callisto could speak; tore away the drapes and smashed out the glass with two exquisite hands which came away bleeding and glistening with splinters; and turned to face the man on the bed and wait with him until the moment of equilibrium was reached, when 37 degrees

---

① for a lark: for fun.
② on the blink: out of order.
③ diminuendo: 音量渐弱。

Fahrenheit should prevail both outside and inside, and forever, and the hovering, curious dominant of their separate lives should resolve into a tonic of darkness and the final absence of all motion.

译文链接：https://book.douban.com/review/8223893

Questions for Understanding

1. Why does Pynchon use the sentences from *Tropic of Cancer* as the epigraph of the story?
2. What's the setting of this short story? Does it have something to do with the theme?
3. Who lives in the downstairs? What are they doing?
4. Why does Callisto living in the upstairs build a "hermetically sealed" hothouse in his apartment?
5. What does Aubade do at the end of the story? Why?
6. What is your understanding of the end? Is it optimistic, pessimistic, or ambivalent?

Aspects of Appreciation

1. This very tightly structured story, moving contrapuntally between Meatball Mulligan's downstairs party and Callisto's upstairs hothouse, is set in a building in Washington, D.C. in early February of 1957. Though the weather changes repeatedly, alternating between rain and sunshine, the temperature remains ominously constant. Such an odd season, together with the pessimistic epigraphy taken from Henry Miller's *Tropic of Cancer*, establishes the tone of this story: changeful, chaotic, and desperate.

2. Although in the *Introduction to Slow Learner*, Pynchon expresses his dislike for "Entropy", claiming that he made a mistake of forcing a theme onto the characters and events rather than having the former develop through the latter, "Entropy" still occupies an outstanding position in his works, for in this short story, Pynchon not only first introduces the term "entropy", the most important concept in his literary universe, but also explores its different uses in thermodynamics, information theory and its theoretical extension to the realms of society and culture as well. He specifically names Rudolf Clausius, Ludwig Boltzmann and Willard Gibbs, all of whom are the representatives of thermodynamic entropy, a theory about energy in which the degradation of molecules makes the universe move into a state of increasing

randomness, chaos and ultimately into the stasis of motion which will culminate in eventual heat-death, and entropy refers to a parameter of disorder in the universe or a closed system; the greater the disorder, the higher the entropy. Besides, he alludes to Henry Adams who applied the theory of entropy to human history, arguing that the whole Western society is a closed system consisting of numerous isolated parties and hence with the increasing amount of entropy, the human society would definitely move towards disorder, chaos and futility. What's more, Phychon also touches upon Nobert Wiener's informational theory in which entropy is a measure of random error or noise in the transmission of information, resulting in redundancy, misunderstanding and failure in communication.

3. Metaphorically, the two situations in the story, that is, Meatball's noisy party downstairs and Callisto's hermetically sealed hothouse upstairs, are apparently "entropic" situations. Downstairs, Meatball is throwing a lease-breaking party which gradually deteriorates into chaos: revelers pass out in every corner of the apartment, drunken Navy officers barge in by mistake, the refrigerator needs repairing, a girl almost drowns herself in the sink and so forth. This wild party could be viewed as the open information kingdom in Wiener's theory, where information and changes pervade but communication breaks down, because people are completely indulged into pleasure and the noises created obviates the possibility of any communication. Meanwhile, upstairs Callisto and his girlfriend Aubade are also trapped in the entropic situation. In order to resist the disorder and decline outside, Callisto spent seven years in constructing a hermetically sealed hothouse which, he firmly believed, can be "alien to the vagaries of the weather, of national politics, of any civil disorder". To some extent, this Rousseau-like fantasy world can be deemed as the closed system in Henry Adams' theory. Castillo and Aubade not only create a sealed hothouse which is insulated from the disorder outside, but also turn themselves into isolated systems, lacking enough mutual communication, which explains the fact that although Castillo tries his utmost to nurse the sick bird back to health (i.e., clutch it to his chest in order to sustain it through the transfer of heat from his body to its body), he ends up in failure, for the entropy has reached the hothouse and there is no transfer of heat.

4. In his masterpiece *The Human Use of Human Beings*, Wiener argues that unlike the universe, human beings might not fall under "nature's statistical tendency to disorder, the tendency for entropy to increase in isolated system", because they are not isolated systems, not only taking in food from the outside, but also taking in information "through the sense organs and acting on information received". Deeply

influenced by this notion, Pynchon firmly believes that communication or love is the only way to resist the entropic decline of the society.

To some extent, the story ends somewhat positive, for Meatball, instead of hiding silently in the closet, decides to take measures to struggle against the disintegration of his party, trying to calm everyone down. For instance, he separates the morra players, gives wine to the sailors, calls someone to repair the refrigerator, helps the girl in the shower and has another talk with Saul. All of these behaviours indicate that he attempts to restore certain order to the party and make the communication possible. And upstairs Aubade is courageous enough to thrust her hands through the window of the hothouse, which suggests that she denies the closed entropic system and affirms her own openness to communication.

5. "Entropy" bears certain postmodern elements. With the epigraph taken from Henry Miller's *Tropic of Cancer*, this short story is full of allusions to many different subjects, scientific, literary, historical, musical and biological, which make the whole story a big collage, and help to reveal the "entropy" theme. For instance, it involves a series of references to literary works, including Henry Miller's *Tropic of Cancer*, Marquis de Sade's writings, William Faulkner's *Sanctuary*, and Djuna Barnes' *Nightwood*. All the works share a common topic, that is, the decadence and forms of dissolution.

Suggested Further Reading

The Crying of Lot 49 (1966); *Gravity's Rainbow* (1973).

Topics for Further Study

1. "Entropy" contains several references to the Bible. For instance, Callisto uses seven years to build a hothouse, which parallels to the biblical seven-day creation. And to some extent, this hothouse shares a lot in common with Eden, with its own Adam and Eve, plus a variety of creatures living in harmonious ecological balance. However, this new Eden fell apart at the end of the story. Try to find the reason why the Eden in "Entropy" ended up in collapse.

2. Pynchon intentionally subverts the traditional quest motif in most of his writings including *V.*, *Crying of Lot 49*, *Gravity's Rainbow* and so forth. Select one of these novels and compare Pynchon's search with the quest convention in terms of the aim, the result, and the figures undertaking such task.

3. How does technology affect the world in *Gravity's Rainbow*? Will our technological innovationslead to our devastation?

Knowledge of Literature

1. Pastiche（模仿）

It refers to a literary piece consisting of the themes, characters and styles borrowed from the previous works of other writers. It is more neutral, compared with parody which uses the imitation to mock and satirize. With its special use to challenge the grand narrative, it is commonly used in postmodern fiction. One of the famous examples is John Fowles' novel *The French Lieutenant's Woman* (1969), which is partly a pastiche of the conventional Victorian fiction.

2. Collage（拼贴）

Derived from French word "coller" (meaning "to gluc"), it rcfcrs to a form of art where various disparate objects are assembled together. Initiated by the Cubist artists, it is widely applied to painting, music, literature and other fields of modern arts. In terms of literature, it generally refers to a technique through which a literary work is assembled partly or wholly from fragments of other writings, including allusions, quotations, foreign phrases and so forth.

3. The Quest Motif（追寻主题）

In the tradition of Western culture, the quest motif is closely linked with the legend of the Holy Grail in which the courageous Round Table Knights set off the quest for the Holy Grail, and only the purest and the most pious one could see the vision of the Grail. Later, it recurs in many works, generally represented as a journey through which the brave, virtuous and wise heroes endure muchtribulation, either spiritual or physical, and finally achieve the triumph as well as the moral or spiritual growth.

4. An Element of Fiction: Theme（主题）

The theme of a novel refers to the central or dominating idea that is made concrete through actions, characters, plot, pointof view, statements, symbols, dialogue, mood, atmospheresetting, figurative language，etc. The idea that a novelist expresses is closely tied to his or her values. No proper theme is simply a subject. It implies a subject and a predicate—not just slavery in general, say, but some such assertion as "Slavery is worse than death".

推荐阅读的论文
[1] 刘雪岚 ."'丧钟为谁而鸣'——论托马斯.品钦对熵定律的应用" [J]. 外国文

学研究，1998(2).
[2] 吕惠. 从秩序到混沌—论品钦作品中的熵主题 [J]. 外交学院学报，2003(4).

Allen Ginsberg (1926~1997)

About the Author

Allen Ginsberg is arguably the most influential poet of the second half of the 20th century. As a leading member of the "Beat Movement", he helped lead the revolt against "academic poetry" and the cultural and political establishment of the mid-20th century.

Born on June 3, 1926 in Newark, New Jersey, Ginsberg had an emotionally troubled childhood that was later reflected in his poetry. He began writing in a journal at the age of 11, and discovered his major poetic influence Walt Whitman in high school. He enrolled in Columbia University in 1943, originally planning to become a labor lawyer, but soon fell in with a literary crowd that included Jack Kerouac, Neal Cassady, and William S. Burroughs.

After graduating from Columbia in 1948, Ginsberg worked as a market researcher in New York and then migrated to San Francisco, where he became a principal figure in the "Beat Generation" literary movement.

In October, 1955, Ginsberg read parts of his new epic poem *Howl* at the Six Gallery of San Francisco, which was written directly at the typewriter in imitation of Kerouac's methods of spontaneous composition. One year later, his first book, the seminal *Howl and Other Poems* (1956) came out. The book's raw, graphic language, its strong discontent and despair at moral and social ills, Ginsberg's homosexuality and his mother's communist beliefs caused an immediate sensation and great astonishment of many traditional critics. As Paul Zweig argued, the poem is "almost singlehandedly dislocated the traditional poetry of the 1950s". Moreover, it transcends literary and intellectual barriers to exert a profound influence on American society and serves as a Beat manifesto.

Ginsberg recorded his first album of poetry readings, also entitled *Howl and Other Poems*, for the Fantasy label in 1959. Over the next decade, Ginsberg became a leading figure of counterculture. In 1961, he published another volume, *Kaddish and Other Poems*, which explores his relationship with his mother. Based on the "Kaddish", a traditional Hebrew prayer for the dead, it expresses the anger, love, and confusion felt towards his mother while rendering the social and historical milieu. Some critics considered this piece to be his most important work.

Ginsberg was a political activist in the 1960s and 1970s. He coined the term and advocated "flower power", a strategy in which antiwar demonstrators promoted positive values like peace and love to dramatize their opposition to the death and destruction caused by the Vietnam War. In 1974, he won the National Book Award for *The Fall of America: Poems of These States* (1965~1971).

Ginsberg is the only Beat writer to sustain a full career. He has accomplished what few writers attain: his acclaim and celebrity were at their height at his death. On April 5, 1997, at the age of 70, just days after being diagnosed with terminal liver cancer, he died.

There are also excellent pieces in his other collections:*Empty Mirror* (1961), *Reality Sandwiches* (1963), *The Yage Letters* (1963) written with William Burroughs, *The Marihuana Papers* (1966), *TV Baby Poem* (1968) and *Planet News* (1971).

A Supermarket in California

About the Poem

This poem, first published in *Howl and Other Poems* in 1956, is generally acclaimed as one of the important works of the Beat Generation. Much inspired by Garcia Lorca's "Ode to Walt Whitman", Ginsberg accomplished his own tribute to his poetic model Whitman, in which he conjured a quitefantastic encounter with Whitman in a modern supermarket. Together with "A Strange New Cottage in Berkeley", it was a part of Ginsberg's early experiments with irregular meter and structure that would be epitomized by his masterpiece "Howl".

What thoughts I have of you tonight, Walt Whitman, for I walked down thestreets under the trees with a headache self-conscious looking at the full moon.

In my hungry fatigue, and shopping for images①, I went into the neon fruit supermarket, dreaming of your enumerations②!

What peaches and what penumbras③! Whole families shopping at night! Aislesfull of husbands! Wives in the avocados④, babies in the tomatoes! —and you, Garcia Lorca⑤, what were you doing down by the watermelons?

---

① shopping for images: searching for the inspiration of writing poems.
② enumerations: 所列举的具体事物细节。
③ penumbra: partial illumination（半阴影）。
④ avocado: 鳄梨。
⑤ Garcia Lorca: (1898~1936) a famous Spanish poet and playwright in the early 20th century. Like Ginsberg, Lorca was greatly indebted to Walt Whitman's innovative style. Here Ginsberg just pays a brief homage to him.

I saw you, Walt Whitman, childless, lonely old grubber, poking among themeats in the refrigerator and eyeing the grocery boys.

I heard you asking questions of each: Who killed the pork chops? What pricebananas? Are you my Angel[①]?

I wandered in and out of the brilliant stacks of cans following you, and followed in my imagination by the store detective.

We strode down the open corridors together in our solitary fancy tasting artichokes[②], possessing every frozen delicacy, and never passing the cashier.

Where are we going, Walt Whitman? The doors close in an hour. Which way does your beard point tonight?

(I touch your book and dream of our odyssey[③] in the supermarket and feel absurd.)

Will we walk all night through solitary streets? The trees add shade to shade, lights out in the houses, we'll both be lonely.

Will we stroll dreaming of the lost America of love past blue automobiles in driveways, home to our silent cottage?

Ah, dear father[④], graybeard, lonely old courage-teacher, what America did you have when Charon[⑤] quit poling his ferry and you got out on a smoking bank and stood watching the boat disappear on the black waters of Lethe[⑥]?

译文链接:《supermarket in california》这篇文章的中文翻译 _360 问答 (so.com)

Questions for Understanding

1. What do you expect to read after viewing the title of this poem?
2. Which poet does Ginsberg think of and converse with? What does the poet look like

---

① Are you my Angel: Here Ginsberg possibly alludes to Walter Benjamin's The Angel of History which predicts that the final result of modernity will be nothing short of the end of civilization.
② artichoke: 洋蓟，朝鲜蓟。
③ odyssey: a famous ancient Green epic poem written by Homer concerning the adventures and ordeals of the Greek warrior Odysseus after the fall of Troy as he struggles to return home. At present, the word is generally used to stand for a long wandering and eventful journey or an intellectual or spiritual quest.
④ dear father: Walt Whitman.
⑤ Charon: In the Greek mythology, Charon is the guardian of Hades who ferries the souls of the dead across the River Styx to their eternity.
⑥ Lethe: a river running through Hades whose waters cause drinkers to forget their past.

and what does he do in the supermarket?
3. How does Ginsberg think of his vision? Does he think it is absurd?
4. What does the last line mean? What does Ginsberg intend to say? What is his opinion about modern America?
5. Does Ginsberg use the device of literary allusion in his poem? If yes, provide examples.

Aspects of Appreciation

1. At the very beginning of the poem, Ginsberg evokes his muse Walt Whitman, bringing him into the poem. The purpose of this evocation is not only to pay tribute to his literary mentor Whitman, but also to show the great differences between the thriving and hopeful America highly eulogized by Whitman and the modern one pervaded with materialism and consumerism.

2. In "A Supermarket in California", Ginsberg recounts an everyday event, that is, going shopping in a supermarket. However, this seemingly plain poem indeed explores certain significant issues concerning consumerism and alienation in modern society, which most of prominent men of letters, including Saul Bellow and John Updike strive to describe and condemn. The supermarket could be viewed as the miniature of the modern American society permeated with material affluence and spiritual loss. Standing in front of the racks loaded with a variety of goods, with their eyes fixed on appealing fruits, the modern men lose themselves in material traps. Although in the crowded supermarket they do always communicate with others, their conversations just center on the goods rather than any meaningful topics. They produce and trade commodities with each other, but never have any meaningful contact. The consumerism and materialism have taken over in the "neon fruit supermarket" as well as the whole society, which alienate modern men and make them forget the value of real human contact.

3. In this masterpiece widely regarded as a fitting memorial to Whitman, Ginsberg sought to continue Whitman's legacy in terms of theme and style. Thematically, Ginsberg inherited Whitman's deep concern for the potential damages caused by industrialized society. And stylistically, inspired by his hero's daring innovation in the meter and rhythm, Ginsberg eschewed the traditional poetic form including stanza and rhyme scheme, and adopted a fresh form, that is, the prose poem with an irregular meter and structures.

Suggested Further Reading

Howl (1956); *America* (1956).

Topics for Further Study

1. Try to describe the poetic form of this poem, and compare its rhythms with those of Whitman's in "Song of Myself".

2. Compare the United States in Whitman's poems, for instance, "I Hear America Singing", with the United States in Ginsberg's writings, and try to tell the differences and the reason for such change. What would be his opinion of modern America If Whitman were alive today?

3. Ginsberg wrote most of his well-known poems in the 1950s and 1960s, a time of great social and cultural upheaval in the United States. Try to explore the historical and cultural context that might have served as inspiration for Ginsberg's poems.

Knowledge of Literature

1. The Beat Movement（垮掉派运动）

The Beat Movement refers to an American social and literary movement of the 1950s and 1960s. Its adherents, derisively called "beatniks", or the beat generation, expressed their alienation from conventional society by adopting a peculiar style of seedy dress, detached manners, and a "hip" vocabulary. Indifferent to social problems, they advocated personal release and sensory awareness that might be induced by drugs, jazz, sex, or the disciplines of Zen Buddhism. Kerouac's *On the Road* (1951) and Ginsberg's *Howl and Other Poems* (1956) are among the best known literary examples of this movement.

2. The Beat Generation（垮掉的一代）

The Beat Generation is a group of American men of letters and artists who came to prominence in the 1950s and early 1960s. Led by Allen Ginsberg and Jack Kerouac, they rejected the conventional social values and searched for the "beatific" ecstasy through drugs, sex and Zen Buddhism. Their works are renowned for confessional candor, spontaneous self-expression and recitation to jazz accompaniment.

3. Prose poem（散文诗）

Taken from the famous French poet Charles Baudelaire's *Little Poems in Prose* (1869), the name "prose poem" refers to a short composition bearing many poetic characteristics, including heightened imagery, compression of thought and emotional effect. To put it simply, it refers to the poetry written in the form of prose.

4. One Element of Poetry: Image（意象）

An image is a literal and concrete representation of a sensory experience or of an object that can be known by one or more of the senses. An image may be visual (pertaining to the eye), olfactory (smell), tactile (touch), auditory (hearing), gustatory (taste), abstract (in which case it will appeal to what may be described as the intellect) and kinaesthetic (pertaining to the sense of movement and bodily effort). It is often the case that an image is not exclusively one thing or another; they overlap and intermingle and thus combine. Thus, the tactile may also be visual. The image is one of the distinctive elements of the "language of art", the means by which experience in its richness and emotional complexity is communicated. The collection of images in a poem is called imagery. A study of a poem's imagery can help us understand the meaning of the poem.

推荐阅读的论文：
[1] 陈新儒.焦虑下的书写——金斯堡《加州超市》意象涵义新探[J].名作欣赏，2014(27).
[2] 刘保安.论狄金森诗歌中鸟意象的象征意义[J].通化师范学院学报，2019，40(07).

Toni Morrison (1931~2019)

About the Author

In 1993, Toni Morrison received the Nobel Prize for Literature. She was the eighth woman and the first African American woman to win the honour. While awarding Morrison the prize, the Swedish Academy described her as a writer "who, in novels characterized by visionary force and poetic import, gives life to an essential aspect of American reality".

In 1931, Toni Morrison was born in the poor, multiracial steel town of Lorain, Ohio. From her parents, Morrison received a legacy of resistance to oppression and exploitation as well as an appreciation of African American folklore and cultural practices. In 1955 Morrison received an M.A. from Cornell University. After that she taught English at Texas Southern University from 1955 to 1957 and at Howard from 1957 to 1964. At Howard she met and married Harold Morrison. During that time she joined a writers' group and wrote a story about a young black girl who wanted blue eyes. From that story came *The Bluest Eye* (1970), her first novel.

Morrison's novels explore issues of African-American female identity in stories that integrate elements of the oral tradition, postmodern literary techniques, and magical realism to give voice to the experiences of black women living on the margins of American society. All her novels have enjoyed critical acclaim and have been the subject of numerous academic books and essays in the fields of gender studies, ethnic studies, postmodern theory, literary theory, and cultural studies. Four of her novels were chosen for the Oprah Winfrey national book club, and *Beloved* was adapted to film as a major motion picture produced by and starring Winfrey.

Morrison's first novel, *The Bluest Eye*, was set in the 1940s and addresses issues of race and beauty standards through the figure of Pecola Breedlove, an eleven-year-old African-American girl who has destructive desire for having blue eyes, a color which represents a flight from blackness and isolation. Like *The Bluest Eye, Sula* (1973) was well received critically, but did not find a large audience. Morrison explores the importance of female friendship in the formation of individual identity, which in reality is often superseded by women's relationships with men.

Toni Morrison's fame and popularity, as well as sales of all of her novels, increased when *Song of Solomon* (1977) was chosen in 1996 by talk-show celebrity Oprah Winfrey for her show's book club. *Tar Baby* (1981), Morrison's fourth novel, has a contemporary Caribbean and European setting. Yet, like her other novels, its principal characters—Jadine, an educated, privileged, westernized model, and Son, a poor African-American who longs for his home in a black Florida town—discover in themselves secrets of the past.

Morrison's subsequent three novels, *Beloved* (1987), *Jazz* (1992), and *Paradise* (1998), are often loosely grouped as another trilogy, each set in a different period of African-American history: *Beloved* takes place during the post-Civil War era, with flashbacks to the years of slavery in the South; *Jazz* is mainly set during the Harlem Renaissance of the 1920s; and *Paradise* is set during the Civil Rights era of the 1960s and 1970s.

The Pulitzer Prize-winning *Beloved*, is the most expressly historical in purpose of all Morrison's novels, as well as the most fantastic in its representation of a world both past and beyond the plotted time. Morrison has been recognized by the *New York Times Review of Books* as having written the best novel of the last 25 years, *Beloved*. It is based on the true antebellum story of a slave mother, Margaret Garner, killing her own children just for them to avoid slavery.

With *Love* (2003), Morrison targets her usual female and black audience, depicting African-American characters and splashing flashbacks of the Civil Rights

Movement sprucely throughout. However, the messages she conveys—the importance of communication, self-esteem, education, soul-searching, relationships and human nature—are universal and timeless, transcending gender and race.

In addition to her novels, Morrison wrote a significant work of literary criticism, *Playing In the Dark: Whitenessand the Literary Imagination* (1992) and also edited two collections of essays, *Racing Justice, En-Gendering Power: Essays on Anita Hill, Clarence Thomas, andthe Construction of Social Reality* (1992) and *Birth of a Nationhood: Gaze, Script, and Spectacle in the O.J. Simpson Case* (1997).

Morrison represented a breakthrough for other black women novelists to succeed in the mainstream publishing industry. She has had a profound impact upon the careers of a range of other black authors. She served as an editor for Random House publishers from 1965 to 1983. As senior editor at Random House, Morrison brought a number of black writers to that publisher's list, including Toni Cade Bambara, Angela Davis, Henry Dumas, and Gayl Jones.

Home

About the Novel

Morrison's tenth novel, *Home,* was published in May 2012. Set in the 1950s, it tells the story of Frank Money, a young Black American soldier returning home from the Korean War, who manages to rescue his sister Cee and build a warm home of love. Chapter One tells about Frank's horrible childhood memories from his perspective.

> Whose house is this?
> Whose night keeps out the light
> In here?
> Say, who owns this house?
> It's not mine.
> I dreamed another, sweeter, brighter
> With a view of lakes crossed in painted boats;
> Of fields wide as arms open for me.
> This house is strange.
> Its shadows lie.
> Say, tell me, why does its lock fit my key?

Chapter One

They rose up like men. We saw them. Like men they stood.

We shouldn't have been anywhere near that place. Like most farmland outside Lotus, Georgia, this one here had plenty of scary warning signs. The threats hung from wire mesh① fences with wooden stakes every fifty or so feet. But when we saw a crawl space that some animal had dug—a coyote maybe, or a coon dog②—we couldn't resist. Just kids we were. The grass was shoulder high for her and waist high for me so, looking out for snakes, we crawled through it on our bellies. The reward was worth the harm grass juice and clouds of gnats③ did to our eyes, because there right in front of us, about fifty yards off, they stood like men. Their raised hooves crashing and striking, their manes tossing back from wild white eyes. They bit each other like dogs but when they stood, reared up on their hind legs, their forelegs around the withers④ of the other, we held out our breath in wonder. One was rust-colored, the other deep black, both sunny with sweat. The neighs were not as frightening as the silence following a kick of hind legs into the lifted lips of the opponent. Nearby, colts and mares, indifferent, nibbled⑤ grass or looked away. Then it stopped. The rust-colored one dropped his head and pawed the ground while the winner loped⑥ off in an arc, nudging⑦ the mares before him.

As we elbowed back through the grass looking for the dug-out place, avoiding the line of parked trucks beyond. We lost our way. Although it took forever to re-sight the fence, neither of us panicked until we heard voices, urgent but low. I grabbed her arm and put a finger to my lips. Never lifting our heads, just peeping through the grass, we saw them pull a body from a wheelbarrow and throw it into a hole already waiting. One foot stuck up over the edge and quivered, as though it could get out, as though with a little effort it could break through the dirt being shoveled in. We could not see the faces of the men doing the burying, only their trousers; but we saw the edge of a spade drive the jerking foot down to join the rest of itself. When she saw that black foot with its creamy pink and mud-streaked sole being whacked⑧ into the grave, her whole body began to shake. I hugged her shoulders tight and tried to pull her trembling into my own bone, because, as a brother four years older, I thought I

---

① wire mesh: 金属丝网、铁丝网。
② coon dog: 猎浣熊的猎犬。
③ gnat: a small fly with two wings that bites (叮人小虫)。
④ withers: 马肩隆（马肩胛骨间的隆起处，马背最高处）。
⑤ nibble: to take small bites of sth, especially food （小口咬）。
⑥ lope: to run taking long relaxed steps （轻松地大步跑）。
⑦ nudge: to push sb/sth gently or gradually in a particular direction.
⑧ whack: (informal) to hit sb/sth very hard.

Chapter 5 American Literature After World War II

could handle it. The men were long gone and the moon was a cantaloupe[①] by the time we felt safe enough to disturb even one blade of grass and move on our stomachs, searching for the scooped-out part under the fence. When we got home we expected to be whipped or at least scolded for staying out so late, but the grow-ups did not notice us. Some disturbance had their attention[②].

Since you're set on telling my story, whatever you think and whatever you write down, know this: I really forgot about the burial. I only remembered the horses. They were so beautiful. So brutal. And they stood like men.

译文参考：托妮·莫里森.《家》[M]. 刘昱含译. 海口：南海出版公司，2014.

Questions for Understanding

1. What's the implied meaning of the epigraph?
2. What does the narrator mean when he says in the second paragraph "We shouldn't have been anywhere near that place"?
3. What do Frank and Cee see when they sneak into the farmland? How do they feel?
4. Why does the narrator say "I only remembered the horses" at the end of the chapter? What's the implication of the horses?

Aspects of Appreciation

1. In the epigraph, the narrator, standing outside of his shabby and shadowy house, expresses his longing and admiration for a sweet, bright and warm house. The epigraph sets the tone for the theme of the novel, looking for one's home, both literally and figuratively.

2. Frank and Cee witness the surreptitious burial of an anonymous Black man. He is the victim of a lynching and hastily buried by a white mob. This shocking opening scene gives readers a glimpse into the harsh life of Black Americans in the 1920s and 1930s who suffered from tremendous violence and oppression in a time of racism and segregation.

3. Chapter One depicts the vivid image of horses. Standing like men, they seem

---

① cantaloupe: (a type of fruit) with a green skin and orange flesh（甜瓜，哈密瓜）.
② some disturbance had their attention: 他们（大人们）在关注别的什么东西。这是指种族主义者以武力威胁，命令弗兰克父母所在的黑人社区居民在一天之内搬走。

to be unfettered, full of power and beauty. However, it turns out at the end of the novel that they are actually prisoners of some men who later sell them to slaughterhouses. To some extent, their experience parallels what happened to Black Americans in a time of racism and segregation. At the end of the novel, Frank and Cee properly rebury the black man and paint the words "Here Stands A Man" on a wooden marker. This final scene well parallels the opening scene that the horses "stood like men".

Suggested Further Reading

The Bluest Eye(1970), *Sula* (1973), *Song of Solomon* (1977), *Beloved* (1987)

Topics for Further Study

1. The novel *Home* is set in a fictional town, Lotus, which alludes to the land of the lotus-eaters in Homer's *Odyssey,* where travelers will forget their homes and families once they eat the lotus. What's the implication of Lotus in the novel?

2. What is the social environment portrayed in the novel *Home?* Howdoes it affect the characters?

3. *Home* is regarded as a novel about how the protagonist Frank recovers from psychological trauma. Try to find some evidence to support the view.

4. It's said that *Home* touches upon many pertinent issues, such as racism in America, the after-effects of the war on a soldier, and the struggle to find a place where you belong. Try to find some evidence in the novel.

Knowledge of Literature

Postcolonial Criticism(后殖民批评)

As a distinctive literary critical approach, postcolonial criticism was not inaugurated until the 1980s. Literary critics use the term postcolonialism as an oppositional reading practice to study the effects of colonial representation in literary texts. The key text in establishing the postcolonial theory was *Orientalism* (1978) by the Palestinian-American scholar Edward Said. In the discourse of Orientalism, the Eastern society is that of barbarism, backwardness, autocracy and corruption, awaiting the European civilization to save; the Oriental people are lowly, cowardly, deceitful, dissolute, sexually immoral, irrational and unreliable, awaiting to be enlightened by education. According to Orientalism, the West is rational, democratic, progressive, etc. In fact, Orientalism is actually a Eurocentric discourse that assumes the normality and preeminence of everything "occidental", correlatively with its representations of the "oriental" as an exotic and inferior other. Orientalism believes that Western culture is advanced and accepting it can do good to Orientals. Obviously, Said's *Orientalism* provides a new perspective for the interpretation of Western writing about the East and of writing produced under colonial rule.

Since the 1980s, there has been an explosion of postcolonial critical practices in Britain, America and other countries. Though critics adopt a great variety of critical stances, they share certain concepts and assumptions, which can be summarized as follows.

1. European colonialism has exerted an decisive influence on all the domains of the colonized lands, including politics, economy, society, culture and so forth.

2. Colonialist ideology is, in essence, a Eurocentric discourse. The colonizers touted European culture as the superior one, considered themselves as civilized, advanced and rational, and regarded the colonized people as barbarian, backward and irrational. By doing so, the colonizers asserted and justified their dominance and superiority.

3. Colonial literature is the product and carrier of colonialist ideology. For instance, nonwhite people, always serving as the marginal and subordinate roles, are distorted into derogatory stereotypes, either demonized as evil and mean heathens, or idealized as noble savages unfettered by social bondage. By reading the literary works, people, including the colonized, internalize colonialist ideology.

4. Postcolonial criticism is a resistance to and subversion of the colonialist ideology with the aim of revealing how it impacts the history, culture and literature of the former colonies.

推荐阅读的论文：
[1] 王巧丽. 最蓝的眼睛和最美的下巴——后殖民视角下《最蓝的眼睛》和"王贝整容事件"之对比 [J]. 名作欣赏，2018(35).
[2] 刘海艳.《柏油孩子》的后殖民生态批评解读 [J]. 名作欣赏，2015(30).

Isaac Bashevis Singer (1904~1991)

About the Author

The fact that Isaac Bashevis Singer was born in a Polish shtetl with a long tradition is perhaps the most important of all the influences that made him what he became: one of the most distinguished American writers and the winner of Nobel Prize for literature in 1978. The Jewish village community where he was brought up has been reshaped as the setting for most of his works. The local dialect Yiddish, an almost dead language after the devastating Holocaust in WWII, is his favorite and exclusive writing language. The Jewish folktales and legends told by his parents at the bed time found their way into his works, which are populated with various types of mythical figures, including demons, dybbuks, witches, angels, magicians and so forth. And his knowledge of the Jewish community life, with its centuries-old Judaictradition and culture, its eventful history of rise and fall from the 17th century to the first half of the 20th century, all fused in his rich imagination and fine craftsmanship, has constituted the essence of Singer's mysterious and fantastic world inspiring both nostalgia and enlightenment in modern readers.

From an Orthodox background, with both of his parents being pious Jews, Singer was expected to become a religious scholar from his early childhood. However, later he developed a keen interest in literature, which pushed him towards a different career as a journalist and writer. By 1935, he had accomplished his first novel *Satan in Goray* and several short stories. At the same year, following his brother Isaac Joshua Singer, a prominent Yiddish novelist exerting a profound influence on his literary career, Singer emigrated from Poland to the United States. He finally settled in New York and began to write essays and reviews for *The Jewish Daily Forward*, America's largest Yiddish newspaper. During the 1940s, Singer's reputation grew steadily among Yiddish-speaking readers with the publication of several journals and articles. In 1950, his second novel *The Family Moskat*, a family saga chronicling the destruction of the Polish-Jewish community from the end of the 19th century up to the Second World War, was serialized in *The Forward* and was then translated into English. Three years later, "Gimpel the Fool", his most anthologized short story recounting a ridiculous yet enlightening life experience of a Jewish "little man", appeared in the *Partisan Review* in English translation by Saul Bellow, which opened a door through which Singer could address the American public and capture their hearts.

Since then, Singer has embarked on his journey of becoming the world first-class writer. From the 1950s till his death in 1991, Singer made great efforts in accomplishing a number of great works, including another two family sagas *The Manor* (1967) and *The Estate* (1969) supplementing the history of the declining old Jewish families from the turn of the century till WWII, eight collections of short stories from the early *Gimpel The Fool and Other Stories* (1957) to the later work *The Death of Methuselahand Other Stories* (1988), with notable masterpieces in betweensuch as *The Spinoza of Market Street* (1961) and *A Crown of Feathers* (1973), as well as several well-received novels best represented by *The Magician of Lublin* (1960), concerning a Jewish magician's journey to find self-identity and faith, and

Enemies: A Love Story (1970), treating the predicaments of Jewish immigrants in America. With the publication of these works, Singer proved time and again his enormous power to transmute the stuff of the Jewish life, past and present, into works of elaborate craftsmanship and universal appeal.

As time went by, his dedicated and meticulous work paid off. The public as well as critics embraced him warmly by awarding numerous literary prizes, including the National Book Award in 1970 and 1974. In 1978, he won the Nobel Prize for literature for "his impassioned narrative art which, with roots in a Polish-Jewish cultural tradition, brings universal human conditions to life".

With the special identity both as a Jew brought up in Eastern Europe and an immigrant in the New Continent, Singer never ceased to use his pen to record the living situation of his countrymen in the given historical period, especially in the modern age under the fierce attack of Nazi persecution and heterogeneous cultures. Though often in the seemingly lighthearted form of parables or tales, his works profoundly explore the individual's search for faith and guidance when suffering the spiritual or identity crises. By these writings, he endeavors to remind all the people, Jew or non-Jew, that the belief in God or returning to tradition could save them out of the spiritual dilemma and lead to the mental tranquility.

In his memoir *In My Father's Court* (1966), Singer recalls with deep emotion his childhood in a poor Jewish quarter of Warsaw, a world where extreme poverty and invaluable cultural heritage were juxtaposed, where sincere piety and blind faith were interwoven. Although this world has gone forever, destroyed by the most barbarous historical catastrophe, it fortunately comes to life in Singer's writings. By means of his natural tongue Yiddish, Singer has successfully revealed the vanished Jewish life to the public, making it an important contribution to American literature. The most important contribution, however, goes far beyond his recreation of this world. It is his deep concern for the predicaments of men trapped in the spiritual crises.

Gimpel the Fool

About the Story

"Gimpel the Fool" is acclaimed as one of Isaac Bashevis Singer's most representative short stories. Set in the imaginary village of Frampol, the story chronicles the life of Gimpel, a kind and innocent Jewish baker, who is often fooled and tricked by those around him, but never gives up his faith in life.

Gimpel the Fool

1

I am Gimpel the fool. I don't think myself a fool. On the contrary. But that's what folks call me. They gave me the name while I was still in school. I had seven names in all: imbecile, donkey, flax-head, dope, glump, ninny, and fool①. The last name stuck. What did my foolishness consist of? I was easy to take in. They say, "Gimpel, you know the rabbi's② wife has been brought to childbed?" So I skipped school. Well, it turned out to be a lie. How was I supposed to know? She hadn't a big belly. But I never looked at her belly. Was that really so foolish? The gang laughed and heehawed③, stomped and danced and chanted a good-night prayer. And instead of the raisins they give when a woman's lying in; they stuffed my hand full of goat turds. I was no weakling. If I slapped someone he'd see all the way to Cracow④. But I'm really not a slugger by nature. I think to myself: Let it pass. So they take advantage of me.

I was coming home from school and heard a dog barking. I'm not afraid of dogs, but of course I never want to start up with them. One of them may be mad, and if he bites there's not a Tartar⑤ in the world who can help you. So I made tracks. Then I looked around and saw the whole market-place wild with laughter. I was no dog at all but Wolf-Leib the Thief⑥. How was I supposed to know it was he? It sounded like a howling bitch.

When the pranksters and leg-pullers⑦ found that I was easy to fool, every one of them tried his luck with me. "Gimpel, the Czar is coming to Frampol⑧; Gimpel, the moon fell down in Turbeen; Gimpel, little Hodel Furpiece found a treasure behind the bathhouse." And I like a golem⑨ I believed everyone. In the first place, everything is possible, as it is written in the Wisdom of the Fathers⑩. I've forgotten just now. Second, I had to believe when the whole town came down on me! If I ever dared to say, "Ah, you're kidding!" There was trouble. People got angry. "What do you mean!

---

① becile, donkey, flax-head, dope, glump, ninny, and fool: all these words share the same meaning, that is, a stupid person.
② rabbi: a person trained in Jewish law, ritual, and tradition and ordained for leadership of a Jewish congregation, especially one serving as chief religious official of a synagogue.
③ laughed and heehawed, stomped and danced: 大笑大叫，又是跺脚，又是跳舞。
④ Cracow:（Kraków）an ancient city in southern Poland where a large number of Jews settled before World War.
⑤ Tartar:（also Tatar）a member of the Mongolian people of central Asia who invaded and harassed Asia and Eastern Europe in the Middle ages. Here "Tartar" refers to a ferocious or violent person with great power.
⑥ Wolf-Leib the Thief: 小偷沃尔夫·莱布。
⑦ pranksters and leg-pullers: mischievous persons who like to play tricks on others.
⑧ Frampol: an ancient town in Poland.
⑨ golem: (Jewish folklore) an artificially created human being that is given life by supernatural means.
⑩ the Wisdom of the Fathers: the biblical books of ancient Jewish forefathers.

You want to call everyone a liar?" What was I to do? I believed them, and I hope at least that did them some good.

I was an orphan. My grandfather who brought me up was already bent toward the grave. So they turned me over to a baker, and what a time they gave there! Every woman or girl who came to bake a batch of noodles① had no fool me at least once. "Gimpel, there's a fair in heaven; Gimpel, the rabbi gave birth to a calf in the seventh month; Gimpel, a cow flew over the roof and land brass eggs." A student from the yesiva② came once to buy a roll, and he said, "You, Gimpel, while you stand here scraping with your baker's shovel the Messia③ has come. The dead have arisen." "What do you mean?" I said, "I heard no one blowing the ram's horn!"④ He said, "Are you deaf?" And all began to cry, "We heard it, we heard!" Then in came Rietze the Candle-dipper⑤ and called out in her hoarse voice, "Gimpel, your father and mother have stood up from the grave. They're looking for you."

To tell the truth, I knew very well that nothing of the sort had happened, but all the same as folks were talking, I threw on my wool vest and went out. Maybe something had happened. What did I stand to lose by looking? Well, what a cat music went up!⑥ And then I took a vow to believe nothing more. But that was no go either. They confused me so that I didn't know the big end from the small⑦.

I went to the rabbi to get some advice. He said, "It is written, better to be a fool all your days than for one hour to be evil. You are not a fool. They are the fools. For he who causes his neighbor to feel shame loses Paradise himself." Nevertheless the rabbi's daughter took me in. As I left the rabbinical court she said, "Have you kissed the wall yet?" I said, "No what for?" She answered, "It's the law; you've got to do it after every visit." Well, there didn't seem to be any harm in it. And she burst out laughing. It was a fine trick. She put one over on me, all right.

I wanted to go off to another town, but then everyone got busy matchmaking, and they were after me so they nearly tore my coat tails off. They talked at me and talked until I got water on the ear⑧. She was no chaste maiden, but they told me she was virgin pure. She had a limp, and they said it was deliberate, from coyness. She had

---

① bake a batch of noodles: 烤面条。指将面条煮后加佐料，盘成团状放进炉中烤成布丁状。
② yesiva: an Orthodox Jewish school of theology（犹太教学堂）.
③ Messiah: in Judaism, a king who will be sent by God to save the Jewish people.
④ blowing the ram's horn: According to the Old Testament, when the Messiah is to come, people will blow the ram's horn in order to assemble their folks.
⑤ Candle-dipper : the person who makes candles.
⑥ a cat music: used to describe people's laughter and shouts which sound just like cats mewing loudly.
⑦ I didn't know the big end from the small: I was completely at a loss.
⑧ They talked at me and talked until I got water on the ear: 他们冲着我唠叨，唾沫星子都溅到我的耳朵上了。

a bastard, and they told me the child was her little brother. I cried, "You're wasting your time. I'll never marry that whore." But they said indignantly, "What a way to talk! Aren't you ashamed of yourself? We can take you to the rabbi and have you fined for giving her a bad name." I saw then that I wouldn't escape them so easily and I thought: They're set on making me their butt. But when you're married the husband's the master, and if that's all right with her it's agreeable to me too. Besides, you can't pass through life unscathed, nor expect to.

I went to her clay house, which was built on the sand, and the whole gang, hollering and chorusing, came after me. They acted like bear-baiters. When we came to the well they stopped all the same. They were afraid to start anything with Elka. Her mouth would open as if it were on a hinge, and she had a fierce tongue. I entered the house. Lines were strung from wall to wall and clothes were drying. Barefoot she stood by the tub, doing the wash. She was dressed in a worn hand-me-down gown of plush[①]. She had her hair put up in braids and pinned across her head. It took my breath away, almost, the reek of it all.

Evidently she knew who I was. She took a look at me and said, "Look who's here! He's come, the drip[②]. Grab a seat."

I told her all: I denied nothing. "Tell me the truth," I said, "are you really a virgin, and is that mischievous Yechiel actually your little brother? Don't be deceitful with me, for I'm an orphan."

"I'm an orphan myself," she answered, "and whoever tries to twist you up, may the end of his nose take a twist[③]. But don't let them think they can take advantage of me. I want a dowry of fifty guilders[④], and let them take up a collection besides. Otherwise they can kiss my you-know-what[⑤]." She was very plainspoken. I said, "It's the bride and not the groom who gives a dowry." Then she said, "Don't bargain with me. Either a flat 'yes' or a flat 'no'. Go back where you came from[⑥]."

I thought, no bread will ever be baked from this dough[⑦]. Butours is not a poor town. They consented to everything and proceeded with the wedding. It so happened that there was adysentery epidemic at the time. The ceremony was held atthe cemetery gates, near the little corpse washing hut. The fellows got drunk. While the marriage

---

① a worn hand-me-down gown of plush: 一件破旧的、大概是从祖宗那传下来的长毛绒袍子。
② drip: a boring or stupid person with a weak personality（怯懦讨厌的人；愚蠢胆怯的人）。
③ whoever tries to twist you up, may the end of his nose take a twist: 谁要是捉弄你，就叫谁的鼻子尖儿歪了。
④ guilder: the former unit of money in the Netherlands（荷兰盾）。
⑤ Otherwise they can kiss my you-know-what: 没钱，就来舔本姑娘的屁股。
⑥ Either a flat 'yes' or a flat 'no'. Go back where you came from: 要就要，不要就拉倒，你滚好了！
⑦ No bread will ever be baked from this dough: It's impossible to bake bread out of this dough. Gimpel thinks Elka's demand for a dowry is more than he can afford and he can not marry her.

contract was being drawn up I heard the most pious high rabbi ask, "Is the bride a widow or a divorced woman?" And the sexton's wife answered for her, "Both a widow and divorced." It was a black moment for me. But what was I to do, run away from under the marriage canopy?

There was singing and dancing. An old granny danced opposite me, hugging a braided white chalah①. The master of revels made "God's mercy" in memory of the bride's parents. The schoolboys threw burrs, as on Tishe b'Av fast day②. There were a lot of gifts after the sermon: a noodle board, a kneading trough, a bucket, brooms, ladels, household articles galore. Then I took a look and saw two strapping young men carrying a crib. "What do we need this for?" I asked. So they said, "Don't rack your brains about it. It's all right, it'll come in handy." I realized I was going to be rooked③. Take it another way though, what did I stand to lose? I reflected: I'll see what comes of it. A whole town can't go altogether crazy.

2

At night I came where my wife lay, but she wouldn't let me in. "Say, look here, is this what they married us for?" I said. And she said, "My monthly has come." "But yesterday they took you to the ritual bath, and that's afterward, isn't it supposed to be?" "Today isn't yesterday," said she, "and yesterday's not today. You can beat it if you don't like it." In short, I waited.

Not four months later she was in childbed. The townsfolk hid their laughter with their knuckles. But what could I do? She suffered intolerable pains and clawed at the walls. "Gimpel," she cried, "I'm going. Forgive me." The house filled with women. They were boiling pans of water. The screams rose to the welkin④.

The thing to do was to go to the House of Prayer⑤ to repeat Psalms, and that was what I did.

The townsfolk liked that, all right. I stood in a corner saying Psalms and prayers, and they shook their heads at me. "Pray, pray!" they told me, "Prayer never made any woman pregnant." One of the congregation⑥ put a straw to my mouth and said, "Hay for the cows." There was something to that too, by God!

She gave birth to a boy, Friday at the synagogue the sexton stood up before the

---

① chalah: 白面包。
② Tishe b'Av fast day: 圣殿节斋戒日。
③ to be rooked: to be cheated or fooled.
④ welkin: (archaic /literary) the sky.
⑤ the House of Prayer: synagogue(犹太教堂).
⑥ congregation: 会众。

Ark①, pounded on the reading table, and announced, "The wealthy Reb Gimpel invites the congregation to a feast in honor of the birth of a son." The whole House of Prayer rang with laughter. My face was flaming. But there was nothing I could do. After all, I was the one responsible for the circumcision honors and rituals②.

Half the town came running. You couldn't wedge another soul in. Women brought peppered chick-peas, and there was a keg of beer from the tavern. I ate and drank as much as anyone, and they all congratulated me. Then there was a circumcision, and I named the boy after my father, may he rest in peace. When all were gone and I was left with my wife alone, she thrust her head through the bed-curtain and called me to her.

"Gimpel," said she, "why are you silent? Has your ship gone and sunk?③"

"What shall I say?" I answered. "A fine thing you've done to me! If my mother had known of it, she'd have died a second time."

She said, " Are you crazy or what?

"How can you make such a fool," I said, "of one who should be the lord and master?④ "

"What's the matter with you?" She said. "What have you taken it into your head to imagine?"

I saw that I must speak bluntly and openly. "Do you think this is the way to use an orphan?" I said. "You have born a bastard."

She answered, "Drive this foolishness out of your head. This child is yours."

"How can he be mine?" I argued. "He was born seventeen weeks after the wedding."

She told me then that he was premature. I said, "Isn't he a little too premature?" She said, she had had a grandmother who carried just as short a time and she resembled this grandmother of hers as one drop of water does another. She swore to it with such oaths that you would have believed a peasant at the fair if he has used them. To tell the plain truth, I didn't believe her; but when I talked it over next day with the schoolmaster he told me that the very same thing happened to Adam and Eve. Two they went up to bed and four they descended.

"There isn't a woman in the world who is not the granddaughter of Eve," he said.

That was how it was; they argued me dumb. But then, who really knows how such things are?

---

① Ark: (Judaism) sacred chest where the ancient Hebrews kept the two tablets containing the Ten Commandments （约柜）.
② the circumcision honors and rituals: 割礼仪式。
③ Has your ship gone and sunk?:Have you lost your fortune?
④ the lord and master: According to the Jewish practice, a wife should obey her husband and call him "lord" or "master".

I began to forget my sorrow. I loved the child madly, and he loved me too. As soon as he saw me he'd wave his little hands and want me to pick him up, and when he was colicky① I was the only one who could pacify him. I bought him a little bone teething ring and a little gilded cap. He was forever catching the evil eye from someone, and then I had to run to get one of those abracadabras② for him that would get him out of it. I worked like an ox. You know how expenses go up when there's an infant in the house. I don't want to lie about it; I didn't dislike Elka either, for that matter. She swore at me and cursed, and I couldn't get enough of her. What strength she had! One of her look scould rob you of the power of speech. And her orations! Pitch and sulfur③, that's what they were full of, and yet somehow also full of charm. I adored her every word. She gave me bloody wounds though.

In the evening I brought her a white loaf as well as a dark one, and also poppy seed rolls I baked myself. I thieved because of her and swiped everything I could lay hands on: macaroons, raisins, almonds, cakes. I hope I may beforgiven for stealing from the Saturday pots the women left to warm in the baker's oven. I would take out scraps of meat, a chunk of pudding, a chicken leg or head, a piece of tripe, whatever I could nip quickly. She ate and became fat and handsome.

I had to sleep away from home all during the week, at the bakery. On Friday nights when I got home she always made an excuse of some sort. Either she had heartburn, or a stitch in the side, or hiccups, or headaches. You know what women's excuses are. I had a bitter time of it. It was rough. To add to it, this little brother of hers, the bastard, was growing bigger. He'd put lumps on me, and when I wanted to hit back she'd open her mouth and curse so powerfully I saw a green haze floating before my eyes. Ten time a day she threatened to divorce me. Another man in my place would have taken French leave④ and disappeared. But I'm the type that bears it and says nothing. What's one todo? Shoulders are from God and burdens too.

One night there was a calamity in the bakery; the ovenburst, and we almost had a fire. There was nothing to do but go home, so I went home. Let me, I thought, also taste the joy of sleeping in bed in midweek. I didn't want to wake the sleeping mite and tiptoed into the house. Coming in, it seemed to me that I heard not the snoring of one but, as it were, a double snore, one a thin enough snore and the other like the snoring of a slaughtered ox. Oh I didn't like that! I didn't like it as at all. I went up to

---

① colicky: 腹绞痛的。
② abracadabras: 咒语，符箓。
③ pitch and sulfur: Here "pitch and sulfur" are used to describe Elka's rude and biting remarks.
④ French leave: an abrupt and unannounced departure(不辞而别).

the bed, and things suddenly turned black①. Next to Elka lay a man's form. Another in my place would have made an uproar, and enough noise to rouse the whole town, but the thought occurred to me that I might wake the child. A little thing like that—why frighten a little swallow, I thought. Allright then, I went back to the bakery and stretched out on a sack of flour and till morning I never shut an eye. I shivered as if I had had malaria. "Enough of being a donkey," I said to myself. "Gimpel isn't going to be a sucker② all his life. There's a limit even to the foolishness of a fool like Gimpel."

In the morning I went to the rabbi to get advice, and it made a great commotion in the town. They sent the beadle for Elka right away. She came, carrying the child. And what do you think she did? She denied it, denied everything, bone and stone③! "He's out of his head," she said. "I know nothing of dreams of divinations." they yelled at her, warned her, hammered on the table, but she stuck to herguns④: it was a false accusation, she said.

The butchers and the horse-traders took her part. One of the lads from the slaughterhouse came buy and said to me, "We've got our eye on you, you're a marked man." Meanwhile the child started to bear down and soiled itself. In the rabbinical court there was an Ark of the Covenant, and they couldn't allow that, so they sent Elka away.

I said to the rabbi, "What shall I do?"

"You must divorce her at once," said he.

"And what if she refuses?" I asked.

He said, "You must server the divorce. That's all you'll have to do."

I said, "Well, all right Rabbi. Let me think about it."

"There's nothing to think about," said he. "You mustn't remain under the same roof with her."

"And what if she refuses?" I asked.

"Let her go, the harlot," said he, "and her brood of bastards with her."

The verdict he gave was that I mustn't even cross herthreshold—never again, as long as I should live.

During the day it didn't bother me so much. I thought: It was bound to happen, the abscess had to burst. But at night when I stretched out upon the sacks I felt it all very bitterly. A longing took me, for her and for the child. I wanted to be angry, but that's my misfortune exactly, I don't have it in me to be really angry. In the first

---

① things suddenly turned black: things became disastrous all of a sudden(事情突然糟透了).
② sucker: (informal) a person who is easily took in and fooled.
③ bone and stone: completely and absolutely.
④ stuck to her guns: (informal) refused to compromise or change, despite criticism.

place—this was how my thoughts went—there's bound to be a slip sometimes. You can't live without errors. Probably that lad who was with her led her on and gave her presents and what not, and women are often long on hair and short on sense, and so he got around her. And then since she denies it so, maybe I was only seeing things? Hallucinations do happen. You see a figure or a mannikin or something, but when you come up closer it's nothing, there's not a thing there. And if that's so, I'm doing her an injustice. And when I got so far in my thoughts I started to weep. I sobbed so that I wet the flour where I lay. In the morning I went to the rabbi and told him that I had made a mistake. The rabbi wrote on with his quill, and he said that if that were so he would have to reconsider the whole case. Until he had finished I wasn't to go near my wife, but I might send her bread and money by messenger.

3

Nine months passed before all the rabbis could come to an agreement. Letters went back and forth. I hadn't realized that there could be so much erudition about a matter like this.

Meanwhile Elka gave birth to still another child, a girl this time. On the Sabbath I went to the synagogue and invoked a blessing on her. They called me up to the Torah[①], and Inamed the child for my mother-in-law, may she rest in peace. The louts and loudmouths of the town who came into the bakery gave me a going over. All Frampol refreshed it's spirits because of my trouble and grief. However, I resolved that I would always believe what I was told. What's the good of not believing? Today it's your wife you don't believe; tomorrow it's God Himself you won't take stock in[②].

By an apprentice who was her neighbor I sent her daily acorn or a wheat loaf, or a piece of pastry, rolls or bagels, or, when I got the chance, a slab of pudding, a slice of honeycake, or wedding strudel—whatever came my way. The apprentice was a goodhearted lad, and more than once headded something on his own. He had formerly annoyed me a lot, plucking my nose and digging me in the ribs, but when he started to be a visitor to my house he became kind and friendly, "Hey, you, Gimpel," he said to me, "you have a very decent little wife and two fine kids. You don't deserve them."

"But the things people say about her," I said.

"Well, they have long tongues," he said, "and nothing to do with them but babble. Ignore it as you ignore the cold of last winter[③]."

---

① Torah: (in Judaism) the law of God as given to Moses and recorded in the first five books of the Bible(摩西五经).
② tomorrow it's God Himself you won't take stock in: tomorrow you won't believe in God.
③ Ignore it as you ignore the cold of last winter: 别理会他们的话，就当作耳边风好了。

One day the rabbi sent for me and said, "Are you certain, Gimpel, that you were wrong about your wife?"

I said, "I'm certain."

"Why, but look here! You yourself saw it."

"It must have been a shadow," I said.

"That shadow of what?"

"Just of one of the beams, I think."

"You can go home then. You owe thanks to the Yanover rabbi. He found an obscure reference in Maimonides[①] that favored you."

I seized the rabbi's hand and kissed it.

I wanted to run home immediately. It's no small think to be separated for so long a time from wife and child. Then I reflected: I'd better go back to work now, and go home in the evening. I said nothing to anyone, although as far as my heart was concerned it was like one of the Holy Days. The women teased and twitted me as they did every day, but my thought was: Go on, with your loose talk. the truth is out, like the oil upon the water. Maimonides says it's right, and therefore it is right!

At night, when I had covered the dough to let it rise, I took my share of bread and a little sack of flour and started homeward. The moon was full and the stars were glistening, something to terrify the soul. I hurried onward, and before me started a long shadow. It was winter, and fresh snow had fallen. I had a mind to sing, but it was growing late and I didn't want to wake the householders. Then I felt like whistling, but I remembered that you don't whistle at night because it brings the demons out. So I was silent and walked as fast as I could.

Dogs in the Christian yards barked at me when I passed, but I thought: Bark your teeth out! What are you but mere dogs? Whereas I am a man, the husband of a fine wife, the father of promising children.

As I approached the house my heart started to pound as though it were the heart of a criminal. I felt no fear, but my heart went thump! thump! Well, no drawing back. I quietly lifted the latch and went in. Elka was asleep. I looked at the infant's cradle. The shutter was closed, but the moon forced its way through the cracks. I saw the newborn child's face and loved it as soon as I saw it—immediately—each tiny bone.

Then I came nearer to the bed. And what did I see but the apprentice lying there beside Elka. The moon went out allat once. It was utterly black, and I trembled. My teeth chattered. The bread fell from my hands and my wife waked and said, "Who is

---

① Maimonides: Spanish philosopher considered the greatest Jewish scholar of the Middle Ages who codified Jewish law in the Talmud (1135~1204).

that, ah?"

I muttered, "It's me."

"Gimpel?" she asked. "How come you're here? I thought it was forbidden."

"The rabbi said," I answered and shook as with a fever.

"Listen to me, Gimpel," she said, "go out to the shed and see if the goat's all right. It seems she's been sick." I have forgotten to say that we had a goat. When I heard she was unwell I went into the yard. The nanny goat was a good little creature. I had nearly human feeling for her.

With hesitant steps I went up to the shed and opened the door. The goat stood there on her four feet. I felt here verywhere, drew her by the horns, examined her udders, and found nothing wrong. She had probably eaten too much bark. "Good night, little goat," I said. "Keep well." And the little beast answered with a "Maa" as thought to thank me for the good will.

I went back. The apprentice had vanished.

"Where," I asked, "is the lad?"

"What lad?" my wife answered.

"What do you mean?" I said. "The apprentice. You were sleeping with him."

"The things I have dreamed this night and the night before," she said, "may they come true and lay you low, body and soul! An evil spirit has taken root in you and dazzled yoursight." She screamed out, "You hateful creature! You mooncalf[①]! You spook! You uncouth man! Get out, or I'll screamall Frampol out of bed!"

Before I could move, her brother sprang out from behind the oven and struck me a blow on the back of the head. I thought he had broken my neck. I felt the something about me was deeply wrong, and I said, "Don't make a scandal. All that's needed now is that people should accuse me of raising spooksand dybbuks[②]." For that was what she had mean. "No one will touch bread of my baking."

In short, I somehow calmed her.

"Well," she said, "that's enough. Lie down, and be shattered by wheels."

Next morning I called the apprentice aside. "Listen here, brother!" I said. And so on and so forth. "What do you say?" He stared at me as though I had dropped from the roof or something.

"I swear," he said, "you'd better go to an herb doctor or some healer. I'm afraid you have a screw loose, but I'll hush it up for you." And that's how the think stood.

To make a long story short, I lived twenty years with my wife. She bore me six children, four daughters and two sons. All kinds of things happened, but I neither saw

---

① moon calf: idiot, fool.
② dybbuks: a condemned spirit who inhabits the body of a living person and controls his or her actions

nor heard. I believed, and that's all. the rabbi recently said to me, "Belief in itself is beneficial. It is written that a good man lived by his faith."

Suddenly my wife took sick. It began with a trifle, a little growth upon the breast. But she evidently was not destined to live long; she had no years. I spent a fortune on her. I have forgotten to say that by this time I had a bakery of my own and in Frampol was considered to be something of a rich man. Daily the healer came, and everywitch doctor in the neighborhood was brought. They decided to use leeches, and after that to try cupping[①]. They even called a doctor from Lublin[②], but it was too late. Before she died she called me to her bed and said, "Forgive me, Gimpel."

I said, "What is there to forgive? You have been a good and faithful wife."

"Woe, Gimpel!" She said. "It was ugly how I deceived you all these years. I want to go clean to my Maker, and so I have to tell you that the children are not yours."

If I had been clouted on the head with a piece of wood it couldn't have bewildered me more.

"Whose are they?" I asked.

"I don't know," she said. "There were a lot…but they're not yours." And as she spoke she tossed her head to the side, her eyes turned glassy, and it was all up with Elka. On her whitened lips there remained a smile.

I imagined that, dead as she was, she was saying, "I deceived Gimpel. That was meaning of my brief life."

4

One night, when the period of mourning was done, as I lay dreaming on the flour sacks, there came the Spirit of Evil himself and said to me, "Gimpel, why do you sleep?"

I said, "What should I be doing? Eating kreplach[③]?"

"The whole world deceives you," he said, "and you ought todeceive the world in your turn."

"How can I deceive all the world?" I asked him.

He answered, "You might accumulate a bucket of urine everyday and at night pour it into the dough. Let the sages of Frampol eat filth."

"What about the judgment in the world to come[④]?" I said.

---

① cupping: 拔火罐，拔罐疗法。
② Lublin: an ancient city in the southeast of Warsaw, Poland.
③ kreplach:（佐以汤食用的）馄饨。
④ the judgment in the world: the last judgment. According to Judaism and Christianity, it is the day of the Last Judgment when God will decree the fates of all men according to the good and evil of their earthly lives. That is to say, those who are righteous will go to Heaven while those who are evil will be punished in Hell.

"There is no world to come," he said. "They've sold you a bill of goods and talked you into believing you carried a cat in your belly. What nonsense!"

"Well then," I said, "and is there a God?"

He answered, "There is no God, either."

"What," I said, "is there then?"

"A thick mire."

He stood before my eyes with a goatish beard and horn, long-toothed, and with a tail. Hearing such words, I wanted to snatch him by the tail, but I tumbled from the floursacks and nearly broke a rib. Then it happened that I had to answer the call of nature①, and, passing I saw the risen dough, which seemed to say to me, "Do it!" In brief, I let myself be persuaded.

At dawn the apprentice came. We kneaded the bread, scattered caraway seeds on it, and set it to bake. Then the apprentice went away, and I was left sitting in the little trench of the oven, on a pile of rags. Well, Gimpel, I thought, you've revenged yourself on them for all the shame they've put on you. Outside the frost glittered, but it was warm beside the oven. The flames heated my face. I bent my head and fell into a doze.

I saw in a dream, at once, Elka in her shroud. She called to me, "What have you done, Gimpel?"

I said to her, "It's all your fault," and started to cry.

"You fool!" she said. "You fool! Because I was false is everything false too? I never deceived anyone but myself. I'm paying for it all, Gimpel. They spare you nothinghere."

I looked at her face. It was black; I was startled andwaked, and remained sitting dumb. I sensed that everything hung in the balance. A false step now and I'd lose Eternal Life. But God gave me His help. I seized the long shovel and took out the loaves, carried them into the yard, and started to dig a hole in the frozen earth.

My apprentice came back as I was doing it. "What are you doing boss?" he said, and grew pale as a corpse.

"I know what I'm doing," I said, and I buried it all before his very eyes.

Then I went home, took my hoard from its hiding place, and divided it among the children. "I saw your mother tonight," I said. "She's turning black, poor thing."

They were so astounded they couldn't speak a word.

"Be well," I said, "and forget that such a one as Gimpelever existed." I put on my short coat, a pair of boots, took the bag that held my prayer shawl in one hand, my

---

① answer the call of nature : the euphemism for "relieve oneself" or "go to the toilet"(解手).

stock in the other, and kissed the mezzuzah[①]. When people saw mein the street they were greatly surprised.

"Where are you going?" they said.

I answered, "Into the world." And so I departed from Frampol.

I wandered over the land, and good people did not neglect me. After many years I became old and white; I heard a great deal, many lies and falsehoods, but the longer I lived the more I understood that there were really no lies. Whatever doesn't really happen is dreamed at night. It happens to one if it doesn't happen to another, tomorrow if not today, or a century hence if not next year. What difference can it make? Often I heard tales of which I said, "Now this is a thing that cannot happen." But before a year had elapsed I heard that it actually had come to pass somewhere.

Going from place to place, eating at strange tables, it often happens that I spin yarns—improbable things that could never have happened—about devils, magicians, windmills, and the like. The children run after me, calling, "Grandfather, tell us a story." Sometimes they ask for particular stories, and I try to please them. A fat young boy once said to me, "Grandfather, it's the same story you told us before." The little rogue, he was right.

So it is with dreams too. It is many years since I left Frampol, but as soon as I shut my eyes I am there again. And whom do you think I see? Elka. She is standing by the washtub, as at your first encounter, but she speaks outlandish words to me, strange things. When I wake I have forgotten it all. But while the dream lasts I am comforted. She answers all my queries, and what comes out is that all is right. I weep and implore, "Let me be with you." And she consoles me and tells me to be patient. The time is nearer than it is far. Sometimes she strokes and kisses me and weeps upon my face. When I awaken I feel her lips and taste the salt of her tears.

No doubt the world is entirely an imaginary world, but it is only once removed from the true world[②]. At the door of the hotel where I lie, there stands the plank on which the dead are taken away. The grave digger Jew has his spade ready. The grave waits and the worms are hungry; the shrouds are prepared—I carry them in my beggar's sack. Another schnorrer[③] is waiting to inherit my bed of straw. When the time comes I will go joyfully. Whatever may be there, it will be real, without complication, without ridicule, without deception. God be praised: there even Gimpel cannot be

---

① mezzuzah: (also mezuzah) a piece of parchment inscribed with biblical passages and fixed to the doorpost of the rooms of a Jewish house (圣卷; 小羊皮纸卷, 上书圣经段落, 被犹太家庭固定在房间门柱上).

② No doubt the world is entirely an imaginary world, but it is only once removed from the true world: 毫无疑问, 这世界完全是幻想的, 但是它同真实世界只有咫尺之遥。

③ schnorrer: (slang) beggar.

deceived.

译文链接：https://www.vrrw.net/wx/43906.html

Questions for understanding

1. Why do people call Gimpel "the fool"? Is he really a fool?
2. Does he see through the lies and tricks of the townsfolk? Why does he allow himself to be constantly fooled by them if the answer is yes?
3. Why does Gimpel momentarily yield to the temptation of the Evil Spirit? How is he delivered from it?
4. Before Gimpel dies, he comes to realize that "No doubt the world is entirely an imaginary world, but it is only once removed from the true world". What does this statement mean?
5. Most of Singer's stories are written in a parable form with exaggerated details common to folktales, which can teach readers some wisdom about life. What moral lessons have you learned from this story?

Aspects of Appreciation

1. On the surface, Gimpel deserves the nickname "Fool". He believes almost everything others tell him and is constantly tricked by the townsfolk as well as his wife Elka. Once he is told that the rabbi's wife is going to have a baby, he believes it without suspicion and skips the class to have a look. However, it turns out to be a trick played by the townspeople. And although twice he finds Elka in bed with another man, he is still blinded to her infidelity by her sly quibbles and fierce curses. So there is no denying that he looks like and acts like a fool. However, he is a wise and kind man by nature. He is not the fool that those who exploit him throughout his whole life believe him to be. He shows his wisdom by having the common sense that a woman can not bear a child only "seventeen weeks after the wedding", knowing very well that those around him "take advantage of" him, and not yielding to the temptation of revenge. Moreover, he is a kind-hearted man who loves the children who are not his seed, keeps sending food and money to his wife after finding her promiscuous sexual relations with others, and forgives those who mercilessly mock and cheat him.

2. In the story Singer uses the first-person narrative technique, which can convey the information directly and help to reveal the major character Gimpel. He reports what he sees, hears, and thinks. Although he is old, he can think logically and describe

details accurately and vividly, which shows that he is not stupid. So readers are inclined to identify with him and observe the people and the world around him from his standpoint. It is easy for them to feel that Gimpel lives in a cruel and crazy world.

Suggested Further Reading

The Magician of Lublin (1960), *Enemies, A Love Story* (1972), *The Son from America* (1973).

Topics for Further Study

1. It is generally acknowledged that Gimpel is a "wise fool". Try to find other examples of "wise fools" in western literature, and explain why they fall into this category?

2. Compare Gimpel with Gump, the leading character in the movie *Forrest Gump*, and try to summarize their similarities and differences.

3. As an immigrant Jewish writer, Singer is very skilled in presenting the Jews struggling between orthodox Judaism and secular modernism. Read one of the recommended works, and try to find some evidence to illustrate this point.

Knowledge of Literature

1. parable（寓言）

A parable is a brief and succinct story, in prose or verse, which illustrates certain moral or religious lessons to readers. It differs from a fable in that fables often use animals, plants, inanimate objects, and forces of nature as characters, while parables generally feature human characters.

2. An Element of Fiction: Characterization（人物塑造）

Characterization is the author's presentation and development of the traits of characters. Authors reveal what characters are like in two ways: directly and indirectly. In the direct method, the narrator simply tells readers what the character is like. In addition, names can be used to indicate the qualities of characters. When the method of revealing characters is indirect, authors show us what characters are like through dialogue, external details(dress, bearing, looks), and characters' thoughts, speech, and deeds. In the case of showing, readers have to infer character on the basis of the evidence presented in the narrative.

推荐阅读的论文：
[1] 胡琴. 从评价理论看《白象似的群山》中的人物塑造 [J]. 西南农业大学学报（社会科学版），2008（2）.
[2] 王明霞."智者"还是"愚人"——简析艾萨克·辛格的《傻瓜吉姆佩尔》[J]. 长江大学学报（社会科学版），2006（2）.

Saul Bellow (1915~2005)

About the Author

In the history of American literature, few writers have garnered more honors than Saul Bellow. During his literary career lasting almost fifty years, he was awarded the Pulitzer Prize, the Nobel Prize for literature, the National Medal of Arts and three National Book Awards, and earned the reputation as "the emerging heir to the Hemingway-Faulkner prestige".

Born as a child of Russian Jewish immigrants, Saul Bellow grew up in the Jewish ghetto of Montreal and then moved to Chicago, the city which later serves as the backdrop of most of his works. In 1933, he attended the University of Chicago, and two years later transferred to the Northwestern University, where he graduated with honors in anthropology and sociology. In the following decade, Bellow held various kinds of jobs, for instance, joining the New Deal Federal Writers' Project, working as an editor at *The Encyclopedia Britannica*, serving in the merchant marine during the WWII, teaching at New York University, Princeton and Bard College. Such rich life experiences made him an intellectual with profound knowledge and an outstanding observer with penetrating insight. In 1962, he settled down in Chicago to teach and write till his death.

Over the course of almost half a century, Bellow created a rich and ample body of works, including eleven novels, several novellas, and a good number of plays, essays and short stories. In 1944, Bellow embarked on his journey to the preeminent writer with the publication of *Dangling Man*. Set in his favorite city Chicago, this novel recounts in the form of a journal the frustrations of a young man seeking to establish a meaningful identity while waiting to be drafted into military service. His second novel *The Victim* (1947) continues to depict a grim story about the agonizing, equivocal relations of Jew and Gentile.

It is the publication of *The Adventures of Augie March* (1953) that made Bellow rise to fame overnight. Unlike his works in the 1940s, this picaresque novel concerning a young Chicago Jew marks a new phase of Bellow's creation in which the rigid and humorless style is replaced by more vigorous and optimistic one, the disciplined form and enclosed structure are changed into apparently loose-jointed plot pervaded with exuberant ideas, flashing irony and hilarious comedy, and what's more, the depressing self-reflection and endless frustration are changed into more positive and uplifting pursuit for the meaning of life. Such daring attempt in the creation paid off. As soon as it came out, this powerfully comic tale was warmly received by critics and universally hailed as a literary masterpiece on a level with *The Adventures of Huckleberry Finn*. Bellow then explored the similar terrain in the following two writings, *Seize the day* (1956) and *Henderson the Rain King* (1959). The former one, universally considered as Bellow's best novella, chronicles a crucial day of Tommy Wilhelm who, despite being a loser in all aspects of his life, strives to redeem his life and seize the day. *Henderson the Rain King* strikes the same chord by presenting the fantastic journey of a millionaire Eugene Henderson into Africa, during which he keeps searching for a sense of fulfillment and finally gains the spiritual rebirth.

Bellow's next masterpiece *Herzog*, ranking even higher than *Seize the Day*, came out in 1964. This fabulous work presents a vivid picture of the disturbing situation of the American intellectuals suffering great spiritual crisis against the background of various social conflicts. Its protagonist Moses Herzog, a middle-aged college professor, is going through the tough phase of life: his career is confronted with a serious crisis, and so is his family life. Greatly tormented by these disasters, he begins to write a series of unposted letters to meditate and reassess the reality and his life. Luckily, he ends up finding solace from the nature and resolving all his struggles with affirmative attitude and rational acceptance. In his subsequent novels, best represented by *Mr. Sammler's Planet* (1970), *Humboldt's Gift* (1975) and *The Dean's December* (1982), Bellow becomes increasingly meditative; his intellectual heroes are more concerned about the general human dilemma than their own troubles. For instance, the protagonist in *Mr. Sammler's Planet*, Mr. Artur Sammler, an aging Holocaust survivor, makes a good number of thought-provoking and clairvoyant observations of a variety of political, economical and spiritual turmoil prevalent in the modern society.

As a writer noted for "human understanding and subtle analysis of contemporary culture", Bellow shows his deep concern towards the spiritual crisis in the modern society pervaded with materialism and mammon worship, creating a series of characters, in most cases the urban Jewish intellectuals, who, besieged by disorder and unrest, suffer great frustration and spiritual loss. However, such negative visions are in the meanwhile modified by his affirmative assertion of the possibility of finding the significance of existence, which is best exemplified by the unremitting quest of the protagonists in his works. As Bellow put it, a man "should have at least sufficient power to overcome ignominy and to complete his own life. His suffering, feebleness, servitude then have a meaning". Most of his heroes, whether in the filthy backyard of the slums, in the chaotic and bustling streets of Manhattan, or in the perilous jungles of Africa, are forever on the move, attempting to find a meaningful life and the freedom to live in dignity during their wandering in the impersonal and alienating world. Although it is unclear whether they have truly found spiritual contentment at last, the novels always end on an optimistic and uplifting note. Thus although Wilhelm in *Seize the Day* has undergone a series of disasters and is almost on the brink of mental breakdown, he finally gains a certain epiphany from a stranger's funeral and then plucks up courage to embrace the society and his new life. And Herzog, confronted with the great spiritual predicament, can in the end realize the importance of sharing his life with others and retreat himself into tranquility.

A Father-To-Be

About the Story

First appearing in 1955 and then collected into *Seize the Day* (1956), "Father-to-be" is generally acclaimed as one of Bellow's most anthologized short stories. Set in Chicago on a snowy Sunday evening, it mainly recounts the thoughtful speculations of a research chemist Rogin on his way to the apartmentof his beautiful and materialistic fiancéeJoan. On the subway, Rogin suddenly has a vision that the dandy seated near him appears to be his son forty years later, incorporating all the shortcomings of Joan and none of his virtues. Such idea frightens him so much that he begins to ponder his relationship with Joan and decides to break up with her. However, when he reaches her apartment and is warmly welcome by Joan, his anger disappears completely.

A Father-To-Be

The strangest notions had a way of forcing themselves into Rogin's mind. Just thirty-one and passable-looking, with short black hair, small eyes, but a high, open forehead, he was a research chemist, and his mind was generally serious and dependable. But on a snowy evening while this stocky man, buttoned to the chin in a Burberry coat and walking in his preposterous[①] gait—feet turned outward—was going toward the subway, he fell into a peculiar state[②].

[①] preposterous: very foolish; ridiculous.
[②] he fell into a peculiar state: he was in a strange psychological state.

He was on his way to have supper with his fiancée. She had phoned him a short while ago and said, "You'd better pick up a few things on the way."

"What do we need?"

"Some roast beef, for one thing. I bought a quarter of a pound coming from my aunt's."

"Why a quarter of a pound, Joan?" Said Rogin, deeply annoyed. "That's just about enough for one good sandwich."

"So you have to stop at a delicatessen. I had no more money."

He was about to ask, "What happened to the thirty dollars I gave you on Wednesday?" But he knew that would not be right.

"I had to give Phillis money for the cleaning woman," said Joan.

Phillis, Joan's cousin, was a young divorcee, extremely wealth. The two women shared an apartment.

"Roast beef," he said, "And what else?"

"Some shampoo, sweetheart. We've used up all the shampoo. And hurry, darling, I've missed you all day."

"And I've missed you," said Rogin, but to tell the truth he had been worrying most of the time. He had a younger brother whom he was putting through college[①], and his mother, whose annuity wasn't enough in these days of inflation and high taxes, needed money, too. Joan had debts he was helping her to pay, for she wasn't working. She was looking for something suitable to do. Beautiful, well-educated, aristocraticin her attitude, she couldn't clerk in a dime store[②], she couldn't model clothes (Rogin thought this made girls vain and stiff, and he didn't want her to); she couldn't be a waitress or a cashier. What could she be? Well, something would turnup, and meantime Rogin hesitated to complain. He paid her bills—the dentist, the department store, the osteopath, the doctor, the psychiatrist. At Christmas, Rogin almost went mad. Joan bought him a velvet smoking jacket[③] with frog fasteners, a beautiful pipe and a pouch. She bought Phillis a garnet brooch, an Italian silk umbrella, and a gold cigarette holder. For other friends, she bought Dutch pewterand Swedish glassware. Before she was through, she had spent five hundred dollars of Rogin's money. He loved her too much to show his suffering. He believed she had a far better nature than his. She didn't worry about money. She had a marvelous character, always cheerful, and she really didn't need a psychiatrist at all. Shewent to one because Phillis did and it made her curious. She tried to keep up with her cousin, whose father had made

---

① …whom he was putting through college: he was supporting his brother financially to finish college education.
② dime store: a retail store selling a wide variety of inexpensive articles(廉价商店).
③ smoking jacket: 吸烟服(男士在室内穿的短款礼服,通常用丝绸或天鹅绒制成,在吸烟时穿)。

millions in the rug business.

While the woman in the drugstore was wrapping the shampoo bottle a clear idea suddenly arose in Rogin's thoughts. Money surrounds you in life as the earth does in death. Superimposition is the universal law. Who is free? No one is free. Who has no burdens? Everyone is under pressure. The very rocks, the waters of the earth, beasts, men, children—everyone has some weight to carry. This idea was extremely clear to him at first. Soon it became rather vague, but it had a great effect nevertheless, as if someone had given him a valuable gift. (Not like the velvet smoking jacket he couldn't bring himself to wear, or the pipe it choked him to smoke.) The notion that all were under pressure and affliction, instead of saddening him, had the opposite influence. It put him in a wonderful mood. It was extraordinary how happy he became and, in addition, clear-Sighted. His eyes all at once were opened to what was around him. He saw with delight how the druggist and the woman who wrapped the shampoo bottle were smiling and flirting, how the lines of worry in her face went over into lines of cheer and the druggist's receding gums① did not hinder his kidding and friendliness. And in the delicatessen, also, it was amazing how much Rogin noted and what happiness it gave him simply to be there.

Delicatessens on Sunday night, when all other stores are shut, will overcharge you ferociously, and Rogin would normally have been on guard, but he was not tonight, or scarcely so. Smells of pickle, sausage, mustard, and smoked fish overjoyed him. He pitied the people who would buy the chicken salad and chopped herring; they could do it only because their sight was too dim to see what they were getting—the flat flakes of pepper on the chicken, the soppy herring, mostly vinegar-soaked stale bread. Who would buy them? Later risers, People living alone, waking up in the darkness of the afternoon, finding their refrigerators empty, or people whose gaze was turned inward. The roast beef looked not bad, and Rogin ordered a pound.

While the storekeeper was slicing the meat, he yelled at a Puerto Rican kid who was reaching for a bag of chocolate cookies, "Hey, you want to pull me down the whole display on yourself? You, chico②, wait a half a minute." This storekeeper, though he looked like one of Pancho Villa's③ bandits, the kind that smeared their enemies with syrup and staked them down on anthills, a man with toadlike eyes and stout hands made to clasp pistols hung around his belly, was not so bad. He was a New York man, thought Rogin—who was from Albany④ him self—a New York man

---

① receding gums: 牙龈萎缩（a sign of growing old）。
② chico: kid.
③ Pancho Villa: Francisco Villa (1877~1923), a prominent figure during the Mexican Revolution.
④ Albany: the state capital of New York.

toughened by every abuse of the city, trained to suspect everyone. But in his own realm, on the board behind the counter, there was justice. Even clemency.

The Puerto Rican kid wore a complete cowboy outfit—a green hat with white braid, guns, chaps, spurs, boots, and gauntlets—but he couldn't speak any English. Rogin unhooked the cellophane bag of hard circular cookies and gave it to him. The boy tore the cellophane with his teeth and began to chew one of those dry chocolate disks. Rogin recognized his state—the energetic dream of childhood. Once, he, too, had found these dry biscuits delicious. It would have bored him now to eat one.

What else would Joan like? Rogin thought fondly. Some strawberries? "Give me some frozen strawberries. No, raspberries, she likes those better. And heavy cream[①]. And some rolls, cream cheese, and some of those rubber-looking gherkins."

"What rubber?"

"Those, deep green, with eyes. Some ice cream might be in order, too."

He tried to think of a compliment, a good comparison, an endearment, for Joan when she'd open the door. What about her complexion? There was really nothing to compare her sweet, small, daring, shapely, timid, defiant, loving face to. How difficult she was, and how beautiful!

As Rogin went down into the stony, odorous, metallic, captive air of the subway, he was diverted by an unusual confession made by a man to his friend. These were two very tall men, shapeless in their winter clothes, as if their coats concealed suits of chain-mail[②].

"So, how long have you known me?" Said one.

"Twelve years."

"Well, I have an admission to make," he said. "I've decided that I might as well. For years I've been a heavy drinker. You didn't know. Practically an alcoholic."

But his friend was not surprised, and he answered immediately, "Yes, I did know."

"You knew? Impossible! How could you?"

Why, thought Roger, as if it could be a secret! Look at that long, austere, alcohol-washed face, that drink-ruined nose, the skin by his ears like turkey wattles, and those whisky-saddened eyes.

"Well, I did know, though."

"You couldn't have. I can't believe it." He was upset, and his friend didn't seem to want to soothe him. "But it's all right now," he said. "I've been going to a doctor and taking pills, a new revolutionary Danish discovery. It's a miracle. I'm beginning

---

① heavy cream: 浓奶油。
② chain-mail: 锁子甲。

to believe they can cure you of anything and everything. You can't beat the Danes in science. They do everything. They turned a man into a woman."

"That isn't how they stop you from drinking, is it?"

"No. I hope not. This is only like aspirin. It's super aspirin. They called it the aspirin of the future. But if you use it, you have to stop drinking." Rogin's illuminated mind asked of itself while the human tides of the subway swayed back and forth, and cars linked and transparent like fish bladders raced under the streets: How come he thought nobody would know what everybody couldn't help knowing? And, as a chemist, he asked himself what kind of compound this new Danish drug might be, and started thinking about various inventions of his own, synthetic albumen, a cigarette that lit itself, a cheaper motor fuel. Ye gods, but he needed money! As never before. What was to be done? His mother was growing more and more difficult. On Friday night, she had neglected to cut up his meat for him, and he was hurt. She had sat at the table motionless, with her long-suffering face, severe, and let him cut his own meat, a thing she almost never did. She had always spoiled him and made his brother envy him. But what she expected now! Oh, Lord, how he had to pay, and it had never even occurred to him formerly that these things might have a price.

Seated, one of the passengers, Rogin recovered his calm, happy, even clairvoyant state of mind. To think of money was to think as the world wanted you to think; then you'd never be your own master. When people, said they wouldn't do something for love or money, they meant that love and money were opposite passions and one the enemy of the other. He went on to reflect how little people knew about this, how they slept through life, how small a light the light of consciousness was. Rogin's clean, snub-nosed face shone while his heart was torn with joy at these deeper thoughts of our ignorance. You might take this drunkard as an example, who for long years thought his closest friends never suspected he drank. Rogin looked up and down the aisle for this remarkable knightly symbol, but he was gone.

However, there was no lack of things to see. There was a small girl with a new white muff; into the muff a doll's head was sewn, and the child was happy and affectionately vain of it, while her old man, stout and grim, with a huge scowling nose, kept picking her up and resetting her in the seat, as if he was trying to change her into something else. Then another child, led by her mother, boarded the car, and this other child carried the very same doll-faced mull, and this greatly annoyed both parents. The woman, who looked like difficult, contentious woman, took her daughter away. It seemed to Rogin that each child was in love with its own muff and didn't even see the other, but it was one of his foibles to think he understood the hearts of little children.

A foreign family next engaged his attention. They looked like Central Americans to him. On one side the mother, quite old, dark-faced, white-haired, and worn out; on the other a son with the whitened, porous hands of a dishwasher. But what was the dwarf who sat between them—a son or a daughter? The hair was long and wavy and the cheeks smooth, but the shirt and tie were masculine. The overcoat was feminine, but the shoes—the shoes were a puzzle. A pair of brown oxfords with an outer seam like a man's, but Baby Louis heels① like a woman's—a plain toe like a man's, but a strap across the instep like a woman's. No stockings. That didn't help much. The dwarf's fingers were beringed, but without a wedding band②. There were small grim dents in the cheeks. The eyes were puffy and concealed, but Rogin did not doubt that they could reveal strange things if they chose and that this was a creature of remarkable understanding. He had for many years owned De la Mare's③ *Memoirs of a Midget*. Now he took a resolve; he would read it. As soon as he had decided, he was free from his consuming curiosity as to the dwarf's sex and was able to look at the person who sat beside him.

Thoughts very often grow fertile in the subway, because of the motion, the great company, the subtlety of the rider's state—as he rattles under streets and rivers, under the foundations of great buildings, and Rogin's mind had already been strangely stimulated. Clasping the bag of groceries from which there rose odours of bread and pickle spice, he was following a train of reflections, first about the chemistry of sex determination, the X and Y chromosomes④, hereditary linkages, the uterus, afterward about his brother as a tax exemption. He recalled two dreams of the night before. In one, an undertaker had offered to cut his hair, and he had refused. In another, he had been carrying a woman on his head. Sad dreams, both! Very sad! Which was the woman—Joan or Mother? And the undertaker—his lawyer? He gave a deep sigh, and by force of habit began to put together his synthetic albumen that was to revolutionize the entire egg industry.

Meanwhile, he had not interrupted his examination of the passengers and had fallen into a study of the man next to him. This was a man whom he had never in his life seen before but with whom he now suddenly felt linked through all existence. He was middle-aged, sturdy, with clean, well formed, but Rogin did not approve of them. The coat he wore was a fairly expensive blue check such as Rogin would never have chosen for himself. He would not have worn blue suede shoes, either, or such a

---

① Baby Louis heels: high heels.
② wedding band: wedding ring.
③ De la Mare: (1873~1956) English poet and novelist.
④ chromosomes: 染色体。

faultless hat, a cumbersome felt animal of a hat① encircled by a high, fat ribbon. There are all kinds of dandies, not all of them are of the flaunting kind; some are dandies of respectability, and Rogin's fellow passenger was one of these. His straight-nosed profile was handsome, yet he had betrayed his gift, for he was flat-looking. But in his flat way he seemed to warn people that he wanted no difficulties with them, he wanted nothing to do with them. Wearing such blue suede shoes, he could not afford to have people treading on his feet, and he seemed to draw about himself a circle of privilege, notifying all others to mind their own business and let him read his paper. He was holding a *Tribune*②, and perhaps it would be overstatement to say that he was reading. He was holding it.

His clear skin and blue eyes, his straight and purely Roman nose—even the way he sat—all strongly suggested one person to Rogin: Joan. He tried to escape the comparison, but it couldn't be helped. This man not only looked like Joan's father, whom Rogin detested; he looked like Joan herself. Forty years hence, a son of hers, provided she had one, might be like this. A son of hers? Of such a son, he himself, Rogin, would be the father. Lacking in dominant traits as compared with Joan, his heritage would not appear. Probably the children would resemble her. Yes, think forty years ahead, and a man like this, who sat by him knee to knee in the hurtling car among their fellow creatures, unconscious participants in a sort of great carnival of transit—such a man would carry forward what had been Rogin.

This was why he felt bound to him through all existence. What were forty years reckoned against eternity! Forty years were gone, and he was gazing at his own son. Here he was. Rogin was frightened and moved. "My son! My son!" He said to himself, and the pity of it almost made him burst into tears. The holy and frightful work of the masters of life and death brought this about. We were their instruments. We worked towards ends we thought were our own. But no! The whole thing was so unjust. To suffer, to labor, to toil and force your way through the spikes of life, to crawl through its darkest caverns, to push through the worst, to struggle under the weight of economy, to make money—only to become the father of a fourth-rate man of the world like this, so flat-looking with his ordinary, clean, rosy, uninteresting, self-satisfied, fundamentally bourgeois face. What a curse to have a dull son! A son like this, who could never understand his father. They had absolutely nothing, but nothing, in common, he and this neat, chubby, blue-eyed man. He was so pleased, thought Rogin, with all he owned and all he did and all he was that he could hardly

---

① a cumbersome felt animal of a hat: a hat that feels as awkward as an animal on one's head.
② Tribune:《论坛报》。

unfasten his lip. Look at that lip, sticking up at the tip like a little thorn or egg tooth①. He wouldn't give anyone the time of day. Would this perhaps be general forty years from now? Would personalities be chillier as the world aged and grew colder? The inhumanity of the next generation incensed Rogin. Father and son had no sign to make to each other②. Terrible! Inhuman! What a vision of existence it gave him. Man's personal aims were nothing, illusion. The life force occupied each of us in turn in its progress toward its own fulfillment, trampling on our individual humanity, using us for its own ends like mere dinosaurs or bees, exploiting love heartlessly, making us engage in the social process, labor, struggle for money, and submit to the law of pressure, the universal law of layers, superimposition!

What the blazes am I getting into? Rogin thought. To be the father of a throwback③ to her father. The image of this white-haired, gross, peevish, old man with his ugly selfish blue eyes revolted Rogin. This was how his grandson would look. Joan, with whom Rogin was now more and more displeased, could not help that. For her, it was inevitable. But did it have to be inevitable for him? Well, then, Rogin, you fool, don't be a damned instrument. Get out of the way!

But it was too late for this, because he had already experienced the sensation of sitting next to his own son, his son and Joan's. He kept staring at him, waiting for him to say something, but the presumptive son remained coldly silent though he must have been aware of Rogin's scrutiny. They even got out at the same stop—Sheridan Square. When they stepped to the platform, the man, without even looking at Rogin, went away in a different direction in his detestable blue-checked coat, with his rosy, nasty face.

The whole thing upset Rogin very badly. When he approached Joan's door and heard Phyllis's little dog Henri barking even before he could knock, his face was very tense. "I won't be used," he declared to himself. "I have my own right to exist." Joan had better watch out. She had a light way of bypassing grave questions he had given earnest thought to. She always assumed no really disturbing thing would happen. He could not afford the luxury of such a carefree, debonair attitude himself, because he had to work hard and earn money so that disturbing things would not happen. Well, at the moment this situation could not be helped, and he really did not mind the money if he could feel that she was not necessarily the mother of such a son as his subway son or entirely the daughter of that awful, obscene father of hers. After all, Rogin was not

---

① egg tooth:（在胚胎中的鸟类和爬行动物的）破卵齿。
② Father and son had no sign to make to each other: Father and son had no common language.
③ throwback: a person, animal, or plant that has the characteristics of an earlier or more primitive type（返祖者，返祖型的东西）.

himself so much like either of his parents, and quite different from his brother.

Joan came to the door, wearing one of Phyllis's expensive housecoats. It suited her very well. At first sight of her happy face, Rogin was brushed by the shadow of resemblance; the touch of it was extremely light, almost figmentary, but it made his flesh tremble.

She began to kiss him, saying, "Oh, my baby. You're covered with snow. Why didn't you wear your hat? It's all over its little head"—her favourite third-person endearment.

"Well, let me put down this bag of stuff. Let me take off my coat," grumbled Rogin, and escaped from her embrace. Why couldn't she wait making up to① him? "It's so hot in here. My face is burning. Why do you keep the place at this temperature? And that damned dog keeps barking. If you didn't keep it cooped up, it wouldn't be so spoiled and noisy. Why doesn't anybody ever walk him?"

"Oh, it's not really so hot here! You've just come in from the cold. Don't you think this housecoat fits me better than Phyllis? Especially across the hips. She thinks so, too. She may sell it to me."

"I hope not," Rogin almost exclaimed.

She brought a towel to dry the melting snow from his short black hair. The flurry of rubbing excited Henri intolerably, and Joan locked him up in the bedroom, where he jumped persistently against the door with a rhythmic sound of claws on the wood.

Joan said, "Did you bring the shampoo?" "Here it is."

"Then I'll wash your hair before dinner. Come!" "I don't want it washed."

"Oh, come on," she said, laughing.

Her lack of consciousness of guilt amazed him. He did not see how it could be. And the carpeted, furnished, lamplit, curtained room seemed to stand against his vision. So that he felt accusing and angry, his spirit sore and bitter, but it did not seem fitting to say why. Indeed, he began to worry lest the reason for it all slip away from him.

They took off his coat and his shirt in the bathroom, and she filled the sink. Rogin was full of his troubled emotions; now that his chest was bare he could feel them even more and he said to himself, I'll have a thing or two to tell her pretty soon. I'm not letting them get away with it. "Do you think," he was going to tell her, "that I alone was made to carry the burden of the whole world on me? Do you think I was born to be taken advantage of and sacrificed? Do you think I'm just a natural resource, like a coal mine, or oil well, or fisher, or the like? Remember, that I'm a man is no reason

---

① make up to sb.: be pleasant to sb. in order to win favors(讨好某人).

why I should be loaded down. I have a soul in me no bigger or stronger than yours."

"Take away the externals, like the muscles, deeper voice, and so forth, and what remains? A pair of spirits, practically alike. So why shouldn't there also be equality? I can't always be the strong one."

"Sit here," said Joan, bringing up a kitchen stool to the sink. "Your hair's gotten all matted."

He sat with his breast against the cool enamel, his chin on the edge of the basin, the green, hot radiant water reflecting the glass and the tile, and the sweet, cool, fragrant juice of the shampoo poured on his head. She began to wash him.

"You have the healthiest-looking scalp," she said. "It's all pink."

He answered, "Well, it should be white. There must be something wrong with me." "But there's absolutely nothing wrong with you," she said, and pressed against him from behind, surrounding him, pouring the water gently over him until it seemed to him that the water came from within him, it was the warm fluid of his own secret loving spirit overflowing into the sink, green and foaming, and the words he had rehearsed he forgot, and his anger at his son-to-be disappeared altogether, and he sighed, and said to her from the water-filled hollow of the sink, "You always have such wonderful Ideas, Joan. You know? You have a kind of instinct, a regular gift."

译文参考：兆霖主编．索尔·贝娄全集第 10 卷 [M]．孙筱珍译．石家庄：河北教育出版社，2002: 285-296.

Questions for Understanding

1. What does Rogin see on the way to Joan's apartment?
2. What do you know about Rogin's fiancée Joan? Why does he hesitate to complain about her?
3. What troubles Rogin most? Why? Does he change his mood later?
4. What does the man sitting next to Rogin look like? Why does he upset Roger so much?
5. What does Roger think of his relationship with Joan? What does he intend to do when reaching Joan's apartment?
6. Why does Roger give up saying "no" to Joan at the end of the story? What is the thematic significance of such an ending?

Aspects of Appreciation

1. On his way to Joan's apartment, Rogin undergoes several emotional ups and downs. When he receives Joan's call requiring him to buy something, Rogin becomes deeply concerned about financial problems besetting him, such as his younger brother's tuition, his mother's daily expenses, and especially Joan's extravagant way of spending money. However, his worry soon turns into delight and relief when he realizes that in such a money-oriented society, all men face money problems. Later, while waiting for the subway, he overhears a confession made by a heavy drinker to his friend, and gets depressed again because of the money troubles. But when he is seated in the subway, he recovers quickly his calm, happy and even penetrating state of mind, for it dawns on him that people should get rid of the negative influence of money. As he puts it, "to think of money was to think as the world wanted you to think; then you'd never be your own master." Such emotional changes reach the highest level when Rogin spots a middle-aged dandy seated next to him. The man's arrogance, indifference and self-complacence remind him of Joan and her father, and make him think that his son might look like the man in forty years, possessing all the shortcomings of Joan and none of his virtues. So he becomes more and more displeased with Joan and decides to end the relationship with her. However, when Joan washes his head affectionately, he indulges himself in such pleasure. His anger is dissipated, and his rehearsed complaints are gone.

2. Though Rogin's thoughts seem to be random and divergent, they are related to his money problems. He is under great financial pressure such as supporting his family and maintaining Joan's extravagant lifestyle. That is why whenever he sees or hears something, he always associates it with the same concern. Luckily, Rogin is accustomed to making up some excuses to deceive himself so that he can forget such troubles temporarily. But the vision of his son-to-be becomes the last straw, forcing him to be determined to escape from being a slave to materialism, and to pursue a meaningful life. However, he ends up in failure and his newly-formed decision gives way to some immediate comfort, which can be best exemplified by the scene of Joan washing his head. Water, always associated with baptism in Christianity, stands for a kind of renewal and rebirth. Therefore, the detailed description of washing suggests that Rogin has already made his compromise, and indulged himself in the sensual pleasure and comfort brought by materialism.

3. To some extent, Rogin could be viewed as a representative of modern American intellectuals. He is sensible and clairvoyant enough to realize the danger of materialism which poses a great threat to the spiritual life of modern people, depriving

them of their own uniqueness and inherent humanity. The pursuit of a materialistic lifestyle will lead to a loss of true love and understanding. With such ideas in mind, he tries to escape from the miserable fate of being enslaved by materialism and make his life meaningful. However, it is a pity that at last he still fails to resist the temptation, and subjects himself to materialism. By deftly employing the stream of consciousness, Bellow vividly delineates the inner thoughts of Rogin, and succeeds in presenting the dilemma of modern American intellectuals, who struggle to live in the contemporary society of material affluence and spiritual poverty, and do their utmost to establish a meaningful identity for themselves in the dilemma. Some like Rogin endup in failure, while others represented by Herzog make it.

Suggested Further Reading

The Adventure of Augie March(1953); *Seize the Day* (1956); *Herzog* (1964); *Humboldt' Gift* (1969).

Topics for Further Study

1. What do you think of Rogin? Do you think he is over sensitive, just making a fuss about trifles?

2. In most of Bellow's works, the intellectuals always appear as the leading characters. With profound knowledge and sensitive feelings, those intellectuals are constantly beset by the turbulent and chaotic society, and find it difficult to live a meaningful life. Read the suggested readings, and try to find some examples to illustrate this point.

3. Try to summarize the characteristics of the protagonists in Bellow's works, and try to compare them with the Code Heroes in Hemingway's writings.

Knowledge of Literature

1. Picaresque Novel（流浪汉小说）

It refers to a subgenre of fiction which describes, from a first-person point of view, the episodic adventures of a roguish hero of low social status. As suggested by its name (in Spanish, "picaresca" means "rogue"), this kind of novel emerged in sixteenth-century Spain. As an early form of fiction, it gained wide popularity in the 17th and 18th centuries. Picaresque fiction is realistic in manner, episodic in structure and often satiric in aim. Although it quickly declined with the development of realistic novels, the picaresque elements or skills are frequently employed in many later novels. Famous picaresque novels include Henry Fielding's *Tom Jones* (1749), and Mark Twain's *The Adventures of Huckleberry Finn* (1884).

2. An Element of Fiction: Irony（反讽）

Irony, used in fiction to convey ideas, makes visible a contrast between appearance and reality. Incongruity is the method of irony. There are three kinds of irony common in fiction: verbal irony, situational irony and dramatic irony. In verbal irony, people say the opposite of what they mean. For example, if the day has been terrible, you say, "Boy, this has been a nice day!" The hearer knows that this statement is ironic because he sees at once the difference between statement and actuality. Verbal irony often displays a mental agility—wit—that people find striking and entertaining. In situational irony, the situation differs from what common sense indicates it is, will be, or ought to be. It is ironic, for example, that someone we expect to be upright—a government official or judge—should be the most repulsive of scoundrels. Dramatic irony involves a situation in a narrative in which the reader shares with the author knowledge of present or future circumstances of which a character is ignorant. It expresses as a difference between what a character says or does and what the reader understands to be true.

推荐阅读的论文：
[1] 曾衍桃. 国外反讽研究综观 [J]. 西安外国语学院学报，2004(03).
[2] 王晓英. 论艾丽丝·沃克短篇小说"日常用品"中的反讽艺术 [J]. 外国文学研究，2005(4).

Maxine Hong Kingston (1940~)

About the Author

In recent Asian American literature, a number of women have emerged as distinct talents, of whom one of the most impressive is Maxine Hong Kingston, whose image well embodies the title of her masterpiece *The Women Warrior* (1976)—a tiny lady with tremendous mind and spirit wielding her pen as a formidable sword to break through deep-rooted constraints of gender and ethnicity, and to bridge the gap between Chinese culture and American one.

Born in a Chinese immigrant family in Stockton, California, Kingston grew up in two worlds, the "solid America" where she lived, and the mysterious China revealed in her parents' "talk-stories". Though struggling for hard existence in the new country,

Kingston's parents, especially her mother, kept on reminding children of their rich cultural heritage by telling mystical Chinese folk tales and family stories. Those fantastic stories and myths, in particular the narratives about women who had been considered privileged or damned, were deeply rooted in young Kingston's heart and would later come into blossoms in the form of writing. However, while intrigued by the magic and mystery of Chinese culture, she strongly felt the pull between it and American culture, and realized her awkward position in the conflicts of these two disparate cultures, which made the question of identity one of her major concerns in her writings as well as in her life.

After having excelled in her high school studies, Kingston attended the University of California at Berkeley, where she graduated with a BA in English in 1962. That same year, she married aspiring actor Earll Kingston and took up work as a high school teacher. After the birth of their son Joseph in 1963, they taught at Sunset High School in California. Though they were once active proponents in antiwar activities in Berkeley, in 1967 the couple decided to go abroad to escape the increasing violence and drugs of the antiwar movement. Finally they moved to Hawaii, where Kingston held various teaching jobs.

Kingston's career as a writer began to flower, as she taught at Mid-Pacific Institute, the University of Hawaii and Eastern Michigan University, and later joined the faculty of the University of California at Berkeley from 1990 till now. In 1976, her first book *The Woman Warrior: Memoirs of a Girlhood among Ghosts* came out and received enormous critical acclaim. Though winning the National BookCritics Circle Award for nonfiction, this book is, in essence, a strikingly original blend of memoir, fiction, history and myth, mainly depicting the special experiences of a young Chinese American girl who grows up within two conflicting cultures. Kingston's next book *China Men*(1980), another blend of fact and fantasy, shifted the focus to Chinese men in America. Using the painful experiences of several generations of her male ancestors, Kingston went on to explore her favorite topics of racial discrimination and self-identity. After gaining tremendous success with these two nonfiction works, Kingston made her debut as a novelist with the publication of *Tripmaster Monkey: His Fake Book*in 1989. Set in a California Chinatown in the 1960s, this densely textured novel describes the life of a hippy, young, fifth-generation Chinese American, Wittman Ah Sing, who is dangling between the two cultures and confused about the future, and accordingly sets out on his journey to find his position in the world.

Incredibly prolific, Kingston also published numerous insightful poems, short stories and articles in her literary career, among which the famous ones include a mixed genre volume *The Fifth Book of Peace* (2003) inspired by the Chinese legend of *Three Lost Books of Peace*, and an anthology of writings by war veterans entitled *Veterans of War, Veterans of Peace* (2006).

"Everyone can be a writer, and everyone needs to find his or her voice." Maxine Hong Kingston once said in an interview, "This doesn't mean that everyone needs to be a professional and publish and all that, but all of us need to find our way to communicate and express ourselves out in the world. Writing, thinking, communicating, it all goes together." Since the publication of her masterpiece *The Women Warrior*, Kingston has managed to find her own unique voice both as a Chinese American and a woman writer through writing, successfully made her voice heard by millions of readers and inspired a new generation of writers, especially those of minority groups, to make their own voices aloud in the American literary field.

Woman Warrior: Memoirs of a Girlhood among Ghosts

About the Novel

Divided into five self-contained chapters, Kingston's masterpiece *Woman Warrior: Memoirs of a Girlhood among Ghosts* records the growing up of a Chinese American girl between two different cultures and explores how she reconciles Chinese cultural history with her emerging sense of herself as an American.

In the first chapter entitled "No Name Woman", the narrator's mother Brave Orchid tells her a tragic story about her deceased aunt, who committed adultery while her husband was working in America, and therefore was forced to kill herself and the newborn baby because of the severe social censure and punishment. Although the narrator is warned by her mother never to mention her aunt again, she invents a history for her in her writing out of sympathy. The second chapter "The White Tiger" begins with the narrator's creative version of the legendary Chinese woman warrior Fa Mulan（花木兰）, who becomes a well-trained fighter and accomplishes a series of great deeds: driving back the barbarians, avenging her village and beheading the vicious emperor. After the battle, she returns home to take on the traditional female role of wife and mother. And in the second part of this chapter, the narrator talks about her painful experience when facing the racial and gender discrimination, and her determination to be a woman warrior. The next chapter "Shaman" mainly focuses on Brave Orchid's legendary life in China as well as in America, including her courageous deed of catching ghosts in a Chinese medical school, her experiences of being a very successful healer, and her hard struggle in adapting to the new life after reuniting with her husband in America. In "At the Western Palace", the fourth chapter, the narrator recounts the tragedy of her aunt Moon Orchid, whose husband went to America alone. Encouraged by Brave Orchid, Moon Orchid chooses to go to America to rejoin her husband. But to her great disappointment, she is rejected again and finally driven to madness. The last chapter "A Song for a Barbarian Reed Pipe" is mainly about the narrator's painstaking childhood experiences to find her personal voice in the conflicts of two cultures. She ends the whole book with a reinterpretation of the legend of Ts'ai Yen, a famous ancient Chinese poetess who was forced to live in a different tribe for twelve years and wrote touching songs to reclaim her identity, from which the narrator gets the inspiration and is determined to use the pen to find her own voice.

Ever since its publication, *The Woman Warrior* has received numerous acclaim. The public as well as critics have embraced it warmly. It is currently considered as the most widely taught book by a living writer in American colleges and universities. However, the book has also received much criticism, especially from some Chinese American authors represented by Frank Chin, who has accused Kingston of adapting the traditional Chinese stories to cater to stereotypes about Chinese people.

The following selection is the first chapter of the book, "No Name Woman", one of the most frequently anthologized and discussed sections, for it encapsulates many themes of the book: silence and voice, women's lowly position in the traditional Chinese society, the difficulty of growing up as a Chinese American and so on.

No Name Woman

"You must not tell anyone," my mother said, "what I am about to tell you. In China your father had a sister who killed herself. She jumped into the family well. We say that your father has all brothers because it is as if she had never been born."

"In 1924 just a few days after our village celebrated seventeen hurry-up weddings①—to make sure that every young man who went 'out on the road'② would responsibly come home—your father and his brothers and your grandfather and his brothers and your aunt's new husband sailed for America, the Gold Mountain③. It was your grandfather's last trip. Those lucky enough to get contracts waved goodbye from the decks. They fed and guarded the stowaways④ and helped them off in Cuba, New

---

① hurry-up weddings: weddings which are held in a hurry (仓促而成的婚礼).
② Went out on the road: 上路。
③ the Gold Mountain: the name given by the Chinese to western regions of North America, particularly the state of California. After gold was first discovered in California in 1848, thousands of Chinese people began to travel to California in search of gold during the California Gold Rush.
④ stowaway: a person who hides in a ship or other conveyance in order to obtain free passage (偷乘者).

York, Bali, Hawaii. 'We'll meet in California next year,' they said. All of them sent money home."

"I remember looking at your aunt one day when she and I were dressing; I had not noticed before that she had such a protruding melon of a stomach. But I did not think, 'She's pregnant,' until she began to look like other pregnant women, her shirt pulling and the white tops of her black pants showing. She could not have been pregnant, you see, because her husband had been gone for years. No one said anything. We did not discuss it. In early summer she was ready to have the child, long after the time when it could have been possible."

"The village had also been counting. On the night the baby was to be born the villagers raided our house. Some were crying. Like a great saw, teeth strung with lights, files of people walked zigzag across our land, tearing the rice. Their lanterns doubled in the disturbed black water, which drained away through the broken bunds. As the villagers closed in, we could see that some of them, probably men and women we knew well, wore white masks. The people with long hair hung it over their faces. Women with short hair made it stand up on end. Some had tied white bands around their foreheads, arms, and legs."

"At first they threw mud and rocks at the house. Then they threw eggs and began slaughtering our stock. We could hear the animals scream their deaths-the roosters, the pigs, a last great roar from the ox. Familiar wild heads flared in our night windows; the villagers encircled us. Some of the faces stopped to peer at us, their eyes rushing like searchlights. The hands flattened against the panes, framed heads, and left red prints."

"The villagers broke in the front and the back doors at the same time, even though we had not locked the doors against them. Their knives dripped with the blood of our animals. They smeared blood on the doors and walls. One woman swung a chicken, whose throat she had slit, splattering blood in red arcs about her. We stood together in the middle of our house, in the family hall with the pictures and tables of the ancestors around us, and looked straight ahead."

"At that time the house had only two wings[①]. When the men came back, we would build two more to enclose our courtyard and a third one to begin a second courtyard. The villagers pushed through both wings, even your grandparents' rooms, to find your aunt's, which was also mine until the men returned. From this room a new wing for one of the younger families would grow. They ripped up her clothes and shoes and broke her combs, grinding them underfoot. They tore her work from the loom. They scattered the cooking fire and rolled the new weaving in it. We could

---

① wing:(建筑物)侧翼、边房或厢房。

hear them in the kitchen breaking our bowls and banging the pots. They overturned the great waist-high earthenware jugs; duck eggs, pickled fruits, vegetables burst out and mixed in acrid torrents. The old woman from the next field swept a broom through the air and loosed the spirits-of-the-broom① over our heads. 'Pig.' 'Ghost.' 'Pig.' they sobbed and scolded while they ruined our house."

"When they left, they took sugar and oranges to bless themselves. They cut pieces from the dead animals. Some of them took bowls that were not broken and clothes that were not torn. Afterward we swept up the rice and sewed it back up into sacks. But the smells from the spilled preserves lasted. Your aunt gave birth in the pigsty that night. The next morning when I went for the water, I found her and the baby plugging up② the family well."

"Don't let your father know that I told you. He denies her. Now that you have started to menstruate, what happened to her could happen to you. Don't humiliate us. You wouldn't like to be forgotten as if you had never been born. The villagers are watchful."

Whenever she had to warn us about life, my mother told stories that ran like this one, a story to grow up on. She tested our strength to establish realities. Those in the emigrant generations who could not reassert brute survival died young and far from home. Those of us in the first American generations have had to figure out how the invisible world the emigrants built around our childhoods fits in solid America.

The emigrants confused the gods by diverting their curses, misleading them with crooked streets and false names. They must try to confuse their offspring as well, who, I suppose, threaten them in similar ways-always trying to get things straight, always trying to name the unspeakable. The Chinese I know hide their names; sojourners take new names when their lives change and guard their real names with silence.

Chinese-Americans, when you try to understand what things in you are Chinese, how do you separate what is peculiar to childhood, to poverty, insanities, one family, your mother who marked your growing with stories, from what is Chinese? What is Chinese tradition and what is the movies?

If I want to learn what clothes my aunt wore, whether flashy or ordinary, I would have to begin, "Remember Father's drowned-in-the-well sister?" I cannot ask that. My mother has told me once and for all the useful parts. She will add nothing unless powered by Necessity, a riverbank that guides her life. She plants vegetable gardens rather than lawns; she carries the odd-shaped tomatoes home from the fields and eats food left for the gods.

---

① the spirits-of-the-broom: 扫帚星。
② plug up: 堵塞,阻塞。

Whenever we did frivolous things, we used up energy; we flew high kites. We children came up off the ground over the melting cones our parents brought home from work and the American movie on New Year's Day—Oh, You Beautiful Doll with Betty Grable① one year, and She Wore a Yellow Ribbon with John Wayne② another year. After the one carnival ride each, we paid in guilt; our tired father counted his change on the dark walk home.

Adultery is extravagance. Could people who hatch their own chicks and eat the embryos and the heads for delicacies and boil the feet in vinegar for party food, leaving only the gravel, eating even the gizzard lining③—could such people engender a prodigal aunt? To be a woman, to have a daughter in starvation time was a waste enough. My aunt could not have been the lone romantic who gave up everything for sex. Women in the old China did not choose. Some man had commanded her to lie with him and be his secret evil. I wonder whether he masked himself when he joined the raid on her family.

Perhaps she had encountered him in the fields or on the mountain where the daughters-in-law collected fuel. Or perhaps he first noticed her in the marketplace. He was not a stranger because the village housed no strangers. She had to have dealings with him other than sex. Perhaps he worked an adjoining field, or he sold her the cloth for the dress she sewed and wore. His demand must have surprised, then terrified her. She obeyed him; she always did as she was told.

When the family found a young man in the next village to be her husband, she had stood tractably beside the best rooster, his proxy, and promised before they met that she would be his forever. She was lucky that he was her age and she would be the first wife, an advantage secure now. The night she first saw him, he had sex with her. Then he left for America. She had almost forgotten what he looked like. When she tried to envision him, she only saw the black and white face in the group photograph the men had had taken before leaving.

The other man was not, after all, much different from her husband. They both gave orders: she followed. "If you tell your family, I'll beat you. I'll kill you. Be here again next week." No one talked sex, ever. And she might have separated the rapes from the rest of living if only she did not have to buy her oil from him or gather wood in the same forest. I want her fear to have lasted just as long as rape lasted so that the fear could have been contained. No drawn-out fear. But women at sex hazarded birth

---

① Betty Grable: (1916~1973) a famous Hollywood actress of the 1930s and 1940s.
② John Wayne: (1907~1973) one of the genuine icons of 20th-century American film, famous as the tough hero in the western movies(约翰·韦恩，美国电影演员，曾扮演若干极具男子汉气概的角色).
③ gizzard lining: 鸡嗉子、鸡内金。

and hence lifetimes. The fear did not stop but permeated everywhere. She told the man, "I think I'm pregnant!" He organized the raid against her.

On nights when my mother and father talked about their life back home, sometimes they mentioned an "outcast table" whose business they still seemed to be settling, their voices tight. In a commensal tradition①, where food is precious, the powerful older people made wrongdoers eat alone. Instead of letting them start separate new lives like the Japanese, who could become samurais and geishas②, the Chinese family, faces averted but eyes glowering sideways, hung on to the offenders and fed them leftovers. My aunt must have lived in the same house as my parents and eaten at an outcast table. My mother spoke about the raid as if she had seen it, when she and my aunt, a daughter-in-law to a different household, should not have been living together at all. Daughters-in-law lived with their husbands' parents, not their own; a synonym for marriage in Chinese is "taking a daughter-in-law!" Her husband's parents could have sold her, mortgaged her, stoned her. But they had sent her back to her own mother and father, a mysterious act hinting at disgraces not told me. Perhaps they had thrown her out to deflect the avengers.

She was the only daughter; her four brothers went with her father, husband, and uncles "out on the road" and for some years became western men. When the goods were divided among the family, three of the brothers took land, and the youngest, my father, chose an education. After my grandparents gave their daughter away to her husband's family, they had dispensed all the adventure and all the property. They expected her alone to keep the traditional ways, which her brothers, now among the barbarians, could fumble without detection. The heavy, deep-rooted women were to maintain the past against the flood, safe for returning. But the rare urge west had fixed upon our family, and so my aunt crossed boundaries not delineated in space.

The work of preservation demands that the feelings playing about in one's guts not be turned into action. Just watch their passing like cherry blossoms. But perhaps my aunt, my forerunner, caught in a slow life, let dreams grow and fade and after some months or years went toward what persisted. Fear at the enormities of the forbidden kept her desires delicate, wire and bone③. She looked at a man because she liked the way the hair was tucked behind his ears, or she liked the question-mark line of a long torso curving at the shoulder and straight at the hip. For warm eyes or a soft voice or a slow walk—that's all—a few hairs, a line, a brightness, a sound, a pace, she gave up family. She offered us up for a charm that vanished with tiredness, a pigtail that didn't

---

① commensal tradition: 共餐传统。
② samurais and geishas: 日本武士和艺妓。
③ wire and bone: 汤亭亭的自创词,可理解为"(姑姑的欲望)就像电流一样,强烈且入骨三分"。

toss when the wind died. Why, the wrong lighting could erase the dearest thing about him.

It could very well have been, however, that my aunt did not take subtle enjoyment of her friend, but, a wild woman, kept rollicking company. Imagining her free with sex doesn't fit, though. I don't know any women like that, or men either. Unless I see her life branching into mine, she gives me no ancestral help.

To sustain her being in love, she often worked at herself in the mirror, guessing at the colors and shapes that would interest him, changing them frequently in order to hit on the right combination. She wanted him to look back.

On a farm near the sea, a woman who tended her appearance reaped a reputation for eccentricity. All the married women blunt-cut their hair in flaps about their ears or pulled it backin tight buns. No nonsense. Neither style blew easily into heart-catching tangles. And at their weddings they displayed themselves in their long hair for the last time. "It brushed the backs of my knees," My mother tells me. "It was braided, and even so, it brushed the backs of my knees!"

At the mirror my aunt combed individuality into her bob. A bun could have been contrived to escape into black streamers blowing in the wind or in quiet wisps about her face, but only the older women in our picture album wear buns. She brushed her hair back from her forehead, tucking the flaps behind her ears. She looped a piece of thread, knotted into a circle between her index fingers and thumbs, and ran the double strand across her forehead. When she closed her fingers as if she were making a pair of shadow geese bite, the string twisted together catching the little hairs[①]. Then she pulled the thread away from her skin, ripping the hairs out neatly, her eyes watering from the needles of pain. Opening her fingers, she cleaned the thread, then rolled it along her hairline and the tops of her eyebrows. My mother did the same to me and my sisters and herself. I used to believe that the expression "caught by the short hairs"[②] meant a captive held with a depilatory string. It especially hurt at the temples, but my mother said we were lucky we didn't have to have our feet bound[③] when we were seven. Sisters used to sit on their beds and cry together, she said, as their mothers or their slaves removed the bandages for a few minutes each night and let the blood gush back into their veins. 1 hope that the man my aunt loved appreciated a smooth brow, that he wasn't just a tits-and-ass man[④].

---

① the string twisted together catching the little hairs: 细线交互缠绞，拔脸上的汗毛。此处指一种古老的美容方式——绞脸，即用线除去妇女脸上的汗毛。过去，我国很多地方都有妇女婚前绞脸的习俗。
② caught by the short hairs: 被某人抓住小辫子（把柄）。
③ have our feet bound: 缠足。
④ a tits-and-ass man: a man who is only interested in women's bodies（一个只对女人的肉体感兴趣的男人）。

Once my aunt found a freckle on her chin, at a spot that the almanac said predestined her for unhappiness. She dug it out with a hot needle and washed the wound with peroxide.

More attention to her looks than these pullings of hairs and pickings at spots would have caused gossip among the villagers. They owned work clothes and good clothes, and they wore good clothes for feasting the new seasons. But since a woman combing her hair hexes beginnings, my aunt rarely found an occasion to look her best. Women looked like great sea snails-the corded wood, babies, and laundry they carried were the whorls on their backs. The Chinese did not admire a bent back; goddesses and warriors stood straight. Still there must have been a marvelous freeing of beauty when a worker laid down her burden and stretched and arched.

Such commonplace loveliness, however, was not enough for my aunt. She dreamed of a lover for the fifteen days of New Year's, the time for families to exchange visits, money, and food. She plied her secret comb. And sure enough she cursed the year, the family, the village, and herself.

Even as her hair lured her imminent lover, many other men looked at her. Uncles, cousins, nephews, brothers would have looked, too, had they been home between journeys. Perhaps they had already been restraining their curiosity, and they left, fearful that their glances, like a field of nesting birds, might be startled and caught. Poverty hurt, and that was their first reason for leaving. But another, final reason for leaving the crowded house was the never-said.

She may have been unusually beloved, the precious only daughter, spoiled and mirror gazing because of the affection the family lavished on her. When her husband left, they welcomed the chance to take her back from the in-laws; she could live like the little daughter for just a while longer. There are stories that my grandfather was different from other people, "crazy ever since the little Jap[①] bayoneted him in the head." He used to put his naked penis on the dinner table, laughing. And one day he brought home a baby girl, wrapped up inside his brown western-style greatcoat. He had traded one of his sons, probably my father, the youngest, for her. My grandmother made him trade back. When he finally got a daughter of his own, he doted on her. They must have all loved her, except perhaps my father, the only brother who never went back to China, having once been traded for a girl.

Brothers and sisters, newly men and women, had to efface their sexual color and present plain miens. Disturbing hair and eyes, a smile like no other, threatened the ideal of five generations living under one roof. To focus blurs, people shouted

---

① Jap: an offensive word for a Japanese person(日本鬼子).

face to face and yelled from room to room. The immigrants I know have loud voices, unmodulated to American tones even after years away from the village where they called their friendships out across the fields. I have not been able to stop my mother's screams in public libraries or over telephones. Walking erect (knees straight, toes pointed forward, not pigeon-toed①, which is Chinese-feminine) and speaking in an inaudible voice, I have tried to turn myself American-feminine. Chinese communication was loud, public. Only sick people had to whisper. But at the dinner table, where the family members came nearest one another, no one could talk, not the outcasts nor any eaters. Every word that falls from the mouth is a coin lost. Silently they gave and accepted food with both hands. A preoccupied child who took his bowl with one hand got a sideways glare. A complete moment of total attention is due everyone alike. Children and lovers have no singularity here, but my aunt used a secret voice, a separate attentiveness.

  She kept the man's name to herself throughout her labor and dying; she did not accuse him that he be punished with her. To save her inseminator's② name she gave silent birth.

  He may have been somebody in her own household, but intercourse with a man outside the family would have been no less abhorrent. All the village were kinsmen, and the titles shouted in loud country voices never let kinship be forgotten. Any man within visiting distance would have been neutralized as a lover—"brother", "younger brother", "older brother"—one hundred and fifteen relationship titles. Parents researched birth charts probably not so much to assure good fortune as to circumvent incest in a population that has but one hundred surnames. Everybody has eight million relatives. How useless then sexual mannerisms, how dangerous.

  As if it came from an atavism③ deeper than fear, I used to add "brother" silently to boys' names. It hexed the boys, who would or would not ask me to dance, and made them less scary and as familiar and deserving of benevolence as girls.

  But, of course, I hexed myself also—no dates. I should have stood up, both arms waving, and shouted out across libraries, "Hey, you! Love me back." I had no idea, though, how to make attraction selective, how to control its direction and magnitude. If I made myself American-pretty so that the five or six Chinese boys in the class fell in love with me, everyone else-the Caucasian④, Negro, and Japanese boys—would too. Sisterliness, dignified and honorable, made much more sense.

---

① pigeon-toed: 脚趾向内弯的，内八字脚的。
② inseminator: 授精人。此处指与姑姑通奸并使其怀孕的人。
③ atavism: 隔代遗传。
④ Caucasian: a member of the Caucasoid race; a white person（白种人）。

Attraction eludes control so stubbornly that whole societies designed to organize relationships among people cannot keep order, not even when they bind people to one another from childhood and raise them together. Among the very poor and the wealthy, brothers married their adopted sisters, like doves. Our family allowed some romance, paying adult brides' prices and providing dowries so that their sons and daughters could marry strangers. Marriage promises to turn strangers into friendly relatives-a nation of siblings.

In the village structure, spirits shimmered among the live creatures, balanced and held in equilibrium by time and land. But one human being flaring up into violence could open up a black hole, a maelstrom that pulled in the sky. The frightened villagers, who depended on one another to maintain the real, went to my aunt to show her a personal, physical representation of the break she had made in the "roundness". Misallying couples① snapped off the future, which was to be embodied in true offspring. The villagers punished her for acting as if she could have a private life, secret and apart from them.

If my aunt had betrayed the family at a time of large grain yields and peace, when many boys were born, and wings were being built on many houses, perhaps she might have escaped such severe punishment. But the men—hungry, greedy, tired of planting in dry soil—had been forced to leave the village in order to send food-money home. There were ghost plagues, bandit plagues, wars with the Japanese, floods. My Chinese brother and sister had died of an unknown sickness. Adultery, perhaps only a mistake during good times, became a crime when the village needed food.

The round moon cakes and round doorways, the round tables of graduated sizes② that fit one roundness inside an other, round windows and rice bowls-these talismans had lost their power to warn this family of the law: a family must be whole, faithfully keeping the descent line by having sons to feed the old and the dead, who in turn look after the family. The villagers came to show my aunt and her lover-in-hiding a broken house. The villagers were speeding up the circling of events because she was too shortsighted to see that her infidelity had already harmed the village, that waves of consequences would return unpredictably, sometimes in disguise, as now, to hurt her. This roundness had to be made coin-sized so that she would see its circumference: punish her at the birth of her baby. Awaken her to the inexorable. People who refused fatalism because they could invent small resources insisted on culpability. Deny accidents and wrest fault from the stars.

After the villagers left, their lanterns now scattering in various directions toward

---

① Misallying couples: 不适当结成的一对。此处指非婚结合的一对，比如姑姑和她的情人。
② the round tables of graduated sizes: 套桌，桌子里套桌子。

home, the family broke their silence and cursed her. "Aiaa, we're going to die. Death is coming. Death is coming. Look what you've done. You've killed us. Ghost! Dead ghost! Ghost! You've never been born." She ran out into the fields, far enough from the house so that she could no longer hear their voices, and pressed herself against the earth, her own land no more. When she felt the birth coming, she thought that she had been hurt. Her body seized together. "They've hurt me too much," she thought. "This is gall①, and it will kill me." With forehead and knees against the earth, her body convulsed and then relaxed. She turned on her back, lay on the ground. The black well of sky and stars went out and out and out forever; her body and her complexity seemed to disappear. She was one of the stars, a bright dot in blackness, without home, without a companion, in eternal cold and silence. An agoraphobia② rose in her, speeding higher and higher, bigger and bigger; she would not be able to contain it; there would no end to fear.

Flayed, unprotected against space, she felt pain return, focusing her body. This pain chilled her—a cold, steady kind of surface pain. Inside, spasmodically, the other pain, the pain of the child, heated her. For hours she lay on the ground, alternately body and space. Sometimes a vision of normal comfort obliterated reality: she saw the family in the evening gambling at the dinner table, the young people massaging their elders' backs. She saw them congratulating one another, high joy on the mornings the rice shoots came up. When these pictures burst, the stars drew yet further apart. Black space opened.

She got to her feet to fight better and remembered that old-fashioned women gave birth in their pigsties to fool the jealous, pain-dealing gods, who do not snatch piglets. Before the next spasms could stop her, she ran to the pigsty, each step a rushing out into emptiness. She climbed over the fence and knelt in the dirt. It was good to have a fence enclosing her, a tribal person alone.

Laboring, this woman who had carried her child as a foreign growth that sickened her every day, expelled it at last. She reached down to touch the hot, wet, moving mass, surely smaller than anything human, and could feel that it was human after all—fingers, toes, nails, nose. She pulled it up on to her belly, and it lay curled there, butt in the air, feet precisely tucked one under the other. She opened her loose shirt and buttoned the child inside. After resting, it squirmed and thrashed and she pushed it up to her breast. It turned its head this way and that until it found her nipple. There, it made little snuffling noises. She clenched her teeth at its preciousness, lovely as a young calf, a piglet, a little dog.

---

① gall: a bitter feeling full of hatred(怨恨).
② agoraphobia: 公共场所恐惧(症)。

She may have gone to the pigsty as a last act of responsibility: she would protect this child as she had protected its father. It would look after her soul, leaving supplies on her grave. But how would this tiny child without family find her grave when there would be no marker for her anywhere, neither in the earth nor the family hall? No one would give her a family hall name. She had taken the child with her into the wastes. At its birth the two of them had felt the same raw pain of separation, a wound that only the family pressing tight could close. A child with no descent line would not soften her life but only trail after her, ghostlike, begging her to give it purpose. At dawn the villagers on their way to the fields would stand around the fence and look.

Full of milk, the little ghost slept. When it awoke, she hardened her breasts against the milk that crying loosens. Toward morning she picked up the baby and walked to the well.

Carrying the baby to the well shows loving. Otherwise abandon it. Turn its face into the mud. Mothers who love their children take them along. It was probably a girl; there is some hope of forgiveness for boys.

"Don't tell anyone you had an aunt. Your father does not want to hear her name. She has never been born." I have believed that sex was unspeakable and words so strong and fathers so frail that "aunt" would do my father mysterious harm. I have thought that my family, having settled among immigrants who had also been their neighbors in the ancestral land, needed to clean their name, and a wrong word would incite the kinspeople even here. But there is more to this silence: they want me to participate in her punishment. And I have.

In the twenty years since I heard this story I have not asked for details nor said my aunt's name; I do not know it. People who can comfort the dead can also chase after them to hurt them further—a reverse ancestor worship. The real punishment was not the raid swiftly inflicted by the villagers, but the family's deliberately forgetting her. Her betrayal so maddened them, they saw to it that she would suffer forever, even after death. Always hungry, always needing, she would have to beg food from other ghosts, snatch and steal it from those whose living descendants give them gifts. She would have to fight the ghosts massed at crossroads for the buns a few thoughtful citizens leave to decoy her away from village and home so that the ancestral spirits could feast unharassed. At peace, they could act like gods, not ghosts, their descent lines providing them with paper suits and dresses, spirit money, paper houses, paper automobiles, chicken, meat, and rice into eternity essences delivered up in smoke and flames, steam and incense rising from each rice bowl. In an attempt to make the Chinese care for people outside the family, Chairman Mao encourages us now to give our paper replicas① to the spirits of outstanding soldiers and workers, no matter whose ancestors they may be. My aunt remains forever hungry. Goods are not distributed evenly among the dead.

My aunt haunts me—her ghost drawn to me because now, after fifty years of neglect, I alone devote pages of paper to her, though not origamied② into houses and clothes. 1 do not think she always means me well. I am telling on her, and she was a spite suicide, drowning herself in the drinking water. The Chinese are always very frightened of the drowned one, whose weeping ghost, wet hair hanging and skin bloated, waits silently by the water to pull down a substitute.

译文链接: https://e.dangdang.com/pc/reader/index.html?id=1901109190

Questions for Understanding

1. Who is "no name woman"? Why is she a "no name woman"? What has happened to her?
2. Why does the mother tell the narrator this story? What message does it send?
3. How does the narrator think of the story of her aunt? Does she approve of her mother's judgment of her aunt? Why?
4. Why does the narrator say that she has participated in her aunt's punishment? What does she do as a compensation to her aunt?
5. What is the living situation of the women in the traditional Chinese culture described in the book? Is it a true description or a distorted one? Defend your answer with examples from the story.

Aspects of Appreciation

1. The narration in this chapter moves back and forth between past and present, fact and fiction, Kingston's life in the new land and the Old China where her aunt lived, serving as a backdrop for Kingston's experience growing up as a Chinese American, torn between the traditional Chinese culture and the permissive American one, and struggling to reconcile the conflict between these two disparate cultures. Since her childhood, her mother Brave Orchid, deeply influenced by the cultural traditions of China, has constantly told her many "talk-stories" in order to pass on

---

① paper replicas: 纸钱。
② origami: 日本折纸艺术。本句指叙述者"我"没有用纸折成房子和衣物来祭奠姑姑,而是用纸记录下她的故事。

to her codes of proper conduct and values. For instance, in this case, Brave Orchid recounts the aunt's story, especially the severe punishment she suffered in order to show the great consequences of promiscuity, and thus discourage the young Kingston from engaging in premarital sex. However, since Kingston was born and brought up in the new land, to her sensibilities, the stories are so confusing that she begins to interpret the story according to the values she has learned, namely, individualism and a strong sense of womanhood, and rewrites the story from her own perspective, providing several sympathetic reasons to justify her aunt's wrongdoing: she might be a victim who was threatened and raped by a certain relative, or perhaps she was a fighter who was courageous enough to go against the restrictions and pursue her true love. What's more, Kingston goes on to explain her aunt's suicide, claiming that her choice of ending her life in the family's well might be a way to take revenge on the whole family by contaminating their drinking water.

2. The theme of silence and voice is revealed by the first sentence of the book, "You must not tell anyone". It's very ironic, for by writing these words down, Kingston is actually telling everyone about her family secret that her aunt gave birth to an illegitimate child and was severely punished by her villagers and family members. From then on, she has been deliberately forgotten by the whole family, and becomes a nameless woman whose story is kept as a family secret. However, by recounting the story of her aunt, Kingston breaks the long-term silence imposed on her aunt. With her fantastic imagination, she adds something more to her mother's version, hypothesizes the impetus for why her aunt was involved in the adultery, and thus saves this silenced woman from obscurity and gives her a voice to justify her behavior.

3. Through the story of "no name woman", Kingston exposes the unfair gender discrimination in traditional Chinese society, which valued men highly while treating women as worthless and inferior. In this patrilineal society permeated with patriarchal ideology, women were doomed to be victims, living in the subordinate status, bearing much burden of looking after family members and obeying all the rules prescribed by the society. Any improper behavior was considered a breach of these rules, and could result in severe punishment. As is shown in her aunt's case, because she violated the code of conduct and committed adultery, the villagers ransacked her family's house, and her family members deserted her. Out of desperation, she was forced to commit suicide by throwing herself and her newly-born infant down into the well. Kingston further argues that actually it is the patriarchal society that should take full responsibility for her aunt's adultery. She might be threatened by some man in the

village, but as a woman accustomed to doing everything she was told, she was unable to pluck up enough courage to resistthe sexual harassment. This submissive behavior well illustrates the low social status of women in Old China: "they did not choose. Some man had commanded her to lie with him and be his secret evil…She obeyed him; she always did as she was told."

Suggested Further Reading

China Men (1980); *Tripmaster Monkey: His Fake Book* (1990)

Topics for Further Study

1. Kingston writes: "Those of us in the first American generations have had to figure out how the invisible world the emigrants built around our childhoods fits in solid America". Consider this statement and the subtitle of the book: "A Girlhood Among Ghosts", and try to find the underlying meaning of the subtitle.

2. *The Woman Warrior* involves several well-known Chinese tales, such as those about Fa Mulan and Ts'ai Yen. However, such tales are not narrated as exactly as what we Chinese are familiar with. Instead, they are, to some degree, rewritten by the author. Choose one of the stories and compare it with the original version, and try to find the differences and the underlying reason of such rewriting.

3. In "Cultural Mis-Reading by American Reviewers", an essay published in *Asian and Western Writers in Dialogue: New Cultural Identities* (1982), Kingston criticizes those critics who find her work exotic and foreign. She states, "*The Woman Warrior* is an American book… Yet many reviewers do not see the American-ness of it, nor the fact of my own American-ness." What are some of the American elements in this work? Do you agree with Kingston's opinion?

4. Throughout *The Woman Warrior*, Kingston explores how her Chinese cultural history can be reconciled with her emerging sense of herself as an American. Is she successful in this endeavor? Support your answer with examples from the novel.

Knowledge of Literature

Feminist Criticism（女性主义批评）

Feminist Criticism was inaugurated in European and American literary circles in the 1960s. Deeply influenced by the Second Wave of feminism, critics such as Kate Millett, Elaine Showalter, and Hélène Cixous, inheriting the rebellious spirit of such precursors as Virginia Woolf and Simone de Beauvoir who have bluntly revealed how patriarchal ideology defines and rules women in all cultural domains, call attention to the unjust and distorted images of females in works of literature, especially works authored by males, attach importance to literary works by females and try to delineate a female poetics.

Although feminist critics' ideas vary, feminists share some assumptions and concepts. Firstly, patriarchal ideology pervades all domains including politics, economy, society and culture. It has given men authority and privilege and put women in a subordinate and oppressed position. Secondly, the prevailing concepts of gender, different from sex, which is biologically determined, are largely cultural constructs. The male has been widely identified as active, dominating, self-assertive, adventurous, rational, creative; the female is the Other, an object whose existence is defined and interpreted by the male. She has been identified as mindless, passive, helpless, timid, submissive, humble, emotional and conventional. Thirdly, under the influence of patriarchal ideology, derogatory stereotypes of women abound in the literary canon. Female characters are distorted into either angels or sirens, acting as marginal and subordinate characters. Lastly, feminist criticism aims to challenge and criticize the patriarchal ideology prevalent in culture and literature, oppose patriarchal sexual norms and gender roles, and create a society in which not only the male but also the female voice is equally valued.

When analyzing a literary text from the perspective of feminist criticism, we can begin textual analysis by asking some general questions, such as these:

1. Is the author male or female? Is the text narrated by a male or female?
2. Are the female characters depicted in the text the leading characters or minor ones? Do any stereotypical characterizations of women appear? Does such portrayal reveal the author's sexism?
3. How do male characters treat female ones? Does the author have the same attitude toward women as the male characters?
4. Does the text disseminate or challenge patriarchal ideology? How does the author's culture influence her or his attitude?

推荐阅读的论文：

[1] 程梅，李静．"无名女子"之名——《女勇士》和《等待野蛮人》中的女性主义叙事 [J]．天津外国语大学学报，2016(4)．
[2] 龙娟，刘蓓蓓．美国早期华人的性别形象建构——以《女勇士》与《中国佬》为镜像 [J]．当代外国文学，2017(2)．

Alice Walker (1944~)

About the Author

In 1952, Alice Walker, at the age of eight, was accidentally wounded by a BB gun. Although this accident has caused permanent blindness in the right eye, life has made up for her in a special way. The experience of this facial transfiguration has prompted her to begin "really to see people and things, really to notice relationships and to learn to be patient enough to care about how they turned out", and to manage to use her blinded eye as a filter through which she has looked beyond the surface of ordinary African American women's lives and discovered the underlying agony and happiness in their struggles in a sexist and racist society.

Born as the youngest of eight children of a southern sharecropper family, Alice Walker spent her childhood in extreme poverty and racism. The adversity didn't hinder her from setting forth the journey to success. As an excellent student, she secured a scholarship to Spelman, a traditional Black college, and later to Sarah Lawrence College in New York, where she got interested in the burgeoning Civil Rights Movement and became an active champion for the rights of her fellows, especially the Black women. After graduation, she continued her involvement with the movement, working for black voter registration drives in Georgia and for the Welfare Department.

Since 1968, Walker has taken up her career as a teacher as well as a writer in residence in a number of colleges, including Jackson State College, Tougaloo College, and so forth. It was during these teaching years that her literary career began to blossom. In 1970, she published the first novel *The Third Life of Grange Copeland*, chronicling the hard life of three generations of an African American family in the society permeated with racial discrimination. Three years later, her first collection of stories *In Love and Trouble* came out. As the subtitle *Stories of Black Women* suggests, it recounts a series of stories centering on the victories and tribulations of African American women, a topic which later recurred in many of her writings. In later years she wrote the novel *Meridian* (1976) and the short-story collection *You can't Keep a Good Woman Down* (1981), in which Walker continued to explore in detail the struggles of African American women amidst the backdrop of social and familial oppression.

It's in her much-admired novel *The Color Purple* (1982) that these themes are deftly interweaved together into an appealing masterpiece. Written in epistolary form, it mainly records an inspiring story of Celie, a southern black woman, who underwent a painful transformation from a submissive victim suffering endless oppression and abuse at the hands of men, into a courageous warrior claiming self-value and self-assertion. Notable for its masterful recreation of black vernacular speech and ingenious use of the epistolary convention, this novel won enormous critical and public success, and was later adapted into a hit movie directed by Steven Spielberg. While garnering warm applauses, the novel also unleashed a storm of controversy. Many critics attacked it for the negative portrayal of Black males, the frank defense of lesbianism and explicit description of incestuous violence.

Since then, Walker has continued her exploration of the unique experiences of black women, and has accomplished a number of works, the most famous ones including a collection of essays entitled *In Search of Our Mothers' Gardens: Womanist Prose*(1983), recording her experiences and observations of black American women's culture, and four novels *The Temple of My Familiar* (1989), *Possessing the Secret of Joy*(1990), *By the Light of My Father's Smile* (1994), and *Now Is the Time to Open Your Heart* (2004). Though as a prolific writer her works cover a variety of genres including poetry, fiction, criticism, screenwriting and children's literature, her major concern has never changed, always focusing on the struggles and spiritual development of African American women suffering "twin afflictions" of sexism and racism.

In the introduction to *In Search of Our Mother's Gardens*, Alice Walker defines "womanist", the term coined by herself for the black feminist, as one who "appreciates and prefers women's culture, women's emotional flexibility…women's strength", And true to her word, as a restless crusader on behalf of women, Walker has managed to use her life and impressive works to prove that she is the most deserved one for this title.

Everyday Use

About the Story

First published in Walker's collection *In Love and Trouble: Stories of Black Women* (1973), "Everyday Use" is generally acclaimed as the most representative of Walker's short fiction. Told in first person by an uneducated African-American mother, it humorously recounts a story of three women's differing views about their cultural heritage.

Everyday Use

For Your Grandmama

I will wait for her in the yard that Maggie and I made so clean and wavy yesterday afternoon. A yard like this is more comfortable than most people know. It is not just a yard. It is like an extended living room. When the hard clay is swept clean as a floor and the fine sand around the edges lined with tiny, irregular grooves, anyone can come and sit and look up into the elm tree and wait for the breezes that never come inside the house.

Maggie will be nervous until after her sister goes: she will stand hopelessly in corners, homely① and ashamed of the burn scars down her arms and legs, eying her sister with a mixture of envy and awe. She thinks her sister has held life always in the palm of one hand, that "no" is a word the world never learned to say to her.

You've no doubt seen those TV shows where the child who has "made it" is confronted, as a surprise, by her own mother and father, tottering in weakly from backstage. (A pleasant surprise, of course: What would they do if parent and child came on the show only to curse out and insult each other?) On TV mother and child embrace and smile into each other's faces. Sometimes the mother and father weep, the child wraps them in her arms and leans across the table to tell how she would not have made it without their help. I have seen these programs.

Sometimes I dream a dream in which Dee and I are suddenly brought together on a TV program of this sort. Out of a dark and soft-seated limousine② I am ushered into a bright room filled with many people. There I meet a smiling, gray, sporty man like Johnny Carson③ who shakes my hand and tells me what a fine girl I have. Then we are on the stage and Dee is embracing me with tears in her eyes. She pins on my dress a large orchid, even though she has told me once that she thinks orchids are tacky④ flowers.

In real life I am a large, big-boned woman with rough, man-working hands. In the winter I wear flannel nightgowns to bed and overalls during the day. I can kill and clean a hog as mercilessly as a man. My fat keeps me hot in zero weather. I can work outside all day, breaking ice to get water for washing; I can eat pork liver cooked over

---

① homely: (of people, faces, etc.,) not good-looking, not attractive（相貌平平的）.
② limousine: a large and very comfortable car, especially one with a glass screen between the front and back seats（豪华轿车）.
③ Johnny Carson (1925~2005): the famous American television host and comedian, known as host of NBC's "The Tonight Show" for over thirty years. 约翰尼·卡森，美国著名的节目主持人，曾主持美国国家广播公司（NBC）深夜时段著名脱口秀节目《今夜秀》。
④ tacky: lacking style or good taste（俗气的）.

the open fire minutes after it comes steaming from the hog. One winter I knocked a bull calf straight in the brain between the eyes with a sledge hammer and had the meat hung up to chill before nightfall. But of course all this does not show on television. I am the way my daughter would want me to be: a hundred pounds lighter, my skin like an uncooked barley pancake. My hair glistens in the hot bright lights. Johnny Carson has much to do to keep up with my quick and witty tongue.

But that is a mistake. I know even before I wake up. Who ever knew a Johnson with a quick tongue? Who can even imagine me looking a strange white man in the eye? It seems to me I have talked to them always with one foot raised in flight[①], with my head turned in whichever way is farthest from them. Dee, though. She would always look anyone in the eye. Hesitation was no part of her nature.

"How do I look, Mama?" Maggie says, showing just enough of her thin body enveloped in pink skirt and red blouse for me to know she's there, almost hidden by the door.

"Come out into the yard," I say.

Have you ever seen a lame animal, perhaps a dog run over by some careless person rich enough to own a car, sidle up[②] to someone who is ignorant enough to be kind to him? That is the way my Maggie walks. She has been like this, chin on chest, eyes on ground, feet in shuffle, ever since the fire that burned the other house to the ground.

Dee is lighter than Maggie, with nicer hair and a fuller figure. She's a woman now, though sometimes I forget. How long ago was it that the other house burned? Ten, twelve years? Sometimes I can still hear the flames and feel Maggie's arms sticking to me, her hair smoking and her dress falling off her in little black papery flakes. Her eyes seemed stretched open, blazed open by the flames reflected in them. And Dee. I see her standing off under the sweet gum tree she used to dig gum out of; a look of concentration on her face as she watched the last dingy gray board of the house fall in toward the red-hot brick chimney. Why don't you do a dance around the ashes? I'd wanted to ask her. She had hated the house that much.

I used to think she hated Maggie, too. But that was before we raised money, the church and me, to send her to Augusta to school. She used to read to us without pity; forcing words, lies, other folks' habits, whole lives upon us two, sitting trapped and

---

① with one foot raised in flight: ready to leave as quickly as possible because of nervousness, timidity and discomfort.
② sidle up: move up sideways, especially in a shy or stealthy manner(悄悄靠近). If you sidle somewhere, you walk there uncertainly or cautiously, as if you do not want anyone to notice you.

ignorant underneath her voice. She washed us in a river of make-believe①, burned us with a lot of knowledge we didn't necessarily need to know. Pressed us to her with the serious way she read, to shove us away at just the moment, like dimwits②, we seemed about to understand.

　　Dee wanted nice things. A yellow organdy dress to wear to her graduation from high school; black pumps to match a green suit she'd made from an old suit somebody gave me. She was determined to stare down any disaster in her efforts. Her eyelids would not flicker for minutes at a time. Often I fought off the temptation to shake her③. At sixteen she had a style of her own: and knew what style was.

　　I never had an education myself. After second grade the school was closed down. Don't ask my why: in 1927 colored④ asked fewer questions than they do now. Sometimes Maggie reads to me. She stumbles along good-naturedly but can't see well. She knows she is not bright. Like good looks and money, quickness passes her by. She will marry John Thomas (who has mossy teeth in an earnest face) and then I'll be free to sit here and I guess just sing church songs to myself. Although I never was a good singer. Never could carry a tune. I was always better at a man's job. I used to love to milk till I was hooked in the side⑤ in '49. Cows are soothing and slow and don't bother you, unless you try to milk them the wrong way.

　　I have deliberately turned my back on the house. It is three rooms, just like the one that burned, except the roof is tin; they don't make shingle roofs any more. There are no real windows, just some holes cut in the sides, like the portholes in a ship, but not round and not square, with rawhide holding the shutters up on the outside. This house is in a pasture, too, like the other one. No doubt when Dee sees it she will want to tear it down. She wrote me once that no matter where we "choose" to live, she will manage to come see us. But she will never bring her friends. Maggie and I thought about this and Maggie asked me, "Mama, when did Dee ever have any friends?"

　　She had a few. Furtive boys in pink shirts hanging about on washday⑥ after school. Nervous girls who never laughed. Impressed with her they worshiped the well-turned phrase, the cute shape, the scalding humor that erupted like bubbles in lye. She read to them.

　　When she was courting Jimmy T she didn't have much time to pay to us, but turned all her faultfinding power on him. He flew to marry a cheap city girl from a

---

① make-believe: a state of pretending or imagining things（假装；想象）.
② dimwit: (infml.) an ignorant and stupid person（傻瓜）.
③ shake her: usually you shake somebody in order to arouse that person to the awareness of something.
④ colored: the black people.
⑤ I was hooked in the side: I was hit in the side by the cow.
⑥ washday: a day set aside for doing household washing（洗衣日）.

family of ignorant flashy people. She hardly had time to recompose herself.

When she comes I will meet—but there they are!

Maggie attempts to make a dash for the house, in her shuffling way, but I stay her with my hand. "Come back here," I say. And she stops and tries to dig a well in the sand with her toe.

It is hard to see them clearly through the strong sun. But even the first glimpse of leg out of the car tells me it is Dee. Her feet were always neat-looking, as if God himself had shaped them with a certain style. From the other side of the car comes a short, stocky man. Hair is all over his head a foot long and hanging from his chin like a kinky mule tail. I hear Maggie suck in her breath. "Uhnnnh, " is what it sounds like. Like when you see the wriggling end of a snake just in front of your foot on the road. "Uhnnnh."

Dee next. A dress down to the ground, in this hot weather. A dress so loud① it hurts my eyes. There are yellows and oranges enough to throw back the light of the sun. I feel my whole face warming from the heat waves it throws out. Earrings gold, too, and hanging down to her shoulders. Bracelets dangling and making noises when she moves her arm up to shake the folds of the dress out of her armpits. The dress is loose and flows, and as she walks closer, I like it. I hear Maggie go "Uhnnnh" again. It is her sister's hair. It stands straight up like the wool on a sheep. It is black as night and around the edges are two long pigtails that rope about like small lizards disappearing behind her ears.

"Wa-su-zo-Tean-o!"② She says, coming on in that gliding way the dress makes her move. The short stocky fellow with the hair to his navel is all grinning and he follows up with "Asalamalakim③, my mother and sister!" He moves to hug Maggie but she falls back, right up against the back of my chair. I feel her trembling there and when I look up I see the perspiration falling off her chin.

"Don't get up," says Dee. Since I am stout it takes something of a push. You can see me trying to move a second or two before I make it. She turns, showing white heels through her sandals, and goes back to the car. Out she peeks next with a Polaroid④. She stoops down quickly and lines up picture after picture of me sitting there in front of the house with Maggie cowering behind me. She never takes a shot without making sure the house is included. When a cow comes nibbling around the edge of the yard

---

① loud: attracting attention by being unpleasantly colorful and bright(俗艳的、花哨的).
② Wa-su-zo-Tean-o: a salutation in an African dialect, meaning "Good morning".
③ Asalamalakim: a salutation in Arabic, meaning "Peace be with you". But here the mother mistook it as the name of Dee's boyfriend.
④ Polaroid: a camera which can produce a photograph within a few seconds(宝丽来照相机).

she snaps it and me and Maggie and the house. Then she puts the Polaroid in the back seat of the car, and comes up and kisses me on the forehead.

Meanwhile Asalamalakim is going through motions with Maggie's hand. Maggie's hand is as limp as a fish, and probably as cold, despite the sweat, and she keeps trying to pull it back. It looks like Asalamalakim wants to shake hands but wants to do it fancy. Or maybe he don't know how people shake hands. Anyhow, he soon gives up on Maggie.

"Well," I say. "Dee."

"No, Mama," she says. "Not 'Dee,' Wangero Leewanika Kemanjo!"

"What happened to 'Dee'?" I wanted to know.

"She's dead," Wangero said. "I couldn't bear it any longer, being named after the people who oppress me."

"You know as well as me you was named after your aunt Dicie," I said. Dicie is my sister. She named Dee. We called her "Big Dee" after Dee was born.

"But who was she named after?" asked Wangero.

"I guess after Grandma Dee," I said.

"And who was she named after?" Asked Wangero.

"Her mother," I said, and saw Wangero was getting tired. "That's about as far back as I can trace it," I said. Though, in fact, I probably could have carried it back beyond the Civil War through the branches.

"Well," said Asalamalakim, "there you are."

"Uhnnnh," I heard Maggie say.

"There I was not," I said, "before 'Dicie' cropped up in our family, so why should I try to trace it that far back?"

He just stood there grinning, looking down on me like somebody inspecting a Model A car①. Every once in a while he and Wangero sent eye signals over my head.

"How do you pronounce this name?" I asked.

"You don't have to call me by it if you don't want to," said Wangero.

"Why shouldn't I?" I asked. "If that's what you want us to call you, we'll call you."

"I know it might sound awkward at first," said Wangero.

"I'll get used to it," I said. "Ream② it out again."

Well, soon we got the name out of the way. Asalamalakim had a name twice as long and three times as hard. After I tripped over it two or three times he told me to just call him Hakim-a-barber. I wanted to ask him was he a barber, but I didn't really

---

① Model A car: a popular low-priced automobile introduced by the Ford Motor Company in 1927.
② ream: here it means "spell".

think he was, so I didn't ask.

"You must belong to those beef-cattle peoples down the road," I said. They said "Asalamalakim" when they met you, too, but they didn't shake hands. Always too busy: feeding the cattle, fixing the fences, putting up salt-lick shelters, throwing down hay. When the white folks poisoned some of the herd the men stayed up all night with rifles in their hands. I walked a mile and a half just to see the sight.

Hakim-a-barber said, "I accept some of their doctrines, but farming and raising cattle is not my style." (They didn't tell me, and I didn't ask, whether Wangero [Dee] had really gone and married him.)

We sat down to eat and right away he said he didn't eat collards and pork was unclean. Wangero, though, went on through the chitlins and com bread, the greens and everything else. She talked a blue streak[①] over the sweet potatoes. Everything delighted her. Even the fact that we still used the benches her daddy made for the table when we couldn't effort to buy chairs.

"Oh, Mama!" she cried. Then turned to Hakim-a-barber. "I never knew how lovely these benches are. You can feel the rump prints," she said, running her hands underneath her and along the bench. Then she gave a sigh and her hand closed over Grandma Dee's butter dish. "That's it!" she said. "I knew there was something I wanted to ask you if I could have." She jumped up from the table and went over in the corner where the churn stood, the milk in it crabber by now. She looked at the churn and looked at it.

"This churn top is what I need," she said. "Didn't Uncle Buddy whittle it out of a tree you all used to have?"

"Yes," I said.

"Un huh," she said happily. "And I want the dasher, too."

"Uncle Buddy whittle that, too?" asked the barber.

Dee (Wangero) looked up at me.

"Aunt Dee's first husband whittled the dash," said Maggie so low you almost couldn't hear her. "His name was Henry, but they called him Stash."

"Maggie's brain is like an elephant's[②]," Wangero said, laughing. "I can use the chute top as a centerpiece for the alcove table," she said, sliding a plate over the chute, "and I'll think of something artistic to do with the dasher."

When she finished wrapping the dasher the handle stuck out. I took it for a moment in my hands. You didn't even have to look close to see where hands pushing

---

① talk a blue streak: to talk much and rapidly（连珠炮似地说话）.
② Maggie's brain is like an elephant's: Elephants are said to have good memories. Here Dee is being ironic. 此处迪在说反话，讽刺梅格记性差。

the dasher up and down to make butter had left a kind of sink in the wood. In fact, there were a lot of small sinks; you could see where thumbs and fingers had sunk into the wood. It was beautiful light yellow wood, from a tree that grew in the yard where Big Dee and Stash had lived.

After dinner Dee (Wangero) went to the trunk at the foot of my bed and started rifling through it. Maggie hung back① in the kitchen over the dishpan. Out came Wangero with two quilts. They had been pieced by Grandma Dee and then Big Dee and me had hung them on the quilt frames on the front porch and quilted them. One was in the Lone Star pattern. The other was Walk Around the Mountain. In both of them were scraps of dresses Grandma Dee had won fifty and more years ago. Bits and pieces of Grandpa Jattell's Paisley shirts. And one teeny faded blue piece, about the size of a penny matchbox, that was from Great Grandpa Ezra's uniform that he wore in the Civil War.

"Mama," Wanegro said sweet as a bird. "Can I have these old quilts?"

I heard something fall in the kitchen, and a minute later the kitchen door slammed.

"Why don't you take one or two of the others?" I asked. "These old things was just done by me and Big Dee from some tops② your grandma pieced before she died."

"No," said Wangero. "I don't want those. They are stitched around the borders by machine."

"That'll make them last better," I said.

"That's not the point," said Wangero. "These are all pieces of dresses Grandma used to wear. She did all this stitching by hand. Imagine!" She held the quilts securely in her arms, stroking them.

"Some of the pieces, like those lavender ones, come from old clothes her mother handed down to her," I said, moving up to touch the quilts. Dee (Wangero) moved back just enough so that I couldn't reach the quilts. They already belonged to her.

"Imagine!" She breathed again, clutching them closely to her bosom.

"The truth is," I said, "I promised to give them quilts to Maggie, for when she marries John Thomas."

She gasped like a bee had stung her.

"Maggie can't appreciate these quilts!" She said. "She'd probably be backward enough to put them to everyday use."

"I reckon she would," I said. "God knows I been saving 'em for long enough with nobody using 'em. I hope she will!" I didn't want to bring up how I had offered Dee

---

① hang back: to be reluctant to advance, as from timidity and shyness.
② tops: referring to quilts. 此处指被子。

(Wangero) a quilt when she went away to college. Then she had told they were old-fashioned, out of style.

"But they're priceless!" She was saying now, furiously; for she has a temper. "Maggie would put them on the bed and in five years they'd be in rags. Less than that!"

"She can always make some more," I said. "Maggie knows how to quilt."

Dee (Wangero) looked at me with hatred. "You just will not understand. The point is these quilts, these quilts!"

"Well," I said, stumped. "What would you do with them?"

"Hang them," she said. As if that was the only thing you could do with quilts.

Maggie by now was standing in the door. I could almost hear the sound her feet made as they scraped over each other.

"She can have them, Mama," she said, like somebody used to never winning anything, or having anything reserved for her. "I can 'member Grandma Dee without the quilts."

I looked at her hard. She had filled her bottom lip with checkerberry snuff and gave her face a kind of dopey, hangdog look[①]. It was Grandma Dee and Big Dee who taught her how to quilt herself. She stood there with her scarred hands hidden in the folds of her skirt. She looked at her sister with something like fear but she wasn't mad at her. This was Maggie's portion. This was the way she knew God to work.

When I looked at her like that something hit me in the top of my head and ran down to the soles of my feet. Just like when I'm in church and the spirit of God touches me and I get happy and shout. I did something I never done before: hugged Maggie to me, then dragged her on into the room, snatched the quilts out of Miss Wangero's hands and dumped them into Maggie's lap. Maggie just sat there on my bed with her mouth open.

"Take one or two of the others," I said to Dee.

But she turned without a word and went out to Hakim-a-barber.

"You just don't understand," she said, as Maggie and I came out to the car.

"What don't I understand?" I wanted to know.

"Your heritage," she said, and then she turned to Maggie, kissed her, and said, "You ought to try to make something of yourself, too, Maggie. It's really a new day for us. But from the way you and Mama still live you'd never know it."

She put on some sunglasses that hid everything above the tip of her nose and chin. Maggie smiled; maybe at the sunglasses. But a real smile, not scared. After we

---

① dopey, hangdog look: 呆头呆脑的表情。

watched the car dust settle I asked Maggie to bring me a dip of snuff. And then the two of us sat there just enjoying, until it was time to go in the house and go to bed.

译文链接：https://zhuanlan.zhihu.com/p/94545584

Questions for Understanding

1. How many main characters are included in this story? Please describe each character's major traits.
2. Consider some of the positive and negative aspects of Dee's character, focusing in particular on her relationship with her family. Is anything implied about Dee in the passage describing the loss of their previous home?
3. In what ways do the two sisters differ from each other? Who do you like better? State your reasons.
4. What is the mother's feeling toward Dee? How does it change in the course of the story?
5. What's the symbolic meaning of the quilt? What are the different attitudes the two sisters have towards the quilt? Why does the mom give it to Maggie?
6. With whom does Alice Walker seem to side on the issue of heritage?

Aspects of Appreciation

  1. The two daughters, Dee and Maggie, form a sharp contrast in many conceivable aspects, for instance, their appearance, characters, and personal experiences. The elder daughter Dee is charming, smart, confident, aggressive and ambitious, while her sister Maggie, seeming to serve as a foil, is rather homely, uneducated, introverted and submissive. However, a closer observation of their values reveals that Maggie outweighs Dee to a larger extent. Deeply influenced by the White culture, Dee is dissatisfied with almost all that she was born with, including the old house, her lame sister, her crude and illiterate mother, and so forth, and knowing little about her root and culture. In contrast to Dee, Maggie inherits the Black tradition from her mother, and greatly honors the Black culture.

  2. The quilt in the story is more than merely a thing for ordinary daily use. Instead, it bears aertain profound meaning. Made from pieces of dresses worn by grand-and great-grandparents of the family and deftly stitched by Grandma's and aunt's hands, the quilts are not only the reflection of the wisdom and diligence of the

black women, but also impregnated with the Black culture and traditions. Hence, Dee and Maggie's different feelings about the quilts could reveal their differing attitudes towards their cultural legacy. Dee covets the quilts so much only because she wants to keep them as extraordinary ornaments to show off, and she doesn't know the true essence of the Black culture. While Maggie honors the quilts as the souvenir of her grandma, knows how to quilt by herself, and uss them in daily life. It's in her hands that the quilts can truly hold family virtues, and pass down from generation to generation, along with the traditional living style and values of the Black. Therefore, in the end, the mother gives the family quilts to Maggie who truly appreciates their real values and can continue the heritage by patching it with new scraps.

3. Dee's image is a direct correlation to many young African Americans in the 1960s. Influenced by the American Black Civil Rights Movement, they adopted a figurative "return to Africa", that is, denying the mainstream white culture once having oppressed their ancestors and oppressing them currently, and celebrating African culture by changing their names, clothing, and a lot of behaviors into the traditional African styles. However, in essence, they only scratched the surface of their culture, merely exploring it for exotic names and ethnic appeal while ignorant of its true values. Dee in the story can serve as a good example. Following the "fashion" of the movement, she gets interested in the house, the bench, the churn and the family quilt which she used to despise much. But it is a pity that she only has a shallow view on her culture. Neglecting the history and the family virtues embodied in these articles of everyday use, she just wants to keep them as ornaments to show off. By portraying the character Dee, Walker shows her deep concern about the dilemma of those Dees in the real life who, struggling to escape the oppression and prejudice, face the danger of deracinating themselves from all that have sustained and defined them. And to some extent, she actually intends to sound the alarm for those people, prompting them to take a scrutinizing look at themselves and to find the best way to seek their identity and celebrate their culture.

4. By entitling the story "Everyday Use", Alice Walkerputs forward a thought-provoking question for the Black as well as other minority groups: how they should treat and preserve their cultural heritage. Through the story of an ordinary Black family, she points up the most suitable way to honor one's heritage is to integrate it into everyday life rather than place it on the shelf to be displayed and admired.

Suggested Further Reading

In Love and Trouble: Stories of Black Women (1973); *The Color Purple* (1982)

Topics for Further Study

1. Do you identify yourself with the narrator in the story? Can you say something in defense of Dee?

2. What is the symbolic meaning of the subtitle? What is implied in it in the form of a dedication?

3. Symbols abound in Walker's masterpiece *The Color Purple*, for instance, sewing, God and the title "the color purple". Select one of the symbols mentioned above, and try to find its symbolic meaning.

4. It is interesting to note that both heroines in Walker's *The Color Purple* and Kingston's *The Woman Warrior* use the narrative, either in the form of letters or of stories, to recount their experiences and lives. Read these two works and try to find the purpose of such an arrangement.

Knowledge of Literature

Epistolary novel(书信体小说)

An epistolary novel is a type of novel in the form of a series of letters written by one or more of the characters, with their dairy entries, newspaper clippings, telegrams and other documents sometimes included. As one of the earliest novelistic forms, it was widely used in the 18th century, possessing such advantages as creating verisimilitude and an immediate sense of reality, narrowing the distance between the readers and the work, allowing the author to employ differing points of view. However, due to the limitation of this special form composed mainly of letters, it relies heavily on coincidences to unfold the story, causing readers tochallenge the authenticity of the plot. Therefore, it gradually fell out of use at the end of the 18th century. The most representative ones include Samuel Richardson's *Pamela* (1740), Rousseau's *La Nouvelle Héloïse* (1761), Tobias Smollett's *Humphry Clinker* (1771) and Pierre Laclos's *Les Liaisons dangereuses* (1782).

Bibliography

Abrams, M. H. *A Glossary of Literary Terms*. Beijing: Foreign Language Teaching and Research Press, 2004.

Baldick, Chris. *Concise Dictionary of Literary Terms*. Shanghai: Shanghai Foreign Language Press, 2000.

Balm, Nina, et al., eds. *The Norton Anthology of American Literature* (Shorter 5th Edition.). New York: W. W. Norton & Company, Inc., 1999.

Bressler, Charles E. *Literary Criticism: An Introduction to Theory and Practice*. Beijing: Higher Education Press, 2004.

Chin, Frank et al. eds. *Aiiieeeee! An Anthology of Asian American Writers*. Washington, D.C.: Howard UP, 1974.

Cuddon, J.A. *A Dictionary of Literary Terms*. London:Andre Deutsch limited, 1979.

Elliott, Emory. *The Columbia History of the American Novel*. Beijing: Foreign Language Teaching and Research Press, 2005.

Elliott, Emory. *Columbia Literary History of the United States*. New York: Columbia University Press, 1988.

Espiritu, Yen Le. *Asian American Women and Men: Labor, Laws and Love*. Walnut Creek: Alta Mira Press, 2000.

Griffith, Kelley. *Writing Essays about Literature:A Guide and Style Sheet*. Beijing: Peking University Press, 2006.

Hart, J. D., and P.W. Leininger. *The Oxford Companion to American Literature*. Beijing: Foreign Language Teaching and Research Press, 2005.

High, Peter B. *An Outline of American Literature*. London and New York: Longman Group Limited, 1986.

Holman, C. Hugh and William Harmon. *A Handbook to Literature*. New York: Macmillan Publishing Company, 1986.

Li, David Leiwei. *Imagining the Nation: Asian American Literature and Cultural

Consent. Stanford, California: Stanford University Press, 1998.

McMichael, George, ed. *Concise Anthology of American Literature*. New York: Macamillan, 1985.

Miller, James E., ed. *Heritage of American Literature*. San Diego: Harcourt, 1991.

Perkin, George, al., eds. *The American Tradition in Literature*. New York: Random House, 1985.

Roberts, Edgar V. and Henry E. Jacobs. *Fiction: An Introduction to Reading and Writing*. New Jersey: Prentice-Hall, Inc.,1989.

Salzman, Jack, ed. *New Essays on The Catcher in the Rye*. Beijing: Beijing University Press, 2007.

Wisker, Gina. *Key Concepts in Postcolonial Literature*. Shanghai: Shanghai Foreign Language Education Press, 2017.

http://en.wikipedia.org/wiki/Main_Page

http://nobelprize.org/literature/laureates

http://www.answers.com

常耀信.《美国文学简史》(第三版).天津：南开大学出版社，2008.

陈世丹等《当代西方文艺批评理论要义》.北京：中国人民大学出版社，2017.

程爱民.《美国文学阅读教程》.南京：南京师范大学出版社，1996.

董衡巽等.《文学文学简史》.北京：人民文学出版社，1986.

杰里米·里夫金，特德·霍华德.《熵：一种新的世界观》.吕明，袁舟译.上海：上海译文出版社，1987.

金莉，秦亚青.《美国文学》.北京：外语教学与研究出版社，1999.

金莉.《美国19世纪文学选读》.北京：外语教学与研究出版社，2008.

金莉，张剑.《文学原理教程》.北京：外语教学与研究出版社，2010.

李公昭.《新编美国文学选读》.西安：西安交通大学出版社，2003.

李宜燮，常耀信.《美国文学选读》.天津：南开大学出版社，1991.

李正栓.《美国文学学习指南》.北京：清华大学出版社，2006.

李正栓，陈岩.《美国诗歌研究》.北京：北京大学出版社，2007.

林六辰.《英美小说要素解析》.上海：上海外语教育出版社，2004.

罗选民.《英美文学赏析教程》(散文与诗歌).北京：清华大学出版社，2002.

邵锦娣，白劲鹏.《文学导论》.上海：上海外语教育出版社，2001.

陶洁.《美国文学选读》.北京：高等教育出版社，2005.

陶洁.《20世纪美国文学选读》.北京：北京大学出版社，2006.

童明.《美国文学史》.北京：外语教学与研究出版社，2008.

王守仁，刘海平《新编美国文学史》.上海：上海外语教育出版社，2002.

沃克.《朗文－清华英汉双解科技大词典》.清华大学出版社组译.北京：清华大学出版社，1996.

吴定柏.《美国文学欣赏》.上海:上海外语教育出版社,2002.
吴定柏.《美国文学大纲》.上海:上海外语教育出版社,2011.
吴伟仁.《美国文学史及选读》.北京:外语教学与研究出版社,2007
杨金才,王海萌.《文学导论》.上海:上海外语教育出版社,2013.
杨仁敬等《美国后现代派短篇小说论》.青岛:青岛出版社,2004.
叶华年,王新球,金辉《英语短篇小说导读》.上海:华东师范大学出版社,1999.
袁洪庚,卢雨菁,杜丽丽《英诗及诗学文选》.北京:北京大学出版社,2008.
袁宪军,钱坤强.《英语小说导读》.北京:北京大学出版社,2004.
翟士钊.《美国文学选读》.开封:河南大学出版社,1994.
张伯香.《英美文学选读》.北京:外语教学与研究出版社,1999.
张冲.《美国文学选读》.上海:复旦大学出版社:2008.
张剑,赵东,王文丽.《英美诗歌选读》.北京:外语教学与研究出版社,2008.